W9-AWV-774

the Unofficial Guide™ to Investing

Lynn O'Shaughnessy

Macmillan • USA

Macmillan General Reference
A Simon & Schuster Macmillan Company
1633 Broadway
New York, New York 10019-6785

ISBN: 0-02-862458-0

Manufactured in the United States of America

10 9 8 7 6 5 4 3 2 1

First edition

To Bruce, Caitlin, and Ben.
And to Jacqueline and Vincent P. O'Shaughnessy, my
parents, who taught me the value of money many years
before I realized it.

Acknowledgments

I will always be amazed at how helpful experts can be when a journalist who just happens to know their phone extensions interrupts their day with a bunch of questions. Why we aren't dismissed as pests more often remains a mystery to me.

Luckily, no one I needed to talk to for this book hung up on me. Rather, the people I thought would add substance to the book were gracious enough to help. Some of the people who shared their valuable knowledge included Ken Landis, co-manager of Firsthand Technology Value Fund; Fritz Reynolds, portfolio manager of the Reynolds Blue Chip Growth Fund; Marc Robbins, editor of the *Red Chip Review;* Noel Maye at the Certified Financial Planner Board of Standards; Stephen Sanborn at Value Line; Mark Hulbert, editor of the *Hulbert Financial Digest;* and Gary Schatsky, a very quotable fee-only certified financial planner in New York. I'd also like to thank Ginita Wall, another certified financial planner, who has written many personal finance books; Patrick Reinkemeyer, the variable annuity whiz at Morningstar; Kevin Lichtman, the brains behind the Web site www.stockdetective.com; Gerri Detweiler, the consumer credit guru; and the many good folks at the Vanguard Group; Peggy Hite, associate accounting professor at Indiana University.

I am also truly indebted to the statisticians at Lipper Analytical Services and CDA/Wiesenberger for providing me with the many mutual fund statistics you will see in this book. I also want to thank the American Association for Individual Investors, of which I am a member, for allowing me to use some of their charts in my manuscript.

In addition, I'd like to thank the technical experts, especially Doug Gerlach and Peter Keating, who pored over each chapter in the book to make sure everything was 100 percent correct. I also appreciate the help of some other experts who graciously agreed to review excerpts of my work. Kenneth S. Janke, Sr., the president and chief executive officer of the National Association of Investors Corp., read my chapters on investment clubs and stock research. Rick Harper, a research analyst extraordinaire at John Nuveen & Co., made some valuable comments on the bond chapter. And Ray Del Cueto, director of business development at Fee for Service, Inc., gave my insurance chapter a good once-over.

I also want to thank Jennifer Farthing, my editor at Macmillan, who remained upbeat and optimistic throughout. With this being one of the first books launched in a brand-new series, the challenges for her and the other editors in New York, including Matthew X. Kiernan, were considerable.

And of course, this acknowledgment wouldn't be complete without thanking my mom and dad, who let me know in many different ways and at many different times that I could be whatever I desired when I grew up. While my career aspirations changed often—a nun, my second-grade career choice; a tap dancer; a novelist living on a Vermont maple-tree farm; a geneticist; and a historian, pretty much in that order—I feel lucky to have chosen journalism as my ultimate profession.

My kids, Benjamin and Caitlin, and my wonderful husband, Bruce Bigelow, deserve the biggest thank you of all. Not to be left out are Berkeley and Benson, two old Golden Retrievers who pretty much slept at my feet during the entire project. And I couldn't forget Tom Handley's third-grade class at Maryland Avenue Elementary School. It was a treat every Wednesday morning to break away from this book to help the great kids in that room with their creative writing.

Finally, I want to finish my thank-yous by borrowing a line we all hear each year at the Oscar ceremonies. I'd like to thank everybody who helped me with this project, and if I forgot anyone, I apologize.

Lynn O'Shaughnessy
San Diego
July 1998

Contents

The *Unofficial Guide* Reader's Bill of Rights

We Give You More Than the Official Line

Welcome to the *Unofficial Guide* series of Lifestyles titles—books that deliver critical, unbiased information that other books can't or won't reveal—the *inside scoop*. Our goal is to provide you with the *most accessible, useful* information and advice possible. The recommendations we offer in these pages are not influenced by the corporate line of any organization or industry; we give you the hard facts, whether those institutions like them or not. If something is ill-advised or will cause a loss of time and/or money, we'll give you ample warning. And if it is a worthwhile option, we'll let you know that too.

Armed and Ready

Our handpicked authors confidently and critically report on a wide range of topics that matter to smart readers like you. Our authors are passionate about their subjects, but have distanced themselves enough from them to help you be armed and protected, and help you make educated decisions as you go through your process. It is our intent that, from having read this book, you will avoid the pitfalls everyone else falls into and get it right the first time.

Don't be fooled by cheap imitations; this is the *genuine article Unofficial Guide* series from Macmillan Publishing. You might be familiar with our proven track record of the travel *Unofficial Guides,* which have more than three million copies in print. Each year, thousands of travelers—new and old—are armed with the brand new, fully updated edition of the flagship *Unofficial Guide to Walt Disney World,* by Bob Sehlinger. It is our intention here to provide you with the same level of objective authority that Mr. Sehlinger accomplishes in his brainchild.

The Unofficial Panel of Experts

Every work in the Lifestyle *Unofficial Guides* is intensively inspected by a team of three top professionals in their fields. These experts review the manuscript for factual accuracy, comprehensiveness, and an insider's determination as to whether the manuscript fulfills the credo in this Reader's Bill of Rights. In other words, our Panel ensures that you are, in fact, getting "the inside scoop."

Our Pledge

The authors, the editorial staff, and the Unofficial Panel of Experts assembled for *Unofficial Guides* are determined to lay out the most valuable alternatives available for our readers. This dictum means that our writers must be explicit, prescriptive, and above all, direct. We strive to be thorough and complete, but our goal is not necessarily to have the "most" or "all" of the information on a topic; this is not, after all, an encyclopedia. Our objective is to help you narrow down your options to the best of what is available, unbiased by affiliation with any industry or organization.

In each *Unofficial Guide*, we give you:

- Comprehensive coverage of necessary and vital information
- Authoritative, rigidly fact-checked data
- The most up-to-date insights into trends
- Savvy, sophisticated writing that's also readable
- Sensible, applicable facts and secrets that only an insider knows

Special Features

Every book in our series offers the following six special sidebars in the margins that are devised to help you get things done cheaply, efficiently, and smartly.

1. "Timesaver"—tips and shortcuts that save you time.

2. "Moneysaver"—tips and shortcuts that save you money.

3. "Watch Out!"—more serious cautions and warnings.

4. "Bright Idea"—general tips and shortcuts to help you find an easier or smarter way to do something.

5. "Quote"—statements from real people that are intended to be prescriptive and valuable to you.

6. "Unofficially…"—an insider's fact or anecdote.

We also recognize your need to have quick information at your fingertips, and have thus provided the following comprehensive sections at the back of the book:

1. **Glossary:** Definitions of complicated terminology and jargon.

2. **Resource Guide:** Lists of relevant agencies, associations, institutions, Web sites, etc.

3. **Recommended Reading List:** Suggested titles that can help you get more in-depth information on related topics.

4. **Important Documents:** "Official" pieces of information you need to refer to, such as government forms.

5. **Important Statistics:** Facts and numbers presented at a glance for easy reference.

Letters, Comments, and Questions from Readers

We strive to continually improve the *Unofficial* series, and input from our readers is a valuable way for us to do that.

Many of those who have used the *Unofficial Guide* travel books write to the authors to ask questions, make comments, or share their own discoveries and lessons. For Lifestyle *Unofficial Guides,* we would also appreciate all such correspondence, both positive and critical, and we will make best efforts to incorporate readers' feedback and comments in revised editions of this work.

How to write to us:

Unofficial Guides
Macmillan Lifestyle Guides
Macmillan Publishing
1633 Broadway
New York, NY 10019

Attention: Reader's Comments

The *Unofficial Guide* Panel of Experts

The *Unofficial* editorial team recognizes that you've purchased this book with the expectation of getting the most authoritative, carefully inspected information currently available. Toward that end, on each and every title in this series, we have selected a minimum of three "official" experts comprising the "Unofficial Panel" who painstakingly review the manuscripts to ensure: factual accuracy of all data; inclusion of the most up-to-date and relevant information; and that, from an insider's perspective, the authors have armed you with all the necessary facts you need—but the institutions don't want you to know.

For *The Unofficial Guide to Investing,* we are proud to introduce the following panel of experts:

Peter Keating has been a member of *Money Magazine*'s writing staff since July 1994. Specializing in consumer issues, Mr. Keating has covered a broad range of financial topics for the nation's largest financial publication. He has won the Investigative Reporters and Editors award for the best investigative journalism of the year; he has also won the ICI Education Foundation/American University Journalism Award for excellence in personal finance reporting.

Before joining *Money*, Mr. Keating worked on other publishing projects, most notably as the researcher for *President Kennedy: Profile in Power* (Simon & Schuster) which was named *Time*'s nonfiction book of the year for 1993. Keating has also written for the *Congressional Quarterly* and has appeared on Nightline, Today, and CNN's Your Money.

Mr. Keating holds a master's degree in public policy from the John F. Kennedy School of Government at Harvard University and is a 1988 magna cum laude graduate of Harvard College.

Victor Levinson is an investment advisor at Weiss, Peck & Greer, a New York City-based investment firm which manages more than $14 billion for its clients. He has been an investment advisor for more than 20 years, following a 13-year career as Chief Financial Officer of a privately owned company.

In addition to his position at Weiss, Peck & Greer, Mr. Levinson lectures extensively on investment topics and teaches continuing education classes on investing at the New School and Marymount Manhattan College in New York City.

Mr. Levinson is a graduate of Cornell, Harvard Law School, and NYU Graduate Law School.

Douglas Gerlach is the author of *Investor's Web Guide: Tools and Strategies for Building Your Portfolio* (Lycos Press/Que Computer Books).

Mr. Gerlach is also the publisher of Invest-O-Rama! (www.investorama.com), an award-winning financial site on the World Wide Web.

In 1998, Mr. Gerlach was named Senior Editor of the Armchair Millionaire (www.armchairmillionaire.com), a savings and investing site developed by Intuit Inc. and iVillage. In addition, he works closely with the National Association of Investors Corporation (NAIC) and was a co-creator of its Web site. Mr. Gerlach is also a member and past President of the Pioneer Online Investment Club, one of the world's first "virtual" clubs.

In recognition of his pioneering efforts to teach people how to invest over the Internet, Mr. Gerlach received the Distinguished Service Award from the NAIC's Investment Education Institute in 1996.

Introduction: Welcome to The *Unofficial Guide to Investing*

Do you remember the first time you had to make a fairly complicated financial decision? I do. When a packet stuffed with information about my company's voluntary 401(k) retirement plan landed with a thud on my desk, I groaned. At the time, I was a young reporter at the *Los Angeles Times,* working long hours to ensure that my editors wouldn't second-guess hiring me. The prospects of spending my free time shuffling through paperwork scattered across my dining table appealed to me as much as washing dishes on Thanksgiving. When I finally did look at it all, I wasn't sure what to do. Should I instruct my employer to put my weekly 401(k) contributions into stocks, or should I play it safe and direct the money into bonds or even an ultrasafe cash account?

Reviewing my choices, I heard a little voice from childhood squeak, *Don't put all your eggs in one basket.* So I didn't. I divided up my future contributions equally among bonds, stocks, and cash. But should I really have based major financial choices on a dumb cliché? Not hardly.

But at this point in my life, I found the topic of personal finance daunting and, frankly, intimidating. When my father-in-law bought my husband and me a subscription to a dry financial newsletter, I'd toss it, unread, in the newspaper recycling pile. What I really needed back then was a reliable guide, short on stuffiness and dull language, that could quickly point me in the right direction. Imagine if I had a book that zeroed in on the inside scoop and essentially said, "Hey, Lynn, you're not going to retire for 30 years. Don't you dare stash any of your retirement money into a cash account! Do that, and it will be much harder to protect your returns against inflation. And if you're not worried about inflation, consider this: A $1 million nest egg in 35 years is only going to be worth, in today's dollars, $119,153." Now that's the kind of warning I would have noticed.

I never bothered to hunt for a book like that. But if *The Unofficial Guide to Investing* had been around, I would have bought it. This is a book designed to provide answers to the most nagging financial questions. You know, the ones that might pop into your head when you're staring at the brake lights of the cars in front of you at rush hour. Or the ones that can sneak up and taunt you when you're slouched across your couch. Unable to find the remote control, you suffer through a commercial featuring an affluent couple who smugly congratulates themselves for picking the right mutual fund family 20 years ago. At times like this, you might even think, *Am I the only one who isn't completely sure what I should be doing with my money?*

Why we need to buckle down

This is a good question to ask, since we are all under more pressure than ever before to be savvy investors. In the past, people like you and me could have managed quite comfortably without knowing the difference between the Standard & Poor's 500 Index and the Dow Jones Industrial Average. It was traditionally our employers who worried about our retirement money. No one gave much thought to their future pension payouts until it was almost time to order the cake for the retirement party. But now fewer and fewer corporations are offering traditional corporate pension plans that provide a tidy monthly check when you leave the premises for the last time. Taking its place are the do-it-yourself 401(k) plans, which are funded by the hard-earned money that comes straight out of your paycheck. And guess who's responsible for how our 401(k) money should be invested? Just like in the lifeboats, it's every man and woman for themselves.

The short-term financial sacrifice you might feel contributing to your company's retirement plan might be dwarfed by the angst you experience choosing your investment options from a cafeteria-style menu. Consider the tale of one Salt Lake City corporation. Responding to employee criticism that five 401(k) choices weren't enough, the company increased its menu to 137 selections. Most of the Utah workers were so overwhelmed that what they did was perfectly understandable. They simply kept their money in the five original choices. And this hardly is an isolated tale.

As if that's not enough to worry about, the prognosis for Social Security is less than encouraging. In one survey after another, Americans express great skepticism about whether Social Security will be around for themselves or their children and grand-children.

But this isn't the only reason why we have to stay on our toes. There are plenty of other times when a solid background in investing ABCs is crucial. Baby Boomers need to know what they should do with inheritances they might receive. Parents struggling to save enough to send their kid to a college that will look impressive on a resume will make their task easier if they know how to make the right financial choices. And we all need to avoid investing in booby traps that can be quite costly. For instance, countless Americans have been ensnared by unfair tax laws that penalize taxpayers who don't withdraw their 401(k) money the *right* way. And being savvy about money can protect us all from the con artists who want to rip us off with bogus investments. If you think you are immune to the shysters, think again. An organization of the nation's top securities regulators recently declared that affinity group schemes represent one of the country's top 10 investment frauds. Affinity group fraud got its name because the swindlers pray on people who belong to the same churches or social organizations or who happen to share the same ethnic background.

Even when we vow to be smart investors, our financial choices can be intimidating. The number of mutual funds available today, for example, is approaching 7,000. That's truly astounding. The year that the Vietnam War ended, just 426 funds existed. Technology also has muddied the water. In the good old days, you might have walked through an elegantly appointed foyer past one oak-paneled office after another to visit your trusted broker.

Today, you can turn on your computer before breakfast and buy stock within seconds through your electronic discount broker. This broker doesn't even have a face.

Of course, the publishing industry—eager to make its own fast bucks—has reacted to this great need for financial tutoring. Many bookstore aisles are lined with enough personal finance books to surely fill up a small-town library in Nevada. But I'd have to argue that *The Unofficial Guide* is different in many ways from these books.

How this book is different

Why should you buy this book when you can get oodles of information free from brokers, mutual fund companies, and other financial institutions? Remember, none of these places are charitable organizations. They don't mail out all those freebies because they aspire to improve the investing IQ of all mankind. Heck, they want your money. So can you blame a brokerage house that never mentions that its fees are the most outrageous in the industry? (It's much easier to tell how much fat is in a package of hot dogs than it is to determine just what fees a mutual fund company is charging.) Or how about a mutual fund that doesn't blurt out that its returns have kept it locked in the basement with the other perennial losers 8 out of the last 10 years? Do you think that an insurance agent or a broker peddling variable annuities will explain to you that recent tax changes make these investments a gloriously bad choice for most people? Hardly. Luckily, however, you can rely on us to tell you these things while giving you the straight, unbiased, independent scoop.

We're not going to force-feed you the same old superficial advice that you might have heard already. If you've read other books, you might have noticed that a lot of experts are awfully vague when they're dispensing advice. For instance, somebody will provide definitions for a junk bond, municipal bond, and U.S. Treasury bond and then scoot on to the next subject. Meanwhile, you're left sitting on your couch with a lot of unanswered questions:

How does the long-term performance of Treasury bonds compare to the other types?

Are junk bonds ever suitable for an individual investor?

Based on my tax bracket, are municipal bonds a smart move for me?

Here's another example: Other books breeze through an explanation of the highly popular index funds. But they don't tell you when they are appropriate and when they are not. They don't share the five indexing myths that you'll find in this book. Are index funds as worthwhile for smallcap and foreign investors? These are the kinds of sophisticated questions that *The Unofficial Guide to Investing* answers on page after page.

Even as we heap lots of morsels on your plate, we know that you don't have a lot of time to linger over the buffet. So we've culled through tons of financial reports, surveys, government statistics, Web sites, newsletters, mutual fund handouts, magazine articles, financial tomes heavier than shot puts, advice from respected financial professionals, and our own experiences to bring you just what's most essential. And most insightful. (If you could only see the paper drift on our desks, you could appreciate just how much heavy lifting has been done to squeeze what's most pertinent into this pocket-sized book.)

You should know that *The Unofficial Guide to Investing* was not created by one born-again journalist who realized a few years back that personal finance was nothing to snicker at. This book truly represents a team effort. When you buy this book, you're getting the combined wisdom of prominent financial pros who lent their thoughts and considerable expertise to every chapter.

The Unofficial Guide to Investing was written with people like you in mind. Since we are consumers ourselves, we think we know the kinds of financial issues you are grappling with because we've been there. Some of your questions could be simple. Maybe you are wondering how you can get your money out of a savings account and into a mutual fund company thousands of miles away. Perhaps you'd like to know how to read the stock tables found in just about any newspaper. Other questions could be more complex. Maybe you are wondering which should be your highest priority if you don't have enough money to fund both your 401(k) and a new Roth Individual Retirement Account. In Chapter 13, we'll provide the answer. Or perhaps you're trapped in life-insurance hell. You're trying to decide whether it's worth replacing an expensive life insurance policy with another one. In Chapter 14, we'll give you three reasons to switch a policy. And if you still aren't sure, we provide you with the phone number and address of a not-for-profit organization that can give you the definitive answer. Maybe you've noticed a trend here; when we answer a question, we don't waffle. We give you straight answers and guide you to other resources when appropriate. While this book contains plenty of solid advice for beginners, it also provides a wealth of strategies for more sophisticated investors who already know the basics and want to learn more to enhance their financial results.

The Unofficial Guide to Investing is written in a style that—with any luck—will keep you turning pages. The book's team of experts mercifully let the professional journalist translate their wisdom onto the printed page. The arcane financial jargon has been stripped out, but the meat is there. Of course, this has its obvious advantages. A dull or incomprehensible investment book that ends up at Goodwill isn't going to do you any good.

In our line of work, we get free financial books sent to us all the time by publishers who are trying to stir up excitement for their latest projects. But quite frankly, many of these books are created by financial stars whose writing abilities exhibit all the flair and style of a driver's ed manual. Many of these books can be traced back to mutual fund managers, stockpicking impresarios, and other financial whizzes who promise that you can duplicate their investing feats by following their easy (yeah, right) formula. Unfortunately, some guy working on the 40th floor of a Manhattan skyscraper with a phalanx of stock analysts at his beck and call, along with enough computer power to short-circuit all the homes in Des Moines, isn't necessarily going to know what's important to you out in the real world. He might not even remember back to the days when a question like "What is a bond yield?" would have stumped him.

Because money is the real reason you're buying this book, we would be remiss if we didn't share tips on how you can stretch those crumpled bills in your wallet and the net asset value of your various accounts. Our editors won't let us extend any crazy money-back offer, but we dare say that they wouldn't lose any money if they did. You'll find money-saving suggestions scattered throughout the book. We'll explain how you can save hundreds of dollars by avoiding insurance agents when you buy policies. We'll tell you how to find the cheapest credit cards. You'll also discover which highly respected company offers mutual funds with the puniest expenses. Want to know how to select the best and cheapest discount broker with the least amount of hassles? Continue turning pages. You won't even have to read this book cover to cover to recoup your $15.95 many times over.

Keep reading for the very latest news

The Unofficial Guide to Investing also will keep you current. Believe it or not, that can be hard to do when you're an investor. We all know that a computer becomes obsolete before a new owner gets a chance to pull off the shrink-wrap. And that killer outfit that looks so fabulous now will be hidden in the back of the closet by the next fashion season. You could actually compile a very long list of wonderful stuff you've carried home in shopping bags that became outdated long before you were ready to replace it. Investing is the same way. Sure, stocks and bonds have existed for hundreds of years, but the rules that govern how they are bought and sold keep evolving.

If you think you know the financial rules of the road, guess again. In recent times, the politicians on Capitol Hill have been as busy as Santa's elves, hacking apart a slew of old laws that will impact every last investor. These busy fellows pummeled the old capital gains tax laws. (No complaints here, we'll all be richer for it.) And they also slipped us an early

Christmas present—Individual Retirement Accounts will no longer be as unappealing as a bowl of stewed prunes. While they were at it, the politicians also handed out goodies to parents saving for college and home sellers who wanted to pocket more of their profits. Meanwhile, Congress also tinkered with the IRS rules that affect how the self-employed and small businesses save for the golden years. And the rules changed for anybody who purchases long-term care insurance to protect their nest egg.

Over all, it's good, good news coming out of Washington. But here's the bad news: You might need an accountant or a $150-an-hour financial planner to make sense of it all for you. When the Taxpayer Relief Act of 1997, which triggered a lot of these changes, was passed, some joked that it could have been nicknamed the CPA Relief Act of 1997. Of course, you can take the cheap way out and buy this book. Relax, and we'll fill you in on the changes.

And here's another bonus for buying this book. We'll explain how you can become a cyberinvestor. If you pay attention to the news media, you might think that the Internet is mostly a breeding ground for guys who like to look at naked pictures. Not true. We know plenty of people who hang out in cyberspace who are strictly interested in boosting their net worth. Actually, if you're the least bit lazy, investing with your computer is ideal. You can pour yourself a drink, lean back in your chair, and with a few clicks of your mouse, you'll own more financial information than you'd find during a whole day at a library with a pocketful of quarters for Xeroxes. If you're not convinced, be sure to read Chapter 8, and I'll bet you'll be itching to plug in.

Can you do it?

You'll find that this book doesn't talk down to you. If you are smart enough to understand a lot of the financial concepts, this book will help you fine-tune your investing strategies. If you are starting from scratch, don't despair. This book can help as well. If you find the task ahead of you too daunting, remember that investing is not rocket science. Anybody with a calculator and a knowledge of simple arithmetic can figure out how to make money investing.

Where's the proof? Your honor, I offer myself as Exhibit A. As I mentioned earlier, I was an investing greenhorn back in the 1980s. But that had to change in 1990 when I left the *Los Angeles Times'* reporting staff. (My husband snagged a wonderful job elsewhere, and we were both ready to escape the City of Angels.) The pivotal moment for me came a few months later when I received the proceeds of my pension and 401(k) plan. At the time, I probably knew less about stocks and bonds than everybody who has ever skimmed through this book. You might recognize the dilemma I faced. I knew I wanted to roll over this windfall, but I wasn't sure how to invest it.

When my husband and I moved, our local broker transferred our files to its Los Angeles office. I made an appointment with a broker who I had never met and who didn't know anything about me. He never bothered to ask what my goals were, what kind of risk I'd be comfortable with, or anything like that. He simply suggested that I dump all the money into zero coupon bonds. I didn't know what zeros were back then, but I had a strong suspicion that they wouldn't be right for me. As I searched for my car in the parking garage, I decided I could do better on my own. I opened up an account with a discount broker. And ever since, I've been investing on my own. Self-taught and happy.

There is nothing particularly unique about my experience. I was talking this morning with a guy who was as clueless as I was several years ago. Doug Gerlach was a fund-raiser for New York theaters when he formed an investment club with friends. The man is a fast learner. Before he knew it, he had launched his own Web site to share what he knows about stocks with perfect strangers. Today 70,000 people a month visit his wildly popular Invest-O-Rama! Web site. In demand as a financial expert, Gerlach now travels the country speaking to groups about investments. And he's been hired to help develop yet another financial Web site.

No one is suggesting that you will quit your day job to become a financial guru. But it should be encouraging that people with an ounce of curiosity and a little determination can prove that investing isn't just for people who sailed through their SATs.

Why should you buy this book? Most important, it could help you become a more disciplined and intelligent investor. And if you can pull that off, you have the potential for a more comfortable lifestyle. Unless you've won a multimillion-dollar lottery or inherited enough money to empty out your desk at work, you're probably going to need to squeeze as much mileage as you can out of every dollar. And frankly, the only way you can hope to do that is by investing. Investing, I might add, with your thinking cap on. Parlaying a fortune with a saving's account passbook doesn't even happen in fairy tales.

Educating yourself—like you're doing right now—is the best way to take control of your own investments. You also should consider taking it slow. If you are investing for the long haul, you shouldn't feel like you have to rush into picking blue-ribbon investments. Making your moves slowly might be boring, but it's safe and you'll ultimately come out a winner. Just ask the tortoise.

A Firm Foundation

PART I

GET THE SCOOP ON...
Give yourself a reality check ▪ Take advantage
of compounding magic ▪ Financial diets and
other investing tricks ▪ The real story behind
investment risks ▪ 401(k)s: Grab that free
money ▪ Investing—your best bet is boring

The Secrets of Successful Investing

There are lots of adults who really seem to believe that America's stock markets—somehow, some way—have been sprinkled with magical pixie dust. Under the spell, the markets can perform feats that even a mastermind like Houdini could not duplicate.

With any luck, the next few pages will put your expectations into perspective. Being realistic about your investments is just one of the guiding principles of successful investing. Stay here and you'll learn other crucial ones as well. In fact, by the time you're finished, you should be able to recite many sure-fire secrets to financial happiness. Establishing your financial goals, finding money for your most ambitious financial dreams, and calculating investment risks will all be explored in this chapter and elsewhere in this book.

Certainly you've heard the classic admonition about risk and reward. You can't keep inflation at bay and prosper financially if you won't take some risks with your portfolio. Risks and rewards, conventional wisdom correctly suggests, go hand in hand. But the prospect of risk is what a lot of timid investors gag on. So they avoid trouble—or so they think—and load up exclusively on bonds and cash investments such as certificates of deposit or money markets. If you recognize yourself in this description, you probably think that you know the answer to this question: Which of the following portfolios has historically been more volatile?

A. A portfolio investing 100 percent in bonds

B. A portfolio investing 60 percent in bonds and 40 percent in stocks

If you picked A as your answer, you'd be right. Fifty years worth of historical data indicates that a portfolio devoted to longer-term bonds can actually be riskier than one containing a healthy dose of stocks. It's this sort of phenomenon that explains why financial experts are always pontificating about the importance of asset allocation. That is, diversifying your holdings among stocks, bonds, and cash to minimize your risk and bolster your return. With any luck, the upcoming short course on risk and diversification will encourage the most reluctant investors among you to become, when appropriate, a little bolder.

The principles that follow can form a solid foundation for your investing strategies. Once these strategies are in place, there should be less chance that your carefully constructed portfolio will topple during a financial crisis. This is relevant for anybody who invests. Whether you've just decided to wean yourself away from a total reliance on your friendly savings and loan or you're a veteran investor in need of a slight financial makeover, these tips are meant for you.

Forget those financial fantasies

We know that invisible strings are not pulling the stock markets up like some kind of marionette. However, anybody who has been investing during the past decade's awesome bull market might not understand that markets can be as dangerous as Molotov cocktails. After all, the biggest, baddest day on Wall Street for most of us was on October 19, 1987. The market got bruised and scraped when it free-fell 508 points in one day. With that stunning decline, 20 percent of the market's value disappeared within hours. But do you remember what happened next? The patient fully recovered in fairly short order. The slide was arguably a pratfall—the opening act for the longest bull run in stock market history.

Financial pundits are running out of fresh adjectives to describe Wall Street's binge during the mid-to-late 1990s. It's obvious to see why. Just look at what's happened lately to the Standard & Poor's 500 Index, which is the most popular benchmark used to measure the stock market's performance. From 1995 to 1997, the S&P 500 gained an average of 31.2 percent annually—breaking an all-time record set back during Franklin D. Roosevelt's first term as president. Quite frankly, this stunning performance might never happen again in our lifetimes.

You'd have to go back a ways to actually study a bona fide financial disaster in the U.S. markets. Of course, the one that sticks in everyone's mind is the great Wall Street crash of 1929. After the market collapsed, the world plunged into a brutal global depression. By 1932, stocks were selling at about

10 percent of their precrash prices. Ironically, the three years preceding the unprecedented collapse almost equaled today's phenomenal bull-run stretch.

Actually, we don't have to rewind back to the flapper days to get a good scare. In 1973 and 1974, the stock market disintegrated by losing 45 percent of its value. The period between 1969 and 1970 was also sobering, as the market plunged 36 percent. Some might have forgotten that financial catastrophes aren't just artifacts relegated to a heart-breaking period of bread lines and bank closings. We shouldn't be terrified by the vicious bear markets of the past, but we should be mindful of the possibilities when we spend a few quiet moments contemplating what to do with our money.

And yet, most of us who are already investing have become a little too smug about our investment returns. Even I, one of those spoiled return hogs, was amazed by a survey conducted late in 1997 by the folks who run the Montgomery family of mutual funds in San Francisco. In the poll, a sampling of investors across the country said they expected average returns of 34 percent a year over the next decade. Yes, that's right: 34 percent! Do you know what the typical stock return has been for most of this century? Try 11 percent. Here are the results of another poll I found on my desk: A survey by Louis Harris & Associates, timed for the tenth anniversary of the 1987 crash, showed that 81 percent of investors didn't think a severe bear market (a market decline of at least 20 percent) could possibly happen during the next 10 years.

Okay, okay, so we are all expecting great things from the stock market. Anything wrong with that?

Well, there can be. The confidence of individual investors is credited with helping to fuel the great run up in stock prices during this decade, so to some extent, optimism is good. If investors cashed out at the first sign of wobbly stock prices, the market surely wouldn't have soared to the heights we are all enjoying today. But the key here to successful investing is maintaining realistic expectations.

Unbridled optimism can get people into trouble by booby-trapping their investing strategy. When we get antsy, we become dissatisfied with what we have, and we tend to ditch solid holdings in favor of flavor-of-the-week investments. A solid-performing mutual fund that returns a respectable 14 percent a year might look too tame when compared to an obscure technology fund that has burst onto the scene with a first-year return of 60 percent.

Assuming that you'll continue to enjoy returns that defy gravity can also skew your financial planning. Let's take, for example, the 34 percent returns the investors answering the Montgomery survey thought they'd achieve well into the next millennium.

If a couple devised a retirement savings strategy based on the 34 percent assumption, they'd be in big financial trouble by the time they were ready to move to Sun City, Arizona. Let's suppose that a thirty-something couple already has a total of $30,000 in his-and-her IRAs. They are investing an additional $300 a month in tax-deferred retirement accounts. They keep this up for 30 years until they retire. With that annual 34 percent turbo-charged return, they'd be millionaires many times over. In fact, their nest egg would be worth a phenomenal $442 million!

Watch Out!
It seems that everybody is searching for instant riches. This no doubt explains why most of us only hold onto a mutual fund for three years. It wasn't so long ago that the typical shareholder was content to own a mutual fund for 10 whole years! Chasing after the hottest funds is never a good idea.

Ah, but let's get real here. Suppose that we plug the historic 11 percent figure into the equation. This, after all, is the average return of stocks in past decades. With this more down-to-earth estimate, the couple would, on the cusp of retirement, have a portfolio worth $1.5 million. That's quite a difference from the cheerier projection.

To avoid nasty and costly surprises, investors obviously need to use realistic figures when calculating their future net worth. You already know how stocks have historically performed. Now here are two other figures to use when making investment projections. Bonds have traditionally earned around 5 percent, while cash invested in such things as certificates of deposits have typically generated just less than 4 percent. You also need to figure in inflation. It's realistic to use a 3 percent inflation rate.

Meanwhile, the best time to examine your own attitudes about money, as well as your expectations, is now. Be sure to check out your own money personality profile in Chapter 16, "Money and Your Psyche."

Compounding—an investor's best friend

In school, there was always at least one kid who smugly completed the big term paper many days in advance. You, on the other hand, might have waited until the last minute and then spent half the night in your dorm room furiously typing. When the graded papers were passed back, perhaps you felt vindicated because both of you got an A. Well, waiting until the last minute to invest in your financial goals just won't cut it. The investment world clearly favors the early birds. It's the people who stash money away early who will be drinking daiquiris on cruise ships, while the rest are wondering how they can possibly afford to retire when they reach 70.

You don't have to be a math genius to appreciate that early investing is clearly superior, thanks to the power of compounding. Compounding is a lot like steroids—it can dramatically pump up your return. With compounding, even the puniest of investments can grow exponentially as long as it's given time to do its magic. At the beginning, the compounded annual returns won't look impressive, but just wait—they will. Here's an example of how compounding works: Let's say a couple invests a total of $4,000 in their IRAs. Earning 12 percent the first year, the couple's $4,000 grows to $4,480. The next year, the couple earns 12 percent again. This is when the compounding kicks in. The couple makes 12 percent on $4,480, not $4,000. That brings them up to $5,018. In 10 years, the initial $4,000 more than triples without ever adding any more money to the kitty.

Here's another way to look at compounding. If you don't start early, you will need a lot more money for whatever your investment goals are. Why? Because you are not giving compounding a long enough period to work. Just take a look at the following table, which assumes that you will make either 8 percent or 10 percent on your money.

Bright Idea
If you put $2,000 annually into an eligible 18-year-old's IRA and stop after six yearly payments, an amazing thing will happen. When she's 65, she'll unwrap quite a retirement present. Assuming a 10 percent return, that initial investment will swell to more than $1 million.

MONTHLY INVESTMENT NEEDED TO BUILD A $500,000 NEST EGG BY AGE 65

Age When You Start Requirement	Monthly Investment 8% Return	10% Return
35	$333	$219
40	$522	$374
45	$843	$653
50	$1,435	$1,196
55	$2,715	$2,421

You can squeeze money from a turnip

No matter how much money we earn, bills can quickly transform the fattest paycheck into a pathetic pile of spare change. I know this all too well. No matter how much I deposit into my checking account, within a short time, it gets eaten alive by good causes—my daughter's art classes, new tires, the baby-sitter, the plumber… the list is only limited by my creditors' imagination. Obviously, debt can torpedo the best-intentioned investment strategy. "When I get out from under all the bills, I'm going to set up a mutual fund for Erin and Tommy's college years." My friend told me that five years ago, and she still hasn't done it.

Of course, one reason why we are suffocating under so many bills is because there are so many temptations. It's only human nature to want to eat out rather than spend an hour or two cooking dinner and then loading the dishwasher. We'd rather buy a child a new pair of jeans than patch the torn pair or let out a hem. Anyway, you get the idea.

Realizing my own lack of discipline, I've put myself on a financial diet. I don't allow myself to touch a portion of the money my husband and I make every month. Instead, it's whisked away through automatic withdrawal plans we have set up with mutual funds. On the eleventh of every month, our short-term bond fund extracts money out of our checking account. We'll use the money to replace my reliable Honda Accord, with 188,000 miles on the odometer, when it finally dies. Later in the month, a stock fund pulls money out for our two children's college years. Meanwhile, at my husband's workplace, Bruce's 401(k) plan automatically extracts 10 percent of his paycheck every week and puts it into his tax-deferred retirement fund.

Every now and then, we review how much is being deposited automatically, and we ask ourselves whether we can squeeze out even more. For instance, when my son stopped wearing diapers, I calculated that I'd be saving about $35 at Target each month. Not a huge sum, but still it presented an investing opportunity. I called the Vanguard Group, where we have a mutual fund for the kids, and increased our monthly automatic investment by $35 a month. We also fattened our contributions when we thankfully no longer had to write those monthly tuition checks to preschool once our children began attending public schools.

Would we have saved as much had we not forced ourselves to do it? Not a chance. And it's not always easy. During some lean months, I curse those automatic deposits, but I'm satisfied when I look at our account statements.

There are other painless ways as well to fatten your net worth. (See more suggestions in Chapter 15, "When You're in Financial Trouble.") If you spend just a little time thinking about it, you can probably pinpoint places where you can tap into some pockets of cash. If you routinely get a Christmas bonus, don't fritter it all away on holiday gift giving. Stash some in savings. If you get a tax refund or a rebate for a major appliance, don't blow it. If you'd feel too resentful putting your entire tax refund into savings, allow yourself to splurge a little.

Meanwhile, when you get a raise, try to pretend that you never received all or most of it. Let's say your boss gives you a $70-a-week raise. You could

Moneysaver
Imagine what you could save by bringing carrot sticks and a tuna salad sandwich to work every day instead of spending $6 on lunch. If you invest that $6-a-day savings during 30 years of time-card punching (and assume it earns 9 percent a year), you ultimately pocket more than $200,000.

have that money whisked away through an auto-matic deposit program with a mutual fund. But trouble is, you might not be sure you can live without the extra cash. Here's an alternative: If you are lucky, your company is affiliated with a credit union. Perhaps it's right in your building. Arrange with the credit union to extract the amount equal to the raise right out of your paycheck each week. It will be put in a savings account. If you have an emergency, perhaps your car needs a new transmission, you can tap into the fund. If you find that you don't really miss the money, even better. In that case, you don't want to keep a lot of money, making an anemic 2 percent or 3 percent, sitting in the credit union. Once you've built up enough in the account for a typical household emergency, skim off the top—maybe $400 at a time—and invest it where the potential return will be greater. A mutual fund is a logical choice.

Get the most out of your 401(k)

Contribute the maximum amounts to your 401(k) or other workplace retirement plan. There is no better financial deal out there. Trust me. With a 401(k), you get to shelter a slice of your salary before Uncle Sam gets a bite. Here's how it can work: Let's say you make $50,000 a year, and you decide to put 10 percent of it into your company's 401(k) plan. Every week, your payroll department will withdraw about $96 from your paycheck before it can be taxed by the IRS or the state. So right from the start, you enjoy a tax break.

Better yet, your company will probably reward you for your admirable savings habit. By one estimate, 88 percent of employers offering 401(k) plans now match all or part of each worker's own contributions. Let's say your company happens to be one of the most generous ones—it provides a 100 percent match. So if you contribute $5,000 a year, your company will throw that amount in the kitty as well. So just for showing up at work each week, you have $5,000 in free money sloshing around in your account. When you add up the tax savings, the company match, and your potential investment gains, your $5,000 contribution will enjoy an initial-year return of more than 100 percent.

The federal government sets limits on how much money you can stash in a 401(k). In 1998, the maximum contribution was $10,000. If you can't manage to put in the maximum allowable, at least try to take advantage of whatever your company's free matching contribution is. A typical employer match is 50 cents on every dollar you kick in. So if you contribute $100 a week, the company deposits an extra $50 into your account. Like I said, free money. Maybe your company will provide this match for your contributions that equal up to 6 percent of your pay. (You are allowed to contribute 10 percent, but your company won't match that last 4 percent.) If this is the case, try to contribute at least 6 percent to capture the whole match.

While you're at it, don't ignore putting money into an IRA. Getting people to fund an IRA became a lot tougher after Congress made it harder for people to deduct their contributions from their taxes in 1986. But today's IRA looks fantastic. In fact, it's hard not to fall in love with the new Roth IRA. (For more details on the new and improved IRAs, see Chapter 13, "Taxes and Investing—What You Should Know.") And as always, the IRA provides a great way to bulk up your savings through the power of compounding. Just take a look at this illustration.

Source: Fidelity Investments

Saving diligently through 401(k) plans is only half the battle. Avoiding the temptation to plunder the nest egg can be even tougher. You'll get the opportunity when you leave a job. When you depart, you can take that tax-deferred money with you. What you should do is have your old employer transfer it directly to an IRA rollover account that you've established with a brokerage account, mutual fund company, or bank. Your IRA rollover account allows your retirement money to continue growing without taxation just like it did when your employer was responsible for it. Once the transfer is made, you'll have to decide how you want the money invested.

Your worst possible move would be to stick the money in your checking account and start spending it. One reason is obvious—this is supposed to provide for you during your golden years. (Without the money, *golden* might not be the best adjective for what lies ahead.) But there's another good reason as well. Let's say you have $60,000 in a 401(k) plan. If you cash that in, Uncle Sam will be waiting for his take. If you are in the 30 percent tax bracket, for example, you will pay that amount off the top. What's more, unless you're at least 59½ years old, you'll owe a 10 percent penalty for the early withdrawal. All of a sudden, your windfall has shriveled to $36,000. If someone stole $24,000 from you at gunpoint, it would probably be one of the most traumatic moments of your life. But amazingly, departing employees who raid their retirement accounts just shrug off this financial debacle. And that, my friends, is one of the biggest investing mistakes you can make.

Even if you intend to stash your retirement windfall—you'll hear your employer call it a *lump sum distribution*—in a rollover, you could lose part of it if you aren't careful. What you don't want is your employer sending the proceeds of your 401(k) or pension directly to your home in a check made out to you. If you do it this way, don't be surprised when you discover that 20 percent of what you saved is missing. The IRS requires that 20 percent withholding—it wants its taxes from you up front just in case you decide against rolling over the amount. Let's say your 401(k) plan has $120,000 in it when you leave. When your check arrives, it totals just $96,000. Unfortunately, you'll only have 60 days to deposit the entire amount in a rollover, even though you're faced with a temporary shortfall. Sorry, but you won't get back that 20 percent until after you file your yearly tax return.

There is an easy way, however, to avoid the 20 percent withholding requirement. You can instruct your old employer to transfer the money directly into a rollover account that you've established. Another way is to keep the money in your old workplace's plan or to transfer it to your new employer's program.

Risk isn't always the bad guy

Remember that not all risk is bad. Actually, risk is a lot like cholesterol. There is good cholesterol, and then there is the bad stuff that can choke your arteries. Risk is bad medicine when it's inappropriate. If you blindly walk into an investment, whether it's a limited partnership, a variable annuity, or a zero-coupon bond, that's a bad risk.

Believe it or not, one of the greatest risks you can face is shying away from any. Why? Consider what could happen if you kept all your money tied up in U.S. Treasury bills or certificates of deposit. Sure, your money will technically be safe, but the financial price will be steep. By avoiding any risks in your portfolio, your money will be eaten alive by inflation. That's been true even during the '90s when inflation has been almost invisible. Need further convincing of inflation's sneaky ways? Look at this example.

Watch Out!
Never transfer money into an investment you don't understand or can't explain. Examining a contract or a prospectus is crucial if you want to make a wise choice. And ask questions if you don't understand something.

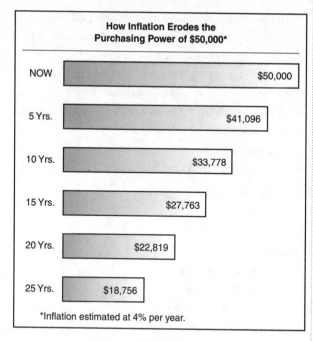

How Inflation Erodes the Purchasing Power of $50,000*

NOW	$50,000
5 Yrs.	$41,096
10 Yrs.	$33,778
15 Yrs.	$27,763
20 Yrs.	$22,819
25 Yrs.	$18,756

*Inflation estimated at 4% per year.

How inflation erodes the purchasing power of $50,000. *Source: Neuberger & Berman*

Here's a concrete example of what could happen if you keep all your cash in a money market, an essentially risk-free investment. You're very disciplined and you don't touch this super-safe investment for decades. Some day, you expect this money to bankroll a cozy retirement. Think again. With taxes (assuming a 28 percent tax bracket) and inflation (at a modest 3 percent) gnawing away at your thin returns, guess how long it could take for you to double your money? You'd die before you found out. Doubling this money could easily take 120 years. Using the same scenario, stocks would likely double in 17 years.

Before you can assess how much risk you can tolerate, you need to know what general categories the main types of investments fall into. For anyone unsure of just how risky some investment opportunities are, here's a quick checklist. You'll learn a great deal more about many of these options later on in the book:

Almost Risk Free
> Certificates of deposit
> Passbook savings
> Money market
> U.S. Treasury bills

Limited Risk
> Municipal bonds
> Blue chip stocks
> Corporate bonds

Moderate to High Risk
> Small-cap stocks
> Foreign stocks
> Rental real estate

Highest Risk
> Commodities
> Futures, options, and other derivatives
> Gold and other precious metals
> Junk bonds
> Initial public offerings of stock

What you should avoid is taking on more risk than you can handle. If your heart flutters whenever you think back to those autumn days in 1987 or 1997 on Wall Street, then maybe you should reconsider how much you have in the stock market. The worst thing you can do, after all, is panic during a downturn and sell out. But before you give up on stocks, remember that the market is really like a wad of Silly

Putty. When it hits the floor, it bounces back up. It might take a few days, weeks, months, or even years, but it has always rebounded. Even after the trouncing in 1987, it took the average stock investor just 18 months to recoup her money.

If none of this sounds the least bit reassuring, there are actually ways to reduce your exposure to risk without sacrificing much in the way of expected return. If you're skeptical, read on for how you can pull this off.

Diversifying can chase away investing jitters

Over the decades, study after study has documented that *asset allocation,* which is an investor's mix of stocks, bonds, and cash, is far more important to financial success than decisions about which individual bonds and stocks to buy. In fact, one famous study published in 1986 suggests that an amazing 91 percent of the performance differences among various investment portfolios can actually be traced back to the asset allocations chosen. So such things as market timing, the securities selected, and even dumb luck had far less of an impact. While some financial experts have quarreled with the 91 percent figure, the real point is undisputed: Diversification is extremely important. And yet despite its virtues, too many people are sitting on lopsided portfolios. They might have all their money tied up in Treasury notes or in a savings account. Somebody else might own three mutual funds, but the funds are all devoted to the same kind of stocks. Other people sink all their money into real estate.

There are excellent reasons why spreading your assets among different types of investments is wise. Stock and bond returns, for example, don't follow

> " Tis the part of a wise man to keep himself today for tomorrow, and not venture all his eggs in one basket.
> —Miguel de Cervantes, *Don Quixote de la Mancha*
> "

Watch Out!
Because your
livelihood is
already closely
tied to the for-
tunes of your
employer, you
should avoid
loading up on
your employer's
stock in your
401(k). Often,
employees tuck
some of their
tax-deferred con-
tributions into
their corpora-
tion's stock. The
company then
matches those
contributions
with more in-
house stock. This
can be a recipe
for disaster.

each other like shadows. If your holdings in blue
chip stocks take a hit one year, it's quite possible that
your bonds will be doing just fine. In this scenario,
your bonds soften the losses your portfolio absorbed
from your equities. When bonds are down, stocks
could be up. Of course, this yin-and-yang bailout
won't happen every time your bonds or stocks get
hammered. But more often than not, the combination has historically dampened the volatility of the
typical investor's portfolio.

Of course, the most conservative investors
among us might remain quite skeptical about the
merits of asset allocation. There are many retirees
living on a fixed income who would insist that stocks
are too risky to touch. But even die-hard bond lovers
could actually reduce their risk by purchasing some
shares in a well-diversified stock mutual fund. Yes,
you heard it right—a smattering of stocks could
reduce a bondholder's risk. To appreciate how this
could happen, you need to glance at the following
table, which lists the average annual returns of
stocks; high-quality, long-term bonds; and combinations during a half-century span ending in 1996.

AVERAGE ANNUAL INVESTMENT RETURNS FROM 1946 TO 1996

	Return	Risk (Standard Deviation)
Stocks	12.4%	16.0%
Bonds	5.4%	10.4%
50/50 Stocks & Bonds	9.2%	10.7%
60/40 Stocks & Bonds	9.9%	11.5%
40/60 Stocks & Bonds	8.5%	10.2%

Source: Frank Russell Co.

When you first look at the table, it might not appear to contain any surprises. Through the second half of the 20th century, stocks have far out-muscled bonds. And portfolios with a mix of bonds and equities have done better than strictly bonds. None of that is shocking news.

But a primary concern of bond holders is volatility, which is why the second column on risk is so important. Looking at this column, you can see what the typical volatility—up and down—is for each investment category. *Standard deviation,* by the way, is simply a statistical measure that indicates how far a return might typically be expected to wander from its average return. Statisticians determine the standard deviation after analyzing decades' worth of returns. As an example, let's see what kind of volatility you could expect from an all-bond portfolio. There is a very good chance that the portfolio will deliver a return that ranges from 15.8 percent on the high side to a negative 5 percent on the downside. If you're wondering how I got those numbers, I added 10.4 (the standard deviation for bonds) to 5.4 to get the greater figure, and I subtracted 10.4 from 5.4 to get the lower one. You might be startled to find that stodgy bonds can be so mercurial.

Let's make things even more interesting by looking at what kind of volatility we can expect from a 60/40 mix of bonds and stocks. In any given year, there is a good chance the return will range anywhere from 18.7 percent down to 1.7 percent. As you can see, this mix has historically provided greater returns, while the downside is generally not as bad. You need to keep in mind, however, that these figures aren't fortune-tellers. In any given year, these investments may do better or worse.

Timesaver
A quick-and-dirty way to diversify is through mutual funds. Each mutual fund can hold stocks and bonds from dozens or hundreds of sources.

When you are deciding what your asset mix should be, you can't do it without establishing your investment goals. You'd never build a house without blueprints, and you can't construct a portfolio without a blueprint, either. It's impossible to select appropriate bonds and stocks unless you know what your investing goals and time horizons are. Here are four key points to consider before deciding what your best investment choices are:

■ **Objective:** You need to establish what financial results you desire. How much money do you want to have, for instance, when you retire at age 65? How much will you need for your child's braces in four years? Then you need to calculate what kind of rate of return you'll need to meet that goal.

■ **Time horizon:** Ask yourself if the investment plans you formulate will fit into your financial timeline. If you'll need money in two or three years, for instance, you don't want to sink it into an aggressive growth mutual fund that can lose as much money as it can make. If you think you'd never do something like that, you'd be surprised how many people eagerly buy a fund just because it earned a spot on some yearly financial honor roll. And the same admonition holds true for stodgier investments. If you purchase U.S. Treasury bills for your child's education, you won't get enough oomph from the return—as I write, the yield is around 5 percent—to do a lot of good. With such a long-term horizon, you can afford to take more risks with stocks. As a rule of thumb, you'll typically expect to use short-term money in one to three years. When saving for long-term goals, give yourself more than five years. Those years in the middle are for intermediate-term goals.

- **Financial situation:** What percentage of your net worth are you planning on investing? If you don't have an adequate amount in reserve for emergencies, you might want to be more cautious with your investments.

- **Risk tolerance:** How comfortable are you with risk? Everybody's answer to this one will be different. One person will be quite comfortable investing 100 percent in stocks. Somebody else will shudder at sinking even a small portion of their assets into stocks.

Don't get too fancy—stick with the basics

A lot has been written and said about the secrets of successful investing. Unread doctoral dissertations and weighty books have been devoted to the topic. Newsletters that purport to know the answer charge people like you and me hundreds of dollars a year. Entire television channels spend all their on-air time discussing it. And yet it really boils down to what Jane Bryant Quinn says. If you want to do well, you don't need to be weaving in and out of the market. You don't need to get hung up with derivatives, options, futures, and other incredibly exotic stuff. And you don't need to worry about whatever utterances come out of the mouth of the Federal Reserve Bank chairman, who wields the power to raise or lower the nation's interest rates. Whenever he speaks publicly, the financial world acts like it's watching extra innings in the seventh game of the World Series. Wall Street is riveted. Before the man

> 66
> Investing should be boring, boring, boring.
> —Jane Bryant Quinn, syndicated personal finance columnist and author
> 99

has even finished his speech, stock prices could be hopping like Mexican jumping beans.

You can tune out all that noise. Instead, what you need to do is pick a small number of investments that offer a historical level of return that you can live with. These investments should also offer a level of risk that won't keep you up at night. Once that's done, you should leave your selections alone most of the time. Do not check on your investments every day or even every week. If you do, you might be tempted to make changes that you later regret. In fact, you'd be surprised at how little time you need baby-sitting your portfolio. Seeing how your portfolio is faring four times a year, or once a quarter, should be sufficient for most. If you own riskier investments, such as individual stocks, you might need to keep closer tabs on what you own. All in all, it's a very boring way to get rich.

Know your tax rate

This might seem way too obvious for most of you. But many people won't necessarily know what their rate is if a preparer completes their annual tax forms. If your income has jumped recently, you might not even realize that you've vaulted into a higher tax bracket. Your bracket more than likely would have jumped if you left your job and cashed in your 401(k) proceeds instead of rolling them over into another tax-deferred account. Or it might not occur to you that you've slipped a notch if you were on disability for a few weeks or you didn't get your usual fat bonus in December.

Not knowing your tax rate can lead you to poor investment decisions. Let's use Nicholas as an example. Nicholas is new to investing, but he has a lot on the ball. After his two kids are asleep, he often reads

Moneysaver
Consider putting much of your money into *index funds,* which are mutual funds that track major stock and bond benchmarks. The most popular are tied to the Standard & Poor's 500 Index, which includes many of the nation's largest corporations.

financial magazines to help him decide how he should diversify his growing nest egg. He has read a lot about how it makes sense to soften the volatility of a portfolio by owning bonds. Consequently, he decides to sink some cash into the Vanguard Long-Term Municipal Bond Fund. It's a solid choice. The fund is highly rated and, as a bonus, its expenses are minuscule. So where did he go wrong?

His tax rate will sabotage his returns. Nicholas's tax bracket is 15 percent, but municipal bonds don't make financial sense for anybody who isn't in a higher bracket. Muni bond issuers get away with paying a lower rate of interest because investors are getting a built-in tax break—they don't have to pay federal taxes on the interest. But if you aren't in a high tax bracket, this tax break won't amount to much. Investors in the higher tax brackets, however, will gladly accept a more modest yield, because they expect a potentially sizable tax break.

Forget about timing the market

Don't fret about whether today, tomorrow, or next year would be the best time to make your move. When is the most opportune time to jump into the market? It's a question the pros struggle with every day. Imagine the poor mutual fund manager who gets an additional $2 million a week to invest. Should he put this in stocks? What if the market is fully valued? As a hedge, maybe he should keep some of it in cash. For him, these sorts of decisions are not idle exercises. Whether he succeeds or fails is readily apparent to any of the thousands of shareholders, who can flip to the back of a newspaper business section to check on his performance. I visited one fund company where each portfolio's

Unofficially...
A surprisingly large number of taxpayers in the 15 percent bracket own municipal bonds, according to John Nuveen & Co. On the other hand, only one-fifth of the tax returns showing adjusted gross incomes of $100,000 to $200,000 reported any income from municipal bonds. Yet it's these wealthier people who could most benefit from the tax-free invest-ment.

results, up to the minute, were posted on a large electronic bulletin board that stretched across the entire floor where the portfolio managers and the stock traders sat. Talk about pressure.

Luckily, we don't have to please thousands of shareholders, and nobody is going to post our investing results on a billboard. If you get a chunk of money all at once—perhaps you received an inheritance or rolled over your 401(k) money when you left a job—proceed slowly. Find yourself a good financial advisor or take the time to educate yourself. When you feel ready, you don't have to jump in all at once. Invest gradually at the pace you feel comfortable with. And don't worry about the timing— even the pros can't get it right.

Ask yourself, "How am I doing?"

Most people aren't sure how well or how badly their investments fare year after year. If you own mutual funds, you can look at the year-to-date and year-end figures in the newspaper listings. Some newspapers also list three- and five-year statistics. What you'll be looking at are a fund's total return figures. This is the best measure of how your fund is doing, because it takes into account not only the fund's appreciation (if there was any), but also the interest or dividends it has generated.

While the fund listings in the newspaper eliminate any guesswork, you can calculate this same total return for any stock holdings you own. Let's assume that the 500 shares of stock you bought for $30 each jump to $50 a share a year later. What's more, you pocket $350 in dividends. To obtain your investment's total return, you add the stock's appreciation—$10,000 and the $350. Next you divide $10,350 by $15,000, the original cost. Your total return for the year is 69 percent.

If you own bonds, you'll also want to know how to calculate the yield. If you buy a $1,000 bond, and it provides $100 in interest, the yield is 10 percent. To get that figure, you divide the annual interest by your cost of the bond. If the market value of a bond changes (this can happen for various economic reasons), the interest payment stays the same, but the yield changes. For instance, if you buy this same bond at a premium price of $1,100, the yield dips to 9 percent.

Knowing your annual return is valuable, because it allows you to know if you are staying on the right financial track. If you are not meeting your financial benchmarks, you might have to play catch up by saving more money the next year. On the other hand, if you surpassed your goal of, say, a 12 percent return, you might lighten up on your equities if you are uncomfortable about the risk they pose.

If you work with a full-service broker or a financial planner, ask one of them to calculate your investment returns. There is also plenty of personal-finance software on the market that can do the calculations, such as Managing Your Money, Microsoft Money, and Quicken.

Don't fall for bad financial advice

Beware of friends and brokers pitching stock tips. Don't assume that the stocks your golf buddy brags about are right for you. Everyone's investment goals are different, so think hard, and then think again before you follow the advice of someone you know. Unfortunately, Gene, an editor I know, fell into this trap. Awhile ago, he bought shares in Iomega, the

Timesaver
Rule of 72 is an easy way to calculate how quickly your money will double. Simply divide 72 by the annual rate of return you expect on your investment. Let's say you invest $25,000 in a mutual fund earning 8 percent annually. According to the equation (72 divided by 8), your fund would be worth $50,000 in nine years.

Bright Idea
You can figure
out the *price-to-
earnings* (P/E)
ratio by dividing
the price of a
stock by its
earnings per
share. For
instance, if a
$20 stock earned
$1 a share last
year, its P/E
ratio is 20. You
can find a com-
pany's P/E in a
newspaper's
stock listings. A
company is usu-
ally fairly valued
if its P/E pretty
much equals its
growth rate.

maker of computer data-storage devices in the bustling metropolis of Roy, Utah. Iomega's fanatical fans on the Internet had whipped up people's enthusiasm for this stock into a frothy frenzy. True believers, particularly those who hung out in investor chat rooms on America Online, pumped up the excitement about this young company with a constant bombardment of positive messages. Amazingly, all this electronic chitchat elevated the stock price well beyond what it was worth, making early holders of this stock rich.

Gene, who subscribed to AOL, had seen some of the Iomega hype, but he was more impressed with the two guys in his office who had made a bundle on the stock. Gene finally decided to join them. However, by the time Gene bought his shares, the stock was so overvalued that the *short-sellers*—people who make financial bets that a stock will plummet in value—were circling like vultures. The end came shortly after Iomega hit a record price of $54 a share, which represented an astronomical price-to-earnings ratio of 100. After that, the stock skidded faster than a kid on a greased slide. Iomega was soon selling for $18. You don't need a calculator to understand what happened to Gene's investment. Soon after, he sold at a loss.

And while you're at it, don't jump for every breathless idea your broker suggests. Remember that these guys dress in Brooks Brothers suits, but they are really car salesmen at heart. They make their money when you buy or trade in what you've got. That seems only fair, but you have to be aware of the built-in conflict of interest. If you are a classic buy-and-hold customer, your broker can't get rich off you. He'll earn respectable commissions, how-ever, if you jump in and out of investments.

If you happily own General Electric stock, and your broker is urging you to dump that and buy a different blue chip company, you should rightly ask a lot of questions. Also grill your broker if he seems eager to sign you up for investments wrapped in high commissions like limited partnerships and annuities. Chapter 3, "Financial Planners and Brokers—The Best of the Bunch," contains much more on brokers and financial advisors.

Just the facts

- Abandon those unrealistic expectations—they can sabotage your investing.

- Finding ways to stretch your investing dollars can make the difference.

- Risk is not a four-letter word; you can't succeed in investing without it.

- Waiting for the "ideal" time to invest your money is bound to fail.

GET THE SCOOP ON...
Organizing inventory—your finances ▪ Cinching
the budget belt ▪ What's important and
what's not ▪ A rainy-day fund strategy ▪
Best places to park your cash

Organizing Your
Finances from A to Z

Chapter 2

S ome thankless jobs always seem just too over-
whelming to tackle. Whether it's organizing
boxes full of old photographs, cleaning out
the garage so both your cars will fit in it again, or
making sense of the clutter hiding your desk, the
tasks are thankless.

Yet getting organized is a lot like giving blood.
It's very helpful to do it, but most people who intend
to roll up their sleeves never bother. So what do
clean desks and tidy garages have to do with money?
Unfortunately, there is a link. You'll have a better
shot at reaching your financial goals if you are organized. Not only should you round up all those stray
receipts, financial statements, life insurance policies, and income tax returns, but you also have to
make sense of it all. Only when you've gotten a good
handle on all of this can you hope to move on to
important and more rewarding jobs like setting
investment goals or polishing your financial game
plan.

You've already accomplished the first step. You are at least thinking about what you might need to do. This chapter will help you accomplish the rest. You'll

- Learn how to determine what you are worth at the outset.

- Look at sources of income that might not have even occurred to you. For instance, when you're adding up your assets, you need to keep in mind what your future Social Security benefits and any pensions will be worth. You'll learn where to go to find this out.

- Get contrarian advice on just how much cash you need to stockpile in a rainy-day fund.

- Discover places you can tap into in a crunch if you get sucked into a financial emergency.

- Examine the first step you should take to develop a solid portfolio from scratch.

Getting organized financially

There are good reasons why we need to be financially organized. At the outset, it's important to know where your starting line is. Throughout our lives, many of us make financial decisions in a vacuum. You might buy a whole life insurance policy from a neighbor, an annuity from a persistent broker, and a mutual fund that some writer, like me, gushed about in a magazine. You sign the documents and then you forget about your actions. Maybe you don't spend any time at all thinking about whether these decisions mesh nicely. And you won't really have a clue unless you have a sense of what your underlying financial foundation is. To do that, you need to have a clear understanding of your cash flow, your insurance coverage, your debt load, and your savings track record. Only after all that's done can you move—guilt free—onto the more fun stuff. Like picking stocks, bonds, and mutual funds.

Luckily it doesn't take long to fill in these blanks. At the most, you will only miss one night's worth of TV by completing an inventory of your net worth. First you need to add up your assets. Then you need to tally up your debts. To get you motivated, I've provided a worksheet. After you've glanced at it, read the advice that follows before filling it out.

When you're filling out this worksheet, it will be tempting to inflate what you own. For instance, you might write down that your sapphire wedding ring is worth $3,000. Your husband's hand might have been shaking 13 years ago when he wrote that $3,000 check to the jeweler, but frankly, the market is not robust for used wedding rings. You'd pocket nothing close to that if you were ever forced to sell it. It would be just as easy for someone to inflate the value of a car. Used-car guides suggest that the top price for your type might be $14,000. But what if it has a dent the size of a grapefruit on the driver's door and the upholstery is splitting at the seams? You wouldn't get anywhere near that. The bottom line: Be realistic about the resale value of your possessions.

You need to be careful with other calculations as well. Let's say a couple bought their house for $130,000 several years ago, but it's now worth $260,000—double the price. Should they use that $260,000 figure on their net worth sheet? No. If they sold the house tomorrow, they'd have to pay a Realtor's commission that could equal 6 percent of the sale price. (The outstanding mortgage will be

WORKSHEET 2.1   YOUR NET WORTH WORKSHEET

Assets

1. Cash

    Checking account _____

    Money markets _____

    Certificates of deposit _____

2. Investments

    Stocks _____

    Bonds _____

    Mutual funds _____

    Life insurance (cash value) _____

3. Fixed assets

    Home _____

    Other real estate _____

4. Retirement assets

    Vested interest in company pension
       or profit-sharing plan _____

    Annuities (cash value) _____

    401(k) plan _____

    Other retirement plans _____

    Future Social Security
       benefits _____

5. Personal assets

    (Fair market or replacement value)

    Cars _____

Computers _____

Jewelry _____

Art and antiques _____

6. Money loaned to others

   (If repayment is expected) _____

7. Other assets _____

   Total assets _____

Debt

1. Home mortgage _____

2. Mortgage on real estate _____

3. Vehicle loans _____

4. Bank loans _____

5. Credit card balances _____

6. Student loans _____

7. Outstanding judgments _____

8. Income taxes due _____

9. Loans on 401(k) plan _____

10. Loans on life insurance
    policies _____

11. Other liabilities _____

Total debt _____

Net worth _____

**Subtract total debt from
total assets** _____

entered in the debt section.) An estimated best guess of the commission and any other costs should be deducted from the $260,000. If you aren't sure what your house is worth, you can call a local real estate office or look at similar listings in your newspaper.

When calculating your net worth, don't forget to plug in your future Social Security benefits. This one might stump you. Most people's knowledge of the Social Security Administration begins and ends with their own Social Security number. To get a feel for what your benefits will be in the future, you'll need to obtain a copy of your *Personal Earnings and Benefit Estimate Statement*. This document includes the amount of Social Security taxes you've paid during your lifetime, as well as how much you've earned. You'll also learn how much you can roughly expect from Social Security if you retire at ages 62, 65, or 70. You can request the free statement by contacting your local Social Security office or by calling (800) 772-1213. You can order the form through the agency's Web site at www.ssa.gov. You'll get the statement by mail in about a month.

And don't forget to check on your workplace retirement plan. Ask your employer for something called the *Summary Plan Description*. This document, which outlines how your company's pension plan works, explains how pension calculations are made. You'll also need your individual benefit statement. This will pinpoint what your pension benefits are currently worth and how many years you've been enrolled in your employer's plan. The statement might include a projection of what your monthly checks will be when you retire. Check for any obvious errors, such as wrong birth date or incorrect

Moneysaver
The Social Security Administration strongly urges people to examine the record of their earnings every two to three years. The federal agency estimates that it accurately posts 99.5 percent of all workers' yearly earnings, but there are occasional glitches.

years of service. And if you are stashing away money in a 401(k), a 403(b), or some other workplace retirement plan, scrutinize those periodic statements as well.

Mistaken pension calculations aren't as rare as you might assume. In a recent survey of 6,000 companies, federal auditors estimated that 8 percent of departing workers were receiving lump-sum payouts that were way too skimpy. While the study only examined small firms, the big guys can be just as guilty at underpaying. Corporations such as Allstate, Continental Airlines, GTE, and the Times Mirror Co. have been caught mailing puny pension checks or handing out incorrect lump-sum payments.

Most of the time, companies don't intentionally underestimate pension benefits. But that would be little comfort if you end up receiving less money during retirement than you are entitled to. If you do spot problems, contact your plan administrator or the company's human resources department. Here are some frequent errors to watch out for:

- The company forgot to include such things as overtime, bonuses, and commissions in determining your benefit level.

- Somebody used the wrong benefits formula. For instance, an incorrect interest rate was plugged into the equation.

- Your employer used incorrect Social Security information in calculating your benefits.

- Your pension calculations are wrong because you worked past age 65.

- Your company's computer software is badly flawed.

Timesaver
If you're worried about your pension accuracy, you can seek help from a certified pension specialist, who typically charges by the hour. To obtain names of actuaries in your area, call the American Society of Pension Actuaries at (703) 516-9300. A free source is the Pension Rights Center, a not-for-profit advocacy group at (202) 296-3776. It maintains a network of actuaries who will help for free.

- You didn't keep your personnel office updated on important changes, such as a marriage, divorce, or death of a spouse, that might affect your benefits.

- The company forgot to include all your years of service.

- Basic math mistakes were made.

What the worksheet can tell you

Let's see how one hypothetical couple does when they fill out their net worth sheet. Jackie, who is 35, vows on New Year's day to significantly increase the amount of money she saves yearly. She and her husband aren't immune to all those gloom-and-doom projections they've been reading predicting that vast numbers of Baby Boomers will be scrubbing dishes at Denny's in 20 years if they don't start saving more money. Jackie's goal is definitely an admirable one. There's only one problem. She and her husband have only the vaguest notion of how much they have saved and how much they owe.

After the drill, the couple's financial picture is a mixed bag. Most of their money is tied up in their home. Based on what their house is valued at today, their equity is $160,000 (minus those future selling costs). Jackie's 401(k) plan contains $31,000, while her husband's has $20,000. They have $8,000 stashed away in a stock mutual fund, as well as $5,000 in their checking overdraft account. Their biggest liability is the mortgage. But they also owe $22,000 on a Ford Expedition they bought last year. And Jackie's credit cards have an alarming $6,500 balance. Excluding the house, the couple has accumulated $64,000 in assets. They agree to continue putting the maximum allowable amount in their

401(k) plans, but in addition, they will try to save an extra $4,000 this year to earmark for his-and-her IRAs. Jackie would like to save more, but after realizing how the credit card debt has piled up, she wants to pay off the four cards as soon as possible. Jackie is smart not to funnel more money into savings when her debt is fueled by an outrageous 19 percent interest rate.

By filling out the worksheet, Jackie is now on the right track. If you come out better than you thought you would after completing it, congratulations. But don't take it too hard if your financial net worth isn't where you'd like it to be. The most important thing is that you have started. If you need to improve your savings and reduce your debt, join the crowd. Just about everybody you'll ever share an elevator with needs to do the same thing.

One way to shed debt and bulk up on assets is to put yourself on a money diet. Your first step is to figure out just where you are hemorrhaging all this money. The next worksheet helps you do that. There are different ways to fill out budgets. Some experts are too fanatical in their advice. Some suggest that you carry a notebook and record all your purchases for a couple of months. Since I wouldn't have the discipline to try that, I'm not going to recommend that you do it either. And actually, I don't think it's really necessary. Estimating expenses should suffice.

Actually, it will be easy to get the exact figures for some expenses. For instance, you probably know how much your mortgage, car payment, children's tuition or day care, and various insurance premiums are each month. By pulling out your canceled checks, you can get a good handle on utilities,

Bright Idea
After you finish your financial inventory and are ready to begin investing, don't forget to ask yourself this question: How much am I prepared to lose? There is no limit to how much money you want to make, but there will be a limit to how much you can afford to lose.

property taxes, telephone, and other such expenses. If you're a heavy credit card user, checking past statements should fill in a lot of the remaining blanks. And your bank statement will tell you how often you are hitting up the *automated teller machines* (ATMs) for cash.

Not everybody needs to put themselves on a budget. If you are saving the maximum amount through your company's 401(k) plan, stuffing $2,000 a year into an Individual Retirement Account, maintaining an emergency cash fund, and socking some money away for college tuition or other goals, you can skip the next worksheet.

Everybody else, pick up your pencils.

If you are lucky, you'll have a surplus. If not, you have your work cut out for you. When Jackie fills out her budget, some of her spending habits shock her. For instance, she was blowing $2,100 a year on Christmas presents and all the trimmings, and her and her husband's lunch tab was even more amazing. They were spending $3,500 a year on chef salads, roast beef sandwiches, and clam chowder. They vow to eat more leftovers. They also decide to find cheaper auto insurance after they learn that they can save several hundreds of dollars by buying insurance through a direct insurance carrier instead of through an agent.

Here are some other quick ideas for cinching the budget belt:

- **Ignore a raise.** When you receive a raise, pretend that you never got it. Invest that extra money instead of letting it disappear into your checking account's black hole.

- **Pretend you still have a car loan.** When your car is paid off, keep making those payments—to yourself. Let's assume that you've just paid off a $190-a-month loan on your Honda Civic. By putting that $190 aside each month (and earning 7 percent interest), you'll have almost $7,500 in three years.

- **Refinance your mortgage.** When interest rates are low, find a cheaper loan. You'll discover plenty of no-points loans to choose from. Because you don't have to pay *points*, or loan charges, you can keep refinancing as long as the interest rates keep declining. Several years ago, my husband and I refinanced our house three times within little more than a year. By doing that, we shaved a total of $400 off our monthly mortgage.

- **Don't buy on impulse.** Do you really need those clunky-heeled shoes that will look ridiculous on your feet in six months when everyone else is slipping back into spike heels or flats? Does your child really need to visit Toys 'Я' Us again?

- **Don't blow your tax refund.** Stick it in an Individual Retirement Account.

Financial spring cleaning

You can put away your calculator now. The worksheets are behind you. Now that you've dug out all your records, you should try to keep them in some kind of order. Saving documents can help you keep on top of just how much you are worth and where you are heading financially. If your record keeping is sloppy or incomplete, you could run into trouble later on with the IRS.

Paperwork can pile up like snowdrifts, but you don't have to keep it all. When the urge to get out

Moneysaver
Save extra paychecks. If you get paid biweekly, there will be two months when you receive a third paycheck. During those two months, channel all or part of that money into your savings.

WORKSHEET 2.2 INCOME STATEMENT

Yearly Cash Income

1. Salary _____

2. Commissions, bonuses, and
   profit sharing _____

3. Dividends and interest _____

4. Proceeds from sale of
   investments _____

5. Alimony or child support
   received _____

6. Pension _____

7. Social Security _____

8. Annuity and life insurance
   income _____

9. Cash gifts _____

10. Other income _____

Total Income _____

Yearly Cash Expenses

1. Housing

   Rent or mortgage _____

   Utilities _____

   Insurance _____

   Property taxes _____

   Repairs _____

   Improvements _____

2. Food _____

3. Clothing (include dry
   cleaning) _____

4. Telephone _____

5. Automobile

   Gas and repairs _____

   Car loan(s) _____

   Car lease _____

   Insurance _____

6. Medical

   Physicians _____

   Dentist _____

   Medicines _____

   Health insurance _____

7. Child-care expenses _____

8. Tuition _____

9. Alimony/child support _____

10. Charity _____

11. Entertainment _____

12. Vacations _____

13. Gifts _____

14. Life insurance
       premiums _____

15. Union dues and professional
       expenses _____

16. Income and Social Security
       taxes _____

Total annual living expenses _____

Surplus or shortfall _____

Subtract expenses from income _____

the trash barrel and dust rag strikes, here's a guide
to follow:

Tax returns and supporting documents	Keep six years.
Canceled checks	Retain for one year, except for those pertaining to tax records, child support, and costly antiques and jewelry.
Paycheck stubs	Keep year-end statements for tax records, but pitch the rest.
Bank statements	Hold onto for one year.
House deed and title papers	Keep as long as you own the house.
Credit card statements	Keep two to three years.
IRA statements	Never throw these out.
Receipts	Hold until a warranty expires or for tax records.
Pension documents	Don't toss out any that your company gives you over the years. Also keep records of the dates when you've worked and your salary.

A rainy-day fund for stormy times

Now comes the fun part—deciding what you should
do with the money you are squeezing out of your
budget. Before you start investing, you need to set
aside a chunk of money for a financial cushion. I'm
going to share with you what the traditional rule of
thumb is for feeding your emergency reserve. And

then I'm going to explain why you might want to ignore it.

Financial experts suggest that you set aside three to six months' worth of your living expenses in an ultrasafe place, like a bank account or money market. This money is for all those potential emergencies that give you nightmares—someone in your family is hospitalized for weeks, you lose your job, you get sucked into an expensive lawsuit... the scenarios are endless. According to one estimate, the cash reserve for the average American household would range from $8,000 to $16,000.

Let's get real here. Is somebody really going to refrain from investing in stocks and bonds while they slowly and religiously accumulate a significant slosh pile of cash? I don't think so. If your combined income is $60,000, for instance, you'd need up to $30,000 before the personal finance wizards say it's safe to venture into the financial markets. If you set aside $500 a month for your reserve, it would take you five years to come up with the dough.

Not many of us have this kind of financial self-control to save for a rainy day. If we did, there wouldn't be so many Americans leasing new cars because they don't have the down payment to buy one outright. What this rigid hurdle can do is discourage would-be investors from ever sticking their toes in the starting blocks. And if you never get started, you'll never appreciate how rewarding investing can be.

I'm not suggesting that somebody without a dime in the bank put his next paycheck in the stock market. It's wise to maintain a safe cash reserve for the inevitable aggravations—your engine needs an overhaul, your property tax is due, the stove burnt its last batch of cookies. Just how much you should stash away depends on your situation, but one month's salary could be a good target for many people. I'd put the rest of your emergency-fund money into a solid stock or bond fund with an excellent pedigree. I mention six great choices in "Setting Your Financial Goals," later in this chapter. Since most people aren't going to have a big lump sum to invest all at once anyway, I suggest that you gradually build up this secondary emergency fund through monthly or bimonthly deposits into a mutual fund. If you don't have the discipline to write those regular checks, establishing an automatic withdrawal plan is an excellent way to start. Once the paperwork is finished, the mutual fund automatically withdraws an agreed-upon amount from your bank account each month on a designated day. This money is deposited into your fund, and you receive a statement with your deposit duly noted.

By sinking money regularly into your equity rainy-day fund, you should, over time, enjoy greater returns than a savings account or money market can offer. And with a mutual fund, you will eventually earn enough money—and more quickly—for just about any emergency. This money, however, should not be used for casual dipping, because it brings the most benefit when bought and held.

Some might find what I'm saying financial heresy. Putting reserve money into the market can be a bad idea if your timing is exquisitely bad. Think back to October 19, 1987, when the stock market, within just a few hours, lost 20 percent of its value. If you desperately needed to pull money out the next day, you were in bad shape.

Even if you need your emergency cash in a hurry, there are ways to limit your exposure to this kind of stock market risk. If the stock market is depressed when you need your money, you might be surprised at where you can find some short-term cash. Of course, these possibilities should only be used in dire emergencies, and the money should be paid back quickly. If you think you'd be too tempted to forget to repay swiftly, do not even consider doing it! The following sections present some options.

401(k) loan

You can typically borrow up to 50 percent of the vested value of your workplace retirement fund as long as the amount doesn't exceed $50,000. The interest rate that the plan charges and that you pay back to yourself is often tied to the prime rate and might be cheaper than what you'd get from a bank. Banks loan their top-notch corporate borrowers their very best—prime—rate.

Most workers are well aware that they can tap into their retirement plans, but sometimes they turn to them too easily. They use their 401(k) money to buy an expensive car, a week's vacation, or a room addition. Many people justify the loan by rationalizing that they are paying themselves interest for the borrowing privileges. But you need to keep in mind that the potential for your money to strike it big during a heated stock market won't exist if it's on loan to you. Anybody who borrowed the money three years ago to pay for a Chevy Suburban, for instance, might be kicking themselves for pulling the money out. After all, the stock market during that time increased in value by almost 100 percent.

Home equity loan or home equity line of credit

With this type of loan, you borrow against whatever equity you have in your house. Using your home as collateral, a bank lends you anywhere from 80 percent to 120 percent of your equity.

Watch Out!
The interest rate you essentially pay yourself when you borrow against your 401(k) plan won't necessarily be as low as you think. Let's say the interest rate is 7 percent. Often, a workplace will pocket 1 percent as a surcharge as well. Read the terms of the loan carefully before proceeding with the loan.

Timesaver
Banks, savings
and loans, and
credit unions will
be glad to quote
you their rates
over the phone.
The process is
quick, and a
bank loan officer
can usually tell
you over the
phone if you
qualify. Ask the
bank to pay for
your home
appraisal—in
competitive mar-
kets, it will.

There are two kinds of equity loans to consider. The traditional home equity loan is the classic second mortgage. You borrow for a set number of years, and the loan is usually offered at a fixed rate. You repay little by little every month. The other kind of loan is a line of credit, and the interest rate varies just like those adjustable-rate mortgages. You aren't borrowing a fixed amount—it's like a credit card in that way. You borrow what you need—up to a cap.

What's attractive about these home equity loans is that, unlike 401(k) loans, the interest you pay is tax deductible. You only enjoy this tax break, however, if you file an itemized tax return.

Insurance policy borrowing

Borrowing against an insurance policy is possible if you own a *permanent life insurance policy*—whole life, universal, and variable life all qualify. Once again, the interest rate is reasonable. You can repay the loan by having the payments added to your premiums. If the loan isn't repaid, the amount is deducted from the death benefit.

Credit card advance

Obviously, the interest rate you pay for this quick cash fix can be stiff—anywhere from 12 percent to 21 percent. While you have a grace period when you make purchases with a credit card, there's no such thing for cash. You also can't deduct your interest payments on your tax returns. If you're constantly getting credit card solicitations in the mail, however, it's likely that you can lock in a much cheaper rate. Issuers who want your business will offer teaser rates like 5.9 percent. If you accept one of these cards, you often can transfer your debt from another card with a steep interest rate. These wonderful rates, however, usually only last a few months. If you intend to take out a cash advance after switching to a more attractive card, you must make sure the lower rate applies to such advances and not simply to purchases. A card with a rock-bottom interest rate for purchases could surprise you by charging 21 percent or some other outrageous interest rate for cash advances.

Remember, no matter which option you choose, these loans are only intended as temporary solutions. You should pay back the loan out of your weekly or monthly salary until the stocks and bonds in your mutual fund have recovered.

Determining how much you should set aside in your emergency fund varies dramatically from person to person. You should ask yourself these questions:

- Is my job at risk because of corporate mergers or downsizing? Or is my work seasonal with periods of unemployment?

- Does my household rely on one income?

- Am I self-employed, a small business owner, or heavily dependent on commissions?

- Do I have disability insurance?

- Is my medical insurance inadequate if someone in my family contracts a catastrophic illness?

If you answered yes to any of these questions, you might want to keep more money on hand for emergencies.

Your cash belongs here

Not all cash is created equal. Once you save up a tidy sum, it makes sense to park your cash in the spot offering the best return. The following sections discuss some choices.

Timesaver
A quick way to find credit cards with low interest rates is through CardTrak. For the latest list, send $5 to CardTrak at P.O. Box 1700, Frederick, MD 21702, (800) 344-7714. Or visit CardTrak's Web site (www.cardtrak.com). Bank Rate Monitor (www.bankrate.com) also provides lists on its Web site.

Money market funds

If you want more pizzazz from your spare cash than a bank passbook can offer, you should definitely consider a money market fund. These funds usually provide greater returns than savings accounts offered by banks and thrifts. In fact, money markets in recent years have often beaten the rates of six-month and one-year certificates of deposit as well.

A lot of people forget that money markets are really mutual funds. Maybe that's because you're not going to see a money market zigzag in price. Day in and day out, year in and year out, the price of one share should always be $1. It's just the yields that will vary. Yes, money markets are boring, but they're dependable. A lot of people like this dependability.

Technically, money markets are not as safe as bank deposits. The *Federal Deposit Insurance Corporation* (FDIC) after all, insures the money invested in certificates of deposit and savings passbooks up to $100,000 per person at any given bank or thrift, but it doesn't protect money markets. No individual investor, however, has ever lost a dime in a money market fund. While the federal *Securities and Exchange Commission* (SEC) tightly regulates these funds, keeping them safe is a zealous preoccupation of the mutual fund industry. Whenever there has been the slightest threat to the $1 share value of any fund, the fund company has scrambled to prop it up. After all, the last thing the industry wants to do is scare away customers.

Choosing a money market can be like shopping for black socks—there isn't much difference in the selection. With the SEC keeping a tight rein on what money managers can invest in, there's not a wide spread between the yields of the best and the worst.

> **"**
> Mutual fund companies go out of their way to make sure their money market funds stay stable. These are the safe havens for mutual-fund companies—the funds with the highest degree of stability.
> —Michelle A. Smith, Managing Director of the Mutual Fund Education Alliance
> **"**

Consequently, when choosing among hundreds of retail money market funds, you need to pay attention to expenses.

With competition among the funds so fierce, funds are slashing their fees to entice you to sign up. Often, the funds with the highest yields are the ones that have cut expenses. When selecting a fund, find out from the investment company how long it expects to keep fees artificially low. Ideally, you will find a money market that doesn't have to resort to waiving fees to earn its status as a top yielder.

Most money markets impose an initial minimum investment that can range anywhere from $1,000 all the way up to $25,000 for some of the highest-yielding funds. You'll also notice a difference in how many checks you may write off your account. Some money markets permit you to write as many as you please, while others impose a ceiling of less than 10. Also beware that some funds won't let you write a check for less than $100, or sometimes less than $500.

You'll also have to choose between taxable and tax-free funds. Tax-free funds offer a skimpier yield, but you do get a tax break. You won't have to pay federal taxes and, in some cases, state taxes. You can skip the state taxes if you live where state-specific, tax-free funds are available. Some of the states where you can find such funds include Arizona, California, Connecticut, Florida, Kentucky, Maryland, Massachusetts, Michigan, Minnesota, New Jersey, New York, North Carolina, Ohio, Pennsylvania, Rhode Island, Texas, and Virginia. Don't assume, however, that a tax-free choice is best just because some fund company is marketing it. For instance, Texas has no income tax, so why would

52 PART I ▪ A FIRM FOUNDATION

a single-state tax-free fund, which typically poses a higher risk than a national tax-free money market, benefit a Texan? The truth is that in many cases, single-state funds don't offer better returns—on a tax-adjusted basis—than national funds unless you live in a very high-tax state with good fund offerings, such as California, Massachusetts, Minnesota, or New York.

A tax-free fund typically makes financial sense for investors in the top tax brackets, but it's not a good choice for taxpayers in the lowest 15 percent bracket. They should stick with a taxable money fund. But you can do the calculations on your own. Let's say you're in the 28 percent tax bracket and you're trying to decide which is a better deal—a taxable fund with an 8.5 percent yield or a tax-free one offering 6 percent. Here is the formula to use:

Tax-free yield ÷ 1 × your federal tax bracket = taxable equivalent yield

This is how you'd plug in the numbers:

6 ÷ .72 (1 × .28) = 8.33 percent

In this case, it is better to stick with the taxable fund.

Certificates of deposit

If you absolutely, positively won't sleep with your money unprotected by the FDIC, your best bet is a certificate of deposit. When you buy a CD, you agree to keep your money in the bank for a specified period of time. The arrangement could last for weeks, months, or years. Most CDs pay you a set rate of interest, though some offer a variable rate, which can move up or down, depending on interest rate conditions.

The interest you can expect to receive from a CD is certainly better than the measly amount you can

Timesaver
A quick way to check on the best money market yields is to look in the financial section of your newspapers or to visit the IBC Financial Data Web site (www.ibcdata. com), which tracks the money market industry. Type in the money market features that interest you, and the IBC site steers you to its top recommendations.

extract from a savings account. But you can get stung if you break your promise and pull your money out early. If you get cold feet, a bank hits you with a penalty. (This can't happen with a money market. As long as you have cash sitting in your money market, you can happily write checks and make withdrawals.) Before you select a CD, be sure to find out what the penalties are.

When CD shopping, you might be able to do better if you pick one outside your neighborhood. Chances are your local bank doesn't offer CDs with the highest yields. One way to find the best rates is to hunt nationwide through a stockbroker, if you have one. (You shouldn't have to pay a commission.) You also can look up charts of CD rates in your local newspaper.

For anybody with a computer, a wonderful place to find the fattest CD yields is at the Web site of Bank Rate Monitor (www.bankrate.com), which tracks not only CD rates, but mortgage and credit card rates as well. At the regularly updated site, you can find "best deal" lists for CDs with varying maturities. The lists provide you with the financial institutions' toll-free phone numbers, their rates, and the minimum deposits required.

U.S. Treasury bills

If you have a lot of cash, you might want to check out U.S. Treasury bills. I'm not talking about dollar bills. These bills are actually "baby bonds" from the federal government. With a bill, your money is tied up for a very short period of time. You buy these short-term Treasuries at a slight discount. For example, you might pay 97 cents on the dollar. When the Treasury matures, you get the entire dollar. You can buy a bill with maturities of three to 12 months.

Watch Out!
Don't be fooled by a CD rate that looks too good to be true. Here's one ploy: A bank will advertise a CD with a generous rate, but it's actually a teaser rate for the tail end of your holding period. The CD might start two percentage points or more lower.

(Just to confuse you, the government calls Treasuries with longer maturities *notes* and *bonds*.)

Some investors prefer Treasury bills to CDs because they come equipped with a built-in tax break. You have to pay federal taxes on Treasuries, but you get to skip the state and local taxes. If you live in a high-tax state, this tax break can be a big deal. Also, there is no penalty for selling these bills early.

Treasuries aren't protected by the FDIC, but trust me, you can sleep like a baby with these bills. The U.S. government would have to crumble under an enemy invasion before it fails to honor its bond obligations. There is one big hurdle to jump, however, if you are interested. You'll learn more about U.S. Treasuries in Chapter 5, "Bond Isn't a Four-Letter Word," and you'll find out how to buy them direct from the federal government in Chapter 10, "Making Your Move—Buying and Selling."

Setting your financial goals

If you haven't invested before, you might be leery about getting started. Maybe you've seen charts with various asset-allocation models. Perhaps you've heard somebody at a party drone on about how you need to balance out your risk with a stock and bond portfolio that has exposure to small cap and foreign stocks. You don't want to know how a yield curve can affect your life. Relax. There's no need to get fancy at the beginning. After all, we don't get hit with calculus the day after we finally memorize our multiplication tables.

If you are an investing novice, one of the best places to begin is at your workplace. If you have a 401(k) or another workplace retirement plan in place, start putting money into it. For starters, the choices won't overwhelm you. By one estimate, the average 401(k) plan offers eight selections. This can be a relief, since there are thousands out there in the market clamoring for a piece of your wallet.

What if you don't have a workplace retirement plan? Don't sweat. The admonition again is to avoid anything too complicated. Actually, your best bet still is with mutual funds. As you'll learn elsewhere in this book, mutual funds are fast, easy ways to achieve instant diversification. If you have $3,000 to spread among bonds, stocks, and cash funds, your money won't stretch far. But it can spread quite a lot with a mutual fund. That's because your $3,000 will buy shares in a fund that is invested in perhaps dozens or hundreds of securities.

If the amount you can invest is limited, stick with one all-purpose fund at the start. This fund will be a core holding as your wealth grows and you eventually spread your money across stocks, bonds, and cash with an increasing level of sophistication. Of course, I just mentioned that there are thousands of funds to choose from. In fact, more than 5,600! But don't let that psych you out. Let's make this as easy as possible. Here are four solid stock funds:

	5-Year Annual Return	Phone
Dodge & Cox Stock Fund	21.5%	(800) 621-3979
Vanguard Windsor II	22.1%	(800) 635-1511
Vanguard Index Trust 500 Portfolio	20.1%	(800) 635-1511
Fidelity Equity Income	20.9%	(800) 544-8888

If you prefer a fund that offers both stocks and bonds, consider these:

	5-Year Annual Return	Phone
Dodge & Cox Balanced	16%	(800) 621-3979
Janus Balanced	15.5%	(800) 525-8983

Bright Idea
Need something to keep you motivated? One way to stay interested is to establish yearly goals. Determine how much you'd like to save each year and then see how close you come to reaching your goal.

Just as important as finding an excellent fund is establishing your investment goals. This will be your financial road map. The investments you pick will depend on your risk tolerance, your time horizon, your return needs, and even tax considerations. As you'll read more than once in this book, it is crucial to choose investments that have a realistic chance of helping you attain your goals. For instance, if you are saving to pay for your child's orthodontia work three years away, you don't want to invest in a junk-bond fund. It's too volatile. At the same time, a Generation Xer isn't going to want to keep any cash in her retirement portfolio. It can potentially drag down her return. (You'll learn more about matching investment strategies with your objectives in Chapter 12, "Strategies for Financial Success.")

Once you have your investments in place, don't obsess about them. In fact, don't even spend much time checking them. If you own mutual funds, you only need to check how they are doing three or four times a year. You want to make sure that the same manager is at the helm, the fund's long-term returns are above average, and its investment style hasn't changed. Flipping to the stock listings in the news-paper each day could also get you in trouble—it might tempt you to make financial moves you later regret. But there are plenty of financial junkies who ignore this advice. Gary Schatsky, a fee-only financial planner and attorney who appears frequently as a guest on CNBC, the business news channel, is astounded at how many people recognize him when he lectures around the country. CNBC's onslaught of financial news, Schatsky observes wryly, "...is the greatest show on earth. Who needs to watch old reruns of *Gunsmoke* when you can switch on the TV and see how your assets have grown each day for years?"

Just the facts

- Getting organized is crucial to success.
- Determine how much you are worth.
- There are many sources of emergency cash.
- With a little research, you can squeeze more yield out of your cash accounts.

GET THE SCOOP ON...
Short-circuiting the information overload ▪
Testing your financial IQ ▪ Finding a great
financial planner ▪ Evaluating brokers ▪
The online brokerage fire sale ▪ Getting the
best tax advice

Financial Planners and Brokers—The Best of the Bunch

Chapter 3

A t first blush, you might think it's easier than ever to be your own financial guru. The bookstore shelves are groaning under the weight of financial self-help books. Visit any computer store, and you'll be astounded by the variety of software programs designed to turn your spare change into a seven-digit figure. Slick newsletters—some good, some embarrassingly bad—clamor for your attention. Even newspaper business sections, which for years seemed to focus exclusively on the ups and downs of corporate America, are now devoting weekly sections on personal finance for people like you and me.

Not to be left out, mutual funds and brokerage houses have developed a cottage industry that produces booklets, worksheets, how-to guides, and cheap software. All of it is designed to help you become richer than you ever dreamed possible.

And, of course, there are thousands of Web sites jam-packed with all sorts of advice on how to buy *initial public offerings* (IPOs), refinance a mortgage, evaluate bonds, and even find stock picks in places like Indonesia. Corporations also are making it easier for investors. Click onto many corporate home pages, and you'll soon be staring at screen after screen of financial figures. Most of the information I've just mentioned is free.

Is this investing nirvana or what? Hardly. Remember when you were a kid and you ate a whole package of Oreos? You didn't feel good. Well, gorging on too much unsolicited financial advice can make you feel queasy, too. Sometimes we need to avoid the temptation to digest every last crumb at the financial smorgasbord. After all, some of this "helpful" advice comes from strangers, and we know how our mothers warned us about strangers.

What should you do? If you are ready to commit some time to the effort, there's no reason why you can't navigate through the briar patch of Wall Street without a helping hand. Some people can tough it out on their own. Thousands of people have started out the same way I did. They buy a subscription to the *Wall Street Journal* and *Barron's,* the weekly financial newspaper. They join the American Association of Individual Investors, an excellent educational organization, and perhaps they become a member of an investment club. They also might subscribe to magazines for beginners, like *Money* or *Kiplinger's.* When they outgrow those, they can graduate to *Smart Money* and *Bloomberg Personal,* which is the most sophisticated magazine of the bunch. For everyone who chooses this route, good luck.

For anybody who needs a helping hand, keep reading this chapter. You'll learn where you can find the best financial advisors. I'll also decode the alphabet soup acronyms that you'll spot on their business cards. And stay tuned for brokerage advice as well. I'll cut to the chase and explain what you need to know before you select a brokerage firm. In addition, I'll tell you how you can save big bucks trading electronically. And here's something you will rarely find—advice on locating a qualified tax professional. The Internal Revenue Service looms so large in our lives, but most of us never think to find a crackerjack tax expert, one who can keep us out of tax trouble but at the same time find all the deductions we can legally claim.

Finding the financial help you deserve

Sometimes what we really need is a financial coach. A professional who isn't distracted by all the extraneous noise and clutter. I know that a lot of people out there believe financial planners are for the poor fools who don't know the difference between a bull market and a bear market. And of course, planners have always been a necessity for the rich, who are too busy making money to be bothered with investing it themselves. Actually, it's probably the people in between who keep financial advisors the busiest. Sometimes people seek an advisor just to make sure they are on the right track. Others end up getting help after they've received a distribution from their retirement fund or when they're interested in estate planning. Some people who have handled their own finances for years might feel uncomfortable going it alone once the assets have grown considerably.

Just a brief description of the sort of people who could benefit from a pro's assistance would fill this book. Just to get you thinking, here are three types

Watch Out!
When you hire a financial advisor, don't get greedy. If you expect a planner to chase away all your money woes and then magically deliver super-human returns every year, you're dreaming. An advisor is really a coach. A good one can provide excellent advice, but you'll still be the one standing at home plate.

of people who could benefit from an outsider's skills.

The newly rich

Out in the Silicon Valley, tech-heads, nerds, propeller heads, whatever you want to call these computer wizards, are collecting stocks options like baseball cards. My friend, Jane, a 36-year-old software executive, is one of them. During the Christmas holidays, I was visiting when she got a call from work. It was her boss with news of her year-end bonus. Grabbing a pen, she wrote some figures on the back of an envelope. She was beaming when she hung up the phone. The payoff for 12 months of hard work was another 10,000 stock options. My friend, who is no slouch when it comes to hardball negotiating, has excelled in extracting stock options from her company. So far, she's amassed the right to buy 200,000 shares at a cheap price.

But Jane is puzzled. She wonders whether she should start exercising her options now and what the tax implications will be. She'd also like to know if it would be worthwhile to obtain a loan to exercise her options. By the way, collecting stock options is a favorite hobby of corporate executives. Stock options are contracts that allow the holder the opportunity to buy company shares in the future at a specified price. If you're lucky enough to own stock options at a company where the share price is skyrocketing, you can become very, very rich. Just ask the many happy millionaires at Microsoft.

Small-business entrepreneurs

Two time zones away, Jack is struggling with a different dilemma. (Actually, we should all have this problem.) Seven years earlier, this certified public accountant launched a medical device company with three partners. The company flourished. In fact, it did so well that the founders couldn't resist a generous offer to sell out a few months ago to a major medical supply corporation. For now, Jack has his share of the sale proceeds—$550,000— sitting in a money market account. Now you might think that a guy who handled the finances for a successful startup could figure out how to invest his money. "Personal finance is different from corporate finance," he says. "It's more complicated!"

Jack not only needs to develop a strategy for investing his windfall, he also requires advice on the tax ramifications. The 58-year-old also has questions about living trusts and other estate planning techniques.

Aging Baby Boomers second-guessing their retirement plans

And then there's Mike and Julie. Mike will be retiring in a few years, and it's safe to say they're feeling anxious. Mike has seen how going cold turkey without a paycheck has crimped the lifestyle of his best friend and his wife. It's prompted him to take stock of his own investments. When a 401(k) plan was unveiled at Mike's company seven years ago, he began making the maximum contribution each month. But always leery about the stock market, Mike and Julie, who is a homemaker, decided to allocate the 401(k) money into a conservative bond fund and a money market. They also own a couple of hefty certificates of deposit generating a mere 5.5 percent. A lot of the couple's retirement money is tied up in a variable annuity, but its returns have been miserable. To bail out, however, they'd have to pay a surrender charge of 6 percent. Here's the question they need help answering: Do they have enough money to last through retirement? And if not, are they playing it too safe?

Test your investing IQ

If you're uncertain whether you need any outside help, why not test your own knowledge of some investing basics? If you don't do well, join the crowd. You'll find the answers at the end of the test.

1. When interest rates go up, what happens to bond prices?

   A. Bond prices drop.

   B. Interest rates do not influence bond prices.

   C. Bond and interest rates always rise together.

2. If you lose money in a mutual fund that you bought at a bank, the *Federal Deposit Insurance Corporation* (FDIC) will protect your assets.

   A. True.

   B. False.

3. How is a fee-only financial planner paid?

   A. He earns a commission when he sells a client stocks and other securities.

   B. The planner typically charges by the hour or project.

   C. He receives a percentage if your holdings gain in value.

4. What is dollar-cost averaging?

   A. It's a tool the U.S. Treasury uses to measure the cost of money.

   B. It's a financial strategy that requires you to invest the same amount of money at regular intervals, such as every month.

Unofficially...
When the Vanguard Group asked 1,476 Americans to take a 20-question quiz on mutual funds, only 16 percent passed. If you want to try your luck with that test, visit the mutual fund company's Web site (www.vanguard.com). Vanguard's Internet test takers have scored better. Their average score is 67%.

C. It's another term for the buy-and-hold stock strategy.

5. If your investment earns an average annual return of 10 percent, how many years will it take before your money doubles?

   A. Ten years.

   B. Seven years.

   C. Five years.

6. Stocks always provide a better return than bonds or money markets.

   A. True.

   B. False.

7. If two bonds are of the same quality, a short-term bond will usually provide a higher yield than a long-term one.

   A. True.

   B. False.

8. If you don't sell your mutual fund shares, you won't have to pay any capital gain taxes.

   A. True.

   B. False.

9. Stock index funds will always do better than other stock mutual funds because they have lower expenses.

   A. True.

   B. False.

10. When you take direct possession of your retirement assets after leaving a job, you will be faced with a withholding tax amounting to

A. 5 percent.

B. 10 percent.

C. There is no withholding tax, but you will owe income tax on the amount.

11. If your spouse doesn't work, the maximum amount he or she can contribute to a yearly Individual Retirement Account is

   A. $250.

   B. $2,000.

   C. None. You can only make a contribution if you are employed.

12. The new tax rate for long-term capital gains is

   A. 25 percent.

   B. 20 percent, but 10 percent for anybody in the 15 percent bracket.

   C. Congress is still bickering over what the new rates will actually be.

13. Congress recently created the Roth IRA. Which description is true?

   A. Your contributions are not tax-deductible, but you will owe no taxes on the money when it's withdrawn.

   B. You can withdraw the money for certain uses if the money stays put for at least five years.

   C. Both A and B.

14. With the new IRA changes, you can avoid incurring a penalty for an early withdrawal if the money is used for

    A. Higher-education expenses.

    B. Covering expenses related to the first-time purchase of a home.

    C. Both A and B.

15. Tax-free municipal bonds and variable annuities are both ideal investments to put in an IRA or other tax-deferred retirement plans.

    A. True.

    B. False.

16. The percentage of bonds, stocks, and cash that you pick for your portfolio will have a greater impact on the success of your investment than choosing the right individual stocks or bonds.

    A. True.

    B. False

17. Parents can realize a tax savings if they use Series EE savings bonds for their children's college education. To qualify, the bonds

    A. Must be registered in the child's name.

    B. Must be in a parent's name.

    C. It doesn't matter.

18. High-yield corporate bonds are

    A. Issued by corporations like Disney and IBM, which enjoy excellent credit ratings.

    B. Junk bonds that are used by companies plagued with poor credit ratings.

19. Under the new capital tax rules,

    A. An investor must hold onto his stock more than 18 months to enjoy the lowest capital gain rates.

B. For tax purposes, there are now three holding periods—short-term, mid-term, and long-term.

C. Both A and C.

20. A sector mutual fund

A. Only belongs in a diversified portfolio.

B. Is only appropriate for aggressive investors, who keep close tabs on the stock market.

C. Only invests in a specific industry, such as banking, electronics, or healthcare.

D. All the above.

Answers: 1: A; 2: B; 3: B; 4: B; 5: B; 6: B; 7: B; 8: B; 9: B; 10: B; 11: B; 12: B; 13: C; 14: C; 15: B; 16: A; 17: B; 18: B; 19: C; 20: D.

If you missed just one question, consider yourself a sharp investor. If you failed to answer two or three correctly, you still know more than most investors. Anyone answering less than 16 correctly could certainly benefit from boning up on their investing knowledge. If you are a self-starter and committed to learning more about personal finance, there is no reason why you can't do it on your own. But it also would be a wise move to consult a financial planner who could help you devise a solid financial strategy.

Not all advisors are created equal

All too often, we wear blinders when we look at our investments. We might obsess about whether we should sink a lot of money into a hot aggressive-growth mutual fund, but it doesn't occur to us to examine how that might affect the mix of assets we have stashed elsewhere. We might focus on saving for our child's college years but fail to stop and think how this might jeopardize our retirement savings goals. We might make investment decisions without thinking about the tax consequences. In other words, we practice jigsaw investing. A good financial planner, however, can earn his keep by gathering up the scattered pieces and snapping them into a big picture. He will not only look at how you should be investing your money, but also whether you are spending it prudently. Before making any recommendations, a good planner will want to know a lot more about you than what's in a folder full of financial documents. A financial planner is a lot like a family physician. While a cardiologist will only be concerned about your heart, a general practitioner will check you out from head to toe.

If you aren't sure what services you can expect from an advisor, here are some routine ones:

- Identifying your investment goals
- Determining your risk tolerance and matching your risk level with appropriate investments
- Recommending solid investments
- Advising you on how to balance various investments within your portfolio to achieve the maximum returns with the least risk
- Monitoring your holdings and keeping you apprised of their performance
- Teaching you the fundamentals of investing
- Staying in touch with periodic written reports and telephone calls
- Providing you with independent analyses of your investments from such organizations as Morningstar, Value Line, and Standard & Poor's
- Troubleshooting

If you conclude that you could use a little advice, the first hurdle will be deciding who to call.

> ❝
> Financial planning is a lot like social work. Personal finance is 70% personal and 30% finance.
> —Gary Schatsky, New York certified financial planner, who made *Worth* magazine's list of the country's 250 best financial planners
> ❞

Stockbrokers will be glad to help you. So will accountants, insurance agents, and lawyers. Some of these professionals might even portray themselves as financial planners. Depending on who you ask, you'll find anywhere from 100,000 to 200,000 people in the Yellow Pages who classify themselves as financial planners. Unlike some other professional fields, financial planning is still in its infancy. Consequently, these folks are not uniformly trained, tested, or regulated in the same way as doctors and lawyers or even beauticians and undertakers. In some states, you can call yourself a financial planner without meeting any professional requirements whatsoever.

If you're not sure who would be the best choice, let me make a recommendation. Your first stop should be with a bona fide financial planner. What you'll probably need is a jack-of-all-trades—someone who possesses a wide knowledge of a variety of personal finance issues. If you later conclude that you need insurance, legal advice, or someone to sort out complicated tax questions, you can call on an insurance agent, an attorney, an accountant, or some other specialist.

Of course, you'll need to narrow the universe even more. To limit the chances of winding up with a clunker, this should be your second step: Find a planner who has earned the designation of *certified financial planner* (CFP). The CFP certification is not easy to get and comes as close as any designation to a badge of honor for the profession. To get one, a planner must prove that he has three years of financial planning experience, along with a college degree, and then he must pass a rigorous two-day exam. The Certified Financial Planner Board of Standards in Denver administers this certification.

The not-for-profit regulatory organization was started back in 1985 out of a frustration that no uniform standards existed for the lawless industry. By 1998, 32,558 planners were licensed to use the CFP designation.

Cynical as it might sound, don't assume that your prospective advisor is a CFP even if he says he is. Check with the CFP Board of Standards (www.CFP-Board.org). By calling its toll-free number, (888) CFP-MARK, you can learn if the planner has credentials and whether he has been the target of the board's disciplinary arm. This also will be a handy number if you think your CFP advisor has been unscrupulous. The Board of Standards, which requires its members to follow a code of ethics, will investigate your complaint. The board has scrutinized the practices of close to 1,000 planners during the past decade.

Your next step will be to find one of these CFPs. This will be a little trickier, because they belong to different professional organizations. Each group has its own requirements for admission. Some are harder to qualify for than others. Typically, applicants have to pass yet another test and agree to enroll in periodic continuing education classes for financial professionals. To make your task easier, I've provided a list of the main organizations. You can contact any of these to receive a list of planners in your area. Many also will typically send out literature on how to best pick a planner.

**National Association of
Personal Financial Advisors**

1130 Lake Cook Rd., Suite 150
Buffalo Grove, IL 60089
(800) 366-2732
www.napfa.org

The National Association of Personal Financial Advisors is certainly the most exclusive group, and some would argue that it's the best one. Only advisors who work as fee-only planners can qualify. You will learn why fee-only planners are more desirable than others in a few moments. Just about the entire membership of 500 or so planners can boast of the CFP designation. The organization will send you an excellent booklet, written by the Consumer Federation of America and the National Institute for Consumer Education, called *Don't Get Burned by the Financial Planner Game.*

The Institute of Certified Financial Planners

Consumer Division
3801 E. Florida Ave., Suite 708
Denver, CO 80210
(800) 282-7526
www.icfp.org

Everybody who belongs to the Institute of Certified Financial Planners—there are 12,500 members—holds a CFP license or is working toward one. While many of the members are fee-only planners, there are also commissioned-based advisors in the group as well.

International Association for Financial Planning

5775 Glenridge Dr. NE, Suite B-300
Atlanta, GA 30328
(888) 806-PLAN
www.iafp.org

The International Association for Financial Planning is the largest organization in its field, and it has more relaxed requirements.

Financial planners, as well as accountants, stockbrokers, lawyers and others can belong to this group of 17,500. Members don't need the CFP designation, but the organization's leadership recently announced that it would like to see more of its members receive it.

American Institute of Certified Public Accountants
Personal Financial Planning Division
1211 Avenue of the Americas
New York, NY 10036
(888) 999-9256
www.aicpa.org

A minority of the certified public accountants who belong to this professional organization are considered tax experts. The organization's Personal Financial Planning division has about 7,000 members. Not all of them hold a CFP license. Those who specialize in financial planning can earn the designation *personal finance specialist* (PFS).

LINC, Inc.
(Licensed Independent Network of CPA Financial Planners)
404 James Robertson Parkway, Suite 1200
Nashville, TN 37219
(800) 737-2727

The professionals who belong to this group are CPAs who work as fee-only financial planners.

American Society of CLU & ChFC
270 S. Bryn Mawr Ave.
Bryn Mawr, PA 19010
(888) ChFC-CLU
www.agents-online.com/ASCLU/index.html

You'll find *chartered life underwriters* (CLUs) and *chartered financial specialists* (ChFCs) belonging to this one. Most of the members are insurance agents who have taken advanced financial courses.

Bright Idea
If you are a conservative investor with a sizable net worth, you can turn to another source of financial advice. Bank trust departments can help you with investing and estate planning.

Here's another source of advice you might not know about. Discount brokerages—which by their very nature don't provide the kind of hand-holding that full-service brokerages do—are now offering financial planning services as well. If you have at least $100,000 to invest, you can locate a fee-only advisor through Charles Schwab AdvisorSource (800) 979-9004. The discount broker will hook you up with one of several hundred advisors participating in the program. To qualify, each advisor must manage at least $25 million and have a minimum of five years of experience in the field. Schwab conducts a background check of its advisors, who pay a fee to participate.

The Vanguard Group—(800) 662-7447/www.vanguard.com—offers another alternative for affluent investors. Vanguard is a well-respected $380 billion mutual fund family in Valley Forge, Pennsylvania, that prides itself on maintaining the lowest expenses for mutual funds in the country. In fact, the company's skinflint ways are legendary in the industry. Through its discount brokerage arm, Vanguard offers a variety of programs. On a one-time basis, Vanguard can analyze your investment, retirement, and estate plans or provide ongoing investment advice. You can also use Vanguard to help establish living trusts, marital and bypass trusts, charitable remainder trusts, and irrevocable life insurance trusts, as well as to serve as a fiduciary. A *fiduciary* is a person or company that holds assets in trust for someone else.

Of course, just because a financial planner has five diplomas framed and hanging behind his desk doesn't mean that he's right for you. Look closely at a person's credentials and don't be immediately impressed just because somebody has an acronym after his name. Take RIA, for instance. It stands for *registered investment adviser.* Someone can obtain this designation after writing a $150 check and filling out a form with the Securities and Exchange Commission. Anybody who charges for advice on trading securities must register. No education, exam, or work experience is required to become an RIA. Many financial planners also will be RIAs because they provide advice on specific stocks, bonds, and mutual funds. You'll also find RIAs in bank trust departments, and money managers are also included in their ranks.

A survey conducted for the Investor Protection Trust, an educational group in Arlington, Virginia, revealed that an amazing 88 percent of investors never bothered to look into the background of their financial planner or broker. The time to do this, of course, is before you make any commitments. As a precaution, call the federal Securities and Exchange Commission to make sure that the friendly person who chatted with you on the phone isn't a quack or a cheat.

Anybody who manages more than $25 million in assets for customers must register with the SEC. Professionals who register with the SEC must fill out Form ADV. Part I outlines any lawsuits or disciplinary actions the applicant has been involved in, while Part II includes such things as the person's educational background and how he will be paid. An advisor is under no obligation to share Part I with you, but you can get it yourself by calling the

SEC at (202) 942-7040. Someone who manages less than $25 million must register with his respective state securities department. You can get the same kind of background information from state agencies.

Fees are more important than you think

Deciding whether or not you need a financial planner is a big decision. One factor to consider is a financial one. These advisors can charge a stiff fee that can range from $100 to $300 an hour, so it makes no sense to spend what could be a lot of money if you don't need an advisor. On the other hand, setting aside $2,000 or more to buy a solid financial blueprint tailored to your needs could be a priceless investment.

How a planner gets paid is more important than you might realize. There are three ways in which advisors are compensated:

- Commission
- Fee-only
- Fee-based

Commissioned planners get paid by selling you investments. The more your advisor buys and sells on your behalf, the more money he makes. But this money doesn't come from you. The planner gets paid by the financial institution that offers the product, such as a mutual fund or an insurance company. This might seem like a great way to get free financial advice, but proceed with caution. The arrangement can create a whopping conflict of interest for your planner. If he expects to pay his own mortgage, he'll be tempted to steer you toward investments wrapped with *loads* or sales charges. The loads, which can run as low as 1 percent or 2 percent to as high as 8 percent or 10 percent or more, provide the money that generates the commission.

These planners will often ignore great investment opportunities if they don't provide a commission. For instance, it would be unusual for a commissioned planner to recommend buying a Vanguard mutual fund, because Vanguard won't pay a red cent for the referral. On the other hand, a planner hungry for a big commission might be tempted to recommend a whole life insurance policy that can provide a 100 percent load during the first year. But guess what? The client might only have needed a cheap term life insurance policy. Think twice before using one of these planners.

Fee-only planners bill you for their services, just as a doctor or dentist would. They don't earn their income through commissions. Consequently, they are free to make the best investment decisions without worrying about their own livelihood. Some advisors price by the hour, while others charge you a flat rate for a complete financial plan. The cost of a comprehensive plan can easily start at $1,500 and cost many times that for a more complex one. Fees vary by location and the background of the advisor.

The financial press clearly favors this sort of planner. In theory, anyway, these advisors can recommend the best investments because you—not some investment firm—are paying for the advice. With the media noisily steering customers to these fee-only planners, the industry is responding. You'll find more and more advisors swearing off commissions. But not all advisors can afford to abandon commissions. It's often the more experienced advisors, who have lots of clients stuffed in their Rolodexes, who can live without commissions.

Unofficially...
Research has indicated that some advisors who proclaim themselves "fee-only" actually accept some commissions. The National Association of Personal Financial Advisors ensures that its members truly spurn all commissions. NAPFA members have to demonstrate through third-party reviews that they practice on a truly fee-only basis.

You'll also find an increasing number of planners trying to have it both ways. You'll hear these professionals refer to themselves as *fee-based,* which is really a misleading term. They earn their living through a combination of fees and commissions. A fee-based planner might charge a reduced rate to draw up a comprehensive plan. Then he'll select mutual funds and other investment products that carry a load, which will bring in more money for him. These same advisors will sometimes agree to work on a fee-only basis for you. But I'd avoid this type of arrangement, because it's hard to see how you could possibly benefit. Since the planner spends most of his waking hours recommending commission products, he'll probably do the same for you, even though you are paying for his advice. Even if he does recommend no-load products, chances are he won't be very familiar with them.

After the introductory meeting, a good advisor will want to do a complete financial inventory before he makes any recommendations. He'll want to look at such things as pension benefits, tax returns, insurance policies, and any estate planning you've done. He'll ask you questions about your assets and how they are spread throughout a portfolio. He'll also pay close attention to your debt—a mortgage, car payments, lines of credit, and credit card balances. After learning what your goals and risk tolerance are, a sharp advisor will provide you with a list of recommendations on how to achieve your targets.

Here's one more thing to keep in mind: Don't be instantly impressed if your financial advisor or broker provides you with a binder filled with glossy charts, all seemingly geared toward your own personal needs. Looks can be deceiving. With financial planning software dirt cheap and abundant, a lazy advisor can create what looks like a detailed, personalized plan within a few minutes. A *Consumer Reports* journalist once derisively called these McPlans. You also should be wary if someone starts pitching investment ideas before you've had a chance to describe your financial situation.

Questions to ask a financial planner

Your job isn't over once you get a list of names of financial planners from a national organization like NAPFA or from friends or associates whom you trust. Your next task is to talk with a few of these planners to get a sense of who would make the best fit for you. If you think this could turn into an expensive fishing expedition, don't fret. Actually, many financial planners will not charge anything for an introductory meeting. If the planner insists on billing you, request that the fee be applied to the development of your financial strategy later. (Of course, you only recoup this money if you ultimately pick this planner.)

When you're sitting face to face with a financial advisor, here are some key questions to ask:

- What are your professional background and credentials? What trade organizations do you belong to?

- How much experience do you have?

- How many continuing education classes have you taken in the past year? How many hours?

- What kind of financial planning services do you provide?

- Do you specialize in any particular areas, such as estate planning, high–net worth individuals, retirement planning, pension plan consulting, and individual stock selection?

- Will you provide a written analysis of my financial situation, along with recommendations?

- What is your investment style? Do you like to swing for home runs or hit a lot of singles?

- Will you recommend specific investments?

- What is your investment track record?

- Can you show me a sample financial plan?

- How often do you suggest we meet to discuss my financial needs?

- Will I maintain control of my assets, and where will they be held?

- Are most of your clients individuals or corporations? What is the typical size of your clients' accounts?

- How will you be paid? Do you have any source of compensation other than fees?

- Do you personally research products you recommend?

- What do you need to know about me?

- Can you provide me with professional references?

- Have you ever been disciplined by a regulatory body or professional organization?

Once you've begun working with a financial advisor, you should never continue the relationship if you feel uncomfortable with it. And there is plenty of evidence to suggest that there are a lot of unhealthy relationships out there. A study by the *American Association of Retired Persons* (AARP), for instance, concluded that many older people don't understand their investments and feel pressured to buy financial products. In the survey, one-third of these investors said they didn't understand the brochures and other written materials that their financial advisors handed them. What's more, one in five said they felt pushed by their advisor to invest in something they didn't want or comprehend. And here's another worrisome sign: One in four of their advisors or brokers didn't tell them how much they would be paying in transaction fees.

There is no reason why this should happen. If you bought a television and the volume knob was broken, you wouldn't hesitate to return the set to the store. You have even more reason to reject a so-called expert who lets you down. Even if a prospective advisor answers all your questions satisfactorily, you have to feel comfortable with him or her. If the planner is haughty or incapable of explaining investment concepts in plain English, he'll be a dud as your financial teacher.

Bright Idea
Once you've selected an advisor, ask her to provide you with what some planners call an *engagement letter*. This spells out in writing what she will and won't do for you.

Do you really need a stockbroker?

While many people will plod along without a financial advisor, it's much harder avoiding brokerage firms if you are going to be an active trader. It is, however, possible. You can buy all your mutual funds directly from a fund company, purchase U.S. Treasuries from the federal government, and pick up shares of stock directly from some companies. But practically speaking, most of us are going to need a broker. A broker can make your financial life much easier. With all your investments being held in one place, trading securities and keeping track of them is much, much easier.

Your brokerage choices can be dizzying. More options exist than ever before, and the range of services, as well as the prices, vary dramatically. It would be wonderful if just one perfect brokerage solution existed for everybody, but it doesn't. Your best fit will depend on what kind of investor you are. If you are plugged into the Internet and consider yourself a confident stock trader, you might want to gravitate to the deep discount brokerage firms that might charge you as little as $8 to $9 for an online trade. Someone who doesn't want to be bothered searching for investment ideas might need to rely on a full-service brokerage house like Merrill Lynch or Bear Sterns. Luckily, there are smart ways to whittle down your options.

Do not pick a broker the way I did back in the 1980s. For several years after college, I didn't need one because, frankly, I never saved a dime. I bought a beautiful handmade quilt in the Ozarks with my MasterCard when my entire net worth was $150. I owned an antique 150-year-old cherry armoire and nightstand, but I had no Individual Retirement Account. When I married my husband, his furnishings weren't as nice as mine, but he was in slightly better financial shape. And he did have an account at a major brokerage house. I can't remember our broker's name because, frankly, he wasn't our broker for long. One day, he'd call up with a stock tip, buy Duff & Phelps, buy General Electric (we bought General Electric and passed on Duff & Phelps), and then he'd be gone. A new fresh-faced broker replaced him, and we'd start getting calls from him.

Obviously, with a small account, we were not what you'd call a good catch. Brokers move on to bigger fish when they can. It wasn't a big surprise then that we always seemed to get stuck with the youngest and most inexperienced broker in the building. Relying on the advice of a new college grad who spends most of the day making cold calls to find clients is not exactly an ideal situation.

Using whichever stockbroker inherits your file makes about as much sense as throwing darts at a newspaper's business pages to pick your stocks. So what do you do? First of all, you need to decide just what kind of broker fits your needs.

If stocks and bonds mystify you, and you aren't motivated to learn the financial ropes, you need someone to guide you through the financial labyrinth. You might do best to stick with a full-service brokerage house. (I say this reluctantly, since I think anybody who is motivated enough to read a personal finance book can figure out what they need to do without one.) A stockbroker will be assigned to you who will make recommendations on how you can invest your money. Your broker can provide you with a wealth of information on just about any investments you're interested in. If you'd like to see reports on stocks or maybe just the overall economy, you can get it free of charge. You pay your broker indirectly through commissions. Some of the fees you pay every time you buy stock, for instance, are used to compensate your broker.

You need to keep in mind, however, that a broker, even if he occupies a fancy corner office in a downtown high-rise, is foremost a salesperson. A broker is trained to sell securities. That's how he makes his money. In fact, that's probably how he got that wonderful view—he pleased his bosses by cranking out a lot of commissions. A broker won't earn extra money if the stocks he recommended for your portfolio soar. Nor will his boss yell at him if the investments he picked for you were dogs.

The names of many of these full-service brokerage firms are instantly recognizable. You can find phone numbers for the nearest offices in your Yellow Pages.

Unofficially...
Don't assume that your broker is an expert financial advisor. Sure, he could tell you how a stock like Microsoft has performed in past years and what the historic yield has been for long-term U.S. Treasuries, but he won't necessarily know how to deftly put a well-balanced portfolio together for you.

- Merrill Lynch
- Morgan Stanley Dean Witter & Co.
- PaineWebber
- Salomon Smith Barney
- Prudential
- Edward Jones
- A.G. Edward

Before you choose a full-service broker, you want to make sure that he has a clean record with the securities regulators. (You can read more about problem brokers in Chapter 17, "Trouble-shooting.") You can check his record by calling the National Association of Securities Dealers, the securities industry's self-regulatory organization, at (800) 289-9999. And call your own state's securities department. If you aren't sure how to locate the appropriate state agency, you can find out by calling the *North American Securities Administrators Association* (NASAA), which is a national organization of state regulators, at (202) 737-0900. NASAA is also a good source to contact about a potential broker, since bad brokers often move from state to state, and any one state agency might not have the records an investor needs. All these sources will provide background on a broker's education and his professional experience, as well as information on complaints filed against him.

The search for a full-service broker can be tricky, because you will be establishing a personal relationship with him. The conventional wisdom is to ask friends, relatives, business acquaintances, your accountant, or somebody like that for a recommendation. That might work, but do you know if Uncle Steve's broker is really no better than mediocre? You probably don't. One way to increase your chances of success is to solicit referrals from people who know a lot about investing and have been successful at it.

When you're interviewing brokers at a full-service firm, you can borrow the list of questions tailored for financial planners. Here are a few more you should ask:

- What is the breakdown on your firm's commissions?

- How has the performance of the stocks on your firm's "most recommended list" fared compared to the Standard & Poor's 500, the standard benchmark? Do you mostly make stock recommendations from this list?

- How many mutual funds can I buy through your firm? Do you sell any no-load funds? (Some are beginning to do this, but they might charge an added fee, such as 1 percent, anyway.)

- How long have you worked at the securities firm?

- How are you qualified to manage my portfolio and give me investing advice?

- Do you recommend the use of options, futures, commodities, or other speculative investments? (Not suitable for most investors.)

- What is your opinion of limited partnerships? (Stay away from these!)

- What is your commission for each type of investment you recommend?

- Do you get most of your investment ideas from your firm? What percentage, if any, do you find on your own? And how do you evaluate these ideas?

- How long will my money be tied up? Will there be plenty of buyers if I decide to sell an investment?

Discounters—the no-frills approach

The cheaper way to go is through a discount broker. If you are comfortable making your own financial decisions, signing up with a discount broker will save you money. One reason why these discounters can charge less is because their overhead is lower. With many branches scattered across the country, full-service brokers must maintain lots of bricks and mortar. The discounters, however, might not operate even one modest suite of offices in the city where you live. And it doesn't really matter, since most customers talk to their discounters by phone, or increasingly by computer modem.

You might have already figured out that you can't expect much personal service from discounters. You won't have your own broker to discuss investment strategies. When you trade stocks, your order will be taken by whichever representative answers the phone. Basically, the discounters exist to help you place trades, whether it's buying 100 shares of IBM or selling some municipal bonds.

Not all of the discounters, however, expect you to conduct your financial affairs in a vacuum. Some provide research on such things as the economy and business conditions, as well as investment recommendations on corporations. These reports can be supplied by outside financial sources such as Value Line and Standard & Poor's. Some discounters generate their own reports with in-house analysts. You need to check with a discounter to see what's available and whether it's free.

CONTACTS FOR PROMINENT DISCOUNT BROKERS

Charles Schwab
(800) 435-4000

Jack White & Co.
(800) 233-3411

Fidelity Brokerage Services
(800) 544-8666

Kennedy Cabot
(800) 252-0090

E*Trade Securities
(800) 786-2575

Quick & Reilly
(800) 672-7220

Waterhouse Securities
(800) 934-4410

T. Rowe Price Discount
(800) 638-5660

Muriel Siebert
(800) 872-0711

Scottsdale Securities
(800) 619-7283

AccuTrade
(800) 494-8946

Discount brokerage firms are not stamped out like cookie cutters. Which one is right for you depends a great deal on your investing profile. For instance, if you buy and sell modest amounts of stocks, it is foolish to sign up with a discounter that rewards only its big traders with deep discounts. A small investor also should know if a discounter levies an extra charge for *odd lots* of stocks. Any trade that isn't a multiple of 100 is considered an odd lot. What's more, some discounters require new clients to open an account with a minimum that ranges between $2,000 and $10,000. If you're a big stock trader, find a firm that offers discounts to customers who buy a large number of shares, say over 1,000 per transaction, or who frequently make large-dollar volume trades.

Obviously, price is a major consideration among discounters. And the good news is that over the past several years, prices have been shrinking. When you are comparison shopping, be sure to ask firms to send you their commission breakdowns and a description of their services.

What kind of prices can you expect? Let's look at the latest annual survey conducted by the *American Association of Individual Investors* (AAII). It asked 100 discounters how much a customer would have to pay to buy 100 shares of a $50-per-share stock. Most of the discounters said they'd charge between $30 and $50 for the transaction.

But if you like the best bargains, you might want to consider heading for the electronic frontier. Online trading is offered by the established discounters, such as Schwab, Fidelity, and Quick & Reilly, but it's also available through strictly electronic brokers as well. The good news is that today's cheap rates will be even cheaper by the time you read this. A 1998 survey by Piper Jaffray, a money management firm, shows that the average commission charged by the 10 leading online brokerage firms in 1998 shriveled to about $16 a trade. And your computer can log on to even better deals. Ameritrade and Suretrade, for instance, offer a basic rate of $8 a trade. How fast are these online prices crumbling? Piper Jaffray concluded that the rates have plummeted 70 percent since early 1996.

These fire-sale prices are luring in millions of price-conscious traders. Online trades accounted for 17 percent of the business in 1997. It's expected that almost one out of three investors will be trading electronically in the near future.

Unofficially...
With prices so cheap, it's only fair to wonder if these online discounters can possibly offer decent service. A survey of 350 AAII members who invest online revealed that only 5 percent of them were dissatisfied.

MOST POPULAR ONLINE TRADING BROKERAGE FIRMS

Broker	Market Share
Charles Schwab	30%
E*Trade	14%
Waterhouse Securities	8%
Datek Online	8%
Fidelity	7%
DLJ Direct	5%
Quick & Reilly	5%
Ameritrade	5%
Discover Brokerage Direct	4%
All others	14%

Source: Piper Jaffray Inc.

A major reason why the prices are plummeting is because the discounters are offering their rock-bottom prices to more people. In the past, there were more hoops to jump through to get the best deal. For instance, you might have to trade large amounts of stock. Now there is less of that. When comparing online brokerage services, don't just look at prices. The broker that seems to be the cheapest could end up dinging you with all sorts of hidden fees. It pays to ask about pricing exceptions. Quite a few online brokers, for instance, will give you the best price only if you trade at the current market price. That is, you place your order via your computer and accept whatever price the broker receives. But if you want to designate what price you are willing to pay for shares in Coca-Cola or some other company, you have to pay a few more dollars. This type of trade is called a *limit order.*

Whether you prefer a full-service broker with Cadillac touches, a major discounter, or a new electronic broker, you might get weary just thinking

Timesaver
If you are contemplating establishing an electronic brokerage account, first check the Web site of Gomez Advisors (www. scorecard.com). Gomez Advisors, a firm that helps financial institutions establish electronic brokerages, rates all the leading Internet stock-trading firms in such categories as ease of use, customer confidence, and service.

about your options. At this point, you might be thinking, "Who has time to do all this legwork? Not I." I understand completely. I've had my money in the same Fidelity brokerage account for seven years, even though I'd save money going elsewhere. It's a hassle finding the right place to park your money. Therefore I'm suggesting a shortcut. Every year, the experts at the AAII and *Smart Money* magazine spend an incredible amount of time accumulating mind-numbing amounts of data so that they can evaluate tons of brokerage firms. My advice is to order the magazine issues devoted to brokerage surveys, read the recommendations, and spare yourself the aggravation.

Where to turn at tax time

Unofficially...
In 1997, the government tweaked the tax code by imple-menting 821 changes.

Once you find a great financial advisor, you can't necessarily expect him or her to handle all your money needs. This is particularly true at tax time. The federal tax code is extremely complicated and challenging even for professionals. And the code became even more nightmarish with the passage of the Taxpayer Relief Act of 1997, which changed many of the tax rules involving investments. (You'll read a lot more about this legislation in Chapter 13, "Taxes and Investing—What You Should Know.")

Here's just one preview of what an investor might be up against with the latest tax wrinkles. Guess how long the federal government estimates that it will take the average taxpayer who enjoyed any capital gains during the past year to fill out the appropriate IRS paperwork? To finish the Schedule D form, you can expect to spend four hours and 19 minutes. (Good luck if you aren't a typical taxpayer.) This 56-line document is the one you'll complete if you experience any capital gains or losses for the year. For instance, if you sold shares in a company and either made or lost money from the investment, this schedule must be filled out. You'll spend more time with a sharpened pencil than you did last year when the Schedule D completion time was generally three hours and 41 minutes.

Obviously, we don't want to overpay our taxes, and underpaying can get us into trouble with some by-the-book IRS agent. But beyond those immediate concerns, it makes sense, particularly for more affluent people, to dedicate time to serious tax planning, such as sheltering your assets through estate-planning methods. Unfortunately, you generally won't find much guidance on how to pick a tax expert to help you do any of this. Should you go the cheap route and visit an H&R Block office near your home to help with your tax return or maybe spend more money with a certified public accountant at a major accounting firm? Perhaps you'd have better luck with a former IRS employee who now works as an enrolled agent preparing your tax return. Or maybe you should try striking out on your own with a tax software program. The most popular one on the market right now is TurboTax from Intuit, while trailing at a distant second place is Kiplinger TaxCut, from Block Financial Corp., a subsidiary of H&R Block.

Whether you need this extra help or not is an individual call. If you annually fill out the IRS's short 1040 form each year, you probably won't require anyone to hold your hand. If you encounter troubles, with any luck, someone at the IRS hot-line number, (800) 829-1040, can answer it. (This number might not work in a few areas of the country. If it doesn't, check for the right number under government listings in your phone book.)

Timesaver
Shun any pre-
parer who still
completes tax
forms by hand.
The process can
take longer (and
that's a concern
if you're paying
by the hour),
and it can
result in more
mistakes.
Computerized tax
software
programs for
professionals can
double-check
work and include
the latest tax
changes.

Even if you use the long 1040 form with attached
schedules, you still might not need anybody. A
rough night wrestling with that Schedule D form,
however, might convince you otherwise. Your return
could still be relatively straightforward if you have
third-party documentation for all or most of your
revenue and expenses. For instance, when you take
a deduction for all the interest you paid on your
home mortgage, the bank provides you with a
yearly proof of those payments. If you are a salaried
employee, you get a year-end W-2 wage and tax statement, and your investments through a brokerage
firm or mutual funds provide a yearly 1099-DIV
form that lists dividends and capital gains. But if
your paper trail isn't so black and white, you could
need assistance. For instance, you might be a self-
supporting entrepreneur, or perhaps you're moon-
lighting by running a small business out of your
home.

Most people who decide they need assistance
often ask friends or colleagues for referrals. That
can be a good way to do it, but don't automatically
assume that a name scribbled down on a piece of
paper will be the best one. Another possibility is to
contact the accounting department at a local university and ask the department chair or another
professor for the names of stellar students who
graduated three or four years ago. You're looking
for someone who has a few years of practical
experience.

While a certified public accountant can be an
excellent resource for your tax needs, you shouldn't
take for granted that any one of them is qualified.
It's true that CPAs have to undergo a grueling set of
tests to earn their respected title, but a lot of what
they know has nothing to do with tax law. What CPAs

learn in the nation's business schools has much more to do with corporate America's needs. Many of them are trained to act, in a sense, as financial killjoys for companies, both large and small. Each year, for instance, CPAs from multinational accounting firms descend on Fortune 500 companies to pore over their financial records. These outside auditors might camp out with a corporation's records for several months before they certify—sort of like a Good Housekeeping seal—that the financial figures are correct. After all that effort and expense, a company can proudly state that the numbers contained in its annual report are correct.

My brother John is a chief financial officer now, but in earlier years, he worked as a CPA auditor for one of the world's largest accounting firms. He readily admits that CPAs are not automatically tax experts. "You don't need to know anything about taxes to be a CPA," he acknowledges. "There isn't even that much in the CPA exam about taxes."

What you really need is someone who lives and breathes the tax code. Not just someone who only prepares tax forms in the weeks leading up to April 15 to earn extra cash. The person could certainly be a CPA, or he could very well be an enrolled agent. If you stick with a CPA, in most cases, you should avoid the solo practitioner or a small firm. Instead, seek the services of a tax specialist who is employed at a large regional accounting firm or at one of the *Big Six,* which refers to the six largest accounting firms in the nation. Why should you stick with the big guys? Because the nation's Byzantine tax laws are constantly changing, and it's nearly impossible for somebody working for himself or in a small office to keep up with all the

Bright Idea
When you get a recommendation, find out what the expert's background is with individual tax returns. Steer away from someone straight out of business school, but also don't assume that a partner in a major CPA tax firm is your best bet. Caught up with administrative duties, partners don't necessarily have time to keep up with the constant barrage of tax changes.

developments. In larger firms, however, there are people assigned to track all the changes, and this information is shared with all the other tax practitioners. These larger firms can also be ideal sources for tax and estate planning.

If you just need someone to fill out a complicated tax form, using an enrolled agent can be another worthwhile alternative. To qualify as an enrolled agent, a person must pass a rigorous two-day tax test administered by the IRS. Once someone earns that title, the IRS requires that he undergo 72 hours of continuing tax education every three years. You find a lot of former IRS agents working as enrolled agents—they qualify if they worked five continuous years at the agency. Obviously, these former agents should know where all the loopholes and trap doors are hidden in the code.

An easy way to find an enrolled agent in your area is to call the National Association of Enrolled Agents at (800) 424-4339, which maintains even stricter continuing education requirements for its 9,600 members. (About 30,000 enrolled agents are practicing across the country.) The association, as well as the IRS, also can tell you if someone claiming to be an enrolled agent has actually met the requirements. To find out about an enrolled agent through the IRS, call (313) 234-1280.

The admonition "buyer beware" certainly applies here. There are a lot of tax preparers out there with no fancy title whatsoever. As with the universe of financial advisors, it's the Wild West. In almost all states, anybody can call himself a tax preparer, and state regulators won't squawk.

A tax pro's credentials aren't your only consideration. Equally important is making sure a preparer is in sync with your comfort level when filing out your return. A study at Indiana University clearly showed that most taxpayers are hardly big gamblers. Those surveyed said they would be willing to take a deduction in a gray area if there was a 70 percent chance that their preparer's interpretation of the regulation was correct. But guess what? According to IRS rules, the guy filling out your taxes only has to be 33 percent sure that the deduction is correct. It's only beyond that point that a tax preparer could face IRS penalties. But if your tax guy is wrong, you're the one who has to square your account with the IRS. You could end up spending thousands more in tax, penalties, and interest.

It's crucial that you have a good understanding of just what kind of risk your tax preparer is comfortable with. If he's willing to make aggressive bets because he knows that only 1 percent of American taxpayers are audited, you might want to look elsewhere unless you are comfortable with submitting a higher-risk return.

When interviewing a prospect, Peggy Hite, an associate professor of accounting at Indiana University, suggests that you don't throw out this softball question: "How aggressive will you be when you're looking for tax deductions on my behalf?" You won't necessarily get an honest answer. Mindful that most taxpayers don't want trouble with the IRS, you won't hear a preparer giving this reply: "I love to push the envelope. I'll claim any deduction that I think we can get away with." If you heard this, chances are you wouldn't hire this tax cowboy.

Instead, ask a question like this: "How certain would you have to be before you would urge me to claim a deduction in a gray area?" Make sure he gives you a percentage when he answers.

There is a definite communications gap between the tax preparer and the client. If you ask a tax preparer do your clients want you to be more aggressive, he'll say, "Yes, yes, yes!" But when we ask clients, particularly those who use CPA firms, they complain that their preparers are too aggressive.
—Peggy Hite, Associate Professor of Accounting, Indiana University

Watch Out!
Thousands of
accountants are
now selling
mutual funds and
other securities
that generate a
commission for
themselves.
Obviously, this
can present a
huge conflict of
interest for an
accountant, who
can make extra
money recom-
mending certain
investments.
About 20 states
forbid accoun-
tants from
doing this.

Here's one last tip. Even though it's tempting to let a $150-an-hour tax professional do all the heavy lifting, you should at least be aware of the tax basics. After all, how will you know if the guy you're paying is worth it? A painless way to bone up on taxes is by visiting a few tax Web sites. Perhaps the mother of all tax home pages is www.taxsites.com. It links other tax Web sites by categories such as Tax Articles and Tax Help and Tips. A professor at the University of Northern Iowa put this one together. You might want to cruise through the American Institute of CPAs site (www.aicpa.org), which is chock-full of tax news. Or perhaps you'd like to wander into www.rothira.com, a cornucopia of Roth IRA information sponsored by a software company.

Just the facts

- Many people can benefit from professional financial advice.

- When choosing financial advisors, don't be confused or fooled by acronyms.

- Full-service brokers aren't necessarily financial planning experts.

- If you want the cheapest stock trades, you must go online.

- Select a tax professional with lots of hands-on experience.

The Financial Markets

PART II

Stock Picking 101

For every investor who can gloat about buying a piece of Microsoft or Intel or Coca-Cola years ago, there is another whose stock market tale is as chilling as a sequel to *Nightmare on Elm Street*. Somebody picked the wrong stock. Maybe it was a horribly bad choice like the once mighty Oxford Health Plan.

What made Oxford's fall onto a bloody knife so terrible was how unexpected it was for so many people. In fact, Oxford is the perfect cautionary tale for individual investors. Not so long ago, the Connecticut managed care company was the darling of Wall Street. There was plenty to love. The company's growth was dazzling. Back in 1993, the numbers of patients enrolled in Oxford could have filled three baseball stadiums. Three years later, you'd have needed 21 coliseums to squeeze everybody inside. Oxford challenged the perceptions that HMOs just hire second-rate doctors who can't hack it on their own. On the contrary, Oxford recruited many of the East Coast's best doctors. The prognosis looked great in the summer of 1997 when shares were selling for $89 a pop. But by autumn, Oxford's stock price had plummeted to a little more than $17 and change. When 1997 ended, Oxford had dropped 73.4 percent for the year.

Oops, somebody screwed up. If experts were fooled, how can you expect to know the truth? Over the decades, stocks have turned janitors into millionaires and driven millionaires into bankruptcy court. Yet despite the stinkers, there are plenty of reasons why stocks have remained so popular during the last half of the 20th century. If you could see a timeline of the U.S. stock market since the end of World War II, you'd notice something very encouraging. During every 10-year period since then, the stock market has posted positive returns. Even better, during the past 15 years, the financial market has annually climbed an average of 17 percent.

As Oxford reminds us all, you have to proceed carefully. Reading about stocks in this book will give you a solid head start. In the next few pages, you can expect to learn plenty about stock market basics. You'll be able to build on these fundamentals as you learn more about analyzing and trading stocks in the following chapters. Meanwhile, in the next minute or two, you'll learn seven tips that should help you become a savvier stock investor. And if you don't want to be bothered with the heavy lifting that stock analysis requires, I'll share a stock-picking strategy that involves no more time than loading a dishwasher.

The ABCs of stocks

When you buy stock, you're purchasing a tiny piece of a company. The emphasis is on the word *tiny*. Let's suppose that you buy 100 shares of IBM. By doing so, you join the ranks of other IBM owners.

How many are there? A ton. The number of shares outstanding, which simply means the number of shares people own, is 972 million. Corporations issue stocks as a way to raise money. Usually companies turn to stocks when they've outgrown their private sources of money, like venture capitalists. Opening the door to anybody who wants a piece of the action can generate a lot more money fast.

Your financial stake in the company is proportional to the amount of stock you own. What do you get for your financial commitment? If the stock price appreciates, you obviously enjoy the ride up. If you decide to cash in on your good fortune, the difference between your original price and the final price is called a *capital gain*. Some stocks also pay dividends. A *dividend* is a portion of a corporation's earnings that is passed on to people who own the stock. Owning stock also entitles you to vote at the company's annual meeting—you can do it by mail if you prefer—and receiving the company's annual report.

The age-old question for anybody interested in stocks is this: How can I make money in the market without getting creamed? Luckily, there are ways that you can invest wisely and protect yourself at the same time. One of the best ways is to plunk your money into stock mutual funds. (You can learn more about mutual funds in Chapter 6, "Mutual Funds—Don't Invest Without 'Em.") With a mutual fund, you let a professional money manager worry about the Oxfords of the world. Be warned, however, that no method is foolproof. Your other choice, of course, is to roll up your sleeves, pull out your calculator, put on your thinking cap, and figure it out for yourself. If you have never done this

Unofficially...
Companies have some say about what their ticker symbol will be. But they don't always get their first choice. For instance, the executives at Ugly Duckling Corp. requested DUCK as its ticker symbol, but it was already taken. After a lot of discussion, the officials picked UGLY.

before, keep reading for tips in this chapter, as well as in Part III, "Zooming In on Your Choices," on how to pull this off.

When professionals refer to the stock market, they aren't necessarily referring to the same thing. There are many different markets that trade stocks. The following sections discuss the best-known U.S. stock markets.

New York Stock Exchange

If you listen to the network news, you'll hear Peter Jennings or one of the other anchors say something like this every night: "In active trading today, the stock market jumped 140 points." What he means is that the *Dow Jones Industrial Average* (DJIA) of 30 companies listed on the *New York Stock Exchange* (NYSE) gained all those points. (With the DJIA hovering at a record 9,100 in the spring of 1998, a 140-point day would represent a gain of just .015 percent.)

The NYSE, the oldest stock exchange in the country, is home to the vast majority of America's biggest and oldest corporate players. Most of the huge brand-name corporations, like IBM, Procter & Gamble, PepsiCo, General Electric, and Exxon, are traded here. The only thing older than the exchange is its address. Back in 1685, Dutch surveyors in lower Manhattan laid out Wall Street along the boundary of a 12-foot-high wooden stockade that had been built to keep out the British and the Indians. More than a century later, two dozen men signed an agreement to begin trading securities while they stood beneath a buttonwood tree on Wall Street. The first corporate stock ever bought or sold belonged to the Bank of New York, which is why it's the first company listed on the exchange to this day.

Unofficially...
On Black Monday, October 29, 1929, the market crashed in historical proportions as panicky investors furiously traded 16 million shares of stock. That huge volume of trading—while a pittance today—was not exceeded for another 39 years.

If you have any mental picture of the New York Stock Exchange, it no doubt is of the stock exchange trading floor. Men and women wearing color-coded jackets wave their hands wildly as they bid for stocks in auction-style trading.

American Stock Exchange

Hardly anybody knows the address of the American Stock Exchange (86 Trinity Place in downtown Manhattan). Actually, for much of its 87-year history, there really wasn't an address—stocks were bought and sold on the street. The AMEX, which used to be called the New York Curb Exchange, literally conducted business on the curb until everybody moved inside in 1921. Most of the stocks traded on the AMEX are medium-sized companies, and there is a large representation of oil and gas companies on this exchange. The AMEX operates in shadows of the mighty NYSE. Recently, the AMEX's trading volume represented less than 3 percent of the country's stock traffic.

NASDAQ

You won't hear people uttering NASDAQ's original name—*National Association of Securities Dealers Automated Quotation System*. Obviously, an English major was not called in as a consultant when names were being suggested. The NASDAQ, which was launched in 1971, is the fastest-growing major stock market in the world and the first electronic-based stock market ever created. The NASDAQ is the watering hole for Microsoft, Apple Computer, Gateway 2000, Oracle, Novell, and many of the other high-tech stocks you read about all the time. Some of the stocks are quite small by Wall Street standards, while others can be as huge as Microsoft and Intel. (During the fall of 1997, the market capitalization of Microsoft and Intel was greater than the combined capitalization of such companies as General Motors, Ford, Kellogg, Sears, and Eastman Kodak.) A healthy dose of telecommunications, financial services, biotechnology, and pharmaceutical companies are represented as well. The NASDAQ, which crows that it's "the stock market for the next 100 years," has more listed companies—nearly 5,550 companies—than any other stock market on the globe. It's also a magnet for more than 87 percent of the country's stock debutantes—companies that decide to trade their stock publicly for the first time.

As you can see in the following table, a majority of the most heavily traded companies listed on the NASDAQ hails from the computer industry.

TOP 10 MOST ACTIVELY TRADED NASDAQ STOCKS

1. Intel
2. Cisco Systems
3. 3 Com Corp.
4. Microsoft
5. Oracle
6. Ascend Communications
7. Dell Computer
8. Applied Materials
9. WorldCom
10. Sun Microsystems

Source: NASDAQ

With momentum clearly on its side, the NASDAQ is positioned to extend its influence even further. The NASDAQ and the AMEX officially agreed in June 1998 to combine forces. Under the terms of the agreement, the AMEX will become a subsidiary of the National Association of Securities Dealers, which operates the NASDAQ. This move, which could take place by the end of 1998, will add hundreds of additional corporations to the NASDAQ's rolls. This could be a plus for individual investors by slightly lowering trading costs.

The NASDAQ differs from the two exchanges in an important way. You won't find frenzied traders working up a sweat on the trading floor. There is no floor. Instead, the National Association of Securities Dealers operates a vast electronic network that allows traders from offices across the country to execute stock transactions. Recently, the NASDAQ generated close to 56 percent of the trading volume, while the New York Stock Exchange handled 42 percent. Amazingly, this is almost a complete reversal of the percentages from just 10 years earlier.

Why stock market indexes matter

Because the stock market is so large and unwieldy, it's broken up into smaller components so investors can get a better idea of what's going on. For instance, the market in general could be on fire, but that won't necessarily tell anybody how utilities are doing. No problem. You can look at the *Wall Street Journal* and find the listing for the *Dow Jones Utility Average* (DJUA), which is composed of 15 gas and electric utility companies spread across the country. Interested in how airline stocks are faring? Check the *Dow Jones Transportation Average* (DJTA).

You might think that knowing the main stock indexes could only help in a game of Trivial Pursuit, but you'd be wrong. You need to be aware of the stock indexes so you can use them as benchmarks when you're evaluating how your stocks are doing. For instance, if you own Northwest Airlines stock, you'd want to see how it has performed compared to the other companies listed in the DJTA. With indexes, you can also quickly compare how different parts of the market are faring. For instance, you can see how small companies are doing as a group compared with larger corporations.

As you can imagine, checking benchmarks is equally important for stock mutual funds. Let's say you own Hotchkis and Wiley International Fund. The fund jumped up 21.6 percent during its 1997 fiscal year. Should you be happy about that? It depends. You need to compare that return with the MSCI EAFE Index *(Morgan Stanley Capital International Europe, Australasia and Far East Index),* which tracks the performance of stocks in developed stock markets overseas. During that same period, the index rose just 12.8 percent. So yes, your fund did super well. You can find a listing of all the major indexes in every issue of the *Wall Street Journal,* as well as in the business sections of many local newspapers. The following sections briefly describe the major indexes.

Dow Jones Industrial Average

The DJIA, also called The Dow, is the granddaddy index. Charles H. Dow began tinkering with the notion of creating an index to make sense of stock market activity back in 1884. He unveiled The Dow in 1896, and in short order, the *Wall Street Journal* began publishing it. The DJIA tracks the performance of 30 of the largest American companies, including General Electric, Exxon, IBM, General Motors, AT&T, and American Express, that are listed on the New York Stock Exchange. These 30 stocks represent about 20 percent of the estimated $8 trillion market value of all American stocks. While this average generally mirrors the health of the entire market, the Standard & Poor's 500 is considered a better benchmark for the overall market.

Unofficially...
The owners of the *Wall Street Journal* occasionally shuffle companies in and out of the Dow Jones Industrial Average so that it reflects the U.S. economy better. In 1997, Westinghouse, Texaco, Bethlehem Steel, and Woolworth were evicted; Hewlett-Packard, Johnson & Johnson, the Travelers Group, and Wal-Mart were invited in.

Standard & Poor's 500

You've probably heard a lot of chatter about this one, but you might not be quite sure why. The S&P 500 is packed with—surprise, surprise—500 companies that are traded primarily on the NYSE. Also included in this index are a few huge corporations from the NASDAQ, such as Microsoft, Intel, and Cisco. These corporate heavyweights represent about 80 percent of the market value of all issues traded on that exchange. Why has the S&P 500 received so much attention? Results. In recent years, it's the Goliaths that have delivered the best investment results. From 1995 through 1997, the S&P 500 soared a phenomenal 90 percent. The only practical way to duplicate the movement of this index in your own portfolio is through an index mutual fund, which you'll learn about in Chapter 11, "Investing on the Run: Sure-Fire Shortcuts."

Wilshire 5000

This is the broadest index of them all. It tracks the prices of more than 6,000 American companies traded on the New York and American exchanges, as well as the NASDAQ. This index is a widely used barometer of broad trends in the overall stock market.

Russell 2000

This index is made up of 2,000 companies that are considered small by financial standards. Their market capitalizations range from $171.7 million to $1.1 billion. The median size is $394 million. A company's market cap isn't tough to figure out. It's determined by multiplying the total number of shares owned by investors by the current price of one share of stock.

MSCI EAFE

This is the abbreviation used for the *Morgan Stanley Capital International Europe, Australasia and Far East Index.* This index, which is pronounced *EE-feh,* tracks foreign companies that are located in 21 developed nations, such as Great Britain, Germany, France, Italy, Ireland, Japan, and Singapore. The benchmark was created in 1968 as a way for institutional investors to gauge how their overseas holdings are doing.

Stocks—pick your flavor

Now that you're familiar with the major benchmarks, let's see what types of stocks you can find when you let your finger do the walking through the financial pages. The following sections discuss stocks categorized by their market capitalization.

Large capitalization stocks

Blue chips. These are the big guys—the largest companies you can find in America. Why the name? It's really quite simple. In poker, the blue chips are considered the most valuable. They are also referred to as *large cap stocks,* which is short for large capitalization. Just to let you know what kind of numbers we're talking about, look at the biggest large caps listed on the New York Stock Exchange.

As a general rule, blue chips are less risky than the Oxford Health Plans of the world. Companies like Johnson & Johnson and Tootsie Roll, which have been profitably selling Band-Aids and cheap lollipops for generations, are generally going to continue running a smooth ship, though there is no guarantee. It's these corporate behemoths that are most likely to offer shareholders tokens of their esteem. That's right, I'm talking about dividends.

TEN LARGEST CAPITALIZATION STOCKS ON THE NEW YORK STOCK EXCHANGE (IN BILLIONS OF DOLLARS)

1. General Electric	$273.9
2. Coca-Cola	$214.9
3. Exxon	$182.0
4. Merck	$140.3
5. Philip Morris	$122.1
6. Proctor & Gamble	$113.5
7. IBM	$112.8
8. Bristol Myer Squibb	$105.7
9. Pfizer	$100.3
10. Johnson & Johnson	$96.6

Source: New York Stock Exchange

Recently, for instance, Johnson & Johnson was paying an 88-cents-per-share dividend. That equals 1.3 percent of its share price, or what's called its *current yield*. Tootsie Roll's dividend wasn't as big— 33 cents a share, which translates to a current yield of 0.5 percent. J.C. Penney Co. was paying a yearly dividend of $2.14 a share. That equals 3.5 percent of its share price—a princely sum compared to the others. (A stock's current yield can change daily, since it's tied to the share price.) In recent years, yields have been steadily shrinking as stock prices have soared—today's average yield is approximately 1.5 percent.

Conservative investors love stocks that pay dividends, because they can provide a cushion if the stock market turns surly. When these stocks start imploding, at least the dividend will usually still be there. The knowledge that they'll continue getting those dividends can give investors the courage to hang tight during a rocky ride. Let's imagine what could happen to a $20 stock that pays an annual $1 dividend (5 percent), when the market slumps. The

Unofficially...
When you buy a stake in some companies, you receive a yearly gift in the mail. Wrigley sends 20 packs of gum to its shareholders. Meanwhile, Chalone Wine Group in California provides private tours of its sister winery, Château Lafite-Rothschild in France. IBM and Tandy send their financial supporters coupons for computers, software, and other goodies. Starbucks shareholders get a free cup of coffee.

stock's price drops 15 percent to $17, but the dividend cuts the actual loss to 10 percent. What's more, corporations that pay a regular dividend tend to experience less volatility in a turbulent market than companies that don't.

Compounding dividends can boost large-cap stock performance. *Source: Scudder Investor Services, Inc.*

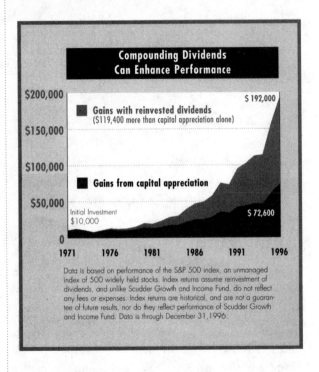

Compounding Dividends Can Enhance Performance

$200,000 $ 192,000

■ **Gains with reinvested dividends**
($119,400 more than capital appreciation alone)

$150,000

■ **Gains from capital appreciation**

$100,000

$50,000

Initial Investment
$10,000 $ 72,600

0

1971   1976   1981   1986   1991   1996

Data is based on performance of the S&P 500 index, an unmanaged index of 500 widely held stocks. Index returns assume reinvestment of dividends, and unlike Scudder Growth and Income Fund, do not reflect any fees or expenses. Index returns are historical, and are not a guarantee of future results, nor do they reflect performance of Scudder Growth and Income Fund. Data is through December 31,1996.

Of course, there can be a downside to dividends. Corporations tend to pay them when their explosive growth years are behind them. With the operations no longer expanding rapidly, less money is needed internally, so a company gives some back to its shareholders. You won't find this happening with high-tech corporations like Microsoft or Cisco Systems, which prefer to plow every loose dollar back into their fast-growing operations. What's more, smaller companies rarely pass out dividends.

Instead, these corporate midgets opt to plow these earnings back into their own operations rather than pay them to stockholders in the form of dividends. So if you favor companies that dole out dividends, you'll find yourself owning a lopsided portfolio, one that could very well be loaded with bank and utility stocks.

Unfortunately, dividend growth has been paltry in recent years. With corporate earnings and stock prices skyrocketing, companies haven't been pressured to bolster their dividends. Thrilled at watching the price of their stocks march steadily upward, investors haven't been paying much attention to dividends. According to Standard & Poor's, the amount of dividends paid by the companies found in the S&P 500 rose a measly 4 percent in 1997. During that same year, dividends represented just 37 percent of the earnings for the S&P 500 stocks. This is the lowest percentage in modern stock market history. But when the stock market resumes to a more normal performance level, investors will no doubt start clamoring for heftier dividends.

Small capitalization stocks

Does anybody ever remember which performers finished third in the Olympic figure-skating competitions? Or who crossed the finish line at the Indianapolis 500 second? Also-rans are often ignored and quickly forgotten. And that's certainly how small cap stocks must feel lately. For most of the 1990s, the biggest stocks have flexed the most muscles and provided the biggest returns. But it would be dead wrong to spurn small cap companies and assume they will never measure up. By the way, financial pros all have their own definition of small cap. Many call a company that has a market

Moneysaver
Don't get stung by taxes when you invest in dividend-paying stocks. Thanks to the big changes in the tax laws, you'll need to keep the tax implications in mind. Unfortunately, dividends are still taxed at your ordinary income level. By holding dividend-rich stocks in an Individual Retirement Account, however, you might postpone or even avoid this tax bit entirely.

capitalization of less than $1 billion a small cap. Much smaller companies, which have a market cap under $250 million, are called *microcaps*.

Small caps are riskier by nature. It's not hard to see why. Many large caps sell products that even a four-year-old can recognize. Often in business for many decades, these companies have proven the Darwinian principle—the fittest survive. Throughout the years, these giants have nurtured a loyal following and attracted more and more customers. So there is a sense of predictability about what these companies can do in the future. It would be hard to imagine, for instance, shoppers hesitating before reaching for a carton of Morton's salt, which as we all know, is decorated with the little girl holding the umbrella.

Many small cap stocks can only hope to attain the same fame as the salt girl. They are still fighting it out with the other Lilliputian competitors for the right to survive. These companies also have to cope with economic demons. Increasing interest rates, for example, can wound a young company with expansion plans, because borrowing money will become far too costly. You have probably never heard of most of these smallish companies. So right from the start, you're at an investing disadvantage. Luckily, that's where small cap mutual fund managers can help you out. A popular way to invest in the Little League companies is through these funds.

What would prompt someone to invest in these companies? Here's the best reason: During much of this century, the nimble small cap stocks have outperformed their bigger corporate brothers by an annual two percentage points. At the same time, small caps can be infuriating. They might poke along for years and then suddenly take off when it's least expected. When it happens, the increase in small stock prices can be explosive. One amazing period came between 1978 and 1982, when small caps provided annual returns of more than 29 percent. A lot of investors have forgotten that the little guys enjoyed another wild and profitable ride in the early 1990s before interest rates started rising.

Small cap companies tend to have a greater growth potential than the big lumbering corporations, but they are also more volatile. While you could buy a huge corporation like Johnson & Johnson and not watch it too closely, you can't adopt that laissez-faire approach with small caps. The fortunes of a small cap can change very quickly.

One of the hazards and, ironically, one of the benefits of trawling for small fry is that fewer people are paying attention to these stocks. You will have a tougher time finding information on the smaller stocks, because fewer institutional investors are monitoring them. Of course, this can present buying opportunities if you discover a great little company that hasn't shown up on Wall Street's radar. One way to learn about solid prospects is to look for ideas in local papers that cover companies in your region.

If you are a tireless researcher and feel up to the task, consider reading *Investing in Small-Cap Stocks*, by Christopher Graja and Elizabeth Ungar, before you start. However, if spending hours poring over Securities and Exchange Commission filings, stock screen results, and stock analysts' opinions leaves you cold, put your small cap money in a mutual fund.

> **"** People are down on small caps and use all this bizarre reasoning. They make arguments that sound good, but they can't back them up with real quality information.
> —John F. Merrill, professional money manager and author of *Outperforming the Market* **"**

It used to be that the experts talked about small cap and large cap, and the vast territory in between was ignored. But now mid-cap stocks are recognized with their own category. While the definition of what constitutes a mid-cap stock can vary, it's pretty well agreed that the market cap ranges from $1 billion to $5 billion. Mid-cap companies are hardly all obscure businesses. Their ranks include Ethan Allen Interiors, Sylvan Learning Systems, and Bed Bath & Beyond. Mid-cap stocks have at times outperformed their larger brethren, and there is usually a greater potential for long-term growth. They are also less risky than small stocks. For anybody anxious about investing overseas, research has indicated that mid-cap stocks tend to conduct a much bigger percentage of their business on American soil than do the bigger companies.

Value stocks

Just like grandmothers and their chicken-soup recipes, stock pickers—the professional money managers and the guys sitting at home—have their own distinct ways of choosing stocks. Some people only get excited if a stock is close to breaking the sound barrier as it appears headed off the charts. People who are fixated on companies that are breaking into new pricing territory are called *momentum investors*. The flip side are folks who would feel at home at a garage sale. They love to buy bloodied, beaten-down stocks—the ones most people don't want to get near. There is always the possibility, after all, that these losers, with nowhere else to go but up, will one day surprise the skeptics.

Not all value stocks are sitting in the cellar. What typically distinguishes these stocks from others is their low price-to-earnings ratio compared with the rest of the market. The P/E ratio, which is listed next to each company's name in a newspaper financial listing, is a handy way to tell at a glance if a stock is priced right. The P/E is determined by dividing the current price of one share of stock by the earnings generated by a single share of stock. In the spring of 1998, the average P/E for stocks in the S&P 500 Index was 26, which is incredibly high. In fact, today's P/Es are at or near record levels. Today's value stock may have P/E ratio several points below that.

Value stocks are often priced cheaply because investors are not enthusiastic about a company's future earnings prospects. Or there is something else lurking in the background that could cause the company to stumble. A great example is Philip Morris, one of the stocks listed in the Dow Jones Industrial Average. Right now, Philip Morris has a P/E of 17. You can probably guess why the stock of this company is pretty cheap. Investors are worried about all the big legal guns aimed at the cigarette maker. The federal and state governments, ex-smokers, and even flight attendants have all been furious at the tobacco giants. You'll also see prominent growth stocks, like WAL-MART and IBM, slip into the value category. WAL-MART, which had been a favorite highflier on Wall Street, skidded into a slump during part of the 1990s, when stock pickers soured on retail stocks. Lately, however, WAL-MART's stock has rebounded. So did IBM's after floundering earlier in the decade.

As you'll discover, there is an endless number of explanations for why some companies are cheap. And you need to find the answer before you make your move. A biomedical company, for example,

Watch Out!
Everybody likes a bargain, but you shouldn't buy a stock just because it's on the bargain table. There are good reasons why some stocks are cheap and stay cheap for years. If you ever sit down with a list of low P/E stocks, you'll be amazed at how quickly you can spot the warts.

might have failed to receive approval from the Food & Drug Administration for its potentially hot new product. A manufacturer could have been accused of inflating its financial numbers. A high-tech startup might be struggling with too much debt. Another company with just a handful of key industrial customers might have just lost its biggest one. As you can see, the possible reasons for a puny P/E are endless.

Bright Idea
If you want to learn more about value investing strategies, read *What Works on Wall Street*, by James P. O'Shaughnessy, the founder of O'Shaughnessy mutual funds. (Just in case you're wondering, I'm not related.) And try *Value Investing Made Easy*, by Janet Lowe.

One reason why finding these stocks is so tough right now is simply because many great deals have disappeared. With the bull market raging for years, it's difficult to find them. Value investors who used to ignore any stock that didn't come with a P/E of 10 or 12 are now reluctantly hunting in the P/E range of 13 to 15 or higher.

But take heart, cheapskates—the stock market is not frozen in time. When a *correction*—the nice word for bear market—arrives, prices will drop. That's a promise. And then the pickings should be plentiful.

Initial public offerings

Watch out for these firecrackers—initial public offerings can blow up in your hands. IPOs, as they are called, simply are privately held companies that want to become publicly traded. Why go public? It can be a great way for a fledgling company to raise money, or for the founding shareholders to sell some of their stock at high prices. An underwriter, which is usually an investment banking firm, handles the arrangements for the company's public debut.

IPOs that do stupendously, at least at the beginning, attract a lot of attention in the media, but they are almost always best to avoid. The only ones who usually make out like bandits are those who are guaranteed shares at the opening-day price. And those just happen to be an underwriter's best customers. Those who get to cut to the front of the line are typically mutual funds, brokerage houses, pension plans, and other institutional investors. It is very difficult for a small investor to get a piece of this. Often, the price of an IPO, which enters the market with lots of hype, will spike up on the first day and stay there until the professional players have a chance to sell their shares for a quick buck. It's often the less-sophisticated individual investors who buy high and then see the value of their hot little numbers cool down. A couple of researchers explored the question of whether IPOs are worth the gamble for the average Joe. After plowing through 20 years' worth of IPO stock prices, they concluded that the average return someone can expect from an IPO is a measly 5 percent. Hardly worth the trouble.

And if that doesn't scare you off, maybe three 1998 studies will. The researchers, from such esteemed business schools as the one at UCLA, suggested that some IPOs are cooking the books. Well, sort of. It's all perfectly legal, but the accounting methods are, shall we say, loose. If you use the same sort of leeway when you balance your checkbook, you'll probably leave a trail of bouncing checks from Blockbuster to your neighborhood grocery store. This is what the finance professors are alleging: At the outset, the number crunchers are manipulating earnings by downplaying expenses and hyping revenue. An IPO's financial figures can look a heck of a lot better on its opening day than they will later on.

Watch Out!
If an IPO plans to use its new cash to grow its operations, that is a good sign. Beware, however, if most of the money will simply go to pay off old debt.

IPOs can be addictive because the payoff can be exhilarating. But as you can see from the following table, they can also wreck someone's best-laid financial plans.

BEST AND WORST IPOS OF 1997

Best Performers	
Rambus	281.2%
LHS Group	273.4%
Complete Business Solutions	262.5%
Star Telecommunications	256.9%
Friede Goldman International	251.5%
Worst Performers	
DTM Corp.	−82.8%
DSI Toys	−76.5%
Axiom	−66.7%
Ionica Group	−66.1%
National Auto Finance Co.	−64.7%

Watch Out!
While researching an IPO, pay attention to what firms are handling the stock debut. While you're reading an IPO's prospectus, you should also look for any mention of investigations or disciplinary actions against the underwriting firms. If the deal is really fishy, often the warning signs will be right there in the document.

Your best approach to IPO investing is to run as fast as you can away from it. But if I can't convince you, at the very least, pick up a copy of an upcoming IPO's *preliminary prospectus*. Everybody in the industry calls these bound documents "red herrings" because portions of it are printed in red ink. The red herring will outline such things as the corporate debutante's financial statements, a description of its management team, its growth prospects, and its mortal enemies—the rival companies that are battling for the same customers. You'll also learn how this market newcomer expects to deploy its cash stockpile after the stock is issued. Don't expect the red herring, however, to divulge a firm price for these new shares. In fact, you won't even spot this important detail if you snag a copy of the final prospectus, which includes even more information. The price won't be set until shortly before the curtains are raised and the stock is trotted out to the buying public.

Investing in exotic time zones

Why would anybody in their right mind buy a stock overseas? A big reason is because, historically, the U.S. market has often not been in sync with foreign ones. So when American stocks are falling down the laundry shoot, equities in countries like Great Britain, China, and Australia might be going gangbusters. So in short, foreign stocks can help diversify a portfolio. What's more, if you only invest in the USA, you'll be ignoring most of the world's corporations. Almost two-thirds of the total value of the globe's stock markets exist outside the U.S. You'd miss out on the future explosive growth possibilities in the Asian consumer markets, as well as the rebuilding of Eastern Europe.

With tens of thousands of professionals bumping into each other as they sift and then resift through all the American stocks for great buys, the most adventurous souls insist that overseas investing is the last frontier. While some believe that undiscovered stocks can only be found in the sorts of countries where quicksand is a bigger nuisance than potholes, other money managers insist that obscure stock gems can just as likely be hiding within the shadows of the Eiffel Tower or the Swiss Alps.

It goes without saying, however, that investing in volatile foreign stocks is very risky and not for amateurs. Here are some of the drawbacks:

- Higher volatility of foreign stock market returns than U.S. market returns

- Less government regulation of stock exchanges
- Political or social instability
- Currency risks
- Possibility of outrageous taxes
- Much less public information about foreign stocks
- Stocks can be less liquid, meaning they are more difficult to sell
- Very different accounting standards

Bright Idea
Interested in overseas investing? That's fine, but don't get carried away. Try to limit your overseas exposure to no more than 20 percent of your portfolio.

For example, even professional money managers can experience trouble finding what they need. Helen Young Hayes, the portfolio manager who enjoys a great track record with Janus Worldwide and Janus Overseas mutual funds, rarely visits Japan, since executives there shroud much of the valuable financial information in secrecy. Perhaps to ensure that nothing too terribly important leaks out in conversations, only mid-level Japanese employees—not the top guns—meet with visiting money managers like Hayes.

All too often, investors jump into foreign stocks for the wrong reasons. Conventional wisdom suggests that foreign stocks are extremely risky, but these stocks are worth the gamble because they can trigger dynamic growth. Actually, financial statisticians have persuasively argued that adding foreign stocks to a well-balanced domestic portfolio reduces its overall risk. Yes, that's right—lowers the risk. Why? Historically, the correlation between American stocks and foreign ones has been quite low. When the price of foreign stocks has escalated, American ones have tended not to go up as much or have even lost value. And the reverse is also true. You can call it the zigzag phenomenon.

Lately, however, overseas investment fans have faced a tough sell. While foreign markets have outperformed American ones during most 10-year periods in this century, this certainly hasn't held true in the 1990s. As you can see from the following table, foreign returns have generally lagged behind American markets.

YEARLY RETURN OF THE EAFE INDEX

Year	Percentage Return
1987	24.63%
1988	28.27%
1989	10.54%
1990	−23.4%
1991	12.13%
1992	−12.17%
1993	32.56%
1994	7.78%
1995	11.21%
1996	6.05%
1997	1.78%

Source: Morgan Stanley Capital International

Buying stocks directly on a foreign exchange can be a nightmare. Quite frankly, many foreign exchanges are geared toward handling trades made by institutional firms, like mutual funds, and not by individuals. You could very well encounter countries that place restrictions on trades by foreigners. Be prepared to absorb higher fees, and the price you expect to pay for stock could be quite different from the actual sale price, thanks to delays in the purchase. If you haven't guessed already, trading foreign stocks directly is foolhardy for all but the most veteran investor.

Luckily, there are ways to invest in a German bank or a Japanese automaker without such hassles.

The easiest way to invest in the rest of the world is through mutual funds. (See Chapter 6.) You also can purchase *American depositary receipts* (ADRs), which are certificates of ownership of foreign shares that are held by American banks. ADRs are traded in dollars on the NASDAQ, as well as the NYSE and AMEX.

Here's how an ADR works: Let's say you want to buy 500 shares in a French company. You contact your American broker and he, in turn, contacts a French counterpart who makes the purchase. The 500 shares, however, never leave France. Instead the French broker deposits the shares in a French branch of an American bank. The bank issues the receipt or ADR to your American broker.

Before you buy through ADRs, consider the following pitfalls:

- Buying through ADRs can be expensive, since intermediaries get a cut of the proceeds.

- ADRs won't protect you from currency risks.

- Foreign companies don't have to answer to American judges.

- Quotes on ADRs can be difficult to get when they aren't traded on the major stock exchanges.

Does foreign investing sound like too much of a gamble? If so, there is one other option. You can buy shares in a multinational corporation. American multinationals are corporate Goliaths that outgrew their own territory. These are corporations that experienced eye-popping growth in past years, but when the market for hamburgers, diapers, or soft drinks was saturated at home, they set their sites on conquering the rest of the world. After all, how

Watch Out!
You're already handicapped when you buy stock in a foreign country, so don't make your task even worse. Limit your research to a handful of very large companies in politically stable and economically solid countries. Let the pros invest in places like Russia and Thailand.

many more Big Mac outlets do Americans really need? Overseas is where millions, if not billions, of potential customers are waiting.

Sticking with McDonald's, 47 percent of the hamburger maker's sales were recently generated overseas. That's up from 20 percent just a decade earlier. Yet those statistics pale when you consider Coca-Cola's global penetration. In the U.S., we're pretty much drinking all the Coke we can stomach—343 cans of the stuff per person each year. But happily for Coke, foreigners are thirsty for flavored brown sugar water. Or at least there's always the hope of turning tea or coffee drinkers into soda fiends. In Hungary, for example, the average person drinks 125 cans of Coke per year, while the average Chinese sips just four glasses. You might be surprised that such an all-American company like Coca-Cola rings up 71 percent of its sales overseas. That foreign sales figure is similar for Gillette, the world's leading maker of shaving products.

Easing into stocks

So you want to be a stock investor? Here's the best advice you can get: Go slow. Picking stocks isn't that different from graduating from a tricycle. Staying balanced on a bicycle that is careening down the street isn't something you know instinctively. Neither is stock investing.

First of all, don't assume that stock picking is an all-or-nothing proposition. It makes perfect sense to keep most or all of your money in professionally managed mutual funds. Actually, owning funds can help you venture out into the stock world. The mutual funds provide the diversification for your portfolio while you test the waters. What can a couple of stocks tucked in a portfolio dominated by

Bright Idea
When you're first starting out, you'll need to spend a lot more time researching stocks than you will later on. But even after you gain some experience as a stock watcher, you should stay alert. At the very least, you should read a company's annual and quarterly reports and watch the financial newspapers for the latest developments on your companies.

mutual funds do for you? It can add a little spice. If you have all your money in mutual funds, over the long term, you stand very little chance of performing any better than the S&P 500.

Okay, let's suppose you're committed to buying individual equities. Where do you begin? One of the safest things you can do is focus on buying a couple of dividend-paying stocks. As I mentioned earlier, these are among the most reliable stocks around. And if your pick doesn't pan out, at least the dividend will break the stock's fall. Another strategy is to focus on a small universe of stocks that you feel strongly about. The strength of your convictions will (hopefully) allow you to concentrate on these equities and make good decisions. This really plays into the advice of Peter Lynch, whose legendary stock picking made Fidelity's Magellan Fund the largest in the country. His mantra is "Invest in what you know." When you've pinpointed a stock to buy, pore over the company's financial data, read articles on the company in magazines and newspapers, and see what financial analysts are saying about its prospects.

You'll learn much more about researching stocks in Part III, but in the meantime, here are seven stock-picking dos and don'ts.

Stick with number one

When the market seems dangerously high, you will hear investors talk about the "flight to quality." They will dump speculative small cap stocks, which historically suffer even worse than the big boys during hard economic times, and head straight for the blue chips. But even better, you should consider investing in the crème de la crème. I'm talking about the number-one corporations in an industry group. Giants that fit this description include such companies as Coca-Cola, Gillette, Intel, and Microsoft. Why mess with second- and third-tier companies when you can buy the best?

Be forewarned that you will usually pay a premium for the stock of these elite companies. But I'm not suggesting that you buy them at any price. No matter how great a company is, there is a price when it's not a good deal. But generally, patient investors will be rewarded. Just hang back and wait for the stock to drop back down to earth. You'll learn more about whether a stock's price is justified in Chapter 7, "Research—The Investing Advantage."

Technology beware!

If you're not a techie, think long and hard before you buy any individual technology stocks. Okay, you know what a modem is and you have Windows 95, but I'm talking about a much higher level of comprehension. For instance, do you understand this first sentence from a press release from Cisco Systems, which is the world's largest maker of computer networking equipment?

> Cisco Systems Inc. today introduced a suite of new Token Ring LAN emulation (LANE) products that boost network backbone and server performance by delivering a scalable, high-speed asynchronous transfer mode (ATM) switched solution.

Wow! If this sounds like gibberish to you, do you honestly think you'd have any chance of properly evaluating the company and its competitors? No way.

When techheads speak, it's almost as if they are communicating in a secret code. It can be hard to understand them in their own insular world of

66
Picking technology stocks is a lot harder than choosing other kinds. You'll feel like you're in a pick-up basketball game with a bunch of seven-footers.
—Kevin Landis, co-portfolio manager, Firsthand Technology Value Fund (a high-tech mutual fund in the Silicon Valley)
99

sun-splashed Silicon Valley, but that could be the least of your worries. Blurring technological changes can infuriate anyone who is trying to figure out whether tech companies are worth their stock prices. Today's hot company can easily become tomorrow's roadkill. For instance, Netscape Communications, which electrified Wall Street with its innovative browser software, saw its stock price disintegrate when Microsoft decided to jump into the browser business.

Bright Idea
If you want to learn more about technology investing, read *Every Investor's Guide to High-Tech Stocks and Mutual Funds,* by Michael Murphy.

This doesn't mean you should banish technology from your portfolio. Far from it. In fact, there is so much economic and market value shifting toward technology today that you probably would increase your risk and decrease your returns by avoiding technology. But unless you can evaluate these stocks intelligently and have the time to follow them diligently, it's best that you get your technology fix through mutual funds. Many stock mutual funds own shares in technology companies, but if you want a fund that invests exclusively in this field, there are some excellent choices. The number-one–rated technology fund during the past five years is Fidelity Select Electronics, with a 35 percent annualized return. Another excellent choice, Fidelity Select Computers, can boast of an annualized return during the past five years of 28.9 percent.

Market timing is for suckers

Forget about market timing. People who insist on this method believe that they can accurately predict when the market will dip and when it will soar. These folks buy stocks when they believe the market is ready to surge forward and dump stocks when they feel the market is ready to get bloodied. But nobody on this planet owns a working crystal ball. So the chances are greatly stacked against you.

Need further convincing? Consider the amazing findings of two different studies. Researchers at the University of Michigan looked at what would have happened to market timers during a 5½-year period in the 1980s. During that time, the average stock increased 26.3 percent each year. But if you had been out of the market for the 10 biggest days, your returns would have dropped to 18.3 percent. You would have lost nearly one out of every three dollars in profit just through lousy timing.

Here's another sobering example that comes from the Frank Russell Co., which is the namesake for the Russell 2000 Index. If you had invested $1,000 in the Standard & Poor's 500 Index during the 10 years ending in 1995, your portfolio would be worth $4,014. But if you had missed the 10 best days on Wall Street during that time, your investment would be valued at a mere $2,653. If you had sat out the 20 best days, your return would have shrunk by about 50 percent to just $2,034. Obviously, none of us wants to experience those sorts of investing nightmares.

Keep your comfort level in mind

If you are nervous about owning individual stocks, you should certainly avoid the riskiest equities. Stay away from small cap stocks, which usually fluctuate more wildly during a market correction. If your comfort level still isn't right, avoid buying stocks and invest instead through mutual funds. After all, the worst thing you can do is panic during a market meltdown and unload your stocks. Ask yourself how you would honestly react if the market tanked by 20 percent to 25 percent, which can happen during a bear market. Some people brush aside that question. After all, they boast, they didn't panic and sell

Recently *Forbes* published its hit parade of the richest people in the world, and I was reminded that there's never been a market timer on the list. If it were truly possible to predict corrections, you'd think somebody would have made billions by doing it.
—Peter Lynch, in *Worth* magazine

Bright Idea
There is no one right way to evaluate stocks. There are tons of people who claim they know how to pick stocks. Don't feel you have to follow their lead. Borrow ideas from others, but develop your own system. Chances are that if you stick with it, your method of evaluating stocks will grow more sophisticated over time.

during that famous market free fall in the autumn of 1987. On October 19, 1987, the Dow Jones Industrial Average plunged 508 points, which represented 22.6 percent of its value. But don't kid yourself. While many investors lost a lot of money during that scary period, it wasn't the kind of sustained bear market that we all have to steel ourselves for. Many people forget that the 1987 stock market actually ended up in slightly positive territory by New Year's Eve. Curiously enough, officials at the Securities and Exchange Commission refuse to even call the 1987 stock debacle a "crash" and instead refer to it as a "market break."

Stay realistic

As mentioned earlier, many of us are getting way too greedy. It's worth repeating that stocks during much of this century have delivered a historic return of 11 percent. Apparently, nobody ever told that to a guy I heard one day on a radio talk show. A listener called to gripe that his stock was only "moving sideways." Yeah, right. The man bought the stock four months earlier at $14 a share. Now he was complaining that after jumping to $28 a share, it was now "treading water." That's a 100 percent increase! But the man wasn't satisfied when the amazed radio host gently suggested that he was nuts. He had taken for granted that his stock would continue to climb. "I'm used to the constant motion up," he groaned.

Don't forget about diversification

It happens time and time again. You can get carried away by Peter Lynch's "invest in what you know" advice. What would happen to a banker who buys what he knows? He loads up on financial institutions—Chase Manhattan, Citicorp, Mercantile Bancorp in the Midwest, and Wells Fargo in

California. Maybe he'll add a savings and loan or two. You probably know why this strategy is dangerous. If this sector of the market heads south, perhaps when interest rates rise, the banker's portfolio will take an extreme hit.

To play it safe, don't let just one or two industries dominate your portfolio. And make sure that a couple of stocks don't overwhelm it either. Try not to let any one equity represent more than 20 percent of your stock holdings unless your portfolio exceeds $100,000. If it's bigger, try to keep any stock from representing more than 10 percent of your holdings. This can happen more easily than you think. For instance, if you were brilliant enough to sink money into Yahoo! Inc. on the first day of trading in 1997, you'd have watched in delight as your pick soared 511 percent during the next 12 months. (This return is not a typo—Yahoo!, the Internet access provider, earned this distinction.) Obviously, with this sort of return, your stock portfolio will be totally out of whack.

Don't abandon your stock prematurely

Maybe you're ecstatic because your great pick, over time, doubles. But once the champagne bubbles fizzle, a feeling of anxiety can gnaw at you. Should you unload your miracle stock? Certainly not if the company's fundamentals still look good. Remember that no glass ceilings exist in the stock market. During a 10-year period, some stocks have actually skyrocketed 3,000 percent or more.

The no-brainer stock-picking strategy

For decades, investors have searched for a sure-fire way to win on Wall Street without perspiring. Fans of the Dogs of the Dow strategy have long claimed they've found the answer. Believe it or not, with this

Timesaver
Each year, the *Wall Street Journal* issues a "Shareholder Scoreboard" that ranks the performance of 1,000 major U.S. companies. To obtain a copy, send $4 to Shareholder Scoreboard, Dow Jones & Co., Inc., 200 Burnett Rd., Chicopee, MA 01020-4615.

strategy you spend more time mowing the lawn than you do determining your stock picks for an entire year. While there are many variations, this is essentially how the Dogs of the Dow works: All you do is purchase equal dollar amounts of the 10 highest dividend-yielding stocks from the Dow Jones Industrial Average. As you'll remember, the DJIA contains 30 companies. Why are these called dogs? Because typically they are the Dow's underperformers.

You hold onto these 10 stocks for exactly one year, and then you reshuffle so that you once again hold only the top 10 dividend yielders. You sell any stocks that no longer make the top 10 list and add those that do. If you embrace this no-brainer approach, be prepared to annually replace 35 percent to 50 percent of your portfolio. To follow this strategy, you don't have to start on January 1—any day will do. If you picked your stocks on September 27, 1998, for instance, you would reshuffle your holdings on September 26, 1999.

Wondering how you'll know which stocks qualify? That's easy. All 30 Dow stocks are listed in each edition of the *Wall Street Journal*. You'll also find the complete list in Appendix E. The task is even easier if you have access to the Internet. The Dogs of the Dow Web site (www.dogsofthedow.com) provides a daily updated list of the 10 stocks you'd pick if you start now. The Internet site also breaks out the Small Dogs of the Dow, which represents the five companies in the original group of 10 that trade at the lowest closing prices.

On January 1, 1998, these were the 10 stocks that made the Dogs of the Dow list.

1998 DOGS OF THE DOW STOCKS

Company	Price	Yield
Philip Morris	45¼	3.54%
J.P. Morgan	112⅞	3.37%
General Motors	60¾	3.29%
Chevron	77	3.01%
Eastman Kodak	60⁹⁄₁₆	2.91%
Exxon	61³⁄₁₆	2.68%
Minnesota Mining & Mfg. (3M)	82¹⁄₁₆	2.58%
International Paper	43⅛	2.32%
AT&T	61⅚	2.15%
DuPont	60⅙	2.1%

Dog Dow believers are a rabid bunch. And it's the historic results that have kept them howling in the past. Since 1972, the strategy has generated an average annual return of 18.6 percent. In contrast, all 30 of the stocks in the Dow Jones Industrial Average have mustered an annual return of 12.4 percent. But the dog results haven't been as impressive lately. In three of the four years from 1994 to 1997, the Dogs of the Dow have underperformed compared to the industrial average.

If you're a Dow Dog player, don't let the IRS ruin your fun. At first glance, that will seem hard to do. You'll face a capital gains tax bill each year for any of the 10 stocks you sell for a profit. The only way to avoid this tax is if a stock loses money. While you'll be writing annual checks to the IRS, your neighbor, who might have held the same IBM shares for 30 years, won't pay a dime of capital gains taxes on his considerable profits. And he won't need to until he sells his shares. This might not seem fair to the active trader, but that's the way our tax system works.

But that actually isn't the end of the Dow dog lover's tax blues. Thanks to the 1997 tax law changes, you can get hammered by stiff capital gains taxes. As you heard, the IRS now extracts the most tax from the impatient investors who can't hold onto a stock for more than 18 months. Dump a stock within one year, and you'll pay at your own individual taxable rate. This can be quite a nasty speed bump for all those cruise-control stock investors. In contrast, buy-and-hold investors will pay 20 percent (and 10 percent for taxpayers in the lowest tax bracket) when they unload their shares. So what's the solution? Keep your dogs in a retirement account. That way, you can buy and sell stocks all you want, but it won't trigger any yearly capital gains taxes.

Unit trust investments—a solution for dog lovers

A big drawback to following the Dogs of the Dow theory is the hassle and the costs. Buying several stocks and then selling them 12 months later, year after year, can get pretty expensive—especially if you use a full-service broker. If you trade online and pay less for a trade than a couple of movie tickets, this is less of a concern. For everybody else, there is an alternative: unit trust investments. While they have been around for decades, these investments have pretty much languished in the backwaters of the financial world. That is, until the dogs started howling.

Since the big brokerage firms began marketing unit investment trusts for dog lovers, the concept has exploded. Billions of dollars are pouring into these products that now invest in various market indexes. Seemingly overnight, they have become one of the hottest Wall Street tickets, but whether they make sense for most people remains debatable.

First a little background. In many respects, unit investment trusts share a lot in common with mutual funds. Just like a fund shareholder, someone who buys into a trust sponsored by a brokerage firm owns units or shares in a bundled portfolio of stocks or bonds. As with mutual funds, unit trust investments allow shareholders to diversify even if they have little to invest. Minimum investments can be as low as $250. But these trusts differ significantly from a mutual fund. Once a money manager selects the securities to be included in a trust, he or she can't change the mix. Securities in a trust generally can't be sold, no matter what happens. If a unit investment trust holds a stake in Philip Morris, for instance, and the tobacco giant gets hammered with the highest punitive damages ever awarded in a civil lawsuit, the portfolio can't unload its tobacco stock. A mutual fund manager, however, can dump tobacco shares and pick them up later at a cheaper price. Once you sign on to a unit investment trust, you're stuck with the portfolio. These unmanaged portfolios are hamstrung in another way as well. Once a unit investment trust is launched, its brokerage sponsor can't add more stocks.

This inflexibility isn't necessarily a bad thing if you love the Dogs of the Dow strategy. After all, if you're a true believer, you aren't supposed to dump these stocks—even if the earth rumbles under Wall Street and swallows the New York Stock Exchange. According to the theory, you must hold onto the entire basket of stocks for one year. And that's what these unit investment trusts do. After a year, the portfolio is liquidated. You can collect your

Unofficially...
Trusts were launched in the 1960s as a way for fixed-income fans to take advantage of municipal bonds. Investors who didn't have enough disposable cash or the financial savvy to purchase individual municipal bonds raved about them. But in the mid-1970s, the love affair was over. That's when no-load mutual funds emerged as a cheaper way to invest in bonds.

money—plus any capital appreciation—or you can roll it over into the next unit investment trust.

A syndicate of the country's biggest full-service brokers—Morgan Stanley, Dean Witter, Merrill Lynch, PaineWebber, Smith Barney, and Prudential—packages these Dogs of the Dow trusts. The best-known one is called the Select Ten portfolio, which contains the 10 highest yielding stocks in the DJIA. The brokerage houses also offer a Flying Five portfolio. The Flying Five contains the five lowest-priced stocks in the Select 10 universe. Keep in mind, however, that the Flying Five trust is inherently riskier because it's less diversified.

Thrilled with all the money chasing these dog portfolios, the brokerage industry quickly dreamed up more and more of them. You can now invest in trusts that have been bundled with stocks of biotechnology firms, global telecommunications companies, healthcare corporations, and even enterprises that are supposed to flourish as the Baby Boomers age. Some unit investment trusts also package foreign stocks. What's more, you can buy into trusts with exotic nicknames like Spiders, Diamonds, and Webs that are traded on the AMEX. Spiders track the S&P 500, Diamonds are tied to the Dow industrials, and Webs track Morgan Stanley's world equity benchmark indexes. The AMEX-sponsored trusts appeal to active traders and speculators who aren't permitted to bounce in and out of mutual funds tied to the S&P 500 and other indexes.

If you're a tightwad like me, you should know that the admission price for a unit trust investment is hardly cheap. That's the case even if you buy one through a discount broker like Charles Schwab, Fidelity, or any other discount broker. You will pay a

> " If you feel the Dogs of the Dow strategy is a good one, investing through a unit investment trust is a way you should consider. If you are a really small investor, the transaction costs to buy the stocks would probably be greater if you did it on your own rather than using a unit trust investment.
> —Albert J. Fredman, professor of finance and author of several mutual fund books "

stiff load that could very well range from 2.75 percent to 5 percent on the broker-sponsored trusts, and you'll be stuck with stock commission costs for the trusts traded on the AMEX.

So are unit trust investments a good or bad idea? If you are a bond investor, sticking with a no-load bond mutual fund remains a better and cheaper alternative. A stronger case can be made if you want to invest in a broker-sponsored Dogs of the Dow trust, since buying into a trust can be less expensive than purchasing five to ten individual stocks. As for investing in the AMEX trusts that track the various stock market indexes, the jury is still out. Because they have a short track record, no one knows for certain how these trusts will perform during a slide in the market. If the popularity of these trusts dries up, shareholders could see their investments lose proportionately more money than the actual indexes.

Just the facts

- There are ways to invest in the stock market and not take unreasonable risks.

- Using stock market benchmarks is one way to evaluate stocks.

- Small cap stocks are more volatile than the blue chips, but the rewards historically have been greater.

- Stay away from initial public offerings.

- Investing overseas is tricky, but there are strategies to avoid the hassles.

- Buying stocks through unit trust investments has become quite popular.

GET THE SCOOP ON...
The ABCs of bond investing ▪
Government bonds—steady as a rock ▪
Municipal bonds—watch your tax rate ▪
Junk bonds can be addictive ▪ Those savings
bonds in your drawer...

Bond Isn't a Four-Letter Word

Chapter 5

Bonds are a snooze. Isn't that secretly what we all think? During the 1990s when stocks have stubbornly defied gravity, bonds have, in comparison, plodded along down here on earth, clearly bound by the rules of physics. Yet even if you ignore the stock market's fabulous romp during the past decade, bonds have historically tagged behind the splashier equities. Any economist will tell you that bonds, during much of this century, have typically trailed several percentage points behind stocks.

Of course, this isn't any reason to boycott bonds. There are awfully good reasons why Americans have been buying bonds for more than 200 years. (It all began back in 1790, when our forefathers issued $80 million in bonds to help pay for the huge Revolutionary War debt.) Bound together in a portfolio, bonds and stocks can behave like yin and yang. For the anxious stockholder, bonds can arguably double as a form of insurance. Bonds might help reduce the losses when the inevitable bear market—yes, it will surely come at some point—begins mauling stock investors. Stashing money into historically less volatile bonds can even out some of the zig and zag of stock market investing. Adding bonds to your stock portfolio can lower the risks, because bonds are not only less volatile, but their returns traditionally haven't been perfectly in sync with stocks. Income is another big reason why investors gravitate to bonds. Retirees like those regular checks that the interest from their bonds can provide. Still others use tax-free bonds to protect themselves from taxes.

With any luck, you should finish this chapter with a better appreciation of bonds. You'll learn what's out there and why you should care. You'll find out what bonds are appropriate for any occasion. Want to know the best way to protect your nest egg from eroding? I'll share the latest research that explains how municipal bonds can help do just that. For any of you not conversant with bondspeak, I'll pierce through the armor of the fixed-income world's dreadful terminology. And you'll be treated to an update on the bad boy of the fixed-income world. Is the junk bond really as terrible for your portfolio as a hot fudge sundae is for your waistline? You'll soon find out. And as an added bonus, find out about the federal government's newest offering—inflation-slaying bonds.

The lowdown on bonds

Let's back up a minute and review just what a bond is. Bear with me if you already know. Bonds are really IOUs. When people buy bonds, they are essentially loaning money to whomever issued them. Who creates all these bonds? The federal government is the colossal debtor. (Does this surprise anyone?) At its frequent auctions, the U.S. Treasury issues $2.3 trillion in debt every year to finance its many functions. Other federal agencies or federally chartered entities with funny nicknames like Ginnie Mae and Freddie Mac, as well as state and local governments, also generate their own IOUs. And not to be left out, corporations rely on bonds for the same reason all the other debtors do.

To understand bonds, you have to appreciate the lingo associated with them. When you buy a bond, the specific sum of money you are lending the debtor is called the *principal*. The bond's face value is referred to as *par*. The length of a bond's life is called its *term*. You can buy short-, intermediate-, or long-term bonds. While the definition of what qualifies as short, intermediate, and long varies, here's a common rule of thumb:

Short term	1 to 3 years
Intermediate term	3 to 10 years
Long term	More than 10 years

    (believe it or not, Disney and a few other companies have actually issued 100-year bonds)

As a general principle, the longer the term, the more volatile the bond. So a 30-year U.S. Treasury bond or a 10-year corporate bond is a lot riskier than a 13-week U.S. Treasury bill. Short-termers are the safest ones. Often providing a higher return than a money market, a short-term bond fund can be an ideal spot for parking money for two or three years.

Obviously, investors need a carrot to buy bonds. What they generally get for their investment is the regular income that bonds spin off. Usually the bond issuer agrees to make regular payments or

> " History shows us that over the long term, a growth stock portfolio with a 20% allocation in bonds can produce competitive returns with less risk than a portfolio concentrated in one or two types of stock investments.
> —James Benham, chairman emeritus of the American Century Benham mutual fund family "

interest to the investor at a rate that is set when the bond is sold. That is why bonds are often referred to as *fixed-income investments*. (There are some notable exceptions. If you hold a zero coupon bond, you have to wait for it to mature before you can pocket the interest. More on these bonds in Chapter 12, "Strategies for Financial Success.")

Typically investors who hold the more volatile longer-term bonds are rewarded with a higher interest or coupon rate. There has to be some financial incentive, after all, to invest money in riskier bonds. In contrast, the interest rate generated by the shorter-term bonds often is punier. You'll also hear investors talking about a bond's yield, but be aware that it won't always be identical to its interest rate. If a person holds a bond until it matures, the yield or the return on the investment will match the interest rate. A $1,000 bond that pays 5.8 percent interest annually ($58) also yields 5.8 percent. But if the investor sells his bond early for a discount or a premium, the yield decouples from the interest rate. Let's say the investor sells his $1,000 bond for $1,100. The new bondholder's yield slips to 5.2 percent (58 ÷ 1,100). If somebody has to dump the same bond for $800, the yield for the new owner is a more attractive 7.25 percent.

The day a bond's term ends is called its *maturity date*. When a bond is held until maturity, the bond is repaid in full. Let's say you buy a $1,000 bond with a 10-year maturity that offers 6 percent interest. Every year, you pocket $60 in interest. By the time your bond matures and you get your $1,000 back, you have pocketed a total of $600 in interest. However, if a bondholder wants to bail out early, the price of the

Unofficially...
About the time we are preparing to head into rush-hour traffic every day, the U.S. Bureau of the Public Debt is gathering data from 50 different sources, including the Federal Reserve Banks, to determine just how big the national debt is. On each workday, the bureau dutifully reports the latest figure at 11:30 a.m. Eastern Standard Time.

bond can be significantly different. Bond prices, which continually change, are influenced by such things as the attractiveness of other investments, such as stocks, the health of the debtor, and the age of the bond.

The biggest boogeyman of all for bondholders, however, is inflation. When interest rates are rising, your bond's principal could very well shrivel. Why? Because your bond becomes about as appealing as a day-old doughnut. It's easy to understand why. Let's say you have a bond with a 6 percent interest rate when inflation hits. If you continue to hold your bond, you miss out on more attractive bonds with higher yields. But if you decide to dump your bond, you take a price hit. After all, who would want to pay full value for your 6 percent bond when the current crop is being offered at heftier interest rates? There could very well be takers for your unpopular bond, however, because it will have to be sold at a discount.

While bonds are allergic to inflation, they love it when interest rates are disintegrating. Imagine owning a bond with an 8 percent yield when new bond issuers are only offering 6 percent. The face value of your bond increases, because other investors are willing to pay a premium for what you're holding.

Before you buy a bond, you'll want to know what impact interest rates will have on it. Obviously, the longer the bond's maturity, the more volatile it can be. As you can see in Tables 5.1 and 5.2, even a slight jump in interest rates can corrode a bond's price. For the purpose of illustration, the face value of the hypothetical bond in the tables is $1,000, with a 7 percent coupon.

PRINCIPAL VOLATILITY OF BONDS

Bond Maturity	Value If Interest Rates Increase By				
(Years)	.5%	1%	1.5%	2%	2.5%
2	$991	$982	$973	$964	$955
5	$979	$959	$940	$921	$902
10	$965	$932	$900	$870	$841
20	$946	$901	$857	$816	$778

As the table above shows, when interest rates inch up 1 percent, about 10 percent of a 20-year bond's value evaporates—from $1,000 to $901. The damage is even greater with a 2 percent interest-rate hike. That same bond loses 18 percent of its value by plummeting to $816. But not surprisingly, the damage isn't nearly as bad with the shorter-term bonds. With a 1 percent interest-rate hike, the price of a two-year bond drops to $982, or less than 2 percent of its value.

On the flip side, the table below shows how a collapse in interest rates is a boon to bonds, especially the ones with a longer shelf life. A 2 percent interest-rate drop makes the price of a 20-year bond soar by 25 percent.

PRINCIPAL VOLATILITY OF BONDS

Bond Maturity	Value If Interest Rates Decline By				
(Years)	.5%	1%	1.5%	2%	2.5%
2	$1,009	$1,019	$1,028	$1,038	$1,047
5	$1,021	$1,043	$1,065	$1,088	$1,111
10	$1.036	$1,074	$1,114	$1,156	$1,200
20	$1,056	$1,116	$1,181	$1,251	$1,327

Because bonds are loans, anybody buying one also needs to check the debtor's creditworthiness. This makes sense if you think about it. You wouldn't loan money to just anybody who asks. And in the financial world, not all debtors are alike. There are wide extremes. Buying a U.S. Treasury bond is like lending money to your mother. These bonds are backed by the "full faith and credit" of the federal government. No matter what your opinion of the inside-the-beltway crowd running Washington, D.C., the chances of the government collapsing into chaos and defaulting on its obligations is nil. On the other extreme, you have people like Donald Trump, famous for his escapades, issuing bonds to fuel his drive to continue changing Atlantic City's landscape with his casinos.

A certified public accountant can dissect a financial statement and get a good idea of whether a would-be debtor is creditworthy. But most of us will need help. Luckily, it exists. Two major independent bond-rating agencies—Moody's and Standard & Poor's—evaluate the financial health of the issuers and give them a letter grade. If these two outfits think a company or a governmental issuer's chances of honoring its obligations are lousy, it doesn't receive a passing grade. That doesn't mean that a flunking company can't issue bonds, it's just that these bad boys have to pay a much higher interest rate to lure you in.

If you're a fixed-income enthusiast, there are plenty of bonds to choose from. On the following pages, you'll see a description of some of the major types.

Bright Idea
When you are buying a bond mutual fund, you should not only ask about the fund's average maturity, but also its duration. If you never part with your bonds until maturity, there is little need to worry about duration. But it's important to people who speculate in bonds, as well as investors who buy shares in bond mutual funds.

BOND QUALITY RATINGS

Moody's	Standard & Poor's
Aaa	AAA
These are the best ratings. These ratings are enjoyed by the U.S. government and U.S. agency bonds, which are considered to offer the highest quality along with the lowest risk.	
Aa	AA
These are also excellent quality—just a step below the very best rating.	
A	A
These are considered to be high medium-grade bonds.	
Baa	BBB
Characterized as a medium-grade bond, this is the lowest investment grade. The bond is creditworthy, but there is a moderate risk.	
Bonds that receive the remaining grades are all considered "speculative." That's why bonds rated this way are called "junk."	
Ba	BB
There could be just a moderate chance that your investment will be safe.	
B	B
These bonds are even iffier. The chances of your principal and interest payments continuing uninterrupted could be small.	
Caa	CCC
Considered poor-quality. The bond issuer might need favorable business and economic conditions to meet its obligations.	
C	CC
This the rock-bottom grade. These bonds could be in default or teetering toward it.	

Sources: Moody's Investors Service and Standard & Poor's

U.S. Treasuries

These bonds, issued by the federal government, win the prize for the highest credit rating. There are no safer bonds on the planet. Issued by the federal Treasury, these bonds come in a wide variety of flavors. Here is a breakdown of what you can buy:

U.S. Treasury bills	Nicknamed T-bills, they have maturities of 13 weeks, 26 weeks, and 1 year.
U.S. Treasury notes	Maturity ranges from 2 to 10 years.
U.S. Treasury bonds	Maturity is 10 years or longer.

The interest paid on Treasuries is exempt from state and local taxes, but holders still owe federal taxes. Because Treasuries are super safe, the return you enjoy is not as great as it is with other types of bonds. But even with the Treasuries, there is a notable difference in returns. Not surprisingly, the bills, which have a much shorter shelf life, typically offer skimpier interest rates. The following table shows returns of different types of U.S. Treasuries.

ANNUAL AVERAGE RETURNS OF U.S. TREASURIES

	5 Years	10 Years
30-Year Treasury	8.34%	9.03%
10-Year Treasury	6.86%	8.05%
2-Year Treasury	5.61%	7.01%

One of the trickiest questions that Treasury investors with a long-term horizon must ask themselves is what maturity should they choose. For most people, the intermediate Treasuries make more sense. During a 50-year period, the long-term and intermediate Treasuries have posted remarkably similar average annual total returns. And yet, the 30-year Treasuries experienced much more upheaval. During that time, long-term Treasuries were saddled with a negative return during 16 of those years. In comparison, the intermediate Treasuries only suffered through six negative years.

If sticking with intermediate Treasuries appeals

to you, you might want to use the *bullet method*. You simply buy five-year T-notes. With a bit more effort, you can also build a ladder of Treasuries by acquiring equal amounts of two-, three-, five-, and ten-year Treasuries. How else can you reach for a higher coupon and limit volatility? You can split your money between ten-year and two-year Treasuries.

Treasuries can be an alternative to certificates of deposit. There's that tax advantage, and Treasuries are highly liquid, which simply means you won't have any trouble finding somebody who'd love to buy your bonds. And if you need to sell your Treasuries before maturity, you won't be zinged with a penalty.

In the past high minimums made Treasuries impractical for many. If you wanted to buy a T-bill, you needed at least $10,000. A Treasury note required $5,000 if the maturity was less than five years. The minimum amount for all other notes, as well as bonds, was $1,000. But happily the Treasury department has lowered the minimum investment hurdle. Today you can by buy T-bills and notes in increments of $1,000 as well.

Buying a U.S. Treasury is almost as easy as getting started in a mutual fund. A broker or bank can sell you these for a small fee, but if you purchase direct from the government, you pay nothing. All you need to do is contact your closest Federal Reserve Bank. See Chapter 10, "Making Your Move—Buying and Selling," for a long list of Federal Reserve branches.

While it's often smarter to buy various types of bonds through a mutual fund, there is no compelling reason to do so with Treasuries. (Unless you can't afford the minimums.) After all, a prime reason why fixed-income enthusiasts flock to bond funds is that they reduce their risk through instant diversification. If you invest $3,000 in a municipal bond fund, for instance, your money is invested in many municipalities, state and local governments, and public works projects scattered throughout the country. If a school district in Kentucky defaults on its bond, the fund barely shudders. But as I mentioned earlier, with Treasuries, there is no real chance of the federal government defaulting on its debt obligations. They are all creditworthy. A Treasury is a Treasury is a Treasury. So you don't need a fund to reduce any credit risk. But a fund that invests in Treasuries whittles down your overall return because of its annual expenses. In fact, the fund could charge you 1 percent or more a year. While this is not outrageous for a hot stock fund that's cranking out a 20 or 30 percent return, it's a real hardship if the fund is generating single-digit returns.

U.S. government agency bonds

While technically they aren't as creditworthy as U.S. Treasuries, U.S. government agency bonds come awful darn close. Some of these bonds are issued by federal agencies, while others can be traced to federally chartered organizations such as the Federal National Mortgage Association (Fannie Mae) and Federal Home Loan Mortgage Corporation (Freddie Mac). Fannie and her friends Freddie Mac and Ginnie Mae (Government National Mortgage Association) specialize in such things as bundling home mortgages from lenders into huge packages that are primarily resold to institutional investors. Each month, the holder of one of these mortgage pools receives interest income and principal from each underlying mortgage. The federal government

Moneysaver
If you decide to buy shares in a mutual fund that invests in Treasuries, make sure it's a no-load fund. That is, it doesn't charge a back-end or front-end sales charge. Purchasing shares in a load fund or one that charges high yearly expenses can gut your return. Try to find a fund with annual expenses well below 1 percent. An excellent source is the Vanguard Group's Treasury bond funds.

stands behind these bonds because Uncle Sam has a vested interest in seeing that the housing market in this country flourishes. The bonds are considered equal or even superior to the creditworthiness of bonds issued by the most reliable corporate borrowers.

But these bonds can be quite volatile. Here's why: When mortgage interest rates dive, people like you and me get excited about refinancing. If you can stomach the paperwork, there are plenty of lenders willing to hand you a no-points loan that can shave $100 or $200 or more off your existing monthly payment. That's great for us, but not for the bondholders. When enough mortgages with those high interest rates are paid off, the returns on the mortgage-backed bonds can plummet. That's exactly what happened in the early 1990s when the country was gripped by a refinancing binge. Adding to the volatility is the speed at which home owners can now refinance thanks to technology. Fannie Mae, for instance, has developed a software program that dramatically shortens the time it takes to approve a refinancing and close a deal.

As a result of the extra volatility, the yields on these mortgage-backed bonds tend to be higher than those that invest solely in U.S. Treasuries or other government securities. Be forewarned: Investors can get clobbered quite quickly with mortgage-backed bonds. Consequently, it's best for bond novices to keep their distance.

Zero coupon bonds

You could call zero coupon bonds naked U.S. Treasury bonds. They come without a coupon. A *coupon* simply refers to the yearly interest rate a bond pays. Zeros earned their name because their interest

Bright Idea
The simplest way to invest in these specialized bonds is through a mutual fund. According to CDA Wiesenberger, which tracks mutual fund returns, there are 77 mortgage-backed mutual funds. In the past decade, the average annual return was 7.7 percent.

is not paid out in a regular income stream to a bondholder. Instead, the interest builds up within the bond until the bitter end when the bond finally matures. When that day arrives, you pocket the zero's accrued interest, along with your original purchase price. The bonds are also called *strips,* because technically, the interest or coupon has been stripped from the Treasury bonds.

The admission price to buy these zeros is what makes them attractive to many. You purchase zeros at a deep discount. In May 1998, for instance, I could have bought a 10-year $1,000 Treasury zero for $575.14. That breaks down to a yield of 5.63 percent. Ten years later—in May 2008—the zero would be redeemed for $1,000. Zeros offering longer maturities are sold at even greater discounts. In contrast, a zero with a short maturity is sold at close to face value.

Zeros can be a logical choice for bond lovers who don't need the regular income that other bonds spin off. If they don't intend to spend their dividend checks, fixed-income investors sometimes struggle to find a spot to park this income that offers a decent rate of return. That hassle is avoided with zeros since you don't get any dividend checks. Zeros are also favored by investors who know they'll need a fixed amount of money in a certain year. And investors who like to gamble on which way interest rates are moving also gravitate to zeros.

Just like the other Treasuries, the creditworthiness of these bonds is as sturdy as the Rock of Gibraltar. But here's where the similarities end. The price of a zero coupon bond is about three times more sensitive to a change in interest rates than the price of a 30-year U.S. Treasury bond. Here's what I

Unofficially...
U.S. Treasury zero coupon bonds are the most popular with investors, but municipal zeros and corporate zeros do exist. Muni zeros can be a draw for individuals in a high tax bracket, while the primary customers of corporate zeros are institutional investors. Unlike holders of Treasury zeros, holders of corporate and muni zeros do face the potential risk of these bonds defaulting.

mean: Let's say you hold a 30-year Treasury that pays 7.04 percent interest and a 30-year zero with an interest rate of 7.27 percent. The worst happens—at least from your perspective—and interest rates during the course of a year increase two percentage points. Oops. The total return for your Treasury drops to a negative 13.12 percent. But that's nothing compared to what happens to your poor old zero. It skids to a negative 38.22 percent return. Why is the zero more allergic to interest-rate hikes? Because it isn't providing biannual income. Without that regular income cushion, these bonds react violently to even the slightest hiccup in interest rates. On the other hand, an investor can make a quick fortune with zeros if interest rates sag.

Holding zero coupons can be a lot like getting stuck on the thirtieth floor of a skyscraper during an earthquake—you're going to get a lot of sway. But if you don't panic and sell, you'll be okay. And there's the irony. The only risk with zeros is selling them prematurely. If you hold onto them, zeros can be as safe as the spare change sitting in your sock drawer. What you need, however, is plenty of patience.

Of course, volatility is no big deal if you're buying for the long term. For instance, if your child is heading to college in 10 years, you can buy a zero that matures when your valedictorian graduates from high school and is ready for college. As long as you hold on until maturity, you know exactly what your return will be. But with such a long horizon, the bulk of any money earmarked for college should be in stocks, not zeros. Zeros, however, can play a useful role in college investing when a child reaches the teen years. When my daughter enters high school, for instance, I intend to put some of her college money into zeros. Since it's too risky to keep money in stocks when college is just around the corner, I'll put what's needed for her freshman-year tuition in a zero coupon that will mature right before we're ready to pack up her CD player and computer. The next year, I'll stash money necessary for her sophomore tuition in a zero, and so on.

It's not just buy-and-hold investors who gravitate to zeros. Kamikaze speculators who like to bet on the movements of interest rates also adore zeros. Speculators snatch up zeros with the longest maturities when they see interest rates softening, and they dump them when rates start heating up. If this kind of gambling appeals to you, the easiest way to mimic this approach is to buy shares in zero coupon funds offered by the American Century Benham funds. (Amazingly, in a universe of thousands of mutual funds, this fund family just about has a monopoly on zero coupon funds.) American Century Benham launches a new zero coupon fund every five years. There are six in all. Each fund, such as American Century Benham Target Maturities Trust 2025, gets its name from the year when its holdings mature. It's the funds with the longest maturities—American Century Benham Target Maturities Trust 2025 and Target Maturities Trust 2020—that attract the hard-core speculators.

Not surprisingly, when interest rates skyrocket, these funds post spectacularly bad returns. But during a year like 1997, when interest rates inched down, Target Maturities Trust 2025 outmuscled every other bond fund in America. Yes, that's right—it was king of all bond funds. During 1997, this fund soared 30.1 percent. In comparison, the median government bond fund posted a return of 8.3 percent. The performance of Target Maturities 2020 was even more impressive in 1995 when inter-

Moneysaver
It takes a little extra effort, but you should consider comparison shopping for zeros to obtain the cheapest brokerage commission possible. Make sure that you ask a broker what the zero's yield to maturity will be after the commission.

est rates fell further. That year, Target Maturities Trust 2020—Target Maturities Trust 2025 wasn't opened to investors until 1996—registered a whopping 61.3 percent return. For the past five years ending in 1997, Target Maturities Trust 2020 earned the title of the leading government bond fund by posting an annualized return of 15.4 percent.

Zero-coupon bonds make the most sense for tax-deferred accounts like an Individual Retirement Account. That's because you must pay federal taxes on the interest that accrues on the zero each year, even though you don't actually receive any of it until your zero matures. Do you really want to pay taxes on money that you won't be able to enjoy for 20 or 30 years? Not likely. If you tuck your zeros into an IRA, however, you can postpone or even eliminate paying the IRS when you retire.

Municipal bonds

Look around when you drive down the highway, and you'll see the concrete monuments of municipal bonds. State and local governments issue municipal bonds to build such things as sewage systems, airports, bridges, hospitals, prisons, highways, and other high-ticket items.

Even with the financial fiasco of the Orange County, California, government's bonds in 1994, this type of bond is generally considered safe. You shouldn't assume, however, that all of these bonds pose a low risk. Holding munis that are located in different regions of the country can help reduce your risks. For instance, if you live in Los Angeles and prefer to buy only California munis, your bond could be endangered if the state gets sucked into a devastating recession. The risk, however, isn't as great if you also hold bonds in Florida, Pennsylvania, Arizona, and elsewhere. Before you invest in individual munis, you should ask yourself this question: "Do I have enough money?" Keeping that need to diversify in mind, you'll need at least $50,000; some experts suggest that $100,000 is a more realistic amount. If your answer is no, try a muni bond mutual fund instead.

When you're shopping for munis, you should pay close attention to a bond's credit risk. The most rock-solid bonds can boast of the highest triple-A designation, but others not quite so creditworthy can compensate for a slightly lower rating. More than half of all new municipal bonds today are insured. The bond insurers provide enough protection to boost these bonds up to a triple-A rating. If you are holding one of these bonds, you can expect the insurer to bail you out financially if the bond is in danger of defaulting. If the worst happens, you recoup the bond's principal value as well as interest payments.

Getting a tax break

A lot of wealthier investors love municipal bonds, because they avoid paying any federal tax on the interest income. In fact, it's one of the few ways left to shelter income from taxes. Because of the tax break, investors load up on munis in their taxable portfolios. Even better, some municipal bonds are classified as double–tax free. If you live in California, for instance, and own Golden State munis, you skip paying state taxes as well. Single-state muni funds can be a boon to investors who are shackled by high state taxes, such as the folks who live in New York. What doesn't make sense is buying a New York muni bond, for example, if you live outside of New York. Sure, you don't have to pay

New York tax on your interest income, but if you're not living there, that isn't going to happen anyway. It also doesn't make sense to own a single-state muni in your own state unless the tax breaks work to your advantage. Indiana, for example, exempts out-of-state munis from state taxes, yet there are still companies that market single-state Indiana bond funds.

Since everybody hates taxes, you might be wondering why munis aren't appropriate for everyone. Here's why: A muni bond's yield is discounted because of the built-in tax break. If you're in a low tax bracket, say 15 percent, your tax savings in a muni are so puny that you're better off with a taxable bond offering a higher yield. In contrast, the people in the highest federal tax bracket—39.6 percent—reap the best tax break.

The following table shows quite clearly that it's the highest-income taxpayers who have the most to gain from muni bonds. Here's how Bruce, who is interested in muni bonds, uses the table to decide whether munis are appropriate for him. Bruce is in the 28 percent tax bracket, which is a tricky tax bracket for deciding whether munis are worthwhile. While it's almost always smart for people in the top tax brackets to own munis, it's often a coin toss for those in the 28 percent tax bracket. Bruce has a chance to buy a high-quality corporate bond yielding 7.5 percent or a muni bond yielding 6 percent. Using the table, Bruce can see that the muni bond looks like a better deal. The taxable equivalent yield of the 6 percent muni is 8.33 percent.

Watch Out!
Not everybody who fills out their IRS tax form will get off scot-free. If your muni bond has increased in value (you bought it at one price and now you're selling it at a higher one), you have to pay federal taxes on your capital gain.

TAXABLE EQUIVALENT YIELD TABLE

Marginal Income Tax Bracket	If the Tax-Exempt Yield Is		
	4%	5%	6%
	The Taxable Equivalent Yield Is		
15%	4.71%	5.88%	7.06%
28%	5.56%	6.94%	8.33%
31%	5.80%	7.25%	8.70%
36%	6.25%	7.81%	9.38%

Source: American Association of Individual Investors

You can also do your own calculations fairly easily. Let's say you want to compare a 9 percent corporate bond with a muni bond yielding 7 percent. Just follow these three steps:

1. Convert your tax bracket into a decimal. If your tax bracket is 31 percent, it would be .31.

2. Subtract the decimal from 1.00 (1.00 − .31 = .69).

3. Divide the tax-exempt yield of the muni by the figure in step 2 (.07 ÷ .69 = 10.1%).

As you can see from this simple math, the taxable equivalent yield of the muni bond at 10.1 percent is superior to the 9 percent junk bond. Unfortunately, many investors never consider municipals because they automatically think their yields are too low. But you don't get an accurate comparison if you compare two yields without taking into consideration how much tax you will dodge with a muni. Also keep in mind that when you buy a muni, you are only earning the muni yield, not the taxable equivalent.

Bright Idea
Financial planners all too often notice that their retired clients who have dropped down to the 15 percent tax bracket still cling to their muni bonds. Many times, these clients accumulated these bonds when they were working and paying higher taxes. It just never occurred to them to unload the munis when the compelling tax reasons for holding them evaporated.

Regardless of your tax status, tax-free muni bonds are a terrible choice for an Individual Retirement Account. In fact, any self-respecting investment company should talk a customer out of doing such a thing. Because you don't pay taxes while your investments are in IRAs, it doesn't make sense to put a tax-free bond into an already tax-advantaged account. Unfortunately, however, this happens all the time.

Spending a minute or two with a calculator, however, won't necessarily tell you whether munis make sense for you. While munis clearly can gut a tax bill, your April 15 obligations shouldn't be the only factor influencing your choice of bonds. For instance, what a lot of people would love to know is what magic combination of bonds, and possibly stocks, will provide them with the steadiest stream of income with the least amount of risk during retirement. Let's suppose that a couple has stockpiled $1 million for their retirement years, and they want it to stretch for 20 years. After giving it some thought, the couple concludes that they can live quite comfortably if they can systematically withdraw $55,000 a year from their $1 million in savings. (They also will receive Social Security and pension checks.)

It just so happens that financial analysts at John Nuveen & Co. in Chicago, a firm that has been peddling bonds for 100 years, spent a great deal of time answering this question. They looked back during a 20-year period beginning in 1977 and created 500 "what if?" scenarios. They examined what would happen to the couple if they held various combinations of bonds and stocks based on different interest rates and stock market returns.

Their task wasn't as simple as determining which asset class generated the highest returns—that distinction would have belonged to the 100 percent stock portfolio. No surprise there. But stocks also pose the riskiest threats to an older couple who intends to regularly tap into their nest egg. Suppose the couple holds a large number of shares of Intel stock, and their scheduled withdrawal just happens to occur when the semiconductor giant is experiencing troubles. When this actually happened in 1998, Intel's stock slipped 21 percent within a few weeks. It was a disastrous time to sell the stock.

Bonds, on the other hand, don't usually move so dramatically. But bonds pose their own threat to this hypothetical couple. While they can provide a fairly steady yield, you can't expect bonds to keep up with inflation. Load up on too many bonds and you sacrifice long-term growth. So what is the ideal portfolio for this couple? After concluding that the straight stock and straight municipal bond portfolios were inappropriate, the Nuveen researchers pinpointed what they determined would be the best combinations for any investors who worry that their money will run out before they die. The ideal portfolio consists of 60 percent to 70 percent municipal bonds, with the rest dedicated to stocks. Stick with those combinations, and the chances of the couple's entire nest egg disappearing ranges from 2.8 percent to 3 percent.

Look at the chart, and you can spot the portfolio that poses the greatest risk for anybody worried about running completely out of money. It's the one most heavily loaded with stocks. With a portfolio containing 80 percent stocks and 20 percent muni bonds, the chances of outliving your savings is almost 11 percent. This kind of risk might make you, as well as your heirs, uncomfortable. But before you sour completely on stocks, the chart also

highlights something you could find important—
the potential payoff for favoring stocks. On the
chart, you see a line that says "Average Residual
Value." In plain English, this boils down to how
much money the hypothetical couple can expect at
the end of 20 years if they pick one of the seven allocation choices. So if they devote 20 percent to stocks
and 80 percent to munis, they have a 50 percent
chance of still having $777,000 at the end. In con-
trast, if they keep 80 percent of their money in
stocks, they enjoy a 50 percent chance of sitting on
a nest egg that eventually swells to $2.2 million by
the end of 20 years.

Ah, but you might be wondering if muni bonds
are necessarily the best choice. What about sticking
with Treasuries or corporate bonds instead? Well,
the Nuveen bond experts anticipated that question.
In another study shown in the table on the following
page, they compared the after-tax return of munis,
corporates, and Treasuries when combined with various amounts of equities. For this example, the statisticians assumed that the original investment
totaled $100,000 and was held by an investor earn-
ing $100,000 a year, between 1978 and 1997.
Looking at the first column, you can see that a portfolio that contained 80 percent stocks and 20 percent muni bonds generated a return of 11.77 percent, while a portfolio of 80 percent stocks and 20
percent of either corporates or Treasuries posted a
slightly lower return.

RETURN COMPARISONS OF BONDS
WHEN LINKED WITH STOCKS

Stock Portion	Munis	Corporates	Treasuries
80%	11.77%	11.30%	11.29%
60%	11.02%	10.07%	10.06%

40%	10.27%	8.73%	8.69%
20%	9.33%	7.39%	7.34%
0%	8.42%	5.95%	5.91%

Source: John Nuveen & Co. Inc.

As you can see, the combination of munis and stocks provides superior returns in every scenario. But there's more. The mix of munis and stocks was slightly less risky than portfolios containing Treasuries or corporate bonds and stocks. "What we discovered is that municipals and equities are a home run," says Rick Harper, a Nuveen investment strategist in charge of the research. "After taxes, munis performed outstandingly."

The Nuveen research hasn't sat on a dusty shelf like so many. More than 300,000 requests for the studies have been mailed. If you'd like your own copy, call the firm at (312) 917-7873. The titles are *Meeting Expectations: Balancing Portfolios to Fund Future Withdrawals; Measuring What You Keep, 1998;* and *Two Is Still Greater than One, Building a Balanced Portfolio, 1977-1997.*

Calling munis

Municipal bonds do have this irritating habit that you should know about. Whether it's the Port Authority of New York and New Jersey, the California prison system, or the Denver Airport Authority, the vast majority of muni bond issuers have the right to ask for their bonds back. When this is allowed, the bond is considered *callable.* Bondholders hate this, because from their perspective, the debtor always calls the bond back at the worst time. It usually happens when interest rates have dropped. By canceling their old debts, a state, county, or other governmental entity can issue new

Timesaver
The Vanguard Group offers a tax-managed fund called Balanced Portfolio. It invests about half of its assets in intermediate-term municipal bonds and the rest in lower-yielding stocks. Nuveen sponsors a similar fund called the Balanced Municipal and Stock Fund. It typically holds munis (60 percent) and stocks (40 percent).

IOUs at a cheaper interest rate. When a bond is called, the issuer returns your principal. Of course, this leaves you looking for a better deal at the worst possible time. Chances are excellent that even after scouring the bond universe, the ones you find will also offer lower yields.

While the vast majority of municipal bonds feature call options, it's not practical to only search for the ones that don't. Investors could pass up many excellent bonds by limiting themselves to the small universe of uncallable ones. And it's also extremely difficult to achieve any type of diversity. The biggest mistake newcomers to muni bonds make is to only focus on the yield to maturity. This represents the yield you get if you hold onto that bond to the bitter end. To protect yourself, you should pay close attention to a bond's *yield to call*. This refers to the yield you can expect if the bond is called at the first opportunity possible. If that figure is considerably smaller than the bond's yield to maturity, search for a better bond.

But you have to worry about more than whether your muni bond will be called. The individual investor will find it hard getting price information on these bonds. What's more, there is intense marketing of available low-quality bonds. These can be especially dangerous when investors are prone to chasing yields wherever they can. And it's happening not only with corporate junk, but with munis as well.

Bright Idea
Get the broker who is buying bonds for you to provide the different yields for each bond you are interested in. In fact, if your broker doesn't offer this critical information up front, it could be time to look for another broker.

High-grade corporate bonds

No surprise here. Highly respected corporations like Disney, IBM, and Merck (the pharmaceutical giant) issue high-grade corporate bonds to generate cash for a lot of reasons. Even though they are issued by instantly recognizable companies that produce such indispensable products as Colgate toothpaste, Tide laundry detergent, and Rice Krispies, corporate bonds are considered riskier than Treasuries or muni bonds, because companies can fail, but the U.S. government cannot. Not surprisingly then, corporations must pay their lenders a higher yield than the government bonds.

Bond ratings are even more critical when you're shopping for corporate bonds. If a county government is struggling to pay the interest on its muni bonds, it can always raise taxes as a last resort. Obviously, McDonald's doesn't have that option if every American kid who has ever devoured a Happy Meal turns vegetarian.

You also have to pay attention to whether the bonds are callable. Like municipal bonds, most corporate bonds can eventually be called or redeemed. So the same admonitions that you read earlier about muni bonds apply here too.

When you're buying a corporate bond, you also should think about how much of a hassle it will be to unload one. In bondspeak, the term *liquidity* is used to measure how easy a sale will be to accomplish. It's better to own a bond with a high liquidity. Once again, to avoid hassles and increase your chances of winding up with the best corporate bonds, stick with a bond mutual fund.

Would corporate bonds fit nicely into your portfolio? To answer that, you need to reflect on your attitudes about risk. If you can't tolerate any risk, you'll feel better with Treasuries. The sterling credit-worthiness of Treasuries, as you know, plays second to no one. But corporations can also warm the hearts of ultraconservative investors who place a

Watch Out!
You can sabotage your returns if you use corporate bonds the wrong way. Play it smart and restrict your corporate bond holdings to your retirement accounts. This way, the bonds can incubate away from the IRS's reach. You should ignore this advice for municipals. Keep them in a taxable account.

premium on safety. After all, what are the chances of General Electric or General Motors going out of business? If you are willing to sacrifice a smidgen of security for a little higher return, corporates can fit nicely into your plans.

High-yield bonds

Don't let the name fool you. *High-yield bonds* is the code term for *junk bonds*. You can trace these bonds to the shakiest corporate borrowers. Companies that might be floundering financially are forced to offer a higher yield—hence the name—to tempt investors. Other companies that resort to junk might be too small or have too short a track record to qualify for an investment-grade rating. Corporations needing a lot of cash to finance a takeover or a leverage buyout—such as the RJR Nabisco merger in the 1980s—also rely on junk bonds. You'll also find fallen angels peddling junk. (A *fallen angel* refers to a blue chip company that has experienced some difficulties in its financial condition.)

Some of the junk issuers are instantly recognizable—Bethlehem Steel, Uniroyal Chemical, and MCI. You'll also see a ton of gaming companies, including MGM Grand, Grand Casinos, and Bally's Grand, using the dough to fuel their expansion in states that have legalized gambling. Companies trying to cash in on the federal deregulation of the telecommunications industry—such as the makers of cellular phones, pagers, and satellites—are also issuing junk bonds.

Unlike most bonds, junk claims a colorful pedigree. These bonds were dreamed up by Michael Milken, the flamboyant and controversial Beverly Hills bond trader. The junk bond king correctly concluded that corporate America, as well as some adventurous investors, were starved for junk. Cash-poor companies without credit would eagerly pay bondholders a premium for taking a chance on them. And sure enough, the bonds thrived. But in the early 1990s, the fledgling junk bond industry ran into difficulty. An amazing 10 percent or so of the junk bonds on the market fell into default. And Milken, junk's number one salesman, was hauled off to jail for federal securities violations. The financial press didn't hold back any invectives when describing the debacle. The *Wall Street Journal* called junk bonds a mediocre investment, while *Barron's* declared the whole affair to be a vast Ponzi of phony bonds.

If he awoke in 1998, Rip Van Winkle would be amazed at junk bonds' rehabilitation. Actually, these bonds have never been more popular. Or, and this might come as a shocker, more respectable—they have become widely accepted today. Amazingly, about a quarter of all corporate bonds issued now are classified as junk. That adds up to about $300 billion worth. With plenty of financial pundits declaring that the stock market is overvalued, many investors are flocking to junk bonds for their high yields.

It's not hard to understand why junk is hot. The yield is far more attractive than other types of bonds. Junk is also attractive because it doesn't behave quite the same as other bonds. Higher interest rates can devastate bonds, but junk isn't as sensitive to escalating rates. Instead these bonds tend to mimic stocks. When a company experiences an upturn, the good news can boost the value of a junk bond, just as it would a stock price. Of course, financial bad news can send this debt spiraling down as well. Junk bonds are less risky than stock in a company, however, because if the worst happens and the business collapses into bankruptcy, bondholders have a priority over stockholders.

ANNUALIZED TOTAL RETURNS OF HIGH-YIELD AND OTHER BOND TYPES

Fund Category	Total Return		
	10 Years	5 Years	3 Years
General U.S. Treasury	9.37%	8.22%	10.83%
A-Rated Corporate Debt	9.08%	7.44%	9.70%
Junk Bonds	10.61%	11.38%	13.61%

Source: Lipper Analytical Services

Because junk bonds are so risky, it makes sense to invest in them through a mutual fund. Fund managers are better equipped to evaluate these bonds. In fact, choosing the best junk is a lot trickier than managing a garden-variety portfolio of government or high-quality corporate bonds. Be sure to compare the track records of junk bond funds before selecting one. Need more reasons to avoid investing in junk on your own? Bond dealers often charge individuals an excessive *price spread*—your cost versus what the bond is actually worth. What's more, junk bonds aren't as liquid when you want to unload them.

Inflation index bonds

You will run across very few show-stopping events in the world of bonds. There aren't any *initial public offerings* (IPOs) to shake things up. But the bond market managed to muster its own excitement recently when it unveiled a brand-new type of bond. Inflation index bonds, which were dreamed up by the U.S. Treasury, offer protection against inflation, that great scourge of bondholders. Investors who buy them will prosper if inflation hits, but they might wish they hadn't bothered if prices remain flat.

Just how good a deal these new inflation-proof bonds are really depends on whether raging inflation makes a reappearance. When inflation was rampant in the 1970s, inflation index bonds would have outperformed almost any other financial investment. But during the 1990s, with inflation just a distant memory, these bonds would have provided mediocre returns.

Here's how they work: Unlike regular Treasuries, the new ones are linked to the *Consumer Price Index* (CPI). The principal rises if the CPI does. For example, if inflation jumps 4 percent this year, the $1,000 face value of the bond now is $1,040. The Treasury uses that figure—not $1,000—to determine what the annual interest payment is. The first round of inflation-proof bonds came with a 3⅝ percent interest rate.

If these newfangled bonds look appealing, you need to be aware of what could be some nasty surprises:

- These bonds are not appropriate for taxable accounts. Why? You will owe taxes on interest payments as well as any rise in the principal thanks to inflation. The only problem is that the government won't distribute the increase in principal until the bond matures. So you are paying taxes for money you might not see for years. People who are caught in the highest tax brackets could conceivably end up owing more in taxes than they get in cash each year. To avoid this, keep these bonds in a retirement portfolio.

Unanticipated inflation is as devastating to bondholders as kryptonite is to Superman.
—Burton Malkiel, professor of economics at Princeton University, writing in *Bloomberg Personal* magazine

Bright Idea
Some conservative investors have gotten downright excited about inflation bonds, because they are the only reliable hedge against inflation. Some people hoard gold or real estate to protect them from the ravages of inflation, but property and the glittery stuff can't always be counted on to keep abreast, much less stay ahead, of increasing prices.

- The rules could change. These bonds are linked to the CPI, but there has been a lot of noise in Washington about tinkering with the index. Critics believe that the CPI overstates the cost of living—one federal commission even suggested that the measurement was off by 1.1 percent. During the past five years, the CPI has inched up an average of 2.7 percent. If the CPI was permanently adjusted downward, inflation bondholders would suffer. Reduce the CPI by 1 percent, and someone holding $50,000 worth of these bonds automatically loses $500.

- Inflation bonds aren't as flexible as the regular U.S. Treasuries. At present, they come in three flavors—5-, 10-, and 30-year maturities.

Are these new bonds right for you? Alas, there is no pat answer. I've heard at least one money manager compare these bonds to buying flood insurance during a drought. Just because inflation has been low for so long doesn't mean the bonds aren't worth buying. An aggressive investor might want to allocate 5 to 10 percent of his portfolio to the bonds. The diversification could soften the scary dips stock owners experience. Here's how: During bouts with inflation, stocks tend to perform pretty miserably. But this is when inflation index bonds shine. On the other hand, if you are convinced that inflation isn't going to resurface, you will probably want to pass on these.

Series EE savings bonds

Have you forgotten about your savings bonds? I know I did until I started writing this chapter. Most of us, especially if we have children, have some stashed away someplace. I found mine in a cubbyhole in my rolltop desk. Relatives and friends bought the bonds for my son and daughter when they were born. Savings bonds are a perfect baby shower gift. (Unlike Treasury securities, you don't need $1,000 to get started.) For just $25, you can buy a savings bond with a face value of $50. Of course, it takes quite a few years before the bond is worth $50.

I'd suggest, however, that you limit savings bonds to baby shower gifts. Sure, some people use these bonds to pay for college. But if you're sinking a lot of money into bonds for a child who can't even crawl yet, you're making a big mistake relying on them. With a time horizon of 18 years, you should be investing your money in stocks.

You can buy savings bonds at your neighborhood bank. You should receive your actual bond within 15 working days. The bonds are exempt from state and local taxes, and the federal tax can be postponed until you cash the bond or when it stops earning interest after 30 years. In addition, federal tax on the interest can be waived when bonds are redeemed for college tuition. For married couples filing jointly, the tax is waived completely if their adjusted gross household income is less than $76,250. The deduction gradually phases out until it's completely eliminated for those earning $106,250 or more.

With the returns on savings bonds modest at best, it takes a long time before they reach face value. As you can see in the following table, the wait can be quite long. The higher the interest rate at the time of the issue, the less time it takes for the savings bond to reach full value.

Moneysaver
Do you know whose name is actually on your bonds? I didn't. But if you expect to use these for college tuition, it makes a difference. The bonds must be registered in a parent's name to realize the tax savings.

MAXIMUM TIME FOR SAVINGS
BONDS TO REACH FACE VALUE

Issue Date	Original Term (in years)
Jan 1980–Oct 1980	11
Nov 1980–Apr 1981	9
May 1981–Oct 1982	8
Nov 1982–Oct 1986	10
Nov 1986–Feb 1993	12
Mar 1993–Apr 1995	18
May 1995–present	17

Timesaver
If you need forms or have a burning question about savings bonds, place a call to West Virginia. That's right. The federal Bureau of the Public Debt—(304) 480-6112—moved not too long ago to Parkersburg, West Virginia. You can also write to the bureau, care of the Savings Bond Department, Parkersburg, WV 26106-1328.

How much are these bonds worth? The short answer is not a heck of a lot. I'm giving you the short answer, because providing the definitive answer could keep you up all night. It seems that every few years, the rules change on how these bonds are valued, so pinpointing what a drawer full of these bonds are worth can be about as easy as programming a VCR. To make it simpler, I'll just share how the value of the latest Series EE bonds is calculated. The government, fretting that people were ignoring savings bonds in droves, decided to make them more attractive in 1997. All the bonds issued after May of that year earn interest based on 90 percent of the average yield of the five-year Treasury. Before the change, the bonds earned interest based on 85 percent of the five-year Treasuries. What's more, in the old days, the interest on these bonds was only compounded semiannually. Now the interest accrues monthly. The most recent rate was just set at 5.59 percent. (The rate is changed twice each year—in May and November.)

If you have some savings bonds, you probably want to know how much they are worth. A bank should be able to tell you quite easily. I found out by visiting the Web site of the Federal Reserve Bank of New York (www.ny.frb.org). The bank has a built-in calculator that can determine how much your savings bonds are worth within seconds. All I had to do was type in the face value of my son's bond ($75) and the month and year it was issued (October 1992). As of February 1998, the bond is worth a whopping $50.40.

It takes decades, but your savings bond eventually stops paying interest. Here is a table that shows when there is absolutely no reason to hang onto them any longer.

WHEN IT'S FINALLY TIME TO CASH IN YOUR SAVINGS BONDS

Series	Issue Date	Final Maturity
E	May 1941–Nov 1956	40 years
E	Dec 1965–June 1980	30 years
EE	All issues	30 years
H	June 1952–Jan 1957	29 years, 8 months
H	Feb 1957–Dec 1979	30 years
HH	All issues	20 years

Don't despair if your savings bonds are lost or destroyed. The Bureau of the Public Debt replaces them free of charge as long as it can establish that the bonds were not cashed. To safeguard your investment, keep records of the bond serial numbers, issue dates, and registration in a safe place, separate from the bonds.

Just the facts

- Bonds are a necessary ingredient for diversification.
- The great enemy of bonds is interest-rate hikes.

- Before committing yourself, check a bond's creditworthiness.

- There is more than one strategy for selecting U.S. Treasuries.

- Don't buy municipal bonds if you're in the wrong tax bracket.

- Junk bonds are gaining more respect, but they still are risky.

GET THE SCOOP ON...
Mutual funds—behind the scenes ▪
Why mutual funds are all the rage ▪
A short list of great funds ▪ Your stock fund
choices ▪ Bonds versus bond funds ▪ Avoiding
mutual fund blunders ▪ Closed-end mutual
funds—not for amateurs

Mutual Funds—Don't Invest Without 'Em

Chapter 6

The first time I visited a mutual fund company, I wasn't sure what I'd discover when the elevator door slid open. Glamour? Excitement maybe? Would I meet men and women with such advanced analytical and mathematical capabilities that scientists someday would want to preserve their brains in formaldehyde?

Alas, there has never been any signs of adventure lurking around the corners of the carpeted corridors I've walked down. What I see on visits as I profile fund companies for *Mutual Funds Magazine* is a lot of people—mostly guys wearing dark suits and starched Brooks Brothers shirts—sitting behind desks. Granted, most of them have nice desks, and the ones with the greatest performance statistics also command the best views. In Denver, for instance, the most successful fund managers get to hang out in offices facing the west, where the magnificent Rocky Mountains soar like exclamation points across the horizon. In San Francisco, another city with a critical mass of fund companies, the favored managers can gaze across the choppy waters of the San Francisco Bay and see such sights as the Golden Gate Bridge and Alcatraz.

Much to my surprise, I learned that what these fund managers do all day isn't so hard to understand. Most spend much of their time working the phones to keep their pulse on what's happening in the stock market. They get a lot of their reconnaissance from their own in-house stock experts, as well as analysts at national and regional brokerage firms. If a manager is considering buying a truckload of Kellogg's stock, for instance, he most likely will call his favorite cereal analyst to glean whatever he can from him. These guys are on the phone so much that voice-mail messages stack up like airplanes on runways during the Christmas season. The amount of faxes, Federal Express packages, press releases, reports, and other paper that continually gets dumped into a fund manager's office is astounding. I have seen money managers at the end of a long day fill a waist-high trash can with paper. By the way, most of this stuff goes unread.

Why am I telling you this? It's my way of explaining to you that mutual funds are not brain surgery. Just about anybody can figure out how to invest in them. If you can keep track of statistics in your office's rotisserie baseball league, compiling a portfolio of solid mutual funds should seem easy. If you're leery about investing in mutual funds or if you aren't sure that you've chosen wisely, keep reading. In the next few minutes, you'll learn just what mutual funds are, what types exist, and how you can successfully invest in them. If you're agonizing about all your choices, I'll help you with that too. I've included a short list of some sterling mutual funds.

I'll also discuss the merits of buying individual bonds or sticking with mutual funds. And I'll share with you some of the worst mutual fund blunders you can make. For veteran fund investors, I'll describe how closed-end funds may be appropriate in some portfolios. Meanwhile, for the scoop on researching funds, as well as buying strategies, see Chapters 7, 8, and 10.

The mutual fund phenomenon

It is undeniable that the popularity of mutual funds is reaching stratospheric proportions. The last time I checked with the Investment Company Institute, the fund industry's trade group in Washington, D.C., 6,976 mutual funds existed. At the current rate, somebody is launching a new one just about every day. The reason is obvious—the demand is insatiable. Investors are pouring money into mutual funds like those slot-machine addicts in Las Vegas. People like you and me have sunk more than $4,334,500,000,000 into funds. For anybody having trouble with all those zeros, that's $4.3 trillion.

Here is a breakdown of mutual fund assets:

Stock funds	$2.3 trillion
Bond funds	$996 billion
Money market funds	$1 trillion

Is all this hard to fathom? Don't even try. Thinking about all your choices could psych you out and lead to brain lock. And besides, I'll explain how you can sift through those 6,976 choices. You'll be surprised how easy it is to whack that number down.

A mutual fund pools the money of thousands of different shareholders just like you. You might send in a $2,000 check and on the same day, the mail

> **"**
> If you want to make money, you have a higher probability of doing that with a mutual fund where you have decision makers who are consumed with making investments. They don't just spend ten minutes a day on it. If you buy one stock instead and it's the wrong one, the game is over.
> —Michael Stolper, prominent mutual fund industry advisor
> **"**

bags will contain hundreds of other checks, some as small as $50 and some many times that amount. Still more money is electronically wired to the fund by other investors who don't want to bother with envelopes. If a fund is successful, the money flows are even heavier. All that money we are sending adds up fast. Tens of millions of dollars can gush into the nation's most popular funds each day.

What happens with all this cash? The fund managers—who have probably been at their desks for hours before you order that first double latté at Starbuck's—spend their days investing it in stocks, bonds, or other assets. The beauty of this arrangement is that you can own a tiny piece of hundreds of individual stocks or bonds just by holding a few shares. In the business, this is called *diversification*.

Here's what I mean. Let's say you invest $2,500 into the Acorn Fund, a well-regarded fund in Chicago that has been investing in smaller-sized companies for more than two decades. (Traditionally this one has been a favorite fund of a lot of professional money managers.) Your money is spread thinly across all the stocks in Acorn's portfolio. Recently, that would have meant that you owned a tiny bit of Harley-Davidson, Borders Bookstores, Royal Caribbean Cruises, Broderbund Software, and dozens of other companies. What's more, you'd own a mini-stake in Acorn's foreign holdings, including a British cosmetics corporation, a Greek bottling outfit, and a Panamanian bank. Obviously, if you invested your $2,500 in the stock market yourself, you couldn't begin to duplicate these investments. In fact, with $2,500, you could buy only about 75 shares of Harley-Davidson.

Why is investing in dozens of companies preferable to betting on just one? Well, what happens if riders start preferring foreign motorcycles? Harley-Davidson's stock tanks, and you lose much of your money. But if you own a mutual fund, Harley-Davidson's misfortune is theoretically neutralized by other companies in the portfolio that are doing just fine. In a nutshell, a fund's diversification reduces your investing risks.

I've been talking about stock funds, but shareholders of bond funds enjoy the same diversification. If you want to own individual bonds, you need at least $50,000 to $100,000 to develop a well-rounded fixed-income portfolio. It's not hard to see why, when you consider that just one municipal bond can cost $5,000, and some bonds require even more than that. A bond fund, on the other hand, can contain hundreds of different bonds. If one bond issuer defaults, the impact isn't nearly as devastating as it is for an individual investor who put all his cash into that bond alone.

What's all the fuss about?

Still on the fence about mutual funds? Here are some compelling arguments for signing on:

- **You don't have to be a financial whiz.** Why not let veteran money managers worry about the best ways to invest your cash? Do you really think you could do better than somebody who is probably slavishly working 60 hours a week to find the best investments?

- **Mutual funds are a cheaper way to go.** If you trade stocks and bonds, commissions and other costs can add up fast.

Bright Idea
For someone with more than $50,000 to invest, five or six funds is usually plenty. Everyone else should be able to suffice with three or four.

Unofficially...
Mutual fund
shareholders
don't have to
be wealthy to
get started.
According to the
Investment
Company
Institute, the
typical new
mutual fund
buyer earns
$44,000 a year.
These investors
put roughly 28
percent of their
savings into
funds.

■ **It's easy to afford.** You need very little cash to begin. Mutual fund companies really want your money, and many don't seem to care how little you have. Some fund families will even let you get started with no money down if you enroll in an automatic savings program. You complete simple paperwork that allows a fund to withdraw an agreed-on amount, say $50 or $100, each month from your checking or savings account. This money is invested in whatever funds you've selected. The withdrawal is made on the same day each month so you won't mess up your checking account balance. Even without an automatic savings program, you can often begin quite cheaply. A few mutual funds will sign you up for as little as $250 or $500. While some funds require higher minimums of say $2,500 or $5,000, these are often waived if you are establishing an Individual Retirement Account or an account for your child's college fund.

■ **Mutual fund companies are solid institutions.** You can make the case that fund companies are safer than banks and savings and loans. After all, plenty of banks failed in the 1980s. But since the passage of the Federal Investment Company Act of 1940, which regulates the industry, not a single fund company has gone under. The money in your mutual funds, however, is not protected by *Federal Deposit Insurance Corporation* (FDIC), which insures savings deposits at banks and S&Ls. If a mutual fund loses much of its value thanks to lousy stocks picks, there will be no one to bail you out.

Whittling down your choices

If you have trouble choosing among the 31 flavors at Baskin-Robbins, selecting the right fund might seem daunting. When you're scouting for a fund, there are plenty of people who want to help. A lot of them are selling something themselves. Magazines will tempt you with tantalizing headlines that scream "Seven Super Funds for a Dream Retirement," "Top Performing Funds at Bargain-Basement Prices," or how about this one: "The Secrets to Making 30% with Your Funds." But what's the best way to pick funds? Here's one strategy:

Draw up a list of possible funds—preferably from well-known and respected no-load fund families, such as Vanguard, Neuberger and Berman, Oakmark, T. Rowe Price, Scudder, Fidelity, Janus, and American Century. One way to zero in on excellent funds is to read personal finance magazines like *Mutual Funds Magazine*, *SmartMoney Magazine*, or *Money*.

You can eliminate thousands of potential fund choices simply by determining why you want to invest. The most important factor to consider is your financial goal. Ask yourself what you want to do with your money and how many years you have to accomplish it. Suppose you need to save for your toddler's college education or for your retirement that's still 25 years away. With such a long horizon, you can afford to be bolder. Consequently your best bet would be a stock fund. A stock fund—which can invest in companies as recognizable as United Airlines and as obscure as the latest Internet company—poses risks. But over the long haul, stock funds have historically provided patient investors with the juiciest returns.

On the flip side, if you don't have much time, say two or three years, you should avoid stock funds. Stick with something much safer, such as a money market or a short-term bond fund. Why? Let's say you want to buy a new car in three years, so you latch onto one of last year's hottest stock funds. You salivate as you watch your fund rack up big gains, but suddenly the stock market gets hit with a major correction. Your car fund loses money. Unfortunately, you don't have the luxury of waiting for the market to rally, because you need that new car. Because of your poor investment choice, the new Honda Accord you dreamed about driving off the lot might instead turn into a Honda Civic.

Here's how you can easily pare down your choices even more. If you have no intention of using a full-service broker to buy your funds, you should stick with no-load funds, which do not come with a sales charge. With load funds, you pay a premium. (See Chapter 10, "Making Your Move—Buying and Selling," for more on the differences between the two.) Automatically, that eliminates close to 3,000 funds from consideration.

Shortcut for cheaters

How many of you out there are thinking, *Just tell me what the good funds are!* Okay, this is for anybody who prefers a list of recommendations. Before you read on, a little caveat.

This is by no means a definitive list of all the wonderful funds available. For starters, I've only included no-load stock funds. This restriction eliminates superb funds like Davis New York Venture and this pair—GAM International and GAM Global. The only drawback to these funds is their respective 4.8 and 5 percent loads. For the same reason, I didn't include Franklin California Growth (4.5 percent load), which recently claimed honors as number one among growth funds during a five-year period.

What you will find on this list are funds that very rarely disappoint. Year in and year out, they out-muscle the competition by posting above-average returns. What's truly impressive and important about these funds is their consistency. They might never be hot enough to make a top 10 list, but they also haven't crashed and burned like many of yesterday's highest flyers during turbulent times. One reason for the consistency is that these funds are largely run by veteran fund managers. This is a definite plus in an era when successful portfolio managers are acting more and more like sports free agents. And here's another bonus: The funds you'll see listed are not fee hogs. They charge average or below-average annual expenses.

As you skim through this list, it is important to keep this in mind: There is no guarantee that any of these funds will continue to perform exceptionally well this year or in the future. Past performance is, well, just past performance. But lacking psychic powers to know which ones will fare best, reviewing a fund's track record, its expenses, and how it is managed are the best strategies we have.

The following are best buys (solid, dependable funds):

LARGE-COMPANY STOCK FUNDS

Dodge & Cox Stock
(800) 621-3979

Neuberger & Berman Partners
(800) 877-9700

Reynolds Blue Chip Growth
(800) 773-9665

Scudder Growth & Income
(800) 225-2470

Vanguard Index Trust 500 Portfolio
(800) 662-7447

Vanguard/Windsor II
(800) 662-7447

Oakmark
(800) 625-6257

Vanguard Equity Income
(800) 662-7447

Torray
(800) 443-3036

Strong Schafer Value
(800) 368-1030

MID-SIZED FUNDS

T. Rowe Price Mid-Cap Growth
(800) 638-5660

Nicholas II
(800) 544-6547

T. Rowe Price New America Growth
(800) 638-5660

SMALL-CAP STOCK FUNDS

T. Rowe Price New Horizons
(800) 638-5660

Vanguard Index Small Cap
(800) 662-7447

Baron Asset
(800) 992-2766

Neuberger & Berman Genesis
(800) 877-9700

INTERNATIONAL AND GLOBAL FUNDS

Janus Worldwide
(800) 525-8983

Hotchkis & Wiley International
(800) 346-7301

Vanguard World: International Growth
(800) 662-7447

Oakmark International
(800) 625-6275

Pick your flavor

Before you begin your own fund shopping, you need to know just what's in those store windows. Here's a glance at the major types of funds you'll find.

Growth funds and value funds

Growth funds are the salt and pepper of the mutual fund world. Just as you'll find salt and pepper shakers on most dinner tables, you'll find a core growth fund in lots of investors' portfolios. If you're a long-term investor, it's smart to build a portfolio around this type of fund. These funds are a perfect fit for all sorts of financial goals—whether you are bankrolling a college education, saving for the years after that retirement party, fattening an inheritance, or stashing away a year-end bonus.

Growth funds invest in corporations that have the potential to grow handsomely over time and provide handsome returns. Typically, growth fund managers gravitate to stocks in larger companies that tend to be well established. In the classic growth portfolio, you find household names that often dominate their industry, such as Coca-Cola, Intel, and Microsoft.

Growth stocks tend to plow profits back into their companies to fuel further expansion. Consequently, you won't see these giants spinning off generous dividends to their stockholders. The flip side to growth funds are value funds. The managers of these funds share something in common with garage-sale scroungers—they like bargains. These professionals want to buy their stocks cheap. Often, value managers snap up shares in unglamorous or out-of-favor companies that they believe will ultimately exceed expectations.

The following were recently the top 10 growth funds based on the highest five-year annualized returns:

1.	Franklin California Growth	25.99%
2.	Legg Mason Value	25.74%
3.	FPA Capital	24.62%
4.	Vanguard PRIMECAP	24.32%
5.	Torray Fund	24.11%
6.	Merrill Growth Fund, A	23.94%
7.	Mairs & Power Growth	23.70%
8.	Oakmark Fund	23.53%
9.	SAFECO Growth	23.52%
10.	Stand Ayer Wood: Equity	23.45%

Source: Lipper Analytical Services

Small cap and aggressive growth funds

Small cap and aggressive growth funds have a lot in common with Tabasco. Never bland, their erratic performance can cause investor heartburn. Like the name suggests, small cap funds sink money into the midgets of the corporate world—companies often worth far less than $1 billion. Chances are you've never heard of a lot of these places, but nonetheless some of them may one day grow into a corporate giant like Microsoft or Intel. Aggressive growth funds aren't restricted to investing in small companies, but many times they do. You'll often find these funds sinking a great deal of cash into companies that produce semiconductors, software, networking equipment, and other high-tech paraphernalia.

How volatile can these funds be? Let's see what recently happened to American Century's aggressive growth fund called Twentieth Century Vista. During the first four months of 1997, the fund lost almost 21 percent of its value. So if you had $5,000 in the fund at the start of the year, you'd have just $3,950 stock by the spring. But in the next two months, the fund had recouped almost 18 percent.

The following are the top 10 small cap funds based on the highest five-year annualized returns:

1.	Barr Rosen: Small Cap	24.1%
2.	Baron Asset Fund	24%
3.	Franklin Small Cap Growth Adv	22.8%
4.	Lord Abbett Developing Growth A	22.8%
5.	Franklin Small Cap Growth I	22.7%
6.	Enterprise Small Co. Growth Y	22.2%
7.	Govett Smaller Companies A	21.9%
8.	Berger Small Cap Value Inst.	21.9%
9.	Berger Small Cap Value Ret.	21.8%
10.	MAS Small Cap Inst.	21.5%

Source: CDA/Wiesenberger

The mission for these funds is rapid appreciation. Historically, investors in these funds have been rewarded with even greater returns than blue chip

Watch Out!
Don't assume that a small cap fund will always remain one. When a small-stock fund makes a spectacular splash in the media, investors inevitably dump many more millions into it. When that happens, the manager often is forced to invest in bigger corporations. Don't invest in a small cap fund that has more than $1 billion or $2 billion in assets.

growth funds. But because of the volatility, you shouldn't consider them unless you can sit on your money for five to seven years or more.

Growth and income and equity income funds

Here's a pop quiz: What's the difference between a growth fund and a growth and income fund? If you're shaking your head, you're not alone. Lately, it's hard even for the experts to tell the difference. Traditionally, growth and income funds have invested in companies that not only expand their operations at a decent clip, but also kick in generous dividends. On the other hand, growth funds have stuck with corporations where the dividend yield is measly at best because the money is reinvested into the companies. Sounds straightforward, but here's the problem. Today, you'll find precious few corporations providing a generous dividend yield of, say, 4 or 5 percent. Instead, a yield of 1.5 percent is typical. Without much income to brag about, that puts these funds in the same league as classic growth funds.

If you like dividends, you could have slightly better luck with an equity income fund, which typically targets large mature companies that aren't considered true growth plays. A portfolio manager might buy shares in big drug companies or perhaps in Philip Morris or British Petroleum. These funds also may invest a small percentage of their cash in dividend-generating bonds. The average dividend yield could be a bit more respectable.

Balanced funds and asset allocation funds

Stocks versus bonds. If you can't decide, you might be asking yourself the wrong question. For some, the answer is both. If you do like stocks and bonds mingled in one place, you're in luck. Balanced funds and asset allocation funds can do just that.

These funds tend to be less volatile than straight stock funds because of the bond holdings, but of course, they'll never be ranked among the great gangbuster funds for the same reason.

Balanced funds are easy to understand. Inside a portfolio, you find a fairly even split between bonds and stocks. This kind of fund can be ideal for a more conservative investor who is leery about having too large an exposure to stocks. It also can be a handy solution for someone who wants exposure to bonds and stocks but doesn't have enough money to open two funds. Balanced funds also attract aggressive investors who have sunk just about everything they own into stocks. A balanced fund gives them a smidgen of bond exposure as a modest hedge against a stock market meltdown.

Asset allocation funds add cash to the equation. The asset allocation manager maintains a pot of stocks, bonds, and cash and can change the mix depending on what's happening on Wall Street. It's kind of like having your own personal finance planner. With this kind of all-purpose fund, you don't have to agonize about whether your investment balance is off-kilter. If you lack confidence in making your own allocation decisions, one of these funds can be a smart choice.

In theory, asset allocation funds are designed to soften the blow of a market slump. If trouble is looming, for instance, managers can quickly sell off stock and convert it into cash. There is a price, however, for this built-in safety feature. These funds don't do as good a job locking in the superlative returns when the market is smoking.

If these kinds of funds interest you, consider checking out fund families that offer life-cycle

Unofficially...
You can now invest in funds of funds. These funds invest in other mutual funds. Portfolio managers typically sink their money into five to ten other funds to provide instant diversification. This new phenomenon is catching on fast—the number of funds has tripled in the past two years. But I think it's best to stay away.

funds. You pick a fund based on your age and when you expect to retire. If you're a Generation Xer, your life-cycle fund could very well be aggressively invested in growth and small cap stocks and even overseas holdings. But as an investor grows grayer, her life-cycle fund becomes more conservative in its mix of stocks, bonds, and cash. (Vanguard is a good source for these funds.)

Which is better—an asset allocation fund or a balanced one? I'd favor a balanced fund for one key reason. Asset allocation funds, by their very nature, practice market timing. Managers shift money around in reaction to changing economic conditions. That sounds great, but over the long haul, market timing never succeeds.

Sector funds

Every package of cigarettes carries a spooky warning label; maybe the literature for every sector mutual fund should too. The message could be "Proceed cautiously, or this fund could be hazardous to your financial health." Sector funds are among the riskiest you can select. They are treacherous because you must place an entire bet on one industry. You can buy into sector funds that invest exclusively in health care, computers, electronics, gold, insurance, brokerages, carmakers, biotechnology, airlines, construction, defense, real estate, consumer products, and more. Believe it or not, there is even a fund that only invests in companies that help connect customers to the Internet!

Because of its concentrated nature, owning a sector fund is a lot like holding individual stocks. Just like single equities, these funds can provide tremendous returns—far greater than the typical stock fund—but they also can self-destruct much

Moneysaver
Want to learn more about sector funds? *Mutual Funds Magazine* has compiled some of its ongoing coverage on the topic into a free booklet. Call (800) 442-9000 for a copy.

easier. Yet the potential payoff is so tempting that some people just shrug off the gamble. You might appreciate why if you've ever looked at any given year's platinum funds. An impressive number of sector funds always seems to be huddled at the top. That's certainly the case with this list of the 10 best stock funds during a recent five-year period. As you'll notice, all the winners are sector funds.

The following are the top 10 mutual funds based on the highest five-year annualized returns:

1.	Fidelity Select Electronics	35.68%
2.	Fidelity Select Home Finance	33.30%
3.	Seligman Communications	31.23%
4.	Fidelity Select Energy Service	30.93%
5.	J. Hancock Regional Bank, A	30.20%
6.	Fidelity Select Computer	29.52%
7.	J. Hancock Regional Bank, B	29.35%
8.	Pilgrim Am. Bank & Thrift, A	28.80%
9.	Fidelity Select Brokerage	28.34%
10.	Fidelity Select Regional Bank	27.74%

Source: Lipper Analytical Services

There is, however, a downside. You'll find a lot of sector funds in the basement as well. The 10 worst performers in 1997 were sector funds. All the bottomdwellers, by the way, were invested in gold. It's not hard to see how sector funds can whipsaw. Let's suppose you own a retail fund that invests in department stores and apparel makers. Guess what could happen to your fund if merchants suffer through a miserable Christmas shopping season? You may very well lose money. It's a similar story for the financial sector. A fund that specializes in banks and thrifts could get walloped if interest rates and inflation rise or if foreign countries begin defaulting on sizable bank loans.

Because of the high volatility, sector funds should only represent a small portion of just about anybody's portfolio. Actually, these funds are only suited for aggressive investors who know what they are doing. Many shareholders prefer sector funds to owning a bundle of stocks in a particular industry, because it is much easier.

Venturing overseas with foreign funds

A lot of people are too petrified to invest their money in a fund that sinks all its cash overseas. Selecting a fund that's loaded with all-American corporations like Gillette or Microsoft is one thing, but choosing a fund that owns stock in a string of Mongolian optical shops is another. I'd certainly not scoff at anybody who is too frightened to try some overseas exposure. In fact, I wouldn't argue with anybody who insists that the harrowing dips in the financial markets do seem scarier overseas.

In the fall of 1997, for instance, stocks trading on the Hong Kong market dropped like a manhole cover. In just four days, this Asian exchange lost 23 percent of its value, which triggered panic selling in Japan as well as on the European stock exchanges. The ripple effect even spooked stock traders as far away as Mexico and Brazil. And then, as you might recall, the U.S. stock market dropped 554 points (7.18 percent of its value) before rebounding. The reason for all this turmoil? Some sort of currency crisis. Thailand was forced to devalue its currency, called the *baht*. While the government aggressively cracked down on speculators who were betting against the baht's strength, other countries in the

Timesaver
If you are interested in sector funds, consider buying them through Fidelity Investments, which maintains an exhaustive selection with dozens of choices. Fidelity sector funds, you should know, all come with a 3 percent sales charge. You will also have to pay a .75 percent trading fee if you dump your sector choice less than a month after you buy it.

region experienced their own currency meltdowns. And months later, the situation in Asia was still a mess. Now, if your life is as harried as mine what with work deadlines, kids' soccer practices, and remembering trash day, there is no time left to understand the complexities of a currency crisis, particularly one 13 time zones away. Foreign funds free you from ever having to personally contemplate such things as the future of the baht. Professional money managers will make the investing decisions instead.

Of course, there are many other solid reasons why foreign funds are appealing. For starters, the United States is rarely the top banana among the world stock exchanges. Here's a sobering statistic: Since 1980, the United States has earned the world-wide title of best-performing stock market just once. In contrast, Hong Kong claimed top honors five times in the past 25 years.

Consider this as well: If you keep your money at home, you'll miss out on some of the bluest of the world's blue chips. That's because 70 percent of the world's' largest automakers, 80 percent of the globe's biggest chemical conglomerates, and 8 of the 10 largest banks are not headquartered on American soil. And here's another reason to invest globally. Hard as this might be to believe, putting some cash in overseas markets can actually reduce the volatility of your portfolio. This isn't just my opinion. Many highly regarded academic studies have documented this phenomenon. Actually, it makes sense if you think about it. The world's financial markets aren't supposed to perform like your car's wheels—they aren't perfectly aligned. So when U.S. stocks are floundering, it's highly possible that other markets are doing just fine. For instance, in

> **"**
> The markets are so much less efficient internationally than in the U.S., so in my opinion you get bigger pockets of opportunities. You can find undervalued stocks that people are either ignoring or they don't understand the story.
> —Helen Young Hayes, portfolio manager of Janus Overseas and Janus Worldwide funds
> **"**

1994, the American market, as measured by the Standard & Poor's 500, plodded along with a 1.3 percent advance. In contrast, the Japanese market sprinted to a 21.6 percent return.

If you want to invest internationally, you should devote no more than 20 percent of your portfolio overseas. Because of the extra volatility, consider investing in a foreign fund through dollar cost averaging. (For a review of dollar cost averaging, see Chapter 11, "Investing on the Run: Sure-Fire Shortcuts.") Here are the main categories of foreign funds that you can choose from:

- **Global funds:** If the thought of investing overseas makes your palms sweat, you might want to ease into it with one of these. The term *global* simply means that a manager may park his or her money anywhere in the world, including the United States. This is not a pure foreign play, since a large chunk of your money might never leave the U.S. If you already own domestic stock funds, there is a danger that a global fund will simply duplicate what you already own. Consequently, if you own funds that invest in American companies, it would be better if you stick with a straight international fund.

- **International funds:** If you're a greenhorn on the world scene, your best move is into one of these all-purpose, one-size-fits-all international funds. And even if you're a seasoned investor, one of these should be your core foreign holding. The typical international fund places bets on stocks scattered in established countries around the world, such as the major European countries, Australia, and Japan. A lot of these funds hold stocks that would be called blue chip in this country, such as Sony, Nestlé, Toyota, and Daimler Benz.

■ **Emerging markets:** If you like casinos, emerging markets might seem like home. By investing in one of these funds, you might end up owning a tiny piece of a Malaysian newspaper chain or an Indian fertilizer company. In the past, stocks from developing countries have delivered both stupendous and disastrous returns. For example, during a recent year, emerging markets actually swept the top 15 spots for annual performance among 76 world stock markets. The top five exchange winners hailed from Bangladesh (196 percent), Russia (156 percent), Venezuela (132 percent), Hungary (95 percent), and China (89 percent). In 1993, emerging markets posted a phenomenal return of 74.8 percent. But like I said, these funds are extremely volatile. The next year, emerging markets plunged negative 7.3 percent.

You need to look no further than the current Southeast Asian meltdown to see what can happen when your financial bet is placed on incubating economies that can seem as sturdy as tinker toys. While Thailand and neighboring countries struggled with their currency woes, for instance, funds investing in the region got walloped. During a single month, for instance, Fidelity's Hong Kong & China Fund lost almost 32 percent of its value.

If you are going to own just one foreign fund, it doesn't make sense to choose one that concentrates in the developing world. If your time horizon is very long and you have a strong stomach, you might consider putting no more than 5 or 6

Watch Out!
No matter how you plan to invest internationally, you need to remember the usual caveat: Consider your time horizon. Foreign funds can take you on a bone-jarring ride, but historically, these funds have paid off for investors who don't panic when markets in places like Hong Kong implode.

percent of your money into an emerging market or regional fund.

- **Regional and single country funds:** With these funds, you're placing your entire bet on just one country, like Japan, or one region, such as Europe or Latin America. If you want to invest in Russia, Indonesia, or many other single countries, you'll more than likely have to purchase shares in a closed-end fund. (More on closed-end funds at the end of this chapter.) Needless to say, these specialized funds are best left to experts.

The following are the top 10 foreign funds based on the highest five-year annualized returns:

1.	GAM International Fund, A	22.79%
2.	Dean Witter European Growth	22.16%
3.	Putnam Europe Growth, A	20.66%
4.	Morgan Stanley Inst. Intl. Equity, A	20.34%
5.	Merrill Lynch Eurofund, A	20.24%
6.	Pioneer Europe Fund, A	19.98%
7.	Harbor Fund International	19.77%
8.	Fidelity Europe	19.58%
9.	Wright EquiFund-Netherlands	19.39%
10.	Vanguard Intl. Equity Index Europe	19.11%

Source: Lipper Analytical Services

Investing in bond funds

Bond funds are considered a safer haven than stock funds, which is why a lot of senior citizens load up on bonds. While even retirees should not abandon stocks entirely, it's generally agreed that as people age, the percentage of bonds they hold in their portfolio should increase. But before you purchase shares in a bond fund, or individual bonds, you need to think about these four questions:

- How much risk am I willing to accept?
- How long will I be investing?
- What tax bracket am I in?
- Is the yield or the credit quality of the bonds more important?

Risk is a crucial consideration when you're trying to figure out whether you want a bond fund that's loaded with long-term bonds or one that comes due in the a few years. You have three choices to choose from:

- Short-term bond funds
- Intermediate-term bond funds
- Long-term bond funds

Short-term bond funds are the safest, because they are best at deflecting interest-rate fluctuations. The mortal enemy of bond funds is high interest rates. When interest rates soar, bond prices drop. (For more details on the peculiarities of bonds, flip back to Chapter 5.) Bonds have a better chance of thriving when inflation is not a threat.

Providing a higher yield than a money market, short-term funds are a great place to park money you'll need in two or three years. On the other hand, long-term bond funds, which hold debt that might not mature for 10 to 30 years, are the most volatile. Sandwiched in between are the intermediate-term funds, which often contain bonds that mature within 5 to 10 years.

Typically, the riskier long-term funds offer investors the highest total returns. After all, there has to be some financial carrot to encourage people to fool with iffier bonds. These more volatile funds, however, are only appropriate for somebody who can hold onto his shares for several years.

Knowing your tax bracket is also essential. Your choice also depends on whether your bond investment will be sitting in a retirement account or a taxable one. (See Chapters 5 "Bond Isn't a Four-Letter Word and 13, "Taxes and Investing—What You Should Know," for the tax consequences of bond investing.)

Lastly, you need to decide whether you want bonds that pose absolutely no chance of defaulting, speculative bonds, or something in between. If all things were equal, we'd of course want the safest bonds in the world. But alas, the yield on these bonds aren't as generous as the riskier ones.

As you mull all this over, here are the main types of bond funds:

- **U.S. Treasuries:** These bonds, issued by the federal government, win the prize for the highest credit rating. After all, there is no chance of the federal government hanging a "Going Out of Business" sign in the window. With a U.S. Treasury bond fund, you do not have to pay state taxes on your income, but Uncle Sam still wants his cut.

- **Municipal bonds:** State and local governments use these bonds to build high-ticket items like water treatment plants, prisons, and airports. The most alluring feature of a muni bond fund is the tax break. Invest in one of these, and you won't pay federal income taxes on your interest. If you invest in a muni fund that only invests in bonds in your state, you avoid state and possibly local taxes as well. While muni bonds aren't as creditworthy as Treasuries or other federal agency bonds, they are generally considered safe. What's more, many of the muni bonds that don't enjoy the highest bond ratings are insured.

All too many taxaphobes, however, make a huge miscalculation when they embrace one of these funds. If you are in the 15 percent tax bracket, your tax break most often won't be worth the lower yield these muni funds typically provide. The only sure winners are Americans in the highest tax brackets. It's often a toss-up whether these funds make financial sense for somebody in the 28 percent bracket.

- **Corporates:** Governments aren't the only big-time debtors. Corporate America issues bonds as well. Don't assume, however, that all bond funds are created equal. High-grade corporate bond funds invest in the cream of the crop. These funds concentrate on companies with excellent grades from the bond rating services. But there are also high-yield corporate bonds. That's just a tricky name for junk bonds, which are issued by companies that aren't nearly as creditworthy. Because these bonds are riskier, they are gift-wrapped with a higher yield. As you can tell from the next chart, junk bonds have captured the majority of the top 10 spots in the latest bond fund hall of fame.

Don't assume that all high-quality corporate bond funds only hold the best bonds. To ratchet up the yield and attract more shareholders, fund managers toss in junk bonds. Before buying, you should check a fund's prospectus to see what percentage of junk is allowed.

Watch Out!
If you blindly seek out a fund with the highest yield, you could end up with a risky fund. Let's suppose two corporate bond funds are advertising yields of 7.2 percent and 7.9 percent. You naturally want the higher yield. But it might not be worth it if that fund is packed with junk bonds and the other is not.

The 10 highest-performing bond funds follow:

1.	GT Global High Income, A	17.99%
2.	GT Global High Income, B	17.22%
3.	American Century Benham Target 2020	16.72%
4.	Northeast Investors Trust	15.21%
5.	American Century Benham Target 2015	14.93%
6.	Fidelity Spartan High Income	14.60%
7.	Loomis Sayles Bond	14.26%
8.	Morgan Stanley High Yield, A	14.24%
9.	MAS Fund High Yield	14.14%
10.	Mainstay High Yield Corp., B	13.98%

Source: Lipper Analytical Services

Moneysaver
Because bond fund returns have historically been far lower than stock funds, selecting a fund with below-average annual expenses is extremely important. Stiff expenses can gobble up a substantial part of your yield. For the same reason, it makes much more sense to pick a no-load bond fund rather than one with a sales charge.

The face-off: bond funds versus individual bonds

Buying bonds individually or through a fund is one of those perennial questions that investment advisors love to explore. Frankly, for most people, bond funds make more sense. But you decide for yourself.

Why bond funds are great:

■ **Your money can stretch farther.** Buying into a bond fund can cost as little as $500 or $1,000. You also can add money in dribs and drabs—say $50 or $100—anytime you please. In contrast, purchasing just one municipal bond can cost at least $5,000. To buy bonds on your own, you really need at least $50,000 to $100,000 for a fairly well-balanced portfolio. (Remember, diversity keeps your risks lower.) With bond funds, you can enjoy the same diversification for a fraction of the price.

- **Funds are convenient and flexible.** To withdraw money, you can write checks off a bond fund or redeem by phone. Selling an individual bond can be harder and more costly, especially since professional bond dealers may prefer trading in blocks of $1 million or more. Fund investors don't have to pay brokerage commissions that are charged for individual bond trades.

- **Funds let others do the work for you.** Do you really want to spend your free time analyzing a casino junk bond or a muni offering from West Virginia? Or how about figuring out the currency implication of a German bond? I didn't think so. Let the fixed-income professionals who get really jazzed about bonds do the research for you. All you have to do is find the right fund, and even this won't be hard if you stick with fund companies well known for their bond offerings, such as the no-load Vanguard Group.

- **Most bond funds distribute their interest income in monthly checks to shareholders.** Of course, you also have the option of automatically reinvesting this interest. If you own a regular bond, however, interest checks are usually only issued twice a year. What's more, the interest income can't be automatically reinvested.

- **Funds also offer bonds with a collection of maturities.** Consequently you don't have to invest a lot of money to enjoy a bond portfolio with different maturities.

Why individual bonds are great:

- **Your income stream is predictable.** When you buy an individual bond, you know up front what your interest payments will be. This can be especially important if you are retired and living on a fixed income. An investor can also purchase an individual bond that matures on a target date, such as the year a child is heading off to college. In contrast, a bond fund manager typically doesn't hold bonds until maturity, so the amount of your dividend checks will vary.

- **You know what you own.** This might seem like a silly reason, but it isn't. If your money is in a high-grade corporate bond fund, some money, more than likely, will be invested in junk bonds as well. Even a government bond fund could hold more speculative debt.

- **You can control the timing of taxable capital gains or losses** since a bondholder can decide when he'll buy or sell.

- **Individual bonds may be cheaper.** The mutual fund investor will be hit with annual expenses (the average is just under 1 percent), but you won't be paying any annual fees if you buy separate bonds.

The biggest mutual fund blunders

Okay, you've gone through all the major mutual fund categories. Maybe you're now itching to either buy a fund or two or tinker with your existing portfolio. But before starting, you need to know how to dodge mutual fund bloopers. Without further ado, here is a list of fund no-nos:

- **Fundaholics:** Unfortunately, too many mutual fund investors—like some of the readers whom I write for at *Mutual Funds Magazine*—behave like the hound dog who chases after every darn truck that whizzes down the street. The pooch just can't help himself, and neither can fund junkies who can't stop collecting mutual funds.

Fundaholics always stumble across funds they think are superior to the ones they already own. If you're skeptical, you should hear the feedback I get from happy portfolio managers after I profile their funds in one of my articles. On the day a magazine containing a flattering story about a portfolio manager is released on the newsstands, readers start flooding the fund's phones. Some of these excited would-be invest-ors can't even wait until daybreak. They call breathlessly at 3 a.m.—no lie—in the hopes that they can sign up immediately.

The managers—their egos pumped up—call to thank me. I graciously accept their gratitude. I don't have the heart to explain that they should be thanking those fund addicts. If you buy every fund you read about, you almost assuredly will have a weird-looking portfolio.

■ **Star struck:** Yes, even the fund industry has its superstars. And placing your bet on them can be risky. Here's a case in point. After a few phenomenal years at Govett Smaller Companies Fund, portfolio manager Garrett Van Wagoner apparently began believing the breathless press clippings and struck out on his own. Thousands of his devoted fans sank money into his new funds. At first, he repeated the magic, but as the money kept pouring in, he struggled to invest it all. In 1997, when the fund industry enjoyed another banner year, Van Wagoner's three funds performed poorly. During 1997, for example, Van Wagoner's Emerging Growth Fund lost 20 percent of its value and ranked an embarrassing 1,043 out of 1,047 domestic

Bright Idea
Thirsty for more on mutual funds? Check out Morningstar's mutual fund ratings publications. You can find them at many libraries. Check their Web site at www.morningstar.net. Or call (800) 735-0700 for subscription information. You might also want to buy Mary Rowland's *A Commonsense Guide to Mutual Funds.*

growth stock funds, according to CDA/ Wiesenberger, the mutual fund rating service.

- **Getting antsy:** When you're in a fund, stay in unless the fund has two lousy years. But even then, you should tough it out if the other funds in the same category are suffering too. That's when it's likely that other factors, such as inflation and overseas turmoil, are keeping a lid on returns.

- **Return worshiper:** Far too many investors buy funds based on their very short-term performance. You should never select a fund just because it shoots to the front of the pack for one year. Or, heaven forbid, for just one quarter. Unfortunately, however, it's a proven fact that cash gushes most heavily into whatever funds are declared the winners of the latest quarter. If you chase the leaders, you could end up with a fund like American Heritage Fund, which posted an incredible 1997 return of 75 percent. That is not a typo. But wait. For the past five years, American Heritage eked out a yearly return of just 1.1 percent. To avoid flash in the pans, you should try to stick with funds that have maintained an above-average return for the past five years. It also makes sense to see how a fund has performed during bear and bull markets.

A yearly review

Finally, here's a list of questions to ask yourself once a year after you assemble your portfolio:

- How is my portfolio divided among stocks, bonds, and cash? Am I comfortable with the percentages?

- Do my funds overlap, or do they represent distinct investing styles?

- Are my funds divided appropriately among large, medium, and small companies?

- Do I understand the holdings in my bond funds and their average maturities?

- Is the money manager who attracted me to the funds originally still running the show?

- How does the total return of my funds compare to the rest of their peer groups for one, three, and five years? And how have my funds done compared with their respective benchmarks, such as the Standard & Poor's 500 Index?

Closed-end funds—not for rookies

I saved the most complicated type of mutual fund for last. Closed-end funds are stuck back here because they are not appropriate for rookies. Since they require a higher degree of commitment and vigilance, most people won't want to bother with them. Nor should they. If you are a gutsy investor, keep reading. Everybody else can jump to the next chapter.

If you've never heard of closed-end funds, it's not a surprise. Usually when you read about mutual funds, the closed-end ones are ignored. And investors also largely ignore them. About $43 billion is sloshing around in closed-end funds, which sounds pretty impressive until you learn that it equals about 2 percent or so of all assets in stock mutual funds.

While closed-end funds are operating in relative obscurity, that doesn't mean they can't play a part in a savvy investor's trading strategies. But first a definition. Closed-end funds differ from regular or

> 66
> Closed-end funds are the ugly ducklings of the fund world—condemned by their big mutual fund brothers and sisters (and most of the media) to the backwaters of the market pond.
> —Norman G. Fosback, editor-in-chief, *Mutual Funds Magazine*
> 99

open-ended funds in a very important way. Unlike most funds, the closed-end variety are traded on the stock exchanges just as corporations are. There is a fixed number of shares available to buy and sell in a closed-end fund, and when an owner wants to dump them, he must sell through a stock broker. You also have to buy shares through a broker.

If shares in the closed-end fund are unpopular, then the price will dip below what its underlying assets are worth. You might, for instance, own shares that are worth $10 each. But on the open market, buyers will only pay $9. This represents a 10 percent discount for the purchaser. (And a 10 percent loss for you!) If the fund is hot, eager investors might pay a premium for shares. New buyers might pony up $12 a share, when each one is actually only worth $10. Regular mutual funds, on the other hand, can never sell at a discount or a premium. Each share is priced at what's called its *net asset value.* In the mutual fund tables in your newspaper, you'll see this term abbreviated as *NAV.* The NAV is calculated each day by dividing all the outstanding shares into the value of the fund's entire assets after liabilities are subtracted.

The number of shares available in an open-ended mutual fund isn't set in concrete like its closed-end cousins. If a fund receives $1 million in the mail from new investors, fund managers add that to their pool of money, and the company issues new shares. What's more, if a shareholder in an open-ended fund wants to sell, the fund company itself is obligated to buy back any shares. The price will equal that day's NAV minus any load or redemption fee.

A lot of investors buy closed-end funds for one simple reason —the discount. Imagine demanding to buy $10,000 worth of Coca-Cola stock or a mutual fund at a 20 percent discount. You'd be nuts. But closed-end investors get discounts all the time. Recently the average discount for closed-end funds was 8 percent. But there is a wide variation. Funds today are selling from a 31 percent discount to a 42 percent premium.

Getting that discount can in some situations really pump up your return. Suppose you buy a closed-end fund worth $10 a share that is trading for $8 (a 20 percent discount). Now let's imagine that the market soars 50 percent, bringing your fund's NAV to $15 a share. Outsiders get excited about your fund, so the demand for shares artificially bumps up the price to $18. It's now selling at a 20 percent premium. Naturally, you're thrilled with your 125 percent gain (from $8 to $18 a share), especially since the actual market advanced by just 50 percent.

Of course, it's great to buy a fund at a discount (who wouldn't love one), but what happens if the discount stubbornly remains? As a shareholder, you want your discount to turn into a premium. But with closed-end funds occupying the financial world's Sleepy Hollow, there is no guarantee that a fund's discount will ever disappear. You can appreciate just how unpopular this way of investing is by seeing how many new closed-end funds were launched recently. During a recent year, just one was created.

Still, not everyone thinks closed-end funds deserve their exile. Not long ago, Norman Fosback made a strong argument for his readers to take a second look. In an analysis of 14 years' worth of

Unofficially...
Back in 1822, King William I of the Netherlands created the first closed-end fund. This newfangled way of investing quickly swept across Europe like wildfire. The Scots were the biggest fans. The idea crossed the Atlantic in 1893 when the first American closed-end fund, the Boston Personal Property Trust, was launched.

Watch Out!
Don't ever buy shares on the first day a new closed-end fund is traded. The opening-day price includes a built-in charge of 5 to 8 percent to pay the fees assessed by brokerage houses to market the new shares.

statistics, the magazine concluded that closed-end funds selling at a discount of at least 10 percent averaged annual returns that were 6 percent fatter than their open-end peers. The closed-end advantage is even greater for someone who buys at a heftier discount. This good news, however, doesn't carry over to funds selling at premiums of at least 10 percent. These funds average returns that are 11 percent less than the open-end funds.

With statistics like that, how come more people don't snatch up discounted funds? For one thing, you don't see closed-end funds advertised in the media the way other funds are. Financial publications are stuffed with mutual fund ads, but you could read the *Wall Street Journal* or *Barron's* for months without spotting a plug for a closed-end fund. And brokers typically don't suggest them to their clients. Remember, closed-end funds, unlike the other kind, are always sold through these middlemen. With so many other publicly traded stocks to choose from, these can get lost in the shuffle.

Only experienced investors should buy into a closed-end fund. If you are interested in one, you need to proceed carefully. After all, the background material on these funds is harder to find than the regular mutual funds. Here are some tips:

- **Never pay a premium for a closed-end fund.** As Fosback's research showed, paying too much for a fund typically guarantees you subpar returns.

- **Limit your purchases to funds that offer a discount.** Deeper discounts usually offer greater upside growth. Sell shares when a fund moves into the territory of its premium high.

- **Do not buy a fund that is too risky for your profile.** You can buy closed-end funds that invest in blue chip stocks and bonds, but a far greater number of these funds concentrate on foreign holdings. You'll find that if you want to invest in just one foreign country, you'll generally have to rely on a closed-end fund. Through these single-country funds, you can invest in the stocks of such countries as Taiwan, Italy, Mexico, India, the Czech Republic, Russia, Malaysia, Spain, Chile, China, Argentina, the Nether-lands, and Sweden. Of course, remember that funds that only invest in one country are extremely risky.

Meanwhile, never buy a fund without thoroughly researching it. It's harder to find information on closed-end funds, but these resources should help:

- Morningstar at (800) 735-0700 or www. morningstar.net provides statistics and analyses on about 200 closed-end funds.

- *Mutual Funds Magazine* and its Internet site, www.mfmag.com, also contains information on these funds.

- *Investing in Closed-End Funds: Finding Value and Building Growth,* by Albert J. Fredman and George Cole Scott, is a good resource.

You can track the value of closed-end funds by checking the business pages of many major newspapers, including the *New York Times,* the *Wall Street Journal,* and *Barron's.* The *Wall Street Journal* and *Barron's* list the NAV of closed-end stocks, as well as their discounts or premiums, weekly.

Just the facts

- Mutual funds are a great way to diversify your portfolio.

- Zeroing in on the appropriate fund isn't as hard as you might think.

- There is a wide variety of stock funds to choose from.

- Mutual funds make bond investing easier.

- Watch out for common mutual fund mistakes.

- Closed-end funds can be lucrative if you know what you're doing.

Zooming In on Your Choices

PART III

GET THE SCOOP ON...
Whittling down your stock choices ▪ Analyzing
stocks—what's important ▪ Value Line comes to
the rescue ▪ Picking small cap winners ▪
Evaluating a mutual fund in three easy steps ▪
Selecting a winning newsletter

Research—The Investing Advantage

Chapter 7

L et's begin with a little quiz. On a scale of 1 to 10, how do you rate Chuck's stock-picking prowess? After college graduation, Chuck hangs out at bowling alleys with his buddies. Sensing an investment opportunity, Chuck pours much of his money into bowling stocks—shoe and ball manufacturers, alley construction companies, the works. Unfortunately, bowling was not the phenomenon he envisioned. I'm not sure if Chuck spent a great deal of time researching his stocks before he plunged headlong into bowling equities, but I doubt it.

Chuck's stock disaster is a handy way to illustrate why doing the legwork before you buy—whether it's a new video camera or a block of stock—is a necessity. But you might be saying to yourself, *I'd never make Chuck's mistakes. He was just plain dumb.* Actually, you wouldn't hear anybody whispering that about the guy today. This is a real story. Just ask the actual stock picker, Charles Schwab, the man who operates one of the premier discount brokerage firms in America today.

Obviously, Schwab's stock mistakes, which he shared with *SmartMoney Magazine* a few years ago, didn't hold him back. He's worth untold millions. And even if he makes a poor investment choice today, it's not going to crimp his lifestyle. Unfortunately, most of us aren't that lucky. We work hard to set aside money we'd probably rather blow at the mall. And we need that financial stockpile to grow much faster than inflation. Of course, we improve our chances of meeting our financial targets if we pick our investments wisely, and that takes research.

For anybody who hasn't had homework assignments for a long time, this chapter will nudge you along. You'll learn some of the basics of analyzing and evaluating stocks and stock mutual funds. You'll also find out how to use the Value Line Investment Survey, which has been helping people just like you tiptoe across those treacherous stock minefields. And how's this for an inside scoop—I'll share how the research director at Value Line uses the stock guides when adding to his own portfolio. Meanwhile, if you are hankering to invest in small cap stocks, keep reading for tips on how to research these equity orphans, which are all too often ignored by the Wall Street crowd. Finally, I'll divulge my secret weapon for selecting the best financial newsletters.

Dissecting stocks your own way

Researching a stock is a lot like putting together a puzzle. There are many ways to do it. Some people start with the straight pieces, others begin in the middle. It doesn't matter, since the puzzle will look identical in the end. It's the same with evaluating stocks. There are different methods, and if you stick with it, you'll find the approach that's right for you. What you should avoid is relying on one source for all your information. Rushing to buy a stock solely on the recommendation of a guest chatting on the set of Louis Rukeyser's *Wall Street Week* television program is not a smart idea. Unfortunately, people rely on hot tips like this all the time.

Logically, you should start with an idea. It might come from a magazine, one of those financial news shows, or a neighbor. You also might find stock ideas by flipping through the annual report of your favorite mutual fund. Inside the yearly update, you'll find an entire listing of a fund's stock holdings. Some managers will helpfully explain why they are thrilled with certain stocks and why they have jettisoned others. Still other folks prefer borrowing ideas generated by Warren Buffett, the brilliant stockpicker from Omaha, Nebraska, who just happens to be the second-wealthiest man in America. Books have been written about Buffett's investing style, though none have been penned by the man himself.

If you believe Peter Lynch, another legendary stockpicker, you can generate ideas just by staying alert. You might notice, for instance, that your daughter and every other impressionable teen is wearing the same polyester clothing and that most of it seems to be coming from the same manufacturer. Or maybe a national pet supply chain has gobbled up the store where you buy your golden retriever's milk bones, as well as other outlets in your city. Hmmm. Maybe there's a growth opportunity there. You might also consider thinking like a

Unofficially...
If you own a computer, you can find out what's on Warren Buffett's mind within a few seconds. When the Sage of Omaha pontificates publicly, he can literally move the stock market. To sneak a peak at Buffett's latest pearls of wisdom, visit www.berkshirehathaway.com.

visionary. Peering into the future, you try to anticipate trends that haven't occurred to most people. What do you think life will be like in 20 to 30 years, and what kind of products and technology are people going to want? Your answer could lead you to a group of companies you'll want to explore.

Don't like predicting trends? Here's an easier way to pick winners. Another stockpicking strategy is simply to team up with America's leading companies. You should reduce your chances of failure if you stick with the world's best corporations. These giants often enjoy global brand-name recognition, worldwide distribution channels, finely tuned research, and development arms that produce cutting-edge technology and extraordinary staying power. Over time, these corporations should produce above-average market returns with below-average risk. If you aren't sure what America's number-one corporations are, here is a sampling of some of the top corporations in some leading industries to get you started. In some cases, I've provided the runner-up company as well.

Drugs
   Merck
   Pfizer, runner-up

Recreation
   Disney
   Time Warner, runner-up

Soft drinks
   Coca-Cola
   PepsiCo, runner-up

Hospital supplies
   Johnson & Johnson
   Abbott Laboratories, runner-up

Household goods
   Proctor & Gamble
   Colgate-Palmolive, runner-up

Food
  Kellogg's
  Sara Lee
  Campbells
  Heinz
  (no runaway leader—
  these are in the top
  tier)

Computer software
  Microsoft

Semiconductors
  Intel

Oil
  Mobil

Deciphering the stock pages

Once you have a list of possibilities, keep in mind these 10 key questions:

- Is the stock reasonably priced?

- Is the stock priced competitively compared with other companies in the same industry?

- What are the company's future earnings prospects? And historically, what kinds of earnings has the company generated?

- What is the corporation's *return on equity* (ROE)? (More on this in a moment.)

- Does the company produce high-quality products or services? Would you want to be a customer?

- What about the people at the top? Are you impressed with their backgrounds?

- Is management's pay tied to the growth of the company, or do the leaders have no personal financial incentive to increase the company's profits?

- What percentage of the company is owned by the very people running the show? Are company insiders buying more shares or dumping them?

- Is the company's brand name recognized and valued?

- Are there any time bombs ready to go off—extensive lawsuits, expiring patents, aggressive competitors?

Your first step toward answering all of these will take 30 seconds. To get a snapshot view of your great prospect, look it up in your newspaper's stock pages. You'll discover even more detailed information in the financial newspapers like *Barron's,* The *Wall Street Journal,* and *Investor's Business Daily.* Flip toward the back of the business section, and you'll find the company listings for the New York Stock Exchange, the American Stock Exchange, and the NASDAQ. For this illustration, I'm going to use Anheuser-Busch, for no other reason than it's in my hometown. This is how a stock is typically listed in a newspaper:

52 Weeks
Hi Lo Stock Sym Div Yld % PE 48 ⅛ 38 ½
AnheuserB BUD 1.04 2.4 18
Vol 100s High Lo Close Net Chg
11170 40 ⅛ 38 ½ 39 7/8 ——

Here's how to decipher it:

- **Stock:** Look for the name. You're not going to find Anheuser-Busch listed—it's too long. So often, you have to find the condensed name, like AnheuserB.

- **Hi Lo:** To the left of the stock name, you see the company's high and low prices during the past year. This gives you a quick idea of what's been happening with the stock. On this chart, Anheuser-Busch's stock has sold as high as 48 ⅛ a share and as low as 38 ½.

- **Sym:** This represents the ticker symbol. The St. Louis brewing giant uses BUD as its symbol ticker. Clever, isn't it? As you can see, the stock symbol isn't necessarily an abbreviation of the corporation. If you are planning to trade through your computer or even by touch-tone on your phone to cut commission costs, you will need to know the ticker symbol.

- **Div:** This is short for *dividend,* which refers to the cash a stockholder can pocket just for owning the stock. Anheuser-Busch pays a yearly cash dividend of $1.04.

- **Yld %:** This just calculates what percentage return that $1.04 dividend represents. This dividend happens to equal 2.4 percent of the beermaker's stock price.

- **P/E:** This is the *price-to-earnings ratio,* which is the ratio of a company's share price to its per-share earnings. Anheuser Busch's P/E of 18 is lower than many. Right now, the average P/E for companies trading on the New York Stock Exchange is about 23. But as you'll see shortly, the P/E ratio is meaningless unless you know how fast (or slowly) the company is growing.

- **Vol 100s:** This refers to how many shares of Anheuser-Busch traded hands the day before. Since the newspaper has a limited amount of space, you have to add three zeros to the number you see. So the total number of shares traded was 11,170,000.

The last three columns show the high, low, and closing price for the previous day. You'll notice that some investors bought shares for as much as 40⅛ ($40.125), while others enjoyed a far better price at

> **"**
> I want to see the managers of the companies I invest in unfit, anemic, tubercular in pallor, single-mindedly striving to become unfathomably filthy rich.
> —Marc Robins, editor-in-chief of The Red Chip Review, a small cap stock advisory service
> **"**

38 ½ ($38.50). When the New York Stock exchange shut down for the day, the closing price was 39⅞ ($39.875). The net change was zero—the ending price didn't budge from the previous day.

The most important nugget on the stock page is the P/E. The P/E is a main tip-off for whether you want to bother with a stock. To get the P/E ratio, today's price of one share of stock is divided by the earnings the company generates for one share of stock. A P/E of 10 means the company has $1 in earnings for every $10 in share price.

Bright Idea
Comparing the P/Es of companies in the same industry is important. A Web site at www. dailystocks.com can provide you with this comparison.

Sometimes you might see two different P/Es for the same company. That's because there are two ways to calculate it. The newspaper stock pages typically list the trailing P/E, which is calculated by using the latest year's reported earnings. A forward P/E uses the analysts' best guess on what earnings will be for the next year. Here's an example of how the numbers can differ. Let's say a company last year earned $1 a share for its stock that is selling for $20 a share. The trailing P/E is 20. However, if the company is expected to boost its earnings to $2 a share next year, the forward or projected P/E for the $20 stock is 10.

Here's a good rule of thumb to remember: A company is fairly valued if its P/E rate pretty much equals its growth rate. So a company that is growing at 15 percent a year is reasonably priced if its P/E is 15. If the P/E far exceeds a company's growth rate, you should look elsewhere. Why? Because the stock is overpriced. This can happen a lot when the stock market keeps marching relentlessly onward and upward. Even excellent companies, such as Coca-Cola, will be unable to keep up with its own P/E when crazy investors keep running up the stock price. Right now, Coca-Cola has a P/E of 43. Yet stock analysts are predicting that the corporation will only grow by 17 percent a year into the next century. So even though it's a great company, the argument could be made that it would be insane to buy it right now. It's the same story with America's number-one beermaker. While Anheuser-Busch's P/E ratio is 18, its projected growth rate into the year 2003 is only 9 percent annually. It's no wonder that the St. Louis company, despite all those cute Budweiser frog commercials, is not popular with new investors right now.

If you are interested in premiere blue chips like Coca-Cola or Procter & Gamble, you will miss the boat if you wait until for a P/E bargain. If you are extremely lucky, you'll be able to buy a company like Coca-Cola when its P/E ratio equals its earnings growth rate. At an industry breakfast meeting not long ago, the portfolio manager of Fidelity's Magellan Fund concluded that his fund hadn't done as well as he'd have liked, because the portfolio didn't hold any Coca-Cola shares. He wistfully chided himself for thinking the soft-drink giant's stock was too expensive. If you really like these blue-blood stocks, keep tracking them until the P/E ratio and the earnings are as close as possible. They will very rarely be well matched. Consider buying these stocks on dips in the price.

Look at these two fictional companies and decide which one you'd rather own:

A. Hillcrest Bank
    P/E: 7
    Annual earnings growth rate: 4%
    Price: $10 a share

B. Silicon Products Corp.

   P/E: 60

   Annual earnings growth rate: 58%

   Price: $52 a share

Congratulations if you said Silicon Products Corp. This fast grower could very well be the better buy, since the P/E just about matches the earnings rate. Meanwhile, Hillcrest Bank's earnings are trailing too far behind its price tag. Don't make the mistake of too many investors. They pick and choose simply by looking at the P/E or the price per share. They think that a company like Hillcrest Bank with a really low price or a puny P/E must be a steal, while they shy away from companies with high ones. But the price and the P/E are meaningless if you don't know what the company's earnings growth rate is.

Of course, fast-flying companies with a high P/E have their own built-in dangers. When the earnings freight train of one of these companies slows, Wall Street can be brutal. For example, if Silicon Products' earnings growth rate slips to 35 percent (still an awfully impressive number), the stock price could drop precipitously because the company couldn't maintain its earnings momentum. It can be risky to buy a stock with a high P/E if there is a possibility of a slowdown in a company earnings trajectory.

Your best bet could be to find a company like this fictional one:

   McCormack Pie Co.

   P/E: 20

   Annual earnings growth rate: 30%

At first glance, this stock looks like a screaming buy. Investors love to snatch up stocks like this. Why?

Because the stock is cheap or, in the parlance of experts, it's not fully valued. If McCormack Pie Co.'s stock price accurately reflected its growth rate, the P/E would be 30.

You could strain your eyes, however, trying to find stocks that combine a high rate of growth with a more modest P/E. With the nation's bull market older than some grade-schoolers, the chances of spying bargains have gotten slimmer. This is particularly true for some of the highly prized blue chips. In this environment, the price of most stocks has risen, if only because of the sheer optimism fueling the financial markets.

Finding a company with an anemic P/E, however, isn't always the same as finding gold in a prospector's pan. Logical reasons can explain why some of these companies appear dirt cheap. Sometimes, the financial soundness of a corporation is actually as flimsy as a Hollywood sound set. For instance, a business might be drowning in debt, while its pipeline of new products has dried up. Or a high-flying company's brand name might not be as prized as it once was. The executives at Nike, the sneaker kingmaker, can tell you all about this one. Fickle teenagers no longer think wearing shoes with a swoosh is a badge of hipness. By 1998, it was obvious to all that Nike's sales had dropped off alarmingly. Among other moves, Nike announced it would eliminate 1,600 jobs. Obviously, the only way to find out if a company on your short list is a dream come to true or an investor's worst nightmare is to research.

Since you can't evaluate a company's P/E without knowing the growth rate, that begs another question. Where do you an find a company's growth

Unofficially...
Corporations can give really lame reasons for disappointing earnings. In 1998, El Niño was blamed a lot. Retailers blamed heavy rains for keeping shoppers away. In the past, companies have even tried to blame O.J. Simpson, the 1996 Summer Olympics in Atlanta, and even Princess Diana. When there's something riveting on TV, people stay home—or so goes the argument.

Timesaver
Public Registers
Annual Report
Service is a free
clearinghouse for
thousands of
annual reports.
Call (800)
4ANNUAL. You
also can order
free annual and
quarterly reports
through the *Wall
Street Journal*.
The companies
that participate
have a club sym-
bol (the one on
a deck of cards)
next to their list-
ing on the stock
pages. Call (800)
654-CLUB, or fax
your request at
(800) 965-5679.

rate? While it's not on a stock page, it is easy to find.
You can look at a Value Line Investment Survey at
your library, which will provide the growth rates of
1,700 leading companies. (You'll learn more about
Value Line later in the chapter.) You also can find
out what the Wall Street analysts' best guesses for
future growth rates are on the Internet. On America
Online, for instance, you can retrieve the latest analyst opinions by visiting the personal finance section
and calling up First Call, which compiles analysts'
opinions of many stocks. And on the Internet, you
can learn what analysts are thinking by visiting
Zacks Investment Research (www.zacks.com). Here's
an option for those trying to do this without a
computer—contact a company's Investor Relations
Department and ask for copies of any current analysts' reports.

As you begin your research, you'll need a copy of
a corporation's annual report. You can get this by
calling the company's toll-free number and asking
for one. (Increasingly, you can download these
reports from corporate Web sites.) Keep in mind
that marketers are paid handsomely to produce
glossy reports that make a company look like a fabulous investment. Despite the glitz, a recent survey
showed that 8 out of 10 professional money managers use these reports when making their trading
decisions. So don't blow them off.

Annual reports give top executives a chance to
reflect (and brag) about the past year's accomplish-
ments as well as to share where the company is heading. You'll also usually find progress reports on a
corporation's various divisions. While you're reading, notice whether a company places unusual
emphasis on the future while saying little about the

present. Or if the corporation plays up its loyal employees or its role in making America a stronger place rather than talking about how successful it is making widgets. Here's another worrisome sign: A division that was highlighted with great gusto in the last annual report is barely mentioned at all this time around.

You'll also want to tackle the annual report's financial statement. First you'll take a peek at the balance sheet. The balance sheet simply lists—well, maybe not so simply—a company's assets, its investments, and its debts on a given date. The assets include cash, the value of its inventory, and the accounts receivable—the money customers still owe it. The liabilities include any long-term debt, including the money it borrowed to build its office complexes; its unpaid bills; and accrued taxes. You'll also find the shareholders' equity on the balance sheet. While the balance sheet will look authoritative, it won't necessarily be accurate. When you are getting ready to sell your home, the appraisal usually pinpoints what your house is worth. But this is a much trickier process for a company. That's because many of the figures in the balance sheet are based on historical numbers. For instance, if a company bought its headquarters and land back in 1955, its worth could appear to be a fraction of what it would bring on the open market today. Some assets that are hard to measure are left out entirely. For instance, Coca-Cola does not report the value of the company's instantly recognizable red-and-white logo, which is thought to be worth more than $50 billion.

So what do you do with this information? The numbers can tell you how much working capital a

> " The trouble with an annual report is that there is a lot of fluff and executives only talk about the positive. But when you get to the back of the report, there are pages and pages of footnotes that are hard to understand.
> —Stephen Sanborn, Value Line's research director "

company has. You can get a good idea of inventory turnover—are the widgets gathering dust, or are they flying out the door? And there is also a useful little indicator called *book value,* which is what you get if the company has a giant liquidation sale and sells all its assets, including its property, equipment, and even those ergonomically correct office chairs. The book value is whatever is left after paying off outstanding bills. Remember that this will be a very rough figure.

Next, you need to look at the income statement. This section starts off by listing the year's sales or revenues and ends with the bottom line—the profit. Most likely, profit will be referred to as *net income.* In between these lines are all the costs of doing business—the research costs of developing a better widget, income taxes, salaries, interest, and so on. Obviously, the higher the profit after paying all those bills, the happier the shareholders are.

The following is a condensed look at a corporate income statement:

Better Widget Corporation

Income Statement

Revenue: $70 million

Cost of sales: $35 million

Gross profit: $35 million ($70 million minus $35 million)

Operating expenses: $15 million

Income from operations: $20 million ($35 million minus $15 million)

Income tax: $6 million

Net income: $14 million ($20 million minus $6 million)

In this example, the Better Widget Corporation generated profits of $14 million. Is this good or bad? A quick way to answer this is to determine the net profit margin. Bear with me, this isn't hard. All you do is divide the net income ($14 million) by the revenue ($70 million). The corporation generated a 20 percent profit margin, which is a great achievement. That means 20 cents of every dollar in sales is pure profit. When you look for stocks, try to stick with companies that have a net profit margin of at least 10 percent. But once again, there is a caveat. Some industries maintain historically low net profit margins, while others enjoy much higher ones. So be sure to compare a company's net profit margin with those in the same industry. Also, a company enjoying a very high profit margin can attract hungry competitors who want to generate the same lucrative numbers.

By sticking to companies with respectable net profit margins, you can weed out a lot of possibilities. One way to find companies with healthy profit margins is to scan the corporate earnings tables listed in newspaper business sections. Each earnings report is smaller than a cartoon panel, but it always contains the two numbers you need—total revenue and net income—to obtain the net profit margin.

Using the income statement, you can also calculate a company's *return on equity* (ROE). Many experts consider the ROE to be the most valuable financial ratio for stockholders to look at. Basically, it provides a quick measure of how well a firm's management is squeezing profits out of shareholders' collective investment. Since most of us aren't going to get the opportunity to size up the top brass during heart-to-heart discussions at a company's

Timesaver
There are plenty
of places where
you can find it.
Standard &
Poor's publishes
numerous stock
guides that list
the ROE. You can
also download a
report from
www.stockinfo.
standardpoor.
com. On AOL,
you can find
ROEs in
Morningstar's
stock reports in
the personal
finance section.
Check the *Wall
Street Journal*'s
Web site at
www.wsj.com.

headquarters, checking the ROE is the next best thing. The ROE, which is expressed as a percentage, examines what would be left of a company's net profits if all the assets were liquidated and the debts paid off. You can obtain this figure by dividing a company's common stock equity or net worth into its net income. It's smart to stick with a company that can boast of a ROE of 20 percent or better. But you should be aware that each industry will maintain its own characteristic ROE. Consequently, you don't want to compare the ROE of a software company with that of a grocery store chain. You need to compare a company's ROE with the standard ROE of its own industry. This allows you to see how well or how badly the corporation is faring compared to its competitors.

You shouldn't make a final decision about a stock based solely on a company's annual report. When you're talking to a company's investor relations representative, ask her to send you recent press clippings, which can alert you to any problems or big successes. (You can also do this background check on the Internet.) And if you're really ambitious, you can request the 10-K, the 10-Q, and the proxies from the company. These are filed with the *Securities and Exchange Commission* (SEC).

Here's a rundown of what's in these documents:

- **10-K:** This contains all the figures in the annual report and more. It's duller reading—there aren't any smiling pictures of executives or gushy writing—but you'll find these once-a-year reports even beefier. Executives must let their hair down a little in this filing. Management will talk about how such things as the economy, taxes, and even the weather affected their business during the past year. In Anheuser-Busch's latest 10-K, for example, executives discussed how rising aluminum prices increased their packaging costs, why the company reduced its massive inventory as part of its fresh beer campaign, and how higher beer excise taxes hurt. If you keep reading, you also learn that Busch's theme parks, including Sea World, experienced record growth despite an unusually ominous hurricane season.

- **10-Q:** Filed every three months, the 10-Qs contain lots of financial figures broken down into quarterly snapshots, which can be very helpful.

- **Proxy statement:** You probably don't know how much your neighbor earns, but you can see how much the head guy at General Motors is making. Proxies give you the scoop on what the corporate honchos and the board of directors are making and how they are compensated. As mentioned before, a stockholder would rather see a chief executive officer's pay tied to performance goals rather than just a very large base salary. A proxy can tell you how it's determined.

If you're in a hurry, you can download all these corporate documents from the SEC's Web site at www.sec.gov. When you get to the SEC's home page, click on EDGAR, which stands for *Electronic Data Gathering, Analysis, and Retrieval* system. Now you know why everybody prefers to call it EDGAR. All these SEC filings, by the way, are free.

Let Value Line hold your hand

If evaluating a corporation's financial filings sounds too time-consuming, a shortcut does exist. The analysts at Value Line have sifted through all of this

Bright Idea
Anyone craving a detailed guide to analyzing financial statements should consider reading the following: *Barron's Finance & Investment Hand Book,* Fourth Edition, by John Downes and Jordan Elliot Goodman; *Financial and Business Statements,* by George T. Friedlob and Franklin Plewa, Jr.; *The Guide to Understanding Financial Statements,* by Geza Szurovy and S.B. Costales; and *How to Profit from Reading Annual Reports,* by Richard B. Loth.

Unofficially...
Arnold Bernhard spent a year developing stock charts on companies, but nobody wanted to buy them. A salesman from *Barron's* persuaded him to advertise his charts in the financial newspaper and offer a trial subscription. It worked. By the late 1970s, Bernhard was on *Forbes'* list of the richest Americans. Value Line is still offering that trial subscription.

material and have recorded the most crucial figures in their one-page guides. Actually, it's always good to run your ideas by an objective source. Value Line has been faithfully fulfilling that role since Arnold Bernhard created the business in the 1930s. Bernhard was convinced that there had to be a way for individual investors to evaluate whether a stock was fairly priced. And he was right. At my local library, Value Line is so popular that the librarians limit users to 30 minutes. They got tired of trying to break up skirmishes among the patrons—mostly retired guys with time on their hands. About 500,000 people consult this stock guide each week.

Once you look at a Value Line analysis like the one you see here for Intel, you'll understand why the guys at my library fight over it. Never have so many useful financial nuggets been crammed onto a single sheet of paper. Let's start at what you see at the top of every Value Line analysis. The first thing many people look at are the two numbers prominently displayed in the top left-hand corner. Value Line rates a company's safety and timeliness on a scale of 1 to 5—5 is always bad. If a stock receives a 5 in timeliness, it means an investor's chances of making money on the stock in the next year are pretty terrible. A 4 ranking isn't much better. That doesn't mean, however, that these companies are mongrels. Take Intel, for example. It's timeliness is a lowly 4 in the latest survey, but it's a great core holding for anybody wanting a technology stock in her portfolio. Value Line analysts, however, believe the current price already reflects the growth the company is expected to experience into the next century. That is, Intel stock price has run away from it, making the gigantic semiconductor chipmaker

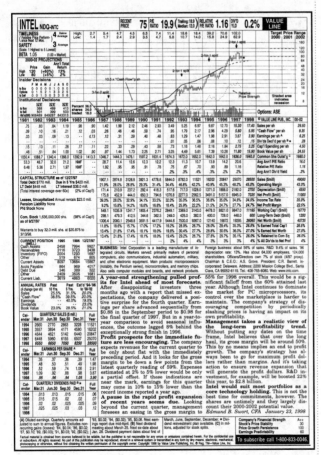

A Value Line stock analysis of Intel.

overpriced today. So who gets the number-one time-liness rankings? Value Line analysts reserve that designation for the companies they believe will enjoy the best stock performance in the next year.

Someone who gravitates to Value Line's lineup of the hottest companies isn't necessarily going to be interested in the companies that are ranked number one for safety. These ultrasafe companies can sometimes be pretty dull, but chances are they won't career off a cliff. In its latest survey, for instance, Minnesota Mining and Manufacturing

(3M), as well as Coca-Cola, earned superlative safety rankings. Investing in these bedrock stocks isn't expected to make you rich in the near term. For instance, Value Line's statisticians gave 3M a 5 for its timeliness. A big reason for the snub was because the company's earnings and sales growth during the past year have been a paltry 3.5 percent. On the other hand, if a company earns a 5 in safety, you can assume it's highly volatile. If it's important for you to own a stake in a company that won't be diagnosed with financial sudden-death syndrome, a company ranked 4 or 5 is not for you.

Quite honestly, many Value Line fans never make it past this simple rating system. They base their trading decisions on those two little numbers. Some investors spurn any stock that isn't rated number one for timeliness. While purists insist that you need to crunch scores of numbers to obtain a realistic picture of a company and its financial trends, Value Line doesn't knock any approach. Try as I might, I couldn't get Stephen Sanborn, Value Line's director of research, to knock this minimalist approach to stock research. In fact, Value Line's historical data suggests that this is not a cockeyed way to invest. Looking at the chart that tracks the New York firm's recommendations, you can see that Group 1 for timeliness has clearly outpaced the others by a very wide margin.

Despite the figures, I'm uncomfortable with an approach that relies on using Value Line's timeliness number or, for that matter, a roll of the dice to make stock picks. After all, if you're only going to invest in a handful of individual stocks, you should be darned sure you've made the right decision. And superficial research could definitely sabotage your

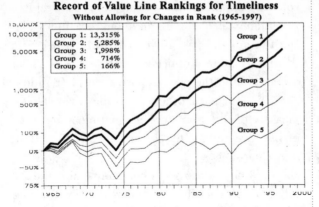

Record of Value Line Rankings for Timeliness
Without Allowing for Changes in Rank (1965-1997)

Group 1:	13,315%
Group 2:	5,285%
Group 3:	1,998%
Group 4:	714%
Group 5:	166%

Record of Value
Line rankings for
timeliness.

portfolio. There are also more pragmatic reasons for not following the dictates of one number. By the time you receive the latest Value Line in the mail or see it in the library, the market has already had time to react. Consequently, the price of a stock could be higher than when the Value Line analysts issued their report. What's more, Value Line will not always be right. If you pick and choose among the number-one–ranked stocks for timeliness, you might be unlucky enough to align with Value Line's mistakes. The only way to replicate Value Line's track record would be to buy all its number-one–ranked stocks and then sell them when the stocks are down-graded. Obviously this is not practical.

Moving along, the chart that stretches across the page gives you a quick picture of what a company's stock price has been doing. As you can see, Intel's stock has been steadily marching up the graph paper. You'll also find the historical high and low prices of the stock going back more than a decade.

Remember how important the P/E ratio is? Well, Value Line includes many, many years' worth. This is a great service, because with these numbers,

Timesaver
If you own stocks but find you have little time to watch them, spend a few minutes every three months reading the Value Line analysis for each of your companies. A new report is released on its universe of stocks every quarter.

you can determine what a company's historical P/E is. With my calculator, I figured out that Intel's average P/E for the past 10 years is 13.1. Armed with that information, I notice that Intel's P/E of 19.9 is higher than in the past. In part, Intel's P/E ratio—and this is true of other companies as well—is a measure of the stock market's sentiment and what people are willing to pay for the stock and its future earnings.

You'll also get to see a company's annual earnings and sales-per-share numbers. Ideally, you love to see these figures climb steadily year after year. Laid out on a bar chart, ever-increasing figures resemble a staircase. On the bottom left-hand side of the Value Line page, these figures are broken down by quarters. In the same section, you can quickly find out what Intel's annual rates of sales and earnings growth have been. During the past five years, sales have grown by 31.5 percent a year, while earnings have soared by 40 percent. An excellent track record that most corporations will never attain.

Value Line's stock analysts also make predictions for each company several years into the future. This is what the analysts at brokerage houses do, too, but it's harder for the average investor to get those opinions. On the sheet, you see future estimates for such critical areas as earnings, sales, net profit margin, long-term debt, and stock price. Getting these crystal-ball projections is very important. After all, you don't want to invest in a company that has little growth prospect in its future.

You shouldn't chide yourself if you find these financial evaluations intimidating at first. Don't be alarmed if it takes you three months or more to feel

comfortable with it. That's quite normal. What's easier to understand is Value Line's written analysis of
companies that appear in the lower right-hand corner of each report.

Wondering how Stephen Sanborn, Value Line's
research director, uses those one-page sheets? Like
a lot of people, he looks at the timeliness rating in
the upper left-hand corner. He prefers the stocks
ranked as 1. He also glances at the box that contains
the annual growth rates found on the left-hand side
of the page. What he looks for are historically strong
performers—companies with vigorous sales and
earnings growth. But he also checks to see what the
company's future growth potential is. And next,
Sanborn does something that most people overlook. He flips to the back of the weekly Value Line
summary and index supplement to the High
Growth Stocks page. Listed on this page are the
companies that have enjoyed an average growth rate
of 13 percent or more over the past decade. What's
more, these companies are expected to keep up that
pace during the next five years. "If I had to find one
place to start, I would personally start with that
screen," Sanborn says. "That's what I do."

Researching small cap stocks

If you're feeling more comfortable at the prospects
of analyzing a stock, don't be too discouraged with
what I say next. No matter how much time you
devote, you won't discover anything that Wall Street
doesn't already know. But this only holds true for
large cap stocks, which explains why many financial
pundits suggest if you're going to spend time scrutinizing financial reports, they shouldn't belong to
the Intels and Disneys of the world. Where you can

Moneysaver
Most people
bring a pocketful
of change to the
library and copy
the pertinent
Value Line pages.
If you don't like
sharing, consider
ordering a 10-
week trial sub-
scription. Call
(800) 634-3583.

strike it big (or lose your shirt) is with the many undiscovered small cap stocks.

These small fry are so busy trying to inch their way up the food chain, they don't have time to court Wall Street. And Wall Street, quite frankly, isn't interested in them. While there are more than 50 highly paid stock analysts shadowing every move that an IBM, Coca-Cola, or Microsoft makes, there often are no more than one or two experts following the small companies. And sometimes there is just nobody out there at all.

But it's this void that presents opportunities, insists Marc Robins, editor-in-chief of the *Red Chip Review*, a premiere small cap newsletter:

> Why would you want to butt heads against these really bright equity analysts following the large caps, when you can research small caps and be almost as smart as they are? When you work in the small and micro-cap arena, the deck is loaded in your favor. The market is essentially operating in a vacuum and anything incremental you can find out is to your benefit.

These corporate midgets are more volatile, and you should absolutely avoid investing in them if you can't handle potentially wild swings in the price. But there is a reward for those Maalox moments. As a class, small caps have historically delivered a bigger punch than their big brothers. Robins, who is perhaps the small-cap world's most eloquent booster, notes that over the past seven decades, the average annual growth rate for small cap stocks has been 19.2 percent. This is almost twice the growth rate of the Standard & Poor's 500.

If small caps intrigue you, your first challenge is to find a handful of prospects. Here are some places to generate ideas:

- **Read through the semiannual reports issued by leading small cap mutual funds.** These managers spend their days talking with small cap companies, evaluating their financial statements, chatting with the employees in the lunchrooms, checking the competition, and generally making pests of themselves. Why not profit from their hard work? In the fund reports, a portfolio manager must list her current top holdings. She might even discuss why she bought her favorite companies and why she thinks the future might look bright for certain companies.

- **Subscribe to the *Red Chip Review*,** which tracks hundreds of small companies that have survived the firm's tough screening requirements. To subscribe, call (800) RED-CHIP; its Web site is www.redchip.com. The companies must pass these requirements:

  1. 20% compounded annual growth
  2. 20% ROE
  3. At least 20% of the company owned by insiders
  4. Less than 20% of the company held by institutional investors
  5. Market capitalization less than $750 million

- **Skim through Value Line's Expanded Survey,** which evaluates smaller companies. The analysis isn't as exhaustive as the surveys of big companies, but there is plenty of meat there.

Timesaver
For the Internet crowd, check out the Small Cap Investor Web site (www. smallcapinvestor. com). It carries a wealth of information about hundreds of smaller companies.

▪ **Purchase the yearly** *Standard and Poor's SmallCap 600 Guide,* which you can find in bookstores. This annual publication lists 600 small companies that have met the S&P screening criteria. Like the Value Line folks, the S&P experts have boiled down in a readable form much of what you need to know about these companies. You also might be interested in the *Standard & Poor's MidCap 400 Guide.* Meanwhile,   for current updates on individual companies contained in these yearly guides, call (800) 292-0808.

Analyzing mutual funds

Analyzing a mutual fund isn't as tough as figuring out whether the stock your dentist raved about is worth buying. And here's even better news. Very soon, the task will become much easier. For years, many critics, including the mutual fund industry itself, have groused that it's a rare person who actually sits down and reads the legally required prospectus that is sent to every soul who is considering opening a new mutual fund. You can buy yourself 100 shares of stock, a portfolio full of bonds, a smattering of futures, and all sorts of exotic securities without ever seeing a shred of information on any of these purchases. (I'm not recommending this!) But technically, as a new customer, you weren't supposed to buy even $100 worth of a fund without having a chance to read the prospectus. The prospectus, which can fill several dozen pages, contains much of the crucial information you need to decide whether a fund is right for you.

All well and good, but there was a problem. The Investment Company Institute, the fund industry's trade group, admitted that half of us never bother to read a prospectus. And no wonder. The prospectus is dense, dull, and dry as burnt toast. Norman Fosback, editor-in-chief of *Mutual Funds Magazine*, wasn't really kidding when he told me recently, "The average guy is more confused after he reads the prospectus than before." So the SEC did us a favor recently by giving fund companies the go-ahead to create shortened prospectuses that are easier to understand.

My guess is most people will still pitch these documents in the trash can unread, but now there is at least another option. The SEC also gave funds permission to create profiles that highlight the most essential data. In fact, all this information will now fit into a newspaper advertisement. Anybody comfortable reading a Morningstar analysis (you'll see a sample later in this chapter) will have no problems with one of these cheat sheets. With all the changes, it should take you less than 30 minutes to evaluate a fund. Not a bad investment of time, considering you might be pouring thousands and thousands of dollars into a fund.

Checking out funds before you buy is critical for many reasons. For starters, spending time sifting through some of your choices should help you easily eliminate many funds that would be disastrous picks. The object of your research, however, shouldn't be to select the very best funds on the planet. If you set that as your goal, you'll be disappointed. You don't need to invest in this year's number-one bond fund or stock fund. The managers who snag these honors change each year. Actually the distinction is really only important to a fund company's marketing department, which can crow about the honor in advertisements. What the research should do is help steer you to above-average performing funds with cheap expenses run by veteran managers. If you do your homework, you also should be able to zero in on funds that fit nicely with your tolerance for investment risk.

Luckily, to properly scrutinize a fund, everything you need is free, and most is available with a phone call. If a fund interests you, use the fund company's toll-free number and request a copy of the prospectus and the profile. (Fund companies aren't required to provide profiles, but many will have them on hand.) I also recommend asking for the annual or semiannual reports.

Besides the literature from the fund, you also need an unbiased evaluation from an independent source. If you were buying a toaster or a washing machine, you could buy an issue of *Consumer Reports* magazine. But you can't expect to find a lot in *Consumer Reports* on mutual funds. Luckily, fund fans can turn to something just as reliable. Morningstar, as well as Value Line, provides fact-filled scoops on tons of funds. What's great about these two rating services is that they can dissect the guts of any fund in just a single page. You should be able to find either Morningstar or Value Line's mutual fund ratings at many libraries. Morningstar is also available on the Web at www.morningstar.net or through America Online. You also can subscribe to either one, but unless you're a fund fanatic, the updates on hundreds of funds will be overkill. For a complete lowdown on Morningstar's products, call (800) 735-0700. For subscription information on the Value Line stock and mutual fund surveys, call (800) 833-0046.

After you gather up the materials you need, there are a few key details you need to zero in on. Since the more user-friendly prospectuses aren't available yet, I'm going to use a current one, from Franklin California Growth, as a guide. All the information I'm going to go over will be in the new prospectuses as well.

Expenses. This is something you should care about. Frankly, fund companies have become quite greedy. They are charging outrageously high expenses. And you know why? Because they know they can get away with it. Few people read that darned prospectus, and many haven't cared about expenses because their returns during the bull-market run have been so impressive.

How do you know what the expenses are? Look in the table of contents for the expense summary. According to its prospectus, Franklin California Growth charges a shareholder 1.09 percent a year for operating the fund.

Here's how it's broken down in the prospectus:

Management fees	.63%
12b-1 fees	.15%
Other expenses	.31%
Total	1.09%

Management fees are pretty much self-explanatory. This is the money the parent company, Franklin Templeton, pockets for taking such good care of your money. This pile of cash is used to pay all those smart stockpickers, their secretaries, the phone reps, the guys who keep the computers humming, and everybody else. The 12b-1 fee is controversial and less justifiable. By paying this fee, you essentially subsidize a fund's marketing machinery.

> 66
> The amount that fund investors have entrusted to mutual funds now exceeds by a substantial amount the total that Americans have in their checking and savings accounts at all of this country's banks, savings and loans, and credit unions combined.
> —Arthur Levitt, chairman of the U.S. Securities and Exchange Commission
> 99

The money can pay for glossy brochures, magazine ads, and slick television commercials that feature attractive Baby Boomers fretting about their retirement years. Even with the 12b-1 fee, however, Franklin California Growth's total expense ratio is reasonable.

Selecting a solid fund with below-average fees is extremely important and can make a big difference in your returns over the long run. The following are the average total expense ratios for different mutual fund categories:

1. Growth funds   1.52%

2. International funds   1.66%

3. Small cap funds   1.49%

4. Sector funds   1.64%

5. Taxable bond funds   .97%

6. Tax-free bond funds   .95%

7. Index funds   .51%

Source: Lipper Analytical Services

A good prospectus is doing its job if it scares you. That's because the fund is legally bound to outline the reasons why you could lose your money. Read all the gory details carefully, then decide whether you can live with the risks. It takes Franklin Growth three pages to explain all its risks. (In the new prospectus, the warnings will probably be condensed.) When you buy this particular fund, you buy a slice of California, which spends a fair amount of time struggling with earthquakes, recession fears, riots, mudslides, and trials of the century. If California, which has a bigger economy than China, dipped into an economic recession, the fund would suffer mightily. Another risk is the fund's love affair with technology stocks. Watch out when the volatile computer industry takes its periodic swan dives. The fund is also exposed to foreign currency risks, since many of the technology companies sell their wares overseas.

Of course the prospectus doesn't describe the lurking dangers in the same way that you or I would. Here's how Franklin Growth explains how its own investment in smaller stocks can be risky:

> Small companies may lack depth of management, they may be unable to internally generate funds necessary for growth or potential development or to generate such funds through external financing on favorable terms, and they may be developing or marketing new products or services for which markets are not yet established and may never become established.

Whew. I only saw one period in all that. Hopefully, these excerpts will be a little snappier in the new prospectus.

Different types of funds pose different risks. If you are looking at the prospectus of a corporate bond fund, for instance, you want to know if the risks include investing in junk bonds. You also are interested to know if a conservative stock fund can invest in foreign corporations and how much is allowable. And you want to know if a large cap fund may invest in small companies that are inherently more risky.

The prospectus will explain what type of securities a fund can invest in. Franklin California Growth must sink at least 65 percent of its money into companies headquartered in the Golden State. Some of

Watch Out!
Here's one worry if you are buying a load fund. The broker will give you the prospectus that contains information on the particular fund and one type of load that he wants you to buy. But you'll need more than one prospectus, even if you're only interested in one fund. That's because, to compare different loads or sales charges you'll need a prospectus for each one.

that money—no percentage is given—will end up in small- and medium-sized companies that are worth no more than $2.5 billion. The fund can also put up to 30 percent of its money in bonds that are just a shade safer than junk bonds.

The prospectus also shares who is making the decisions. You'll find a brief biography of the fund managers. At Franklin Growth, the two main portfolio managers are Conrad B. Herrmann and Nicholas Moore. The prospectus tells you where they went to college. Herrmann got an MBA at Harvard, while Moore, who is tall, lanky, and the more talkative of the two, got his bachelor's degree from Menlo College. A long list of degrees isn't necessarily relevant, but what you should pay attention to is how long these guys have been on the job. Both Herrmann and Moore have been running the fund since mid-1993 and have worked at Franklin Templeton since the 1980s.

A portfolio manager's tenure is important for two reasons. First, if he's relatively new, you should stay away unless he has developed a solid track record at another fund. You don't want to be the guinea pig for some new guy's mistakes. Second, you want to be sure that the manager who generated a fund's fabulous returns is the person who is still at the helm.

Annual reports

While the writing in the prospectus is dry, a fund's annual report can be a bit looser. The annual report gives the company a chance to explain what happened during the past 12 months. Some funds are shameless about tooting their own horns, while others remain quietly modest. Some of the best reports provide an in-depth look at why major stocks in the

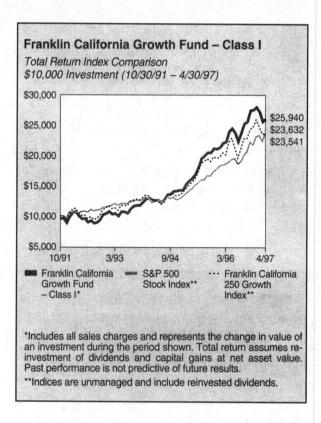

Franklin California Growth Fund – Class I

Total Return Index Comparison
$10,000 Investment (10/30/91 – 4/30/97)

$25,940
$23,632
$23,541

■ Franklin California   ■ S&P 500   ⋯ Franklin California
Growth Fund   Stock Index**   250 Growth
– Class I*   Index**

*Includes all sales charges and represents the change in value of an investment during the period shown. Total return assumes reinvestment of dividends and capital gains at net asset value. Past performance is not predictive of future results.
**Indices are unmanaged and include reinvested dividends.

Franklin
California Growth
Fund's total
return chart.
*Source: Franklin
Templeton.*

portfolio were bought or sold. The yearly report also includes a list of the fund's top holdings, as well as all the other ones. But keep in mind that the list will likely be outdated by the time you read it, because the holdings can be changed by the manager at any time.

What's the fund's track record? That's the main question you want answered in the annual report. Look for the table that lays out a fund's performance over the past 10 years. (Or the life of the fund, if it's not that old.) Also check for a nifty chart that shows how much $10,000 sunk into the fund would have grown over many years. The fund's performance is compared to a benchmark. For blue chip growth funds, the benchmark is the Standard & Poor's 500 Index. Compare the track record of small company funds with the Russell 2000 Index. If the fund consistently lags behind the benchmark, stay away from it.

What's with the five stars?

If you've shown the least bit of interest in mutual funds, you have no doubt seen funds bleating about their five-star ratings. Earning five stars is like graduating from college magna cum laude. It's a big deal. Morningstar decides who gets the stars and who doesn't. Anyone who remains befuddled by a

A typical Morningstar fund analysis. *Source: Morningstar.*

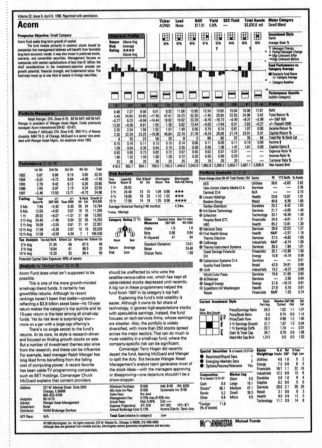

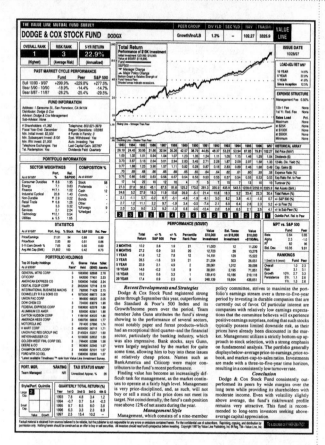

A typical Value Line fund analysis. *Source: Value Line.*

mutual fund's own literature should be grateful for Morningstar, which cuts through all the baloney to concisely provide investors with what they need to know.

Morningstar's one-page reports on more than 1,500 mutual funds look suspiciously like the Value Line stock guides. In one corner, a brief summary provides an update of the fund, a discussion of its investing style, and whether buying shares is a smart idea. The rest of the page is filled with enough pint-sized charts, tables, and statistics to satisfy even the most voracious number cruncher. Impressed with

Morningstar's success, Value Line launched a report of its own. Value Line Mutual Fund Survey looks remarkably like Morningstar's, but it has fewer subscribers.

There is a danger in relying too heavily on Morningstar's or Value Line's rating system. Investors can get star-crossed. Chasing exclusively after five-star funds will get you into trouble. Let's say that after you consult with Morningstar, you decide to buy the three following funds:

▪ Selected American Fund

▪ Vanguard Growth & Income Fund

▪ Muhlenkamp Fund

These are all excellent choices. The managers at the helm have been steering a steady course for years. Morningstar is in love with them. And as a bonus, the expenses are reasonable. But buying all three would be a big mistake. Can you guess why?

They are all growth and income funds. You don't need three funds that all invest in the same kind of stocks. The duplication will cost you more money in fees, the extra paperwork will drive you crazy, and worst of all, your portfolio won't be diversified. Beware of picking funds just because they have the highest number of stars. You could later regret it.

Learning beyond the classroom

There are many other ways you can learn more than you'd ever want to know about investments. Here are some suggestions.

Education

Many brokerages and mutual funds sponsor educational forums that can be worthwhile. Fidelity Investments, which has offices scattered throughout the country, holds small educational seminars for investors. During the past year, American Century, the mutual fund family, has also sponsored seminars in more than 20 cities. Top headliners have included Jane Bryant Quinn, the personal finance author, and Don Phillips, president of Morningstar. To find out about American Century's upcoming events, call (800) 345-2021 or visit its Web site at www.americancentury.com.

Community colleges, adult-education programs, and university extension divisions also offer reasonably priced money management courses. Keep this in mind, though: Many of the instructors are local financial planners, insurance agents, or brokers who spend nights at the blackboard as a way to find new clients. Don't assume that the broker who is teaching your class is a financial genius. He just might be the only one who volunteered to work for little or no money.

You also can teach yourself at home. The *American Association of Individual Investors* (AAII) offers a series of educational booklets and video cassette tapes geared toward teaching investing fundamentals. The Investing Basics Videocourse (the tapes last 3⅛ hours) explains what investment risk is and how to reduce it, teaches basic stock evaluation methods, and discusses bond investing. Another video cassette series is devoted exclusively to mutual funds. Contact AAII, which also hosts investment seminars in major cities each year, for a list of all its educational products. Call (800) 428-2244.

Another great resource for learning how to evaluate stocks is the *National Association of Investors Corp.* (NAIC). This is the umbrella group for 36,000 investment clubs operating across the country. You don't have to belong to a group, however, to use the NAIC's educational material. For much more on

> " You need disinterested, unbiased third-party information. Brokers aren't going to say commissions are bad and loads are bad.
> —John Markese, president of *American Association of Individual Investors* (AAII) "

investment clubs, see Chapter 9, "The Investment Club Phenomenon."

Financial newsletters

If you are unsure of what stocks, bonds, or mutual funds to buy, there are plenty of financial gurus who would love to help you out. That is, for a price—you have to buy their financial newsletters. There is a misperception that newsletters are strictly for hyperactive traders who buy and sell at a furious rate. Actually, they also appeal to do-it-yourselfers who don't want to relinquish control of their investments to anyone else. These folks often see investing as a challenge and use newsletters as just one source of information.

After eliminating tip sheets with meager followings, there are between 400 and 500 financial newsletters that cater to every type of investor, from buy-and-hold blue chip fans to market timers. Whether you will make a fortune following the advice of one of these newsletters is anyone's guess. But if you do buy a subscription, stick with an advisory letter with a winning track record. An orangutan with a red crayon can make better picks from the stock listings than some of these publications.

How will you know whether a newsletter's model portfolio is worth duplicating? *The Hulbert Financial Digest,* the newsletter industry's watchdog, is the one easy source. Mark Hulbert started this newsletter in 1980 after attending an investment seminar in New Orleans. He listened in disgust as he heard editors from dozens of investment letters promising listeners that they could double and triple their investment without risk if they followed their advice. When he returned home, he checked the editors' actual market performance and found their claims were wildly exaggerated. Today Hulbert, who is a columnist for *Forbes* magazine, follows more than 160 newsletters, along with the 450 portfolios these newsletters recommend.

For the best results, Mark Hulbert recommends that you seriously consider following the recommendations of whatever newsletter you choose. (It should be one that dovetails nicely into your investment philosophy.) By doing that, there is less risk in bailing out of the market at the worst possible times. "We think there is a lot of virtue in following the advice religiously," he says. "It's often uncomfortable to do the right thing in the market, and you may need someone to impose some discipline. Discipline is the great unsung virtue of investing."

You can obtain a five-month trial subscription to *The Hulbert Financial Digest* for $37.50. The toll-free number is (888) HULBERT. The newsletter's Web site is www.hulbertdigest.com.

Unofficially...
In the financial newsletter business, it takes all kinds. Arch Crawford, who runs the *Crawford Perspectives*, provides his financial gems by looking toward the heavens. This market timer believes eclipses, sunspots, comets, along with volcanoes and earthquakes, can move markets. Crawford was actually one of the few financial seers who predicted the stock market crash of 1987.

THE HULBERT FINANCIAL DIGEST'S LIST OF THE BEST AND WORST NEWSLETTERS

Top Five Newsletters	Annualized Gain (Past 15 Years)
The Prudent Speculator	18.3%
The Chartist	16.7%
Zweig Performance Ratings Report	15.3%
Investor's World	14.7%
The Value Line Investment Survey	13.9%

Bottom Five Newsletters	Annualized Gain (Past 15 Years)
International Harry Schultz Letter	1.3%
The Dines Letter	.7%
The Professional Tape Reader	-.9%
The Option Advisor	-7.7%
The Granville Market Letter	-25.2%

Source: *The Hulbert Financial Digest*

CNBC

If you're a stock junkie, this network, which is devoted to covering every Wall Street hiccup, is for you. When the market takes those harrowing dips, you can be assured that even professional money managers are tuning in to watch the minute-by-minute action. The station, which has grown in stature through the years, enjoys the kind of clout necessary to convince the finest financial minds to appear on their shows. Tune in, and you'll very likely see the head of one of the exchanges, a chief economic forecaster for a brokerage house, and other experts calmly trying to answer questions over the din of a trading floor. The network also sponsors hokier fare. In one regular segment, callers can ask a guest expert if their pet stocks should be considered a buy, sell, or hold opportunity.

Investment clubs

The main focus of these clubs is to learn more about stocks. For more information on how they work and how you can join one, read Chapter 9.

Financial press

Here's a list of magazines and newspapers devoted to making people like you smarter and richer:

The Wall Street Journal	(800) 568-7625
Investor's Business Daily	(800) 831-2525
Barron's	(800) 544-0422
Bloomberg Personal	(888) 432-5820
Mutual Funds Magazine	(800) 442-9000
SmartMoney Magazine	(800) 444-4202
Money	(800) 409-8437
Individual Investor	(800) 383-5901

Kiplinger's Personal Finance	(800) 544-0155
Forbes	(800) 888-9896
Business Week	(800) 635-1200
Fortune	(800) 621-8000

Just the facts

- Winnow down your stock choices by asking 10 important questions.

- Know how to properly evaluate a stock's P/E ratio.

- Using Value Line can make stock evaluations easier.

- It can be wiser to devote more time to researching small cap stocks.

- Focus on what's important when evaluating mutual funds.

GET THE SCOOP ON...
Finding your way through the cyberspace maze
▪ Exploring stocks online ▪ Evaluating mutual
funds on the net ▪ Finding tax help in
cyberspace ▪ Online banking arrives

Chapter 8

Investing on the Net

Back in October 1997, when the stock market tanked 554 points in just a few hours—the biggest one-day drop in history—my first reaction was one that a lot of investors must have had. "You've got to be kidding! Really? Are you sure?" Not a very original reaction, but I didn't know what else to say. After I hung up with my husband, who had called with the news, I did what many thousands of others were doing at that very minute. I logged onto the Internet to see just what kind of mess the stock market was in.

I was curious about my own stocks. Had they fallen hard enough to present a buying opportunity? And what about those overpriced stocks that I had been following on the sidelines waiting for a dip in price? With the stock market seemingly turning into an equity garage sale, was it time to make a move?

I guess I should say that I *tried* to log on to my Internet provider. My modem kept getting a busy signal. Next I tried my America Online account.

Busy again. Then CompuServe. No luck. I'm not sharing this story to whine about cyberspace. Rather, I think it helps illustrate how the Internet and investing have become intertwined. The instinct of many, many people was to do just what I was doing. And it's no wonder.

Investing by way of the Internet is incredibly convenient. Anybody with a computer no longer has to trot to the library to research stocks, bonds, and mutual funds. Nor do you have to wait until the morning paper hits the driveway to learn what happened in the financial markets the day before. (In fact, if I want to, I can read tomorrow's *Wall Street Journal* tonight by visiting its Web site.) No longer do you have to be dependent on your broker and his firm's inside research to evaluate stocks. You now can have electronic access to some of the same charts, graphs, and reams of other financial data for which the professionals pay big bucks. Zacks Investment Research (www.zacks.com), which publishes analysts' opinions of the earnings and growth potential of thousands of stocks, for instance, is just one of the services now available that most individual investors never used to see.

If you're eager to learn how the Internet can make investing easier for you, join the rest of us on the net. There are no dues or membership requirements. If you can click a mouse, you are welcome. In this chapter, you'll learn how to navigate the World Wide Web, and I'll tell you some of the best places to park. The cyberinvesting universe is so vast that most people will need a compass to make any sense of it. Use this chapter as your navigator. I'll explain what some of your choices are and tell you where you should logically start. You'll learn what some of the best sites are on the Web—the main focus will be on the free ones. I'll also introduce you to personal finance software and online banking. You'll learn what you need to be aware of before you abandon your traditional bank account. And lastly, with any luck, you'll finish this chapter with an appreciation of how the Internet can make you wealthier, but only if you remain cautious and alert. It's not just the cyber con men that you have to worry about, but the well-intentioned folks as well. They spread a lot of hype about stocks and other investments, and much of it should be instantly forgotten.

A snapshot of cyberinvesting

To get started on this grand adventure, you need a computer with a modem that allows your computer to link up with the Internet through a phone line. You also need an *Internet service provider* (ISP). Lastly you must have a Web browser—you can choose between Netscape Navigator or Microsoft Internet Explorer. The browser is a software program that translates the gibberish language of Web sites, called *Hypertext Markup Language* (HTML), into readable words and pictures. You can buy this software at any computer store, or you can download it for free off the Internet. The browsers are so easy to use and so intuitive that my third-grader can tool around the Internet quite easily.

Once you're plugged in, you'll find that most of the places you will be visiting are free, free, free. A few sites, however, are worth their nominal subscription fees. To whet your appetite, here are just a few goodies you can expect to find on your cybercruises:

- Built-in financial calculators that can project what you will need for retirement or college

Timesaver
Look in the Yellow Pages, newspaper classifieds, or your community's free computer newspapers for the names of computer consultants. They can hook your computer up to the outside world in a matter of minutes. Before you hire someone, ask what their hourly rates are.

- An e-mail news service that alerts you to breaking news that might affect your stocks

- Screening devices that hunt for companies with low P/E ratios, high dividends, high insider ownership, small or large capitalization, and dozens of other variables

- Constantly updated stock quotes

- Latest updates on federal tax legislation

- Annual reports on thousands of companies

- Bond market news and research

- Corporate filings with the U.S. Securities and Exchange Commission

- Glossaries of financial terms

- The latest corporate earnings projections by analysts

- Tons of college financial aid information

- Historical stock data for any company you'd like

- The scoop on insider-trading activity

- Yet more built-in calculators that will pinpoint the value of your savings bonds, tell you what type of IRA is appropriate for you, or determine whether debt consolidation is a good idea

- Portfolio tracking of your investments

- Financial analyses of third-world stock markets from Egypt to Slovakia

You can also read what some of the most thoughtful financial journalists are writing about in the big wide world of investing. These sites can be especially helpful if you are fairly new to investing, but even veteran investors can benefit by boning up on areas they are unfamiliar with. One of the neatest things about these media sites is the archives.

Some let you scrounge for any past articles, while others limit your searches. Relying on a magazine or newspaper's archives can be invaluable when you are collecting background on a stock or are trying to familiarize yourself with investing basics, whether they are retirement planning strategies, bond investing, or closed-end mutual funds. No longer do you have to keep stacks of musty magazines in the garage when you can search for an old article on your computer.

And the best part is that there is no catch—you don't need to buy a subscription. These Web sites are almost all free. Here's just a partial list of some of the popular publications that are just a click away:

The New York Times	www.nytimes.com
Worth	www.worth.com
Business Week	www.businessweek.com
Fortune and *Money*	www.pathfinder.com
Mutual Funds Magazine	www.mfmag.com
SmartMoney Magazine	www.smartmoney.com
Investor's Business Daily	www.investors.com
CNNfn	www.cnnfn.com
The Economist	www.economist.com
Individual Investor	www.iionline.com
Bloomberg Online	www.bloomberg.com
Forbes	www.forbes.com
USA Today's money section	www.usatoday.com/ money/mfront.htm
Kiplinger's	www.kiplinger.com
Barron's	www.barrons.com
Reuters	www.moneynet.com

Bright Idea
If this chapter doesn't quench your thirst for cyberinvesting, pick up a copy of *Wall Street City, Your Guide to Investing on the Web,* by David L. Brown and Kassandra Bentley. The book includes a CD-ROM that gives you free 30-day access to Wall Street City (www. wallstreetcity. com), an investing supersite.

Research Magazine	www.researchmag.com
Euromoney	www.euromoney.com
Financial Times	www.usa.ft.com
Standard & Poor's Headlines	www.stockinfo. standardpoor.com/ today.htm
Business Wire	www.businesswire.com
PR Newswire	www.prnewswire.com

For an investor, using the Internet is like winning a 15-minute shopping spree at a grocery store. There are so many goodies lining the aisles that the poor shopper is overwhelmed and paralyzed by her choices. If the thought of 6,976 mutual fund choices unnerves you, watch out. That number is a joke compared to the endless armies of financial sites marching across the Internet.

Before you begin searching the Web, you need to remain skeptical. All sorts of investors come online with high expectations and often believe everything they read. The Internet is no different from TV, newspapers, and magazines. A lot of what you see is opinion. Just because it's online doesn't mean it's right. There are other reasons as well to remain vigilant. On cyberspace's Infobahn, you'll run across financial charlatans who will try to lure you into dubious investment schemes by promising ridiculously high returns. People have actually been tricked into buying stakes in such things as eel farms and a coconut chip factory through the Internet. (You'll learn more about investing scams in Chapter 17, "Troubleshooting.") One way to play it safe is to stick with Web sites sponsored by well-known institutions, such as the following:

Watch Out!
Before you believe anything you read on the net, check to see who is providing the information. You'll discover that all too many Web sites are useless, mostly filled with advertisements for brokers, money managers, and all sorts of financial bit players on the fringes.

U.S. Securities and Exchange Commission	www.sec.gov
Internal Revenue Service	www.irs.gov
American Association of Individual Investors	www.aaii.com
NASDAQ	www.nasdaq.com
Standard & Poor's Investor Services	www.stockinfo. standardpoor.com
Morningstar	www.morningstar.net
The Wall Street Journal	www.wsj.com
National Association of	www.better-investing. org

Investors Corp. (NAIC)

One of the Internet's handy features is being able to hop from a lousy site to a useful one within seconds. Links help you do that. Here's how they work: Let's say you are visiting the Quicken Web site (www.quicken.com), a nice oasis that can provide a hodgepodge of financial advice from retirement planning to tax strategies. As you're exploring, you'll see the links—they are highlighted, under-lined words. Click on one, and you're instantly whisked to a different home page. For example, while at the Quicken site, you can click on the links to the Silicon Investor (www.techstocks.com), Hoover's Online (www.hoovers.com), or the Mutual Fund Education Alliance (www.mfea.com). If you are visiting Bonds Online (www.bonds-online.com), you'll run across links to the Federal Reserve Bank of New York (www.ny.frb.org) and the American Association of Individual Investors (www.aaii.com). If you keep jumping from link to link, it's easy enough to get back to where you started. Just click the back button on the browser.

Bright Idea
Keep in mind that Web site addresses, which are commonly referred to as *uniform resource locators* (URLs), can change from time to time. If you reach a dead end, use a search engine such as Yahoo! to find the new address. If that fails, you can always call the organization to get the new address.

Ready, get set, go...

Before you turn on your computer, you need a game plan or you'll blow a lot of time wandering aimlessly. What I would avoid at this point is using one of those souped-up search engines. As you might already know, search engines are a great tool for finding sources for just about anything under the sun. If you are researching a term paper on the Loch Ness monster, you could use a search engine to no doubt find a Loch Ness Monster home page somewhere on the planet.

Here are the addresses for some of the most popular search engines:

Yahoo!	www.yahoo.com
AltaVista	www.altavista.digital.com
Excite	www.excite.com
Infoseek	www.infoseek.com
Lycos	www.lycos.com
Webcrawler	www.webcrawler.com

For an investor, the search engine can be a little too helpful. For instance, when I typed IBM into the AltaVista search engine just now, it spit out 557,191 different sites! The search engine found another 133,451 possibilities for Coca-Cola. But most of this stuff won't help at all. Some of AltaVista's top picks included Jay and Cathy's Coca-Cola Page, and another location was dedicated to somebody's Coke bottle collection. When I searched for Microsoft on the Webcrawler search engine, I got 46,922 hits, including a link to a teacher at the Massachusetts Institute of Technology who has developed a Bill Gates personal wealth clock. (For those who are curious, Gates was reportedly worth $46.1 billion on the day I checked.)

Okay, so where should you start? There are many great places, but I'd recommend that you steer your browser to Invest-O-Rama! (www.investorama.com). Invest-O-Rama! was created by Doug Gerlach, a guy who probably knew less than you do about stocks just a few years ago. He started researching equities on the Internet back in the early 1990s, arguably when the net was still in its primordial-ooze period. Hooked on the Internet, Gerlach eventually created his own cyberhome and laced it with thousands of financial links. For the novice, Invest-O-Rama! is loaded with tutorials to help you figure out how to evaluate stock possibilities. A lot of Web sites already assume that you know how to scrutinize a company's balance sheet or cash flow statement. Gerlach, who is a high muckety-muck with the NAIC (www.better-investing.org), doesn't make that assumption.

It's all those good links to other places that also make Invest-O-Rama! such an invaluable launching pad for anybody with a laundry list of stock tips. Gerlach has links to stock investing, *initial public offerings* (IPOs), bonds, discount brokerages, financial organizations, insurance and annuities, investing supersites, and lots more. All those links come in handy when you're researching an individual stock. When I typed in the stock symbol for Disney in the Research a Stock section, for instance, Invest-O-Rama! listed 75 to 80 links for me to try.

Researching stocks electronically

There are plenty of worthwhile pit stops on the cyberbahn for stock investors. Here are some of the most notable ones that you might want to visit as you cruise the net.

Bright Idea
Not sure how to read a corporation's financial statements? Let IBM (www.ibm.com/financialguide) be your tutor. In this cyberclass, you learn the basics and are treated to how professionals, such as the dean of Emory University's Goizueta Business School (named after the late Coca-Cola CEO), personally use the numbers to evaluate stocks.

EDGAR database (www.sec.gov)

Who is EDGAR? It's the acronym for *Electronic Data Gathering Analysis and Retrieval* system. Aren't you glad it's just called EDGAR? Unlike a lot of other sites with flashy advertisements and slick home pages, EDGAR is as ugly as its name. But it makes up for its dullness with its vast storehouse of financial data. EDGAR, a creation of the federal government, is the repository for all the documents that publicly traded companies are required to file with the SEC. EDGAR is fast—all filings are posted 24 hours after they are received. You can find a company's 10-K, which is the yearly filing that includes more than what you'd find in an annual report, the quarterly reports (10-Qs), the proxies, and many other documents. All you need to do is type in the name of the company, and a list of all the filings scrolls down your screen.

Yahoo! finance (www.quote.yahoo.com)

This is just one section of the vast Yahoo! search engine, but it's quite an undertaking. With the financial Yahoo!, you can pretty much navigate on autopilot as you effortlessly research stocks, receive the latest market news, and even check what's going on overseas. Its Market Guide area keeps track of 8,000 or so public companies and provides links to more than 31,000 companies and mutual funds. *SmartMoney Magazine* called it the most finely tuned financial search engine on the Internet.

Microsoft Investor (www.investor.com)

Using this site, you'll feel like you have a robotic broker working for you. If you want a thorough backgrounder on a corporation, Microsoft Investor can do everything but staple the report. Within seconds, it can compile a company profile; current trading price, earnings estimates, analyst recommendations, charts, financial highlights, and financial statements, including the balance sheet, income statement, and cash flow numbers. On this site, you can also track dozens of stocks and mutual funds in your own portfolios. And its databases are so comprehensive that you can research a stock all the way back to the 1920s if it makes you happy. This site does cost $9.95 a month, but you can get a free 30-day trial offer.

Wall Street Journal (www.wsj.com)

Though it's not free, another boon for research is the *Wall Street Journal* Web site. For what I consider a reasonable annual price—$49, or $29 for subscribers to the *WSJ, SmartMoney Magazine,* or *Barron's*—you can read the electronic version of the newspaper, search for previous articles, and fine-tune your investing knowledge in its Personal Finance Center and Tax Classroom. You can also easily track your own investments here. What I like best is a feature called the Company Briefing Book, which provides a slew of information on just about any company you're interested in. Particularly helpful are easy-to-follow charts on such things as quarterly and yearly earnings, and the stock's performance. There are also plans in the near future to add audio and video coverage of key financial news events.

Mutual funds meet the Internet

Mutual fund investors can find plenty of useful information on the net. Here are two of the better-known information sites. Mutual funds also hang out at their own electronic homes. There are excellent sites and yawners. We'll look at two examples.

Timesaver
You can avoid a lot of aggravation by creating a *bookmark* (Netscape) or *favorite* (Internet Explorer) for each of your best-liked financial sites on the Web. It's like setting the speed-dialing feature on your phone. Next time you want to visit, just click your cursor on the name in your Bookmarks or Favorites list, and your browser heads straight for it.

Morningstar (www.morningstar.net)

Anybody who even vaguely knows what a mutual fund is has probably heard of Morningstar, the premier fund-rating service. Portfolio managers pray that they will receive one of Morningstar's coveted five-star ratings. Want to know what Morningstar thinks about your fund? Head this way.

The fund wonks can load you up with all sorts of tidbits on a fund's price, annual returns, and how its returns compare to others. Morningstar also brags that it can "x-ray" a fund by peering beyond the usual stats. It can tell you such things as what industries a fund is most heavily invested in and provide a portfolio's percentage of foreign stocks. Don't be fooled by its name. Morningstar's Web site also generates in-depth analyses of thousands of stocks as well. At last count, Morningstar's database included more than 13,000 stocks and funds. You won't find just performance stats here. You'll find plenty of commentaries and how-to articles.

Mutual Fund Magazine (www.mfmag.com)

If you're a fund fan, you should also visit this magazine's ambitious home base. Among the many features of this site is your ability to search for articles on any topic or fund you're interested in. You'll also find lots of nifty interactive functions here. For instance, there's a calculator that helps you determine what the cost of a load will really be and which type would be the cheapest. You'll also find a calculator that is great for pinpointing exactly how well any of your mutual funds have been doing. Of course, you can look in the mutual fund listing of any newspaper and learn how your fund has performed during some key periods, such as the past 12 months, year-to-date, or the past three or five years.

But most of us don't buy a fund on the first business day of the year, so we won't know exactly how well we are doing.

No problem with this calculator. It was amazingly easy to use when I tried it. I typed in the day I bought my shares in Strong Common Stock mutual fund—February 22, 1993. Then I used March 26, 1998 as the ending date for the calculation. In two seconds, the calculator provided me with the results. The fund had jumped 166 percent since I bought it, which breaks down into an annual rate of 21.25 percent. What's even better is that the calculator compares your return with a slew of benchmarks, such as the Russell 2000, which is the best comparison for small cap stocks. During the same time period, the Russell 2000 climbed 131.4 percent, so I'm way ahead. The calculator also compared Strong Common Stock's return with the universe of other small cap funds. Since February 26, 1993, the average small cap fund increased 147 percent—not nearly as good as mine.

Janus funds (www.janus.com)

The Web site for the Janus funds is illustrated with pictures of the snow-covered Rocky Mountains and kamikaze skiers. That's nice, guys, we already know you are close to the slopes, but how about a little meat to your Web site? At the very least, you can typically download fund applications and prospectuses from these sites and check on the performance of individual funds. A lot of companies have also packaged on their sites very basic—to the point of being pretty worthless—advice on such things as saving for retirement or college. To their credit, many funds are trying hard to dispel the confusion over the new federal rules on Individual Retirement Accounts.

Bright Idea
Try visiting this mutual fund newcomer: Fund Spot (www.fundspot.com), which provides weekly news from the world of funds, a directory of every mutual fund company and links, and fund articles culled from lots of publications.

Some fund companies provide worksheets online that can help you decide which IRA option makes sense for you.

Vanguard Group (www.vanguard.com)

There is no question which mutual fund company earns the Olympic gold for its cyberheadquarters. The Vanguard Group, those frugal folks from Valley Forge, Pennsylvania, wins hands down. Vanguard maintains a vast library of articles and commentaries on mutual funds and other types of investing. For instance, if you are wondering whether you should invest in a bond fund or just buy it directly yourself, Vanguard can help you make that decision. Vanguard, which is best known for its extensive choice of index funds, can also provide authoritative backgrounders on such topics as foreign investing, Roth IRAs, and small cap stocks. The site also provides great planning tools that focus on retirement distributions. Using Vanguard's built-in software, for instance, you can figure out how long your nest egg will last. There is so much information at Vanguard's site that they've labeled one section of it The University. You won't earn a degree here, but you'll be a lot smarter by the time you graduate.

The following are Internet addresses of mutual fund companies:

Fidelity Investments	www.fidelity.com
Invesco Funds	www.invesco.com
Lindner Funds	www.lindnerfunds.com
Neuberger & Berman Funds	www.nbfunds.com
Royce Funds	www.roycefunds.com
Scudder Funds	www.scudder.com

Timesaver
If you want to find a fund's home page, but you don't know the Internet address, don't fret. You can try guessing—the addresses are usually pretty obvious, like www.fidelity.com for the Fidelity mutual fund family. Or you can turn to www.gsionline.com. This Web site lists links to hundreds of mutual fund companies.

SteinRoe Funds	www.steinroe.com
Strong Funds	www.strong-funds.com
TIAA-CREF	www.tiaa-cref.org
T.Rowe Price	www.troweprice.com
Vanguard	www.vanguard.com

Your take-home assignment

If you'd like to learn more about using the Internet to increase your mutual fund investing IQ, consider reading these two books.

Mutual Funds on the Net: Making Money Online, by Paul B. Farrell, explains how you can analyze funds and then track them without ever leaving your computer. The author also guides you through the maze of online mutual fund brokers and shows you where you can find some of the leading mutual fund families on the Internet.

Then there's *Mutual Fund Investing on the Internet,* by Peter G. Crane. Written by an editor at IBC Financial Data, which generates truckloads of mutual fund data, the book grades many relevant Web sites and even tells you how much time you should linger at each one.

Incidentally, you can order both books online from www.amazon.com or www.barnesandnoble.com.

Boring, boring bonds

Sorry, bond lovers. The Internet hasn't been kind to you. When stock lovers prowl around on the Internet for the first time, the experience is like opening a closet on a Saturday morning cartoon— all sorts of things come flying out. While stock investors must grapple with too many choices, bond buyers have too few. I don't know if that's because bonds aren't sexy, or maybe it's that their returns have lagged behind stocks for so long. Whatever the reason, I won't leave you completely empty-handed—I'm recommending three sites. And you can always check with Vanguard, which provides a wealth of information about bond mutual funds.

Bonds Online (www.bonds-online.com)

Thanks to a feature called the Bond Professor, you can bone up on some of your fixed-income basics. Ask any question you want, and the kind professor finds the answer or refers you to some place that can. He sends the answer to you via e-mail. This is truly a bond supersite that provides handy links to other fixed-income home pages, including the U.S. Bureau of Public Debt. You'll also find market commentaries, rankings of taxable and tax-free bond funds, dates for U.S. Treasury auctions, weekly reviews of the bond market, and free muni bond valuations. Maybe it's just my computer, but I find that this site can be rather cantankerous. Sometimes my computer freezes up while I'm with the bond professor, but if you really love bonds, it should be worth the aggravation.

John Nuveen & Co. (www.nuveenresearch.com)

This site, sponsored by the 100-year-old Chicago bond firm, is for the more sophisticated fixed-income investor or those who'd like to be. For your downloading pleasure, Nuveen maintains a library of its fixed-income research, which is geared more toward bond wonks. At this site, you can read reviews of individual state's credit issues and other developments of significance to bondholders, and treat yourself to an analysis of transportation bond financing through airports, tolls, and mass transit.

Amid the more technical writing, you can find a beginner's primer on the $1.3 trillion muni bond market. If this site is too stuffy, try Nuveen's other Web site, www.nuveen.com. Here you'll find Nuveen's daily take on the economy and market trends, a section on investment ideas and tips, its investor newsletters, and loads of bond links.

U.S. Bureau of Public Debt (www.publicdebt.treas.gov)

The friendly bureaucrats have tried to anticipate all the questions you might have about Treasuries and savings bonds. In its savings bonds section, there is a long list of *frequently asked questions* (FAQs). The site can also link you to appropriate IRS documents that you might need.

Is it tax time again?

Nobody likes to think about taxes, but where would accountants be without the federal tax code? Not surprisingly then, it's those fun-loving CPAs who operate some of the best pit stops for weary taxpayers. At these sites, you can find tax tips, the latest tax law changes, and a variety of forms:

Deloitte & Touche	www.dtonline.com
Coopers & Lybrand	www.taxnews.com
Internal Revenue Service	www.irs.gov
Intuit	www.turbotax.com
Ernst & Young	www.ey.com/pfc/rca.htm
SecureTax	www.securetax.com

Surely the IRS, the source of all those confusing forms, can't be much help when you're struggling with your yearly tax ritual. (You've probably seen media accounts of honest taxpayers calling the IRS

Timesaver
If you are into buying books on investing, you can simplify your search by visiting Amazon.com (www.amazon. com) or Barnes and Noble (www. barnesandnoble. com), the gigantic cyberbooksellers. Here's just one example of what you can find. When I typed **financial statements** into Amazon's search function, it yielded more than 100 book titles.

Unofficially...
If you're a regular Internet user, you know what FAQ means— *frequently asked questions.* There is a financial Web site strictly devoted to FAQs (www.invest-faq. com). You'll find dozens of FAQs on such topics as dividends, money markets, annuities, real estate investment trusts, hedging, and Dogs of the Dow.

help line and getting different answers for the same question.) But you might be surprised. You can get scores of forms from this Web site, as well as a bumper crop of pamphlets and publications. If you are confused about all the changes triggered by the Taxpayer Relief Act of 1997, you can find a full explanation here. Amazing as this might sound, a reporter for the *New York Times* actually declared that the site is "lively and amusing." Honest.

The mother of all calculators (www.smartcalc.com)

If you have spent any time at all cruising the Web, you have spotted some built-in financial calculators. Sites sponsored by insurance companies, personal finance magazines, banks, and many other sources let you calculate all sorts of financial what-if scenarios right on the spot. What if I want to retire to the south of France at age 50? How much money will I need to save? How much will my daughter—class of 2010—need for Princeton? Just by punching in a few figures, these calculators can do the math that allows you to pinpoint your own magic number. These calculators also can help you decide such things as whether refinancing your home makes sense, how much life insurance you need, and whether your credit card debt should be consolidated.

While these efficient calculators are scattered throughout the Internet universe, you can save a lot of time by simply visiting the mother of all calculator sites—www.smartcalc.com. The site was created by FinanCenter, Inc., a Web pioneer from Tucson, Arizona, which began developing these SmartCalc calculators several years ago. It makes its money selling them to scores of Web sponsors, such as Allstate Insurance, Yahoo!, *USA Today,* and *Money Magazine.*

When you visit, you can choose from well over 100 different calculators all in this one place. The calculators, which can actually be more sophisticated than the ones personal finance advisors and mortgage loan officers use, were developed by an emeritus professor of finance and a Ph.D. candidate in physics.

Here's a piece of trivia that might interest you. The site's most popular calculator answers this question: What will it take to become a millionaire? Other really popular calculators determine what the payments on a car loan would be, as well as how much someone can realistically borrow for a home mortgage.

The calculators cover such topics as mutual funds, stocks, bonds, Roth IRAs, budgeting, home loans and refinancing, credit lines, auto loans, and insurance. Here's a sample of the kinds of financial dilemmas FinanCenter can help with:

- Which is better financially—a new or a used car?

- Should I lease or purchase a car?

- Should I convert my regular IRA into a Roth IRA?

- What will it take to save for a car or home?

- How will interest rate changes affect my bond's value?

- Which are better—tax-exempt or taxable bonds?

- Should I buy a zero coupon bond?

- How much will it cost to raise a child?

- How advantageous is increasing my savings?

- Should I consolidate my debts?

- Should I use a home equity loan instead of a home loan?

- Is a lower rate on a credit card worth an annual fee?

- Which is better—a load or a no-load fund?

- What will my expenses be after I retire?

- What selling price for my stocks will provide my desired return?

- How will exchange rates affect my foreign stocks?

How long will it take to be a millionaire—a sample calculation from FinanCenter. *Source: FinanCenter, Inc.*

FinanCenter's consumer Web site is actually www.financenter.com, but I prefer the SmartCalc Web site, because there are more calculators to choose from. To view the complete list of calculators, click on the list of online software offered to businesses.

Indexes galore!

Indexes can be invaluable for people who want to compare their portfolio's performance with a benchmark. Go ahead and compare to your heart's content. These Web sites are great sources for all sorts of benchmarks:

Standard & Poor's Corp.	www.stockinfo.
	standardpoor.com
Russell Index	www.russell.com
Wilshire Associates	www.wilshire.com
NASDAQ	www.nasdaq.com
J.P. Morgan	www.jpmorgan.com

Wandering closer to home

What if you are intimidated by the Internet and prefer to stick with one of the big online services? You will find a decent amount of financial information in a nicely packaged format on America Online, CompuServe, and Prodigy. You can find stock quotes, business news, and stock market updates on all three. Each online service also provides you with a variety of financial publications, such as *Money, Fortune,* and *Business Week.* All three also serve as financial matchmakers of a sort. They bring together people who are just bursting to talk to anybody who will listen to their investing feats. All three offer electronic bulletin boards where you can post messages to fellow investors. If you don't like investing alone, you can join one of the scores of chat groups devoted to investing junkies. Perhaps the most famous are the chat groups within AOL's Motley Fool section. You can also visit the Motley Fool at www.motleyfool.com. And of course, all three provide their own access to the Internet.

Those wild and crazy sites

Usenet groups congregate around those unedited and uncensored bulletin boards that are devoted to every possible subject you can imagine. If that sort of thing interests you, there happen to be about 20 Usenet groups devoted to investing. The purpose of

> **“**
> Usenet is the wild frontier of the Internet. Anything goes (and usually does) in these investing newsgroups. If you can get through the noise, you'll find some smart investors who are willing to share their knowledge with you. The trouble comes in trying to tell the good guys from the bad.
> —Doug Gerlach, author of *The Investor's Web Guide: Tools & Strategies for Building Your Portfolio*
> **”**

these groups is to share ideas, offer advice, and provide insights on the market. But often you have to
sift through a lot of irrelevant and off-the-wall messages to get to the good stuff. You also have to be
extremely cautious about whatever you hear. People
are hyping or trashing stocks for all sorts of financial
reasons.

If you are game, here are some of the newsgroup
addresses:

misc.invest.stocks

misc.invest.mutual-funds

misc.invest.emerging

misc.invest.financial-plan

misc.taxes

misc.real-estate

An easy way to visit a Usenet group is through
Deja News (www.dejanews.com), the ultimate search
engine for Usenet groups. Deja News can link you
up with thousands of discussion groups.

Another way to bond with other investors is
through electronic mailing lists. Dozens of these
mailing lists, which are also called *list servers,* focus
on personal finance. You'll find that the mail lists
aren't as wild as the in-your-face Usenet groups. For
one thing, it takes a bit of effort to join, which
should discourage visitors from dropping in to contribute something obscene, irrelevant, or completely wrong. Electronic mailing lists also have
rules to maintain order. For instance, you might not
be able to use a pseudonym, and the organizer
might screen out unacceptable posts. Be forewarned
that if you join, you'll receive every message that
anyone on the mailing list posts. If it's a lively group,
you might gets dozens of e-mails a day. A good way

Watch Out!
If you go on
vacation, be sure
to ask the mail-
ing list coordina-
tor to stop
forwarding your
messages. If
you forget, when
you return, your
e-mail basket
might have shut
down because it
was jammed
with too many
messages.

to find a suitable mailing list is to visit www.liszt.com or www.reference.com.

Financial software to keep you on track

Cruising the Internet isn't the only way you can use your computer to improve your investing prowess. No farther than your nearest computer superstore, you'll find software that can help you keep on top of your household finances, track your portfolios, and screen stocks. You can download a lot of software programs from the Internet. Some of them are free, while some can be purchased and retrieved online. Here's a brief rundown of what you can expect.

Financial planning software

If you need a budget to stay financially disciplined, this type of software might be just what you need. Some people swear by Quicken, Managing Your Money, and the other types out on the market. These programs can be scary—they will pinpoint just how much you are blowing on such things as restaurants and vacations. To get the most from these programs, you'll need to enter all your expenditures into the computer. You will also be able to send your checks electronically, and the programs will assist you with tax preparation. In addition, the software can help you track and analyze just how well your investments are doing, but if that's your only interest, you would do better to buy software that is strictly devoted to portfolio management.

Portfolio management software

These programs go beyond just following your investments. All of them can keep you posted on the changing value of your portfolio and can sum up what sort of capital gains and dividends your investments have generated. But beyond that, they can assist the savvier investor with tougher investment decisions. The software, for instance, can help you analyze if your portfolio is properly diversified and whether your asset allocation is on the mark.

Screening your stocks

In the old days—which for the computer industry could mean a few days ago—only the professionals used computerized stock screens. But now anybody with a computer can do the same thing as well. Stock screening can help cut through all the stock tips and investing ideas that bombard us all the time. If you chase every dead-end tip that you hear or read about, you'll have little time to do anything else. And that doesn't sound like fun, does it? What you need to keep in mind is that stock screening merely reduces your universe of stocks to a manageable amount. It won't select the perfect stock for you.

Stock screening makes your hunt less aimless. These screening services help you filter out lousy stocks effortlessly. Let's say you'd love to find a small company that is growing at a 25 percent clip, maintains a P/E ratio no higher than 20, and has very little debt. If you were on your own, how long do you think it would take you to sift through 8,000 stocks to find those that match your criteria? I'd rather stand in a department store's return line on December 26 than do that. Ah, but with a stock screener, your picks should appear on your screen almost instantaneously. Stock-screening services on the Web used to be pricey. And two major screening resources—Wall Street City (www.wallstreetcity. com) and Market Guide (www.marketguide.com)— still cost. (Market Guide's online version, though, is free.) But there are now alternatives for anybody who hates to pay. For free screening, visit these

Web sites: Hoover's, a major source of corporate profiles (www.stockscreener.com), Morningstar (www.
morningstar.net), and Quicken (www.quicken.com).

Stock screen programs, however, can't substitute
for your brain. After you filter out some possibilities,
your research begins. Don't ever buy a stock just
because it was detected by the stock screener.

Online banking—the teller's always there

Remember back to the days when automatic teller
machines were exotic? Of course today, ATM
machines are as ubiquitous as pay phones. You can
find them in grocery stores, video stores, and malls.
I've even spotted one in a McDonald's.

No doubt, online banking—the newest banking
phenomenon—will be just as popular someday.
Actually, online banking has been around for more
than 10 years, but it's only been more recently, with
the explosion of cheap personal computers and the
Internet craze, that banks are starting to push the
service. Hundreds of banks are already offering
online banking to their customers, and more programs are being launched all the time.

What's the allure of online banking? For starters,
it's convenient. You can have access to your checking, savings, and investment accounts around the
clock from the comfort of your own home. Through
the computer, you can transfer money between
accounts, initiate withdrawals, and check on balances. Another big draw is electronic bill paying.
You'll never have to lick another stamp. While some
banks use their own proprietary software, others
provide planning programs that can help you manage other aspects of your finances. NationsBank, for

Timesaver
Before you
attempt to sort
out which finan-
cial software
packages are
best for you,
consider ordering
*The Individual
Investor's Guide
to Computerized
Investing,* 14th
edition, from
the American
Association of
Individual
Investors at
(800) 428-2244
or www.aaii.
com.

Unofficially...
According to a
recent cyberpoll
conducted by
Bank Rate
Monitor, two-
thirds of online
and Internet
users say they
are considering
using online
banking to help
balance their
checkbooks and
pay bills.

example, gives Microsoft Money out free to customers who bank electronically.

If online banking intrigues you, here are some
questions you should ask before plunging in:

- How long does it take to complete each transaction? If you electronically instruct the bank to
  pay your $84 utility bill, will it be done imme-
  diately? Some banks, while they act like they
  are cybersavvy, have operations stuck in the
  Cretaceous Period. At some institutions, a check
  still has to be printed and then mailed to the
  utility. The process can take several days.

- What security procedures are in place at the
  bank to protect my account? Encryption is used
  to scramble your account information.

- What happens if I make a mistake? Imagine, for
  instance, that it's midnight and you're winding
  up a night of electronic bill paying. Suppose you
  erroneously pay your mortgage twice. Can this
  be easily corrected, and will you have to pay any
  penalties?

- How difficult is it to close an account? Are there
  any costs involved?

- What are the fees? Many banks offer cut-rate
  prices to attract customers. A nationwide survey
  by Bank Rate Monitor indicated that banks
  charge just a nominal fee or none at all for this
  electronic banking convenience. Bank of
  America, which is headquartered in San
  Francisco, prices its electronic services at $6.50
  a month. But even that is waived for customers
  who use the bank's direct deposit features or
  maintain a high checking account balance. You
  can get by even cheaper with Citibank in New

York, which aggressively markets its online services, including stock quotations. Some banks charge for their bill-paying feature. For instance, NationsBank in Charlotte, North Carolina, charges customers $5.95 per month to pay 20 bills. This is a little cheaper than buying the stamps.

Just the facts

- When exploring the Internet, have a strategy.
- Avoid getting snookered by cybercrooks—stick with reputable Web sites.
- Doing stock research on the Web can give you the tools the professionals use.
- Thanks to the Internet, you can track your mutual fund portfolio like a pro.
- Know what questions to ask before you try online banking.

GET THE SCOOP ON...
Forget the Beardstown Ladies ▪ Three key
principles of club investing ▪ Getting beyond
the hype ▪ Evaluating stocks the NAIC way ▪
Avoiding common mistakes ▪
Starting your own club

The Investment Club Phenomenon

Chapter 9

I s there anybody out there who hasn't heard
about the Beardstown Ladies? You know who
I'm talking about. They're the ones who share
casserole recipes, clip coupons, and baby-sit grand-
children. But they are best known—at least until
recently—for repeatedly embarrassing some of Wall
Street's shrewdest money managers with their investment club's spectacular stock market returns. They
cashed in on their fame to write *The Beardstown
Ladies' Common-Sense Investment Guide* and three
other personal finance books, star in a video, and
speak before many a television audience. Ah, but
the ladies no longer seem so brilliant. Lately the
only ones who have been embarrassed are the ladies
themselves.

Gathered around a dining room table, the sep-
tuagenarians are still committed to buying and
selling stocks that are as all-American as the corn
fields that line the two-lane highways in Middle

Unofficially...
Many might assume that the Beardstown Ladies became media stars because their stated returns were superior to other clubs. Not so. A network television producer called the National Association of Investors Corp. looking for a club in Middle America to profile. Somebody suggested the Beardstown group, which had been mentioned in an issue of the NAIC's magazine. Eventually a publisher called with a book contract.

America. The women love stocks like Quaker Oats, Rubbermaid, and Colgate-Palmolive. Blue chip companies that sell the kinds of products you'll find if you open your kitchen drawers or medicine cabinet. But thanks to an inquisitive reporter, Beardstown's finest were dethroned rather abruptly. As it turned out, their yearly stock returns were nowhere near the 23.4 percent they had claimed for a 10-year period. With media hound dogs sniffing out the story, Price Waterhouse, the accounting giant, was called in to sort out the mess. An audit of the books revealed that the club's returns were a mere 9.1 percent. The professional money managers could once again act smug.

But it would be a mistake to assume that you can't beat the professionals just because the treasurer of the Beardstown Ladies' Investment Club was a bit befuddled. (Everyone agrees that their accounting mistakes were honest.) Joining an investment club is still an excellent way to increase your chances of winning on the stock market. It's also a safe way to learn about the markets for anybody who knows little about stocks. If you belong to an investment club, you won't have to develop your buy and sell signals from scratch. Your cheap club membership in the National Association of Investors Corp. entitles you to share stock-picking guidelines that have performed admirably through bear and bull markets for decades. Relying on these time-tested investing rules has given thousands of people the courage to buy stocks for their own personal portfolios. Typically only a couple of people in a new club already own stocks when they join, but usually just about everybody does once a club hits the five-year mark. And here's another benefit: Once you're following a disciplined investing approach, you won't be as tempted to blindly buy shares in the stock flavor of the month.

With any luck, this chapter will help you decide whether joining an investment club is right for you. Find out what these clubs can offer and what you should know before you join or create one. This is crucial, since many of the people who are anxious to get started will all too soon view the experience as a huge waste of time. About 50 percent of all new clubs disband before reaching their second anniversary. A big reason for the failures is that people accept as truth all the investment club myths they hear. By the time you finish reading this chapter, you should be able to separate the reality from the investment club hype. And trust me, there is a lot of hype. I know because I started an investment club with a friend back in the early 1990s. Consequently, you're going to hear the inside scoop on investment clubs—information you won't necessarily see in all those newspaper and magazine stories.

Stick around and you'll also learn just how successful investment clubs pick stocks. In media accounts, you'll find very few, if any, details on how the best clubs pull this off. You'll also learn how to avoid common, boneheaded mistakes my club and many others have committed over the years. Finally, if you're still excited about communal investing by the end of the chapter, you'll learn what simple steps you must take to start your own club.

The popularity is out of sight

To their credit, the Beardstown Ladies' homespun schmaltz fueled the appetite for investment clubs. Since they became media stars, interest in investments clubs has exploded. By mid-1998, 730,000 persons belonged to the not-for-profit NAIC, which

Moneysaver
Want to avoid financial miscues of Beardstown proportions? The NAIC sells a software program that can track the performance of your own individual portfolio. Personal Record Keeper sells for $129 and can be obtained by calling (248) 583-6242. You can download a free demo from the NAIC's Web site: www. better-investing. org. Quicken 98 software programs, produced by Intuit Inc., have the same kind of features.

represents an incredible 253 percent increase in membership in just three years. Today the NAIC keeps tabs on 37,000 clubs, which is up from about 8,000 about a decade ago. (Many more than that exist, but no one tracks clubs that don't affiliate with the NAIC.) Every month, more than 40,000 callers, many eager to make a fortune on the stock market, overwhelm the NAIC's switchboard in Madison Heights, Michigan. In fact, it can take you several minutes just to get through to the operator.

None of this hubbub existed at the beginning. While the oldest known investment club started 100 years ago in Texas, the modern investment club movement can be traced to 1940. In that year, Frederick C. Russell, a college grad who couldn't find a job, launched the Mutual Investment Club in Detroit. He had hoped to make enough money in the stock market to start his own business. The original club is still around. Fifty-eight years later, the portfolio of this pioneering club is worth $4.5 million. (Club members have withdrawn another $2.9 million for such things as their children's college education and bigger house mortgages.) Not bad for a total investment of just $440,000. It was the members of this first club who helped create the NAIC in 1951.

The guiding principles

The stock-picking philosophy of the pioneering group lives on through the NAIC. The Michigan organization acts much like a mother who coaxes her toddler into the swimming pool for the first time. Its big mission is to convince people that buying stocks isn't as scary or as complicated as it looks. For a modest sum—membership is $14 per person and $35 per club—you can immerse yourself in the organization's tried-and-true stock-picking techniques. One of the truly amazing things about this organization is that it is run, in large part, by volunteers across the country who seem truly delighted to help beginners. If Norman Rockwell were alive today, he'd probably feel compelled to paint a picture.

The goal of these clubs isn't to make a quick profit on the hottest stocks. After all, a group can't furiously buy and sell stocks when it only meets once a month. Rather, the cheery folks at the head office and in local councils throughout the nation try to steer people to Wall Street's steady performers, the ones that can brag about solid long-term track records. And I do mean long-term. When you are analyzing stocks the NAIC way, you find yourself penciling in such figures as stock prices, dividends, book value, net profit, and revenue that go back 10 years. Follow its rules, and the NAIC likes to say that a club should be able to double its money every five years. If your club can pull this off, that performance breaks down to a 14.9 percent compounded annual growth rate. Perhaps not a flashy figure during an overheated bull market, but certainly it's far superior to the historical 11 percent return that stocks have enjoyed through much of this century.

In a nutshell, the NAIC's stock-buying advice can be broken down into three pieces of advice:

- **Invest regularly, no matter how grim the market looks.** If a club tries to time the market by guessing when Wall Street's on the verge of a collapse or a wild ascent, it will fail most of the time. Instead, members are encouraged to regularly pump money into the market no matter what kind of shape it's in. And no investment, by the

> 66
> Our feeling is, if you're smart enough to be out there making a living, you can also make some pretty good investment decisions.
> —Kenneth S. Janke, Sr., NAIC president and chief executive officer
> 99

way, is too small. Nationally, the average club member contributes just $29 a month to his or her club's kitty. The typical portfolio is now worth $89,573.

- **Reinvest all earnings.** This is pretty obvious. If a club wants its portfolio to grow through compounding, it needs to reinvest. Clubs are supposed to sink their dividends, as well as any capital gains, back into stocks. Of course, in today's market, healthy stock dividends seem more like a quaint artifact from a bygone era. But even modest dividends can help soften the blow when a stock skids.

- **Stick with growth companies.** Hunt for the best-managed companies in rapidly growing industries. These gems are usually the ones with the highest profit margins and earnings on invested capital. NAIC officials acknowledge that trolling for buys in the hottest industries is risky, so they offer a fall-back position for the more timid: Find companies that are simply growing at a 10 percent clip or better.

The following are the 10 most popular holdings among investment clubs in 1998:

1. PepsiCo
2. Intel
3. Motorola
4. Tricon Global Restaurants
5. Merck
6. Aflac
7. Diebold
8. McDonald's

9. Coca-Cola

10. Lucent Technologies

The NAIC is also a big booster of diversification. As you can see from the table, the most popular stocks among clubs nationwide include some of the biggest corporate names in the world. But the NAIC really wants its stock pickers to branch out. According to the NAIC, the ideal portfolio is more or less equally divided among large, medium, and small companies. By its standards, a corporation is considered big if its sales reach at least $4 billion a year. A company is considered small if it generates revenues of $400 million or less a year, and everything else belongs in the middle territory.

Debunking investment club myths

Thousands of investors have concluded that these NAIC principles make a heck of a lot of sense. Every month, club members pour $50 million into the stock market. More than $60 billion in the stock market today can be traced back to investment clubs. You, in fact, might be getting ready to join them. Learning how to invest in stocks with a bunch of colleagues can be more than educational. It can actually be fun. Even better, the pressure is off. Investing in stocks can be a nerve-wracking experience for someone who is depending on that money for retirement or to finance a kid's college education. You might be kicking in just $25, $50, or $100 a meeting—money you might have blown anyway on movies and Chinese dinners. With this discretionary money, you can afford to make mistakes as the club gets its bearings in the stock market.

Certainly investment clubs have a lot to offer. But before you get too excited, you need to acquaint

Timesaver
Wondering what stocks meet the NAIC's growth guidelines? A quick way to generate ideas is by reading the NAIC's magazine, *Better Investing*. It might look awfully dowdy, but every month it features companies that have been steady growth performers. Companies profiled in the magazine's "Stock to Study" section have, on average, doubled their value within five years.

yourself with the misconceptions. There are a lot of myths out there, and I'll mention seven notable ones. The Beardstown Ladies made investing look fun and easy. But perhaps they've made it look too easy. Actually, it can be hard and tedious work, and the dynamics of these individual clubs can make Christmas dinner with the in-laws seem like a cinch.

I'm going to get filthy rich.

"All I need to do is join a club and I'll enjoy fantastic returns." It's easy to see why so many people believe this. First, they've been reading the NAIC's press clippings. According to the Michigan group's own surveys, the clubs appear, by and large, to be enjoying quite a bit of success. In 1997, for instance, 58.3 percent of all the investment clubs equaled or beat the S&P 500 Index. (This is mighty impressive when you consider that the famous benchmark was up 33.4 percent that year.) Most professional money managers couldn't even pull this off.

But what a lot of people don't understand is that these numbers come only from the clubs that send in their annual tallies. Most clubs never bother with it. In fact, only 700 to 800 groups mail them in. And human nature being what it is, I'll bet that most of the clubs that do address those envelopes have something to brag about. If your club loses, say, 10 percent of its value in one year or ekes out a 1 percent gain, do you think you'd want any outsiders knowing about it? Not likely.

Kenneth Janke, the NAIC's CEO and treasurer of the original NAIC club, which is worth $4.5 million, readily acknowledges that he's no George Gallup. The surveys are not scientifically valid. "I'm not a polling expert. I'm not sure if we get the right numbers or not. But I don't think we want to hire a polling outfit to do it for us."

Yet it's those amazing returns, dutifully reported in the press, that help lure newcomers into the fold. All too often, eager new members fully expect that they'll soon be driving a Mercedes-Benz, thanks to the collective stock-picking prowess of their clubs. Here's a more realistic picture of what can happen: Let's assume that you belong to a club of 15 members, who each invest $20 a month. At the end of five years, a club that follows the guidelines could expect to be managing a portfolio of about $22,000. A respectable sum, but it's certainly not enough to change anybody's lifestyle. (Of course, the club's assets will grow faster if members contribute more each month.)

Clubs buy and sell stocks at a fast pace.

In this era of almost instantaneous electronic stock transactions, consider this scenario: Buying stocks by mail. With the market so volatile, would you want to purchase stocks by snail mail when the share price could be dramatically higher by the time the mail carrier delivers your payment? Well, get used to it. Most new clubs must resort to this because they don't have much cash. At the beginning, your club won't have the big bucks necessary to make major purchases and absorb those stockbroker commission costs. If you have $400 to spend, for instance, you'll get less than six shares of AT&T after you pay the commission. If the commission is $35, the stock's return at the starting gate will be close to negative 9 percent.

The only way to avoid stiff commissions on these small trades—you get charged more for trades of less than 100 shares—is to buy on the cheap. One

> 66
>
> We are not all trying to beat Warren Buffett or Peter Lynch. The question is are you making a decent return and learning things that will help you with your own personal investing? Actually why should the majority of clubs do better than most fund managers when they are getting paid a heck of a lot more?
> —Kenneth S. Janke, Sr.
>
> 99

way to accomplish this is through NAIC's low-cost investment plan. For a $7 setup fee and the price of a share of stock, you can purchase a tiny piece of any company that participates in the plan. The NAIC handles the arrangements, but once that initial stock purchase is registered, a club mails future checks for additional shares directly to the company.

That's how our club got started. We scoured the list of companies participating in the NAIC's cheapskate plan. We did chafe over how this limited our choices through these DRIPs, or *dividend-reinvestment plans*. (See Chapter 10, "Making Your Move—Buying and Selling," for more on how DRIPs work.) About 150 companies participate in the NAIC plan, and most of them are not what you'd consider aggressive growth stocks. There is a big assortment of utility stocks to choose from, along with such stolid companies as La-Z-Boy Chair, Maytag, Whirlpool, Dow Chemical, and Quaker Oats. One of my first purchases was Intel, which is an anomaly. High-tech stocks almost never participate in the NAIC program, though Lucent Technologies was recently added to the list.

Clubs can invest in the entire universe of stocks.

Realistically, this doesn't happen. Nationally, the 100 top holdings of investment clubs are dominated by large cap stocks, the ones that are instantly recognizable. A big reason for this embrace of the gigantic companies is because newcomers feel more comfortable buying into something they know. After all, a lot of us wear Nike shoes, drink Pepsi, pass out Tootsie Rolls at Halloween, and buy fast computers powered by Intel's Pentium chips. But beyond this natural instinct, the NAIC setup favors the Goliaths. One reason is because of the heavy reliance on

Bright Idea
Clubs find stock ideas the same way individual investors do. They read financial newspapers and magazines, look at Value Line or Standard & Poor's reports, and some use computerized stock-screening programs. Members can also uncover gems thanks to specialized knowledge they possess of their own industries.

Value Line, the stock-rating service, which is available at most libraries. Value Line provides a statistical analysis of 1,700 large corporations, but that still leaves out the vast majority of publicly traded companies. (See a sample Value Line analysis in Chapter 7, "Research—The Investing Advantage.") The Value Line Expanded Survey covers many more smaller companies, but this publication doesn't include such things as analysts' commentaries or future earnings estimates. The Extended Survey also isn't in a lot of libraries. Consequently, if Value Line doesn't evaluate a stock, many investment clubs don't bother to do the legwork themselves. Investment clubs, however, don't snub small cap stocks entirely. Some clubs accumulate shares of smaller regional companies in their own areas. For instance, Californians gravitate toward less well-known stocks in the Golden State.

So what's the harm of ignoring stocks that don't attract Value Line's attention? Without diversification, a club's portfolio is lopsided. A club won't own the smaller stocks, which historically have performed even better than their bigger brothers. It's this built-in investment club bias toward big stocks that makes some financial experts groan. Back in 1994, for example, a *Wall Street Journal* reporter asked the chief investment strategist at Merrill Lynch to review the 100 stocks most favored by investment clubs. Looking at the holdings, the strategist sniffed and declared it was a "stagnant list." The man holding the same post at Dean Witter Reynolds concurred, "They are concentrated in the success stories of the 1980s."

Of course, the joke was on those experts. We all know that the big stocks have done fabulously well in recent years, but no one is suggesting that this large cap boom can last forever.

A club can start trading immediately.

Not so fast. A new club needs money before it can begin buying. If members pitch in just $25 a month, you can imagine how long it could take before a club can assemble a respectable stock portfolio. Unless a club uses DRIPs to buy shares, it often shows a loss during its first year because of the commission costs. I can tell you from experience that this can be extremely frustrating.

I'll find a club that wants me as a member.

One reason why the Beardstown Ladies got noticed is because the national media thought it was precious to see a club composed of sweet grandmothers. But the Beardstown group—the average age is now 70—is quite similar demographically to many other clubs that go by such silly names as Cover Ur Assets, Money Honeys, Moneywi$e, and the Dow Janes. If you try to join an existing club, you'll discover that senior citizens run the majority of them. Interestingly, about 46 percent of clubs only accept women, while 12 percent of clubs just accept men. Women represent 65 percent of NAIC's total membership. The gray demographic of America's investment clubs, however, appears to be slowly changing. More and more young people are joining the ranks. I've even heard of kiddie investment clubs.

If I'm not in a group, I can't belong to the NAIC.

Plenty of people join the NAIC solo—about 64,500 people have. There is no reason why somebody can't follow the organization's guidelines and do quite well picking stocks all by herself.

Following the NAIC's guidelines won't be hard.

Actually, it's not as simple as it sounds in those glowing newspaper profiles. You'll find the guidelines spelled out in the *NAIC Investors Manual*, a handbook crammed with page after page of deadly dull text. You can call NAIC's headquarters to order a copy. I must confess, I never did make it to the end. Don't feel too guilty if you don't either. Another alternative is to read *Starting and Running a Profitable Investment Club,* which you can find on many bookstore shelves. It was co-written by Kenneth S. Janke, Sr., and Thomas E. O'Hara, chairman of the NAIC's board of trustees.

The NAIC stock-picking rules

Before you join an investment club, you need to be comfortable with its stock-picking strategy. This is not the kind of organization that will cheer wildly if you dabble in initial public offerings. If you expect to bounce in and out of stocks a lot, this also isn't your kind of crowd. And the NAIC isn't enthusiastic about buying cyclical stocks, such as automobile, steel, and oil stocks, since timing the purchasing and selling of these manic stocks can be tricky.

If the NAIC had a mantra, it could be this, "It's the management, stupid." Investing in a company with poor management is sacrilege to the folks at the Michigan headquarters. Stick with companies run by top-flight managers, and you should do all right financially. Of course, you might be thinking, management is a subjective thing. How can somebody living in California, for instance, know if the highest-paid executives at Coca-Cola in Atlanta are really earning their stratospheric salaries? Chances are, you'll never meet these guys, but there are ways to at least partially answer the question with a calculator. Here are the clues to excellent management:

- Are the company's sales and earnings growing at a healthy pace? Is the record of growth in sales and earnings consistent? Most corporations experience rough patches every now and then, but reliable, steadily upward earnings are what you want.

- Is there a high return on stockholder equity? You might remember the *return-on-equity* (ROE) ratio in Chapter 7, "Research—The Investing Advantage." It's an excellent and quick way to measure how well management is using its cash.

- Does the corporation enjoy a high pretax profit? Since corporations pay different tax rates, the NAIC thinks it's better to see what kind of profit a company generates before it pays the IRS. Be careful how you use these numbers. Some industries, such as supermarket chains, have a very low profit margin, while others, such as software companies, have much higher ones. When comparing two companies in the same industry, look for the one with the higher pretax profit margin.

While you're evaluating management, ask these questions, too:

- Are much of the earnings plowed back into the company? While the NAIC likes companies with dividends, it thinks no more than 50 percent of the earnings should be funneled into dividends. The rest should be plowed back into the company.

- Does the company produce superior products or services?

- Is the company nurturing a robust research and development department that continues to roll out innovative new products?

Even if you answer yes to all these questions, you shouldn't overlook asking yourself this: Is the current share price reasonable? It's not hard to figure this one out once you have the historical figures, which you can get from Value Line or Standard & Poor's. First, you should check to see if the earnings are keeping pace with revenues. What you don't want is a company with booming sales and stagnating earnings.

To make this clearer, let's look at a hypothetical company's financial snapshot.

Year	Sales per Share	Earnings per Share
1996	$1.25	25 cents
1997	$1.75	26 cents
1998	$2.00	28 cents

You can immediately see that something is wrong. In three years, sales have jumped 60 percent. Meanwhile, earnings have only increased 12 percent.

While there can be logical explanations for lagging earnings (the company might have had some unusual one-time expenses), this is often a warning sign that a corporation is doing a lousy job. If a company is generating more sales, it should be generating more profits as well.

You also should check to see what a stock's trading range has been for the past several years. Once again, Value Line provides this information. By reviewing the price history and its typical P/E ratios, you'll get a rough idea of when the stock is in buy, sell, or hold territory.

You won't be able to answer some of the questions you've just read without filling out standard NAIC forms. The first form you need to tackle is the *Stock Check List.* (After you've been analyzing stocks for awhile, you can skip this first form.) The form, as shown below, is just two pages, and actually this one isn't hard to fill out. The first time you complete one, it should take no more than 20 minutes. This form is supposed to ensure that you don't fritter away a lot of time researching inherently flawed stocks. You simply plug in figures on revenue and earnings to determine if a company's growth rates

The front and back pages of the NAIC stock check-list. *Source: National Association of Investors Corp.*

NATIONAL ASSOCIATION OF INVESTORS CORPORATION

NAIC®

INVESTMENT EDUCATION FOR INDIVIDUALS AND CLUBS SINCE 1951

Stock Check List ® for Beginning Investors

Company _____
Prepared by _____
Date _____

See Chapter 7 of the NAIC Official Guide.

While Investors are learning to use NAIC's Stock Selection Guide, it is suggested the following Check List be used for each stock considered for investment.

1 PAST SALES RECORD

Sales for most recent year were	(1) $ _____	
Sales for next most recent year were	(2) $ _____	
Total of above (1 + 2)	(3) $ _____	
Figure above divided by 2		(4) $ _____
Sales 5 years ago were	(5) $ _____	
Sales 6 years ago were	(6) $ _____	
Total of above (5 + 6)	(7) $ _____	
Figure above divided by 2		(8) $ _____
Increase in sales in above period (8 from 4)		(9) $ _____
Percentage increase in sales (9 divided by 8)		(10) _____ %

CONVERSION TABLE

This % Increase in Sales Gives →	27	33	46	61	76	93	112	129	148	205	271
This % Compounded Annual Growth Rate →	5	6	8	10	12	14	16	18	20	25	30

Look for the percent increase that meets the objective you have set.

COMPOUND ANNUAL RATE OF SALES GROWTH WAS _____ %

2 PAST EARNINGS PER SHARE RECORD

Earnings Per Share for most recent year were	(1) $ _____	
Earnings Per Share for next most recent year were	(2) $ _____	
Total of above (1 + 2)	(3) $ _____	
Figure above divided by 2		(4) $ _____
Earnings Per Share 5 years ago were	(5) $ _____	
Earnings Per Share 6 years ago were	(6) $ _____	
Total of above (5 + 6)	(7) $ _____	
Figure above divided by 2		(8) $ _____
Increase in Earnings Per Share in above period (8 from 4)		(9) $ _____
Percentage increase in earnings (9 divided by 8)		(10) _____ %

See **Conversion Table** above to determine _____→

Earnings Per Share have increased _____ than sales in this period.
                                    (more)   (less)

COMPOUND ANNUAL RATE OF EARNINGS PER SHARE GROWTH WAS _____ %

Explain Apparent Reason for Difference in Sales and Earnings Per Share Growth: _____
_____
_____

© 1996. National Association of Investors Corporation; 711 West Thirteen Mile Road, Madison Hgts., Michigan 48071

Discuss Possible Reasons for Past Growth:

A new product was very successful_____.

A cyclical business that experienced recovery_____.

A research program has produced several new products or uses for older products_____.

Purchase another company_____.

Has taken larger share of business in its field_____.

Skill of management_____.

Will Factors Which Produced Past Growth Continue Effective

for the next five years_____ yes,_____ yes, but less effective,_____ no.

3 PRICE RECORD OF THE STOCK

Present Price $_____. Present Earnings Per Share_____.

List Last 5 Years	High Price Each Year (A)	Low Price Each Year (B)	Earnings Per Share (C)	Price Earnings Ratio at High (A ÷ C)	at Low (B ÷ C)
Totals					
Averages					

Average of High and Low Price Earnings Averages for the past five years.	

Present Price is _____ than high price five years ago.
(higher)   (lower)

Present Price is _____% higher than the high price 5 years ago. Compare this figure with the percent sales increase in 1 (10) and percent earnings per share increase in 2 (10).

The price change compares with sales growth and earnings per share growth _____.
(favorably or unfavorably)

This stock has sold as high as the current price in _____ of the last 5 years.

In the past five years the stock _____ sold at unusually _____ price earnings ratios.
(has)   (has not)   (high)   (low)

The Present price earnings ratio is _____.

In relation to past price earnings ratios the stock is currently

_____ selling at a higher ratio

_____ selling about the same

_____ selling lower

The average price earnings ratios of the past might be expected to continue _____,

or should be adjusted to_____ high, _____ low.

4 CONCLUSION

1. The past sales growth rate _____ meet our objective.
   (does)   (does not)

2. The past earnings per share growth rate _____ meet our objective.
   (does)   (does not)

3. Our conclusion has been that possible earnings per share growth rate_____ meet our objective in the coming five years.
   (will)   (will not)

4. The price of the stock is currently _____.
   (acceptable)   (too high)

This form is not meant to give you an adequate analysis of the stock, but is meant to help the beginner ask questions to indicate whether the company is likely to become more valuable and if it can be purchased reasonably. As Investors gain practice, a more thorough study of the stock is suggested using NAIC's Stock Selection Guide and Report as a guide.   ST-1040

during the past several years justify further digging. If both figures are at least 15 percent, you can move on to the tougher analyses.

It's the long form called the *Stock Selection Guide* that presents a bigger challenge (see next page). At first, it might take you several hours to fill out the SSG—that's what people call it—and when you're finished you could very well be perplexed about whether you did it right. The NAIC acknowledges that it might take a new club six months before its members can feel comfortable even trying the SSG.

The front and back pages of the NAIC stock selection guide. *Source: National Association of Investors Corp.*

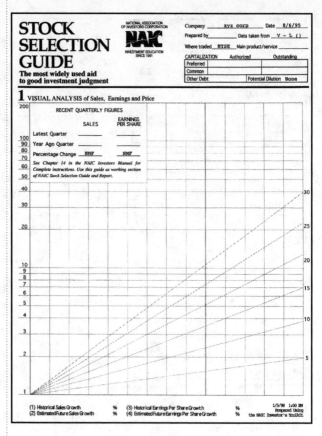

For starters, you have to record 10 years' worth of a company's financial statistics—such things as its yearly earnings per share, net profit, tax rate, sales, and high and low stock prices. This will be easy, since you can transfer the figures from Value Line. You also have to fill in more recent quarterly sales and earnings figures.

Based on all that information, you make your own projections on the company's future growth prospects, and you have to plot trend lines on the SSG's front page. This can be intimidating at first. If you persevere, however, the data will lead you to formulating your own buy, sell, and hold ranges.

2 EVALUATING MANAGEMENT Company _____ xyz corp _____ 8/6/95 _____

									LAST 5 YEAR AVE.	TREND UP	DOWN
A	% Pre-tax Profit on Sales (Net Before Taxes ÷ Sales)										
B	% Earned on Invested Capital (E/S ÷ Book Value)										

3 PRICE-EARNINGS HISTORY as an indicator of the future

PRESENT PRICE _____   HIGH THIS YEAR _____   LOW THIS YEAR _____

	A	B	C	D	E	F	G	H
	PRICE		Earnings Per Share	Price Earnings Ratio		Dividend Per Share	% Payout F ÷ C X 100	% High Yield F ÷ B X 100
Year	HIGH	LOW		HIGH A ÷ C	LOW B ÷ C			
1								
2								
3								
4								
5								
6 TOTAL								
7 AVERAGE								
8 AVERAGE PRICE EARNINGS RATIO				9 CURRENT PRICE EARNINGS RATIO				

4 EVALUATING RISK and REWARD over the next 5 years

A HIGH PRICE - NEXT 5 YEARS
Avg. High P/E _____ (3D7) x Estimated High Earnings/Share _____ = Forecast High Price B-1 $ _____ (4A1)

B LOW PRICE - NEXT 5 YEARS
(a) Avg. Low P/E _____ (3E7) x Estimated Low E/Share _____ = $ _____
(b) Avg. Low Price of Last 5 Years = _____ (3B7)
(c) Recent Severe Market Low Price = _____
(d) Price Dividend Will Support $\frac{\text{Present Divd.}}{\text{High Yield (H)}}$ = _____ = _____
Selected Estimated Low Price _____ B-2 $ _____ (4B1)

C ZONING
$\frac{\text{(4A1)}}{\text{Lower }^1/_3 =}$ _____ (4B1)   High Forecast Price Minus _____ (4B1) Low Forecast Price Equals _____ (C)   Range. $^1/_3$ of Range = _____ (4CD)
To _____   (Buy) (4C2)
Middle $^1/_3 =$ _____ (4B1)   To _____   (Maybe) (4C3)
Upper $^1/_3 =$ _____   To _____ (4A1)   (Sell) (4C4)
Present Market Price of _____   is in the _____ (4C5)   Range

D UP-SIDE DOWN-SIDE RATIO (Potential Gain vs. Risk of Loss)
$\frac{\text{High Price} \quad \text{Minus Present Price}}{\text{(4A1)}}$ _____
$\frac{\text{Present Price} \quad \text{Minus Low Price}}{\text{(4B1)}}$ = _____ (4D) =To 1

5 5-YR POTENTIAL

A Present Full Year's Dividend $ _____
$\frac{}{\text{Present Price of Stock} \quad \$}$ = _____ x100 = _____ Present Yield or % Returned on Purchase Price

B AVERAGE YIELD OVER THE NEXT 5 YEARS
$\frac{\text{Avg. Earn. Per Share Next 5 Years}}{\text{Present Price } \$}$ _____ x Avg % Payout _____ (3G7) = _____ %

© 1994. National Association of Investors Corporation; P.O.Box 220, Royal Oak, MI 48068   1/5/98 1:07 PM

Investment club bloopers and how to avoid them

I'm always telling my eight-year-old daughter that it's okay to fail the first time she tries something. She crashed her bike the day the training wheels came off, and her bed looked like a disaster the first time I asked her to make it. You can expect to make mistakes in your investment club, too. Unfortunately, they can be a little more serious than a lumpy bed. Luckily, you can reduce your mistakes by avoiding the ones that tripped up our club. To shorten your learning curve, I'll share what some of our lulus have been, as well as some things we've done right.

- **Be choosy.** Don't accept just anybody who wants to join. When my friend Michelle and I first started the club, we posted notices on the bulletin boards at the local newspaper. (Our husbands happened to work as reporters there.) We were grateful for anybody who showed up and happily accepted them as members. We continued this policy far too long. We let anybody wander into our meetings, then join. We passively sat by and let the newcomers make the decisions. Consequently, we ended up with some members we might have done better without. We no longer have the same open-door policy.

- **Don't get all your members from one place.** If everyone works at the same company, you won't have a diverse group. It's best to find people with different occupations who can rely on their expertise to follow different types of stocks. For instance, the dentist in my club follows one of our long-term holdings—Patterson Dental. He not only uses Patterson products, but he passes along the latest scoops he hears from Patterson salespeople that he talks with. He also keeps us informed about what Patterson's chief rival is doing.

- **Be firm.** Joining a club is easy. Staying committed is the hard part. Our investment club, like so many others, has been plagued over the years by some habitually absent members. Our bylaws state that anybody who can't attend a meeting must contribute $5 to the club's kitty. (The kitty pays for stamps, brokerage account fees, and occasional pizzas.) No one in our club has ever paid this penalty, because we've been too chicken to enforce the rule. No-shows are a problem for a couple of reasons. First, absentee members can endanger the quorum. They also can build resentment among members who are doing all the work.

■ **Be patient.** A club's first year or two is a lot like a new marriage. It's tough and you'll be tempted to dissolve the group. At first, I thought that was going to happen to our club, too. We tried to recruit an aerospace engineer for our first treasurer, but he turned out to be way too conservative. Fretting about our ability to pick good stocks, he wanted the club to select equities as a paper exercise. Needless to say, he didn't last. A new mother, exhausted by her infant, got discouraged by how much time she was spending on the NAIC stock forms and quit. One couple bought a house and didn't feel they could afford buying stocks. Luckily for us, a solid core group hung in there.

■ **Be prepared for personality clashes.** Every investment club I know would make for a great psychological study. Happily, our group has finally achieved a reasonable balance of yin and yang. Our secretary writes funny meeting minutes that make everyone chuckle. And our members come from different walks of life (journalists, a securities lawyer, a university administrator, a dentist, an accountant, a nurse, a cardiologist, a real estate broker, a property manager), which makes for interesting discussions. What you don't want are too many chiefs.

These are the folks who bring in most of the stock tips and do most of the talking. Our group has survived some of these ego clashes as well.

■ **Keep a lid on your membership.** Our group has had up to 14 members and as few as nine. I think anything beyond 15 is unmanageable. And as a practical matter, you have to consider where you can meet with all these people. Fifteen people do not fit comfortably in most living rooms.

■ **Keep your treasurer happy!** One of the biggest reasons why clubs give up is because their treasurers leave. We adore our treasurer, and just the thought of Mike quitting someday terrifies us. The treasurer is really the club's cement. He puts in the buy and sell orders, deposits money in the brokerage account, and prepares the club's monthly financial statement. And then every spring, he's stuck with the thankless task of preparing each member's tax forms.

In some clubs, members will designate that a small fraction of their monthly contribution go toward buying their treasurer's extra stock. You might try this, especially if members are reluctant to take on the job. Even if your treasurer declines the offer, broach the subject a couple of times a year. Your treasurer might feel too sheepish to tell you that she feels underappreciated. It's also a smart idea for the members to pitch in to buy the treasurer a gift during the holidays or for her birthday.

What is crucial is buying your treasurer the NAIC's accounting software. (This is different from the stock selection software.) As your club's stock portfolio grows, keeping track of it all by hand is really too much of an imposition. An added plus is

Timesaver
It's still possible to run a club even if no one wants to assume all the responsibilities of a treasurer. There are consultants who will manage a club's books for less than $10 a month. You can find these people through the NAIC's regional councils, and some advertise in *Better Investing* magazine.

that the software makes a club's financial documents look professional.

Stick with your club's investing principles. Not long ago, Jim, a university administrator, arrived all excited about a company that puts pheromones into perfume. *Pheromones* are chemicals secreted by animals to attract mates. Admittedly, it's a weird niche. Jim presented some company's financial figures, and he relayed a conversation he had with a Macy's perfume clerk. She had raved about the scent. Most of us seemed to think it would be lunacy to buy shares in a company with a dubious product, particularly since Jim couldn't explain why the share price had dipped recently. But since we hadn't found any good buying opportunities lately—and maybe because a full moon was shining—we disregarded our doubts and voted to buy the stock. Our hasty vote even startled Jim. Sure enough, a few days later, Jim discovered that the company was actually struggling, and its perfume sales had been propped up by expensive marketing. Without the benefit of a slick marketing campaign, sales of the company's latest perfume were evaporating. The next month, we sold our stock and promised each other we wouldn't do anything that dumb again. Luckily our lesson cost us less than $100.

Don't limit yourself to DRIPs. As I mentioned earlier, you'll probably need DRIPs at the start. Once you build up your cash, it can make more sense to buy through a discount broker. This is especially true if your club trades electronically, which really brings the commission down. As you might remember from Chapter 3, "Financial Planners and Brokers—The Best of the Bunch," Internet brokerage fees are dropping dramatically, with some trades

Moneysaver
When a new member joins a club, she doesn't have to play catch-up financially. It's not necessary to contribute a large lump sum so that her investment approximates the others. The value of a newcomer's contributions will just be much lower than everyone else's.

actually possible for as little as $8 or $9. When we started our club, the first five purchases were all DRIPs—Century Telephone, Charles Schwab, Colgate-Palmolive, Intel, and U.S. West. We still own Intel and Schwab, but we no longer use the DRIP program. We buy additional shares in Charles Schwab and Intel through Jack White & Co., our discount brokerage. We are no longer willing to leave to chance what our purchase price will be.

Keep it fun. Once a year, our club holds a potluck meeting at the beach. Everybody brings their kids and spouses and enough food to attract seagulls. Somehow we find time to conduct a little business and, of course, collect the checks.

A club's first baby steps

Does an investment club still sound good to you? If so, here are the first concrete steps you need to take:

- **Call the NAIC headquarters for your free package of investment club materials.** While you're on the phone, ask for the contact numbers of the NAIC officers in your community. One of these volunteers can put you in touch with someone locally who helps new clubs get started. You can reach the NAIC at (248) 583-NAIC, 711 W. Thirteen Mile Rd., Madison Heights, MI 48071.

- **Buy a copy of *Starting and Running a Profitable Investment Club*,** the book I mentioned earlier. This book provides detailed information on such things as the NAIC stock-picking protocol, record keeping, partnership considerations, and analyzing the financial statements you find in an annual report.

- **Ask friends, relatives, or coworkers if they are interested in learning about investment clubs.** Hand them one of the pamphlets you receive in your packet.

- **Hold an informational meeting.** Invite the local club organizer as the guest speaker. After the meeting, ask those who attended if they'd like to join.

- **If there is enough interest to keep going, a couple of people will need to write the club's bylaws.** You can get a sample copy of the typical bylaws from your local contact or the national group.

- **At the first official meeting, discuss what the stock-picking philosophy of the club will be.** Pick a name for the group. Review and approve the bylaws. Collect NAIC dues and send off enrollment forms. Elect a president, vice president, secretary, and treasurer. While the treasurer has the toughest job by far, there is one consolation. She will probably learn more than anybody else.

- **Once the treasurer is elected, she'll need to request a tax identification number for the group.** The Internal Revenue Service considers your club a business. The club receives a tax ID after the treasurer fills out the IRS's Form SS-4. Your club's broker needs that tax ID number to report the club's purchases and sales. Without that number, the brokerage would be obliged to withhold 20 percent of the earnings generated by the stock trades for taxes.

If forming a club sounds like too much work, there is an alternative. If you don't want to go to all

Watch Out!
You don't want to use a member's Social Security number for the club's tax ID. The member would have to explain to the IRS why certain income, which was really the club's, wasn't reported on her tax return.

that trouble, search for a club near you that is open to new members. A local NAIC volunteer can give you contact numbers of groups. Before you make any commitment, make sure the club is a good fit for you.

Just the facts

- Investment clubs are a booming trend.

- Follow the guidelines, and you might be able to double your money in five years.

- Don't let the hype about investment clubs fool you.

- Avoiding common club mistakes can improve your chances of success.

- There are simple steps you need to take to launch a new club.

GET THE SCOOP ON...
Why no-load funds are better ▪ Questions to ask
before you buy ▪ Stock sell signals ▪ DRIPs—the
cheapskate's way to buy stocks ▪ Executing
stock trades ▪ Buying Treasuries direct

Making Your Move— Buying and Selling

Chapter 10

Your hunt has ended and now comes the fun part. You're ready to buy, or at least you're pretty sure you are. All those magazines and newspaper articles you've relied on for fabulous tips have been filed away. You've cleared off your desk all the fund prospectuses, annual reports, and perhaps a page or two from Value Line or Morningstar. After finishing your research, you might feel like a law school graduate who has crammed so hard for the bar exam that she can't wait to pick up that number-two pencil on test day.

If you're ready to buy, congratulations. The really tough work is behind you. But before you buy, or even sell, you should review whether the decision is a sound one. In this chapter, you'll learn some solid reasons for purchasing stocks and mutual funds. You'll also learn some telltale warning signs that might encourage you to unload a disappointing investment. And then there are some niggling little rules of the road you should know before you proceed with your transactions. You can't just call up a broker and say, "I want 5,000 shares of Intel stock!" and think you're done. There are guidelines for buying or selling stocks, mutual funds, and bonds. And I'll explain what those are. Lastly, for any bargain hunters out there, you'll learn about two nifty ways to buy stocks or bonds for practically nothing. And no, this isn't a gimmick.

Load versus no-load mutual funds

The first decision you must make when shopping for a mutual fund is whether you want a load or a no-load fund. While there are close to 7,000 mutual funds on the market, they can all be lumped into these two categories. Which one you select will primarily depend on how much help you need finding that perfect fund.

Buying a load fund simply means it comes with a sales charge. You can compare it to valet parking. Just as you tip the person parking your car, you pay an extra built-in fee to have a stockbroker or financial planner choose your fund. These sales charges can range anywhere from 1 percent to 9 percent. The average load is 4.35 percent.

You can thank the fund industry's marketing departments for making your load choices as clear as river water. The marketers would like everyone to believe the world is a better place because of their wonderful array of loads. But don't believe it. Once upon a time, the only type of load was a *front-end* one. You'll also hear brokers refer to these as *Class A shares*. With these shares, you pay the load up front. For instance, somebody who invests $10,000 into a fund with a 5 percent load pays $500. Since the broker keeps the $500, your initial investment drops to $9,500. So you are in the hole at the start.

But there's more. You can also select Class B, C, or D shares, and for all I know, there could be W, X, and Y shares as well. (Z shares really do exist!) Some load fund companies are actually dreaming up their own names for shares. If you select a *back-end load,* or *B shares,* you don't pay the fee until you sell your mutual fund. And if you hold your B shares for several years, you might skip paying any load at all. That might sound good, but the fund still gouges you by charging higher yearly fees. As for C shares, the load can be quite low, but it's like an unwanted houseguest—it never goes away. The load is charged on your investment every year. Because B and C shares can hit you with higher expenses for a long, long time, you're smart, in most circumstances, to stick with A shares.

No-load funds, on the other hand, don't have any strings attached. You don't get stuck with a sales charge. If you buy $10,000 in the no-load Strong Schafer Value Fund, for instance, that whole amount starts working for you. Unlike a load investor, you aren't handicapping your returns at the start. Consequently, unless you have no interest in picking funds or you feel overwhelmed by the process, stick with no-loads.

Do you need convincing that no-load funds are the best way to go? Here's an example from the guys with the calculators at Price Waterhouse, the accounting giant. The number crunchers looked at what would happen to a $10,000 investment that sits in a no-load fund charging expenses of 1 percent for 26 years. If the fund does as well as the Standard & Poor's Index, the money grows to $97,200. But oops, look what happens if that $10,000 goes into a load fund that charges 2 percent annually—this can happen with Class B and C shares. The investment is worth just $76,300. That's a 27 percent difference!

Since you will be paying a bundle for load funds, get your advisor, who will reap the benefits of your purchase, to explain the different types of loads available in plain English. When buying a load fund, be sure to ask your broker or financial planner how much he'll be pocketing. If the price sounds too exorbitant, just pass.

Most funds sold in this country still come with a load and are often sold through brokers. There is nothing wrong with relying on a broker's advice to pick funds, but a healthy amount of skepticism is advisable. When your broker pesters you to buy a fund, ask him a few questions to reduce your chances of getting stuck with a lousy fund. If you are a do-it-yourselfer, you should also ask the following questions before making any decisions.

What is the one-, three-, and five-year track record of the fund?

Compare those figures with the fund's benchmark. For instance, a large cap growth fund's return should be compared with Standard & Poor's 500 Index.

If a broker is raving about a fund, tell him you want to see the one-page analysis of the fund from Morningstar or Value Line, the independent rating services that were discussed in Chapter 7, "Research—The Investing Advantage." Both firms provide an easily understandable summary of thousands of funds, as well as many measurements of past performance. Also ask your broker how Lipper Analytical Services and CDA/Wiesenberger, which rank mutual funds by statistical performance, rate his recommendation. For instance, if your broker is recommending AIM Aggressive Growth Fund, CDA/Wiesenberger data shows that this small cap fund recently ranked third out of the entire universe of aggressive growth funds for the past five years and number one during the past decade. You can't get much better than that!

What are the fund's annual expenses and sales charges?

With the stock market's returns amazing us for so long, many people don't bother to look at a fund's expenses. This is a major mistake. And guess what? The mutual fund industry is counting on this. Frankly, fees for the fund industry have been getting heftier because customers aren't complaining. Anybody who ever took Economics 101 in college can appreciate that fees should really be slimming down. With the customer base swelling, the economy-of-scales principle would suggest that the costs of doing business are dropping, not going up.

The following are the average annual mutual fund expense ratios:

1. Growth funds   1.52%
2. Bond funds   .96%
3. Small cap funds   1.49%
4. Foreign funds   1.7%
5. Index funds   .51%

Source: Lipper Analytical Services

While you're checking fees, also look for this hidden gem—the 12b-1 fee. This controversial fee pays for a fund's marketing costs. If a fund charges one, I'd think twice before choosing it. Why should we pay a premium so that mutual funds can pelt

Bright Idea
If you have two funds you like and they seem equal in every way, pick the one with the lowest fees. You should steer clear of funds that generate fees that exceed the industry's average.

prospective investors with slick, unsolicited junk mail or pay for television commercials? Believe it or not, fund companies have even advertised during Super Bowl games.

How does this fund fit in with my time horizons and my tolerance for risk?

Will this fund provide better diversification or duplicate something I already own? Unfortunately, most people don't ask these sorts of questions. They look for the hot funds and then jump aboard without determining if it's a smart move. You can read more about fund investing blunders in Chapter 6, "Mutual Funds—Don't Invest Without 'Em."

How long has the fund manager been running the show?

Maybe you've located a fund with low expenses and a sterling track record and you're itching to buy shares.

Make sure that the person who is running the fund is actually the one responsible for the great performance. It's not unusual for a fund manager blessed with a golden touch to be recruited by another fund company so he can perform his magic there, too. That's fine and dandy unless you're stuck at the old fund with an untested new replacement. Avoid a fund with a new manager unless his own record is equally good.

Is the fund I like already too crowded?

Yes, funds can get too big. Fidelity's Magellan fund provides the most famous example. While Peter Lynch, the fund world's equivalent of basketball's Michael Jordan, was at the helm from 1977 to 1990, Magellan was smoking. It finished up the 1980s as the decade's top-performing fund. This amazing performance was hardly a secret. With so many

Unofficially... When portfolio managers hop from one fund company to another, their track records sometimes accompany them. For instance, when Elizabeth Bramwell left Gabelli Growth Fund, she transferred her old Gabelli track record to her new fund, Bramwell Growth Fund. The SEC has been reviewing whether this practice should remain kosher.

wannabe millionaires signing on, Magellan swelled into the biggest fund in America. That was great for Fidelity, but not so great, as it turned out, for its customers. The fund, which today has $72 billion in assets, could no longer be nimble. So what was the problem? Too much cash. If Lynch's predecessors found a handful of great stocks to buy, it wouldn't move the fund's price up. With so many billions to invest, Magellan didn't need a few nifty stock ideas, it needed hundreds of fabulous stocks. Here's another way to look at this dilemma: It's a lot easier to name the five most special people in your life than it is to name your 1,000 favorite people. Not surprisingly, Magellan's returns began lagging, and Lynch's successors found themselves unable to come close to duplicating his feat. Ultimately, Fidelity, in a move that acknowledged that the fund was too big, finally closed it to new investors.

Magellan isn't an aberration. Not long ago, for instance, the company that runs the Franklin Templeton funds swallowed up the highly celebrated Mutual Series mutual funds. With energetic marketing, billions more have flowed into these funds since the merger. But as the money keeps coming, Michael Price, the creator of the six Mutual Series funds, has been talking out loud about closing one or more of them. Once again their performance is dragging. And just this month, Fidelity announced it was closing three more of its most popular funds. This was great news for me, since I've owned shares in one of the funds, Fidelity Contrafund, since 1991. Contrafund has always been one of my favorites—with a 10-year record of 23 percent annual gains—the fund is the number-one growth performer of the decade. Yet with Contrafund's size ($30.8 billion in assets) too

Watch Out!
Size is especially important for funds that specialize in small cap companies. Ideally, you'd like to be in a small cap fund with no more than $1 billion in assets, because it would be hard for the manager to invest all that money in excellent companies.

unwieldy, its once superb numbers were beginning to erode. I had toyed with pulling out of the fund, but now I'll sit tight.

When should I bail out of a fund?

Selling a fund can be tougher than buying, and you can blame it all on those darn emotions. If a fund has been nothing but a curse for years, you might be tempted to hang on until you can at least break even. This is not a good idea. But there are plenty of good reasons to abandon a fund.

Here are some simple sell signals:

- Your fund has posted mediocre returns for at least two years, while other, similar funds have done much better.

- The manager who produced great results has left the fund.

- The fund's investment style has radically changed.

Buying and selling mutual fund shares

Okay, once you've made your decision, the next steps are pretty easy.

To buy mutual fund shares, just fill out the application form you received after calling the fund company's toll-free number for the sales literature. On the form, you are asked to check off certain options, such as the ability to redeem shares by telephone.

Another alternative is buying mutual funds through a brokerage firm's mutual fund supermarket. You'll learn all about this one-stop shopping by reading Chapter 11, "Investing on the Run: Sure-Fire Shortcuts."

Don't be discouraged if you don't have much cash at the start. Some fund companies that require minimum initial deposits of $2,500 or $3,000 make exceptions. If you agree to set up a $50-a-month (or higher) automatic investment with the fund, the higher minimums sometimes are waived. You'll also find that your initial investment often is lower for an Individual Retirement Account or an account you establish for your child.

Redemption

If you are lucky, you will be able to redeem your shares by telephone. If not, you need to send in a written request. Be sure to include in the letter your name, address, account number, fund name, and the dollar amount or number of shares you want to redeem. If you and your spouse's names are on the account, you both need to sign the letter. Before you mail it, call the fund's toll-free number to see if any other information is required. While you're on the phone, double check which address the redemption needs to be sent to. A fund can take up to seven days after it receives your redemption request to send your money.

Wire transfers

If you need your cash in a hurry, have it sent to you by wire. If you make the request before 4 p.m. Eastern Standard Time, you can usually have your money in your own bank account the next day. To take advantage of this quick method, you have to make arrangements in advance. The best time to do this is when you are purchasing a mutual fund. The paperwork you fill out typically asks if you want to be able to wire any proceeds to your bank. (You can wire deposits, too.) If so, you fill out your bank account information and send along a voided check with your account number on it.

Watch Out!
Think twice about purchasing mutual fund shares late in the year. This is usually when funds distribute their capital gains to share-holders. You might end up having to pay a whole year's worth of capital gains on an investment you've only owned a short time. It doesn't matter, however, what time of year you buy a fund in a retire-ment account, since you don't have to pay income taxes until you with-draw the money.

You can also pull cash out of a fund by transferring it to a money market within the same fund family. With check-writing privileges through the money market, you can withdraw your proceeds this way, or keep the money in the money market until you need it. Another possibility is to transfer the money from one fund to another in the same fund family.

Trade date

The day the fund receives your sell order isn't necessarily the day you sell it. If the request is received on a weekend, holiday, or after the stock market closes, the sale is posted on the next business day.

The ultimate investing decision: buy, sell, or hold

Do stockpickers trade too much? It's an interesting question that perhaps only a guy working on his Ph.D. would have time to explore. And what do you know, somebody at the University of California, Berkeley, did devote his thesis to the question. After poring through trading records for 10,000 accounts at a large—unnamed—discount brokerage, his conclusion was, yes, we are selling way too often. This is what he discovered: The stocks that were sold in those 10,000 portfolios actually outperformed the ones that were bought to replace them. What does this mean? You are better off holding your securities for the long term rather than trading frequently. And it certainly reinforces the admonition to give every stock trade a lot of careful, unemotional thought.

Now with that cautionary tale behind us, I'm going to share the nitty-gritty mechanics of buying and selling stocks. Buying stocks is obviously the first part of the equation.

For most people, buying and holding makes the most sense. If the stock you own keeps growing at a steady pace, continues to introduce innovative products, and remains a leader, there is little reason to sell. You also shouldn't sell solid stocks when they drop along with the entire market. (You'll find a lot of stock-buying tips in Chapter 7, "Research—The Investing Advantage.") There will be times, however, when selling is advisable.

Here are a few classic sell signals to consider:

- **A bad change in management occurs.** One of the most reliable predictors of a company's growth and success is its management team. Consequently, Wall Street often rewards a struggling company with a bump up in its stock price when a mediocre chief executive officer leaves. But management musical chairs isn't always a good omen. You personally won't be able to assess whether the new guys in the boardroom are first-rate, but you can keep track of what experts are saying in the press about a shift in the regime. When the former Hollywood super-agent Michael Ovitz left Disney after a controversial tenure, crocodile tears were shed. But if Disney's CEO and Mickey Mouse's indispensable partner, Michael Eisner, walked away, the stock price would surely tumble.

- **You hear about declining profit margins and other bad news.** Even the best companies experience a bad quarter or two. Maybe the profit margin shrinks a little. Sales falter a bit. If misfortune seems to strike in more than two consecutive quarters, you could be facing a real problem. I've heard this referred to as the *cockroach theory*. When there is one piece of bad

Bright Idea
If you're not sure whether to sell, you can always hedge your bet. Sell part of your holdings and keep the rest. Not sure whether to buy? Consider acquiring stock through dollar cost averaging, which you'll read about in Chapter 11.

news, often others are hiding under the refrigerator.

▪ **The competition is gaining ground.** A company can have the best product in the world, but stockholders shouldn't assume that it will maintain its leadership edge forever. Competitors will be working furiously to knock the number one leader off its pedestal.

U.S. Surgical, which was the king of the surgical-staple market, provides a classic example of this phenomenon. Back in the 1991, U.S. Surgical was the darling of momentum traders. At the start of that year, the stock was trading in the mid 50s, but by January 1992, the bloated stock sold for as high as $134½. Thrilled with the stock's performance, investors—including surgeons who used U.S. Surgical's products—were blind to the company's big vulnerability. Johnson & Johnson, the medical-supply behemoth, had launched an attack on U.S. Surgical with its own product.

By February 1994, U.S. Surgical's stock price plummeted to less than $16, which amounted to a stunning 88 percent decline over just two years. And U.S. Surgical is still trying to dig itself out of that deep hole. Recently, the company earned the dubious distinction of winning a spot on the top 10 list of worst stock performers for the past five years. Its five-year average return was negative 15.3 percent.

▪ **The company becomes too dependent on one product.** That's what happened in the 1960s when Brunswick Corp., the bowling-alley supplier, was considered a hot stock. It's an old example, but still a great one. The automatic bowling-pin remover was a real boon to the company, but they had nothing splashy in the wings. After every bowling alley installed them, the growth stopped.

- **The investing herd has bid the price up to outrageous levels.** If the P/E ratio is running well ahead of a stock's annual growth rate, it's time to think about dumping it. If you really like the stock, you might consider selling some of your shares at the high price to lock in some profits. If the price does fall back down, you can get in at the cheaper price.

The stock-buying (and selling) guide for cheapskates

My friend Ted trades stock all the time. Charles Schwab, his discount broker, loves him. In fact, it's given him its equivalent of a gold card. As a heavy hitter, Ted can get all sorts of stock reports faxed to him free. One time, I mentioned to him a company that intrigued me that happened to be the number one seller of cordless headsets in the country. Later in the day, my fax machine was tied up for 15 minutes—until it ran out of paper—with research reports on the California company that Ted had gotten from Schwab.

People like Ted are keenly interested in getting the cheapest discount brokerage rates because they trade a lot. If you're interested in discount and Internet trading, flip back to Chapter 3, "Financial Planners and Brokers—The Best of the Bunch." But most investors aren't as fixated on stocks as my very helpful friend. There are plenty of people who are content to buy one or two stocks a year with every intention of holding on for a long, long time. If you

Moneysaver
Do you know what your trade is going to cost? It will trigger commission costs, but what you owe your broker could be puny compared to your tax bill. If you haven't owned your stock very long, it can sometimes make sense to hold on just a little bit longer. You'll owe less capital gains tax if you keep the stock for more than 18 months.

fit that category or you'd like to add small amounts to your holdings on a regular basis, you might be interested in the cheapskate way to buy stocks. (Don't expect your broker to tell you about it.) It's called a *dividend reinvestment plan,* or DRIP. The name can be something of a misnomer, because DRIPs can go beyond allowing you to reinvest dividends in stocks you own. In fact, some companies that sponsor these plans don't even generate dividends.

What's appealing about these plans is that you don't need a broker to buy shares. Obviously, you can save a lot of commissions doing it this way. If you buy 200 shares of a $50 stock the old-fashioned way, for instance, it can cost you $150 to $200 through a full-service broker and perhaps $60 for a discount brokerage.

For many DRIPS, however, you need a broker's help to buy the first share. But the good news is that there is an increasing number of companies that will sell you that initial share directly. You often see these programs referred to as *direct purchase plans.* These plans have become more popular in the last two or three years, as the Securities and Exchange Commission eased restrictions that had kept companies from selling shares directly to the public. At least 200 companies now offer direct purchase plans, and more are joining in all the time.

Here's a partial list of prominent companies that allow you to bypass a broker and buy your first shares directly from them. You'll also see what the minimum initial purchase is.

COMPANIES' MINIMUM INITIAL STOCK PURCHASE

AFLAC: $750

AirTouch Communications: $500

Ameritech: $1,000

Amoco: $450

Bell Atlantic: $1,000

Chevron: $250

Gillette: $1,000

Home Depot: $250

IBM: $500

Lucent Technologies: $1,000

Mattel: $500

McDonald's: $1,000

Merck: $350

Procter & Gamble: $250

Tribune Co.: $500

Tyson Foods: $250

Here's a glimpse at how one of these purchase plans works. Let's say you want to buy stock in Sears, Roebuck & Co. Luckily, this Illinois retailer will sell you shares directly. You call the company shareholders' toll-free number—(800) 732-7780—and say you want information on its reinvestment plan. Within 7 to 10 days, you receive Sears's prospectus in the mail, along with paperwork to get you started. The prospectus explains the process for buying shares, how they are priced, the process for selling shares, and any fees. Be sure to read it. After you complete the paperwork and mail in your check, you receive a confirmation when your initial shares have been purchased. Sears requires that your first purchase be at least $500. If you want, you can buy shares from Sears as often as once a week. And if you have deep pockets and really love Sears, you can purchase up to $150,000 worth each year. And all this is commission-free.

Timesaver
The American
Association of
Individual
Investors pub-
lishes an annual
DRIP directory,
*The Individual
Investor's Guide
to Dividend
Reinvestment
Plans.* Call (800)
428-2244.
There's also the
*Standard & Poor's
Directory of
Dividend
Reinvestment
Plans,* which you
can get by
calling (800)
221-5277. For a
great book on
the topic, read
*Buying Stocks
Without a Broker,*
by Charles B.
Carlson.

Sears, like a lot of participating corporations, offers all sorts of options to make investing with them more tempting. For instance, you can designate that your dividends not be reinvested. You'll receive those dividends in the mail instead. Or you can split it up. You can tell Sears that you want to reinvest some dividends and pocket the rest. Sears also lets you set up an automatic investment plan. The company withdraws an agreed-on amount of money from your bank each month to buy more shares. Sears is one of the few companies that allows you to set up an Individual Retirement Account through its direct purchase plan.

Amazingly, you can even buy some DRIPs at a discount. A few companies, Sears isn't one of them, sell you shares with discounts of up to 5 percent. One company, York Financial Corp., gives you a 10 percent discount on your dividend reinvestment purchases. Of course, buying stocks is not the same as hunting for bargains at a garage sale. Investing in companies just because you get a break on the sale price is a terrible way to pick stocks. You should know that the companies that offer the discounts are not exactly household names. The discounters include ADAC Laboratories, Aquarion Co., Bay View Capital Corp., Blount International Inc., ReliaStar Financial Corp., and United Mobile Home, Inc.

The beauty of these plans is that you can accumulate small amounts of stocks on a regular basis without being gouged by brokers. Buying $100 worth of Sears stock every month wouldn't make financial sense if you did it another way.

One of the gripes you'll hear about this stock-purchasing strategy, however, is that penny pinchers can't hold a diversified portfolio of companies. For starters, the nimble small cap companies don't show up on the lists. So putting all your money in DRIPS automatically prevents you from investing in what historically has been the most dynamic part of the market. The DRIP lists are jam-packed with utility and bank stocks. The latest DRIP survey by the *American Association of Individual Investors* (AAII) revealed that banks and utilities represent 43 percent of the 853 firms it surveyed. This is completely out of whack with their actual presence on the stock exchanges. These plans are also slanted toward instantly recognizable consumer juggernauts like Johnson & Johnson, Procter & Gamble, and General Mills. On the other hand, choices in some sectors are scarce. You'll have an especially tough time finding many technology stocks or healthcare choices.

The following are prominent no-load stocks in various industries:

Bright Idea
If you are a DRIP fan and are plugged into the Internet, try visiting www.netstockdirect.com. This Web site provides you with an exhaustive list of participating companies. Through the site, you can learn everything you need to know about a particular company's DRIPs.

Computers/Technology
Intel
Lucent Technologies
IBM

Consumer Goods
Mattel
Kimberly-Clark
Anheuser-Busch
American Greeting

Media
Knight-Ridder Inc.
Time Warner
Tribune Co.
Times Mirror

Utilities
Public Service Co. of Colorado
Wisconsin Energy
Carolina Power & Light
New England Electric System

Energy
Exxon
Texaco
Mobil

Financial
Chase Manhattan
Wells Fargo
American Express

Looking at a sampling of no-load companies on these pages, you might be thinking, *It sure looks like there are plenty of choices, what's terrible about sticking with them?* A lot of companies in the DRIP universe, to put it kindly, are mature. They pay dividends because their fastest-growing years are behind them. So sure, DRIP investors get dividends, but at a cost. The growth-and-earnings rate might very well be subpar. The AAII analysis of DRIP stocks, for example, showed that the annual earnings-per-share growth of DRIPS was 11 percent, compared to 14.4 percent for non-DRIPs. For DRIP corporations, sales were expanding at 6.3 percent a year, compared with 12.6 percent for the others.

Buying stock this way is not necessarily free. Some companies levy a fee, such as $15, to join, and you might have to pay transaction charges. Traditionally, the maximum charge has often been no more than $2.50, but the fees have increased lately. For instance, Merck, the pharmaceutical giant, charges $5 for any new DRIP purchase. It pays to find out what the costs will be up front so you can decide whether buying this way makes sense.

Before you buy, you should find out how fast you could dump the stock. In the past, buy and sell transactions were limited to what computer users derisively call *snail mail*. Relying on the mail carrier to be the middleman was an achingly slow process. And a crap shoot. Especially with the markets so volatile, would you feel comfortable mailing in a sell order? Probably not. Luckily, many companies now let you phone in your sell orders.

DRIPs overseas

DRIPs are not just an American trend. Foreign companies also compete for your dollars. According to one head count, at least 136 overseas corporations will sell you shares without a broker. Don't worry—you won't have to make any international calls. The foreign DRIP programs operate on American soil. Sony, Volvo, British Airways, Ericsson Telephone, and Royal Dutch Petroleum are a few of the huge multinationals that participate. Instead of buying shares directly in overseas markets, you can buy them through *American Depository Receipts* (ADRs) in the United States.

The receipts for the foreign shares are held in the vaults of U.S. banks. ADRs are traded on the New York and American stock exchanges, as well as the NASDAQ. Someone who buys an ADR for British Airways, for instance, is entitled to the same dividends and capital gains that a shareholder in Great Britain enjoys. Most companies that sell shares through ADRs are the more established, global corporations. ADRs are listed in the *Wall Street Journal* and other newspapers in dollars so they reflect the current currency exchange rates.

Mechanics of stock sales

If you don't trade with DRIPs, you need to know more about stock trading. Before calling your brokerage firm, you have to know how you want to execute your trade. It's best to understand what your two main choices are so you don't have to make a snap decision on the phone.

Market orders

If it's really important that you buy or sell stock immediately, this is the way to go. By placing a market order, you instruct your broker to make the trade at the best price available at the time you call. With a market order, you can often pick up shares or dump some within minutes after hanging up the

Timesaver
Two main sources for ADR DRIPs are the Bank of New York and Morgan Guaranty Trust. Here's how to reach both: J. P. Morgan Guaranty Trust, Shareholder Services, P.O. Box 8205, Boston, MA 02266-8205; (800) 749-1687; www.jpmorgan. com. Bank of New York, Global Buy Direct, Shareholder Relations Department, P.O. Box 11258, Church Street Station, New York, N.Y. 10286-1258; (800) 943-9715; www.bankofny. com/adr.

phone. By far, this is the most popular way to trade stocks.

Limit orders

Nervous Nellies often prefer to use these. If you're worried that a stock will explode in price before your broker can buy it, a limit order can protect you. You can use a limit order when you're selling stock as well. With a limit order, you set your own price. For example, let's suppose that Coca-Cola is trading at $66 a share, but you won't touch it unless it inches down to $64 a share. If you place a limit order at $64, you won't own Coca-Cola unless the price drops that low or lower. With limit orders, however, you run the risk of never making a trade. For instance, if Coca-Cola is trading at $64\frac{1}{8}$ on the New York Stock Exchange, your broker cannot pick up the shares for you. Yet if you are buying 100 shares, the difference between the two prices is puny.

The investment club I belong to learned the hard way how limit orders can backfire. Not so long ago, we were congratulating ourselves for being smart enough to buy a California health maintenance organization called PacifiCare Health. Investing when the shares were selling for $49 each, we watched delightedly as the value of each one escalated to $96. But that's when we started to get worried. We decided the stock was overvalued and we should bail out. Our instincts were correct, but our limit order was lousy. We instructed our broker—Jack White & Co.—to sell our stake for $99 a share. As it turns out, we missed unloading our shares by 25 cents. Boy, were we sorry! What happened next wasn't pretty. PacifiCare's stock price disintegrated. We eventually unloaded the stock at $52 a share.

Using a limit order could have been a smart trading strategy the day after that 554-point stock market free fall in October 1997. With so many stocks decimated, lots of people were eager to snatch up shares at fire-sale prices the following morning. But with the market regaining 337 points the next day, the bargain you thought you were buying with a market order might not have been a good deal after all. With a limit order, you could have set a ceiling for how high you were willing to pay.

Stop orders

Brokers usually don't tell you about this option. Why? Because it's more of a hassle for them. Stop orders simply protect gains or limit the losses. When the markets are quite volatile, stop orders might help restless investors sleep soundly. Worried about the turbulence of technology stocks, you place a stop sell order on your Intel shares for $58. The price right now is $70. If the market tanks, you pretty much know what your worst loss will be. The stop order won't ensure that your stock will be sold at the exact price you set. In a fast-declining market, your shares could be executed at a lower price. Some investors place stop sell orders that are 10 percent below the current value of a share. You should ask yourself if you want to be a seller when prices are plummeting.

You can place a stop order for just one day, or you can keep it in effect indefinitely. These kind are referred to as *good-till-canceled orders*. There is a downside to stop orders. If you have one in place when the market takes a momentary dive—just a blimp on the radar screen—you will have sold your shares prematurely.

Bright Idea
Placing orders in off-hours can be dicey. Crazy things happening overnight in the Asian or European markets might trigger the U.S. markets to open dramatically higher or lower. To protect yourself, you can place a limit order.

Buying bonds without a broker

Unfortunately, trading bonds can be more difficult than buying and selling stocks. For starters, you won't find many bond prices in the newspaper. To buy or sell most bonds, you typically need a broker. (Both full-service and discount brokers can help you.) But be prepared to pay more than brokerage fees if you like individual bonds. A hidden cost lurks each time you buy and sell individual corporate and municipal bonds. You aren't paying what the bond is actually worth on the open market; rather, you're paying a little more. In the bond world, that difference—between the value of the bond and the actual sale price—is called the *spread*.

Luckily, there is one kind of bond you can buy direct and there is no nasty markup. In fact, there's no sales charge. Yes, I'm talking about U.S. Treasuries. Treasuries, which come with differing maturities, are the country's most creditworthy bonds. While the federal government has never been a poster child for efficiency and innovation, the nation's bond bureaucrats have done something right. They recently made buying Treasuries, which was already fairly painless, even easier for you folks at home.

To buy Treasuries direct from the source, just call the nearest Federal Reserve branch and order the forms. You also can download the necessary forms from the U.S. Treasury's Web site at www. publicdebt.treas.gov. In the fall of 1998, investors actually began buying Treasuries over the Internet.

The following is a list of Federal Reserve bank branches and contact numbers:

Atlanta   (404) 521-8653

Baltimore   (410) 576-3300

Birmingham	(205) 731-8708
Boston	(617) 973-3810
Buffalo	(716) 849-5000
Charlotte	(704) 358-2410
Chicago	(312) 322-5369
Cincinnati	(513) 721-4794
Cleveland	(216) 579-2000
Dallas	(214) 922-6770
Denver	(303) 572-2473
Detroit	(313) 964-6157
El Paso	(915) 521-8272
Houston	(713) 659-4433
Jacksonville	(904) 632-1179
Kansas City	(816) 881-2883
Little Rock	(501) 324-8272
Los Angeles	(213) 624-7398
Louisville	(502) 568-9238
Memphis	(901) 523-7171
Miami	(305) 471-6497
Minneapolis	(612) 340-2075
Nashville	(615) 251-7100
New Orleans	(504) 593-3200
New York City	(212) 720-6619
Oklahoma City	(405) 270-8652
Omaha	(402) 221-5636
Philadelphia	(215) 574-6680
Pittsburgh	(412) 261-7802
Portland	(503) 221-5932
Richmond	(804) 697-8372

Salt Lake City	(801) 322-7844
San Antonio	(210) 978-1305
San Francisco	(415) 974-2330
Seattle	(206) 343-3605
St. Louis	(314) 444-8703
Washington, D.C.	(202) 874-4000

Timesaver
Do you have a burning question about U.S. Treasuries or savings bonds and don't know where to turn? Check out these government Web sites for the answers: www.publicdebt.treas.gov or www.savingsbonds.gov.

The Federal Reserve sends you an information packet to get you started. You need to fill out a tender form that asks for the type of security you want to buy (see the figure on the next page). Let's say you want a three-year note. On the line that says **par amount,** you fill in how much you want to invest. In this case, you could write **$3,000.**

Next you have to instruct the Federal Reserve whether your bid is noncompetitive or competitive. You are bidding for your securities, because you'll be buying them at an auction—these IOUs will be hot off the presses. The federal Bureau of Public Debt holds more than 150 auctions a year to sell its assortment of bills, notes, and bonds. If you check the Noncompetitive box, you simply agree to buy the note at whatever yield is set at the auction. This is the only way you are guaranteed a note. Most individual investors prefer this route. It's the institutional players who try to get a better deal by naming their price.

The rest of the form is pretty much self-explanatory. You're asked to indicate how you intend to purchase the securities. Personal checks must be certified, and cash can only be accepted if you pay in person. You also can pay by reinvesting Treasuries that mature on or before the auction. You need to pencil in your bank account number so that all the money generated by your holdings can

A form for buying U.S. Treasuries direct.

PD F 5381
Department of the Treasury
Bureau of the Public Debt

OMB No. 1535-0069

TREASURY BILL, NOTE & BOND TENDER

TREASURY DIRECT®

For Tender Instructions, See PD F 5382

TYPE OR PRINT IN INK ONLY – TENDERS WILL NOT BE ACCEPTED WITH ALTERATIONS OR CORRECTIONS

DEPARTMENT USE

TENDER NO.

RECEIVED BY/DATE

1. BID INFORMATION Tender amount must meet or exceed the minimum for the term selected below. (Must Be Completed)

Par Amount:

Bid Type: (Fill in One)

$ _____

○ Noncompetitive

○ Competitive at |_|_|_|.|_|_|_| %
(Bid bids must end in 0 or 5.)

ENTERED BY

2. TREASURY DIRECT ACCOUNT NUMBER
(If NOT furnished, a new account will be opened.)

|_|_|_|-|_|_|_|-|_|_|_|

3. TAXPAYER ID NUMBER (Must Be Completed)

|_|_|_|-|_|_|-|_|_|_|_| OR |_|_|-|_|_|_|_|_|_|_|
Social Security Number (First-Named Owner)   Employer ID Number

APPROVED BY

4. TERM SELECTION (Fill in One)
(Must Be Completed)

Treasury Bill   Circle the Number of
$10,000 Minimum   Reinvestments

○ 13-Week.........0   1   2   3   4
           5   6   7   8

○ 26-Week.........0   1   2   3   4

○ 52-Week.........0   1   2

Treasury Note/Bond
$5,000 Minimum

○ 2-Year Note

○ 3-Year Note

$1,000 Minimum

○ 5-Year Note

○ 10-Year Note

○ 30-Year Bond

○ Inflation-Indexed

      Term

5. ACCOUNT NAME Please Type or Print! (Must Be Completed)

6. ADDRESS (For new account or if changed.)   ○ New Address?

     City   State   ZIP Code

ISSUE DATE

CUSIP 912794-

CUSIP 912827-

CUSIP 9128-10-

FOREIGN ☐

BACKUP ☐

7. TELEPHONE NUMBERS (For new account or if changed.)   ○ New Phone Number?

Work ( ) ____ - ____   Home ( ) ____ - ____

8. DIRECT DEPOSIT INFORMATION (For new account only.)   Changes? Submit PD F 5178.

Routing Number |_|_|_|_|_|_|_|_|_|

Financial Institution Name _____

Account Number |_|_|_|_|_|_|_|_|_|_|_|_|_|_|_|_|

Name on Account _____

Account Type: (Fill in One)   ○ Checking   ○ Savings

9. PURCHASE METHOD
(Must Be Completed)

○ **Automatic Withdrawal**
(Existing Treasury Direct Account Only)

○ Cash: $_____

○ Checks: $_____

       $_____

○ Securities: $_____

Total Payment
Attached: $_____
CHECKS ARE DEPOSITED IMMEDIATELY

REVIEW ☐

CHECK #

10. AUTHORIZATION (Must Be Completed – Original Signature Required)
Tender Submission: I submit this tender pursuant to the provisions of Department of the Treasury Circulars, Public Debt Series Nos. 2-86 (31 CFR Part 357) and 1-93 (31 CFR Part 356), and the applicable offering announcement. As the first-named owner and under penalties of perjury, I certify that the number shown on this form is my correct taxpayer identification number and that I am not subject to backup withholding because (1) I have not been notified that I am subject to backup withholding as a result of a failure to report all interest or dividends, or (2) the Internal Revenue Service has notified me that I am no longer subject to backup withholding. I further certify that all other information provided on this form is true, correct and complete.

Automatic Withdrawal: (If using this purchase method.) I authorize a debit to my account at the financial institution I designated in TREASURY DIRECT to pay for this security. I understand that the purchase price will be charged to my account on or after the settlement date. I also understand that if this transaction cannot be successfully completed, my tender can be rejected and the transaction canceled. If there is a dispute, a copy of this authorization may be provided to my financial institution.

_____
Signature(s)

_____
Date

SEE BACK FOR PRIVACY ACT AND PAPERWORK REDUCTION ACT NOTICE

be electronically deposited into your account. After the form is filled out, you send it to your nearest Federal Reserve or the federal Bureau of the Public Debt. You get a list of all the addresses in your information packet.

Here are some new features that make Treasury investing even easier:

■ Customers with existing accounts can direct the Treasury to withdraw money from their bank accounts to pay for their new securities. This eliminates a visit to the bank to get a certified check.

- You can now reinvest maturing Treasuries 24 hours a day, every day—even Christmas. Just call (800) 943-6864 and follow the step-by-step directions.

- Selling Treasuries has become a breeze. In the past, an investor faced the hassle of transferring the securities to a bank or broker. Now you just need to complete a form and send it to the Chicago Federal Reserve Bank. The Federal Reserve in Chicago obtains three price quotes from dealers and accepts the highest one. Your cost is $34.

Just the facts

- If you are picking mutual funds yourself, avoid load funds.

- Before buying a load fund, ask your broker six questions.

- Look for several warning signs before you sell a stock.

- For buy-and-hold investors, DRIPs can be a cheap way to purchase stocks.

- Before trading stocks, you need to know the rules of the road.

- You can save money buying Treasury bonds from the source.

PART IV

Decision-Making
Made Easy

GET THE SCOOP ON...
Indexing—the couch potato's answer ▪ Top
indexing myths ▪ Dollar cost averaging—Easy as
Simple Simon ▪ One-stop mutual fund shopping

Investing on the Run: Sure-Fire Shortcuts

I started taking shortcuts back in grade school. My friend and I would climb the fence of a neighbor, scoot down an alley, and then sneak through another backyard if we didn't spot the home German shepherd. It shaved five minutes off our walk to school. Kids, especially under the threat of no TV, create all sorts of shortcuts to clean their rooms or finish their homework. Yet even after we toss out our old Cliff notes, we never outgrow our love of cutting corners.

Whole industries cater to our addiction to shaving minutes from our chores. Automated teller machines are spreading like fungi in video stores, grocery stores, and hair salons so we don't have to visit the bank. In a van loaded down with balls, cleats, shin guards, and their respective owners, a stressed-out soccer mom can pull up to a grocery drive-through to buy a gallon of milk. You stop in front of a home for sale, tune into a certain

Chapter 11

frequency on the car radio, and hear a Realtor's spiel without ever wiping your feet on the welcome mat. Ironically, the lazy man's drive-through window at the fast-food restaurants is so clogged that the shortcut is now just ordering inside.

In love with shortcuts, it's only natural that Americans might feel indignant if there weren't quicker and easier ways to invest. Well, look no further. In this chapter, you'll find three huge time-savers for the chronically busy. Here are my nominations for the investing world's best time-management ideas:

- Indexing

- Dollar cost averaging

- Fund supermarkets

We'll explore why index funds are more popular with the American public than the quarterback of the Super Bowl champion could ever hope to be. I'll also share some common indexing myths and explain what percentage of your portfolio you might want to put into these funds. Despite academic critics' snickers, you'll also learn why dollar cost averaging is such a great way to invest. In addition, you'll find out why so many Americans are scrambling to put all their money into fund supermarkets. They are the perfect solution for all but the most impulsive investors. And in keeping with the theme of this section, I promise to keep this chapter short!

Index funds—the ultimate shortcut

On a busy day when George U. Sauter, who runs the second-most-popular mutual fund on the planet, had pitched in to answer customer service calls at the Vanguard Group, a critic was patched through. Sauter manages Vanguard's Index Trust 500

Portfolio, which has lately been humiliating thousands of other fund mangers with its spectacular returns. Everyone, however, is not impressed with his work. As Sauter listened, a caller, unaware of who he was talking to, blurted out, "Listen, you and I both know a monkey could run an index fund."

No actually, that's stretching it a bit. Somebody at the helm of an index fund can't be a dim bulb, but the rest of us can be. When you invest in index funds, you can pretty much cruise on autopilot. Once you stash your money in index funds, many of your decisions about investing are over. With your money tucked into one of these funds, you don't have to worry about whether the manager of your mutual fund is losing his golden touch. You don't have to fret about whether your portfolio is diversified. You don't even have to agonize about whether the fund's expenses are ridiculously high.

While index funds are now incredibly popular, this hasn't been so during most of their existence. The public largely ignored index funds, and the financial pundits scorned them. After all, they will never be flashy, and very rarely will they burst onto the lists of the hottest-performing funds. On the other hand, you can count on them to rarely be stuck in the cellar. Arguably, the index fund is a solid-B student. With index funds, you are guaranteed of doing just about as well as the stock market, year in and year out. If the market performs marvelously, so will you. When the market stinks, your returns will smell like last week's garbage. If this volatility unnerves you, remember that the stock market, despite occasional nasty bear markets, has always marched upward.

Here's how index funds work: An index fund seeks to match the returns of whatever benchmark its fate is tied to. By far, the most popular index funds are linked to the Standard & Poor's 500, which happens to contain 500 corporate heavyweights. With an S&P Index fund, a manager generally buys and holds stock in all 500 companies. Simple, isn't it? By mimicking the index, a manager can't hope to perform better than the index, but he can just about duplicate it. (A shareholder's returns will lag slightly behind the benchmark, because she'll have to pay the fund's annual expenses.) If you buy shares in a small cap index fund, it will often be tied to the performance of the Russell 2000, the classic benchmark for small stocks. There are also widely used benchmarks for foreign and bond index funds.

This passive investing approach remains an alien concept for most funds. In actively managed funds, money wizards try to outwit the market by furiously buying and dumping stocks. Unlike their index colleagues, these managers don't want to match the index, they want to pulverize it. But there's one problem. The vast majority of managers can't regularly beat the indexes. As you can see from this list, most funds don't even come close.

PERCENTAGE OF ACTIVELY MANAGED STOCK FUNDS THAT UNDERPERFORMED THE STANDARD & POOR'S 500 INDEX

Year	%	Year	%
1997	89.5%	1991	45%
1996	75%	1990	64%
1995	85%	1989	82%
1994	78%	1988	59%
1993	40%	1987	76%
1992	46%		

Source: Lipper Analytical Services, Inc.

But even this chart doesn't convey just how soundly indexers, with their autopilot strategy, can annihilate their peers. Recently, CDA/Wiesenberger, another mutual fund tracker, decided to find out how many funds beat the S&P 500 during each of the past 15 years. Guess what? Nobody did. Only one came even close. Davis New York Venture Fund, a load fund, outperformed the benchmark during 12 of the past 15 years. Only a handful outsmarted the index 9 out of 15 years.

There is another key reason why index funds can trample the competition. With index funds, you get a Mercedes on a Hyundai budget. While your index fund should generally do better than most of the competition, it can deliver those kinds of returns for a fraction of the other guy's costs. Throughout the industry, the average expense ratio for index funds is .51 percent. In contrast, the average growth fund charges 1.52 percent. The difference can be much wider than that. Customers in some actively managed foreign funds must pay more than 3 percent a year in expenses.

The expense spread might not seem like a big deal, but in the competitive mutual fund world, a one, two or even three percentage point advantage can make a huge difference. Imagine an Olympic sprinter having to start the 100-yard dash 10 feet behind everyone else. It's highly unlikely he'll win the race. That's the kind of disadvantage actively managed funds have. Here's another way to look at how expenses can erode a fund's performance. If your fund returns 12 percent and its expenses are 1.5 percent, fully 12.5 percent of your gain is consumed by expenses. And that doesn't include inflation or any applicable taxes.

Unofficially...
When Vanguard launched the country's first index fund in 1976, financial gurus, couldn't stop laughing. Between chuckles, they accused Vanguard of creating a fund that was doomed to mediocrity. Well, the joke's on them.

The cost advantage is even more important in the bond world where, let's face it, even the most talented, ambitious fixed-income genius is going to find it extremely difficult to pull away from the pack. Here's what I mean by that. With stock funds, you might have managers who post negative returns in the same year that some of their peers enjoy gains of 20 or 30 percent or more. With bond returns far less volatile as a rule, fixed-income managers' results tend to bunch up. So if you have 50 bond funds, which all rose 7 percent for the year before expenses were deducted, the one with the tiniest expense ratio soars ahead of the pack. The annual expense for the Vanguard Bond Index Fund, as an example, is close to a whole percentage point below the average competitor. In the bond world, this gulf might as well be as big as the Grand Canyon.

The incredible returns of the Vanguard Index Trust 500 Portfolio (30.4 percent annually during the past three years) and its many copycats have converted a lot of skeptics. Recently, $50 million or more a day was reportedly pouring into the Vanguard's flagship fund. In 1987, only five funds that track the S&P 500 existed. Today your choices exceed 80. The biggest source of index funds is Vanguard, which now offers 20 different kinds, including a mid cap, a variety of small cap funds and international ones.

Indexing's biggest myths

While index funds are hot, some true believers could very well be buying them for the wrong reasons. Before you invest in an index fund, acquaint yourself with these five common myths.

Index funds aren't as risky as other kinds.

Not true, and here's why: While a cautious manager of a regular fund might keep 5, 10, 15 percent, or more of his assets in cash for fear of a market correction, the index fund manager scorns cash. The aim of every index fund is to quickly put every last $50 check it gets into the stock market. Consequently when the market dives, index funds could decline more than many other funds because they don't have cash cushions.

This is what happened during that terrible fall of 1987. Back then, the average S&P 500 Index fund dropped 32.1 percent, while other stock funds slid, on average, 29 percent. It was the cash that the active fund managers had stashed in their portfolios that made the difference. It's not just nervousness that prompts these managers to cling onto some cash. Money managers may also keep some on hand to pay off investors who decide to sell their holdings. Cash also can build up while managers take their time looking for great stocks to invest in.

So far you've only heard why index funds can bruise easier than most when stocks are tanking. But on the flip side, index funds can rebound more quickly when the financial gloom evaporates and stocks perk back up. Why? Once again, cash is key. The indexers don't have any cash, which in turbo-charged markets would only drag the return down. In the year after the 1987 crash, for example, the S&P 500 indexers clocked a 25.4 percent return, beating the rest of the stock fund pack by almost 3.5 percent.

All index funds track the S&P 500.

It's easy to understand why so many people believe this. With the S&P 500 Index funds generating such

> 66
>
> I worry that since people focus on the S&P 500, when it has a mediocre year—as it inevitably will—people will say, "See indexing doesn't work." What they really mean, though they may not know it, is that large cap stocks did not outperform during that time.
> —George U. Sauter, Vanguard Group
>
>

Unofficially...
When the S&P
500 was intro-
duced in 1957,
all the compa-
nies in the pool
were traded on
the New York
Stock Exchange.
Later, companies
listed on the
American Stock
Exchange and
the NASDAQ were
invited to join
the elite group.
Today, the index
contains stocks
in approximately
103 different
industries, rang-
ing from pharma-
ceuticals to
aerospace to
trucking.

explosive returns, no one seems too curious about the other alternatives. And there are plenty. For instance, you can also purchase shares in indexes that attempt to mimic the return of the entire U.S. stock market, such as Vanguard's Total Stock Market Portfolio. Or you can invest in smaller companies with the Vanguard Small Capitalization Stock Portfolio or the Schwab Small-Cap Index Fund. There are even international and bond index funds. The Vanguard Total International Portfolio, for instance, invests in stocks in Europe, Asia, and emerging markets. Meanwhile, the Vanguard Bond Index Fund aims to mimic the entire bond market as measured by the Lehman Brothers Aggregate Bond Index.

Everyone seems to agree that placing indexing bets on large cap stocks works. But you should know that the jury remains deadlocked on the merits of small cap and foreign indexing. Picking out a small cap or foreign index fund is easier than hunting endlessly through the huge fund universe. But some experts say that individual stockpickers can outperform the mechanical stock selections of index funds because these markets are quirkier. Actually, economists prefer to call them "inefficient." The market for large American corporations is considered by many to be efficient—hordes of financial analysts follow the companies—so there are usually few surprises, and any news on these giants is swiftly reflected in their stock price. In contrast, small cap companies and many, many foreign outfits—particularly in Asia and the emerging markets—can often be ignored by analysts. Shrewd stockpickers can flourish in this kind of environment. By selecting the gems among the universe of under followed companies, a smart fund manager can pull ahead of the competition, as well as the appropriate index.

Arguably, foreign index funds are the most controversial. And strange as it might seem, you can blame Japan for that. Here's the explanation: To track the most popular foreign benchmark—the Morgan Stanley Capital International Europe, Australasia, and Far East Index—an index fund must include Japanese stocks. But with the Japanese market mired in a funk for years, active fund managers have kept Japanese corporations out of their portfolios. Consequently, index funds haven't looked good in comparison. But if you look at more specialized index funds (say the ones that invest in Europe and emerging markets), the scenario is much rosier for index boosters. During the past three years, for instance, Vanguard's European index fund has beaten 88 percent of its competitors.

What's the recommendation? If you aren't motivated to research actively managed funds in the more volatile sectors but you want the diversification, I'd stick with the index funds. The odds, despite Japan, favor indexes. Even if you get lucky and pick a great-performing foreign or small cap fund this year, it could very well do poorly the next year. Picking a fund that consistently beats its index is next to impossible. You also increase your chances of faring better with indexes because the costs of actively managed small cap and foreign funds are quite high.

S&P 500 Index funds will always wallop the competition.

Nobody at Vanguard dares to suggest that the dramatic returns of the S&P 500 Index funds will

Unofficially...
Despite all the publicity, indexing is still a midget player in the mutual fund universe. Today stock index funds only account for 3 percent of all the assets invested in equity mutual funds. Bond index funds represent only 1 percent of the fixed-income fund pie.

continue. In fact, John C. Bogle, Vanguard's founder, takes every opportunity on the talk circuit to warn fans that index funds are not a slam dunk.

One reason why the S&P Index funds have performed so well is because the Goliath corporations found in the index have had a tremendous run. (The S&P 500 represents 70 percent of the stock market's capitalization.) But in the early 1990s, when smaller stocks were the darlings of Wall Street, the S&P 500 Index funds didn't fare as well. In 1991, for example, 55 percent of actively managed stock funds beat the S&P 500 indexers. You can expect this phenomenon to repeat itself again in the future. That's because, over time, small cap stocks have consistently returned more than large caps, presumably because they must compensate investors more for their riskiness.

An index is an index is an index.

Not true. Just because index funds track a particular market doesn't mean they'll all post the same results. Believe it or not, there is some skill involved, but beyond that an index's expenses can ultimately decide the winners from the losers. The expense ratios for S&P 500 Index funds range as low as .18 percent to as high as 1.1 percent. If you want the cheapest expenses, stick with Vanguard.

One reason why Vanguard remains the undisputed indexing king is its Kmart prices. Since the returns of index funds, by their very nature, don't differ much, it's crucial to find one that operates with rock-bottom expenses. Vanguard, which enjoys about 60 percent of the index business, offers the lowest prices around.

Performance is the only reason to choose an index fund.

Anybody who hates paying a lot of taxes will also love these funds. Index funds buy and hold their stocks for a long time, so you are unlikely to ever see much selling. A large cap index fund will sell its shares in a company leaving the S&P 500 and will pick up shares in a corporation that is joining, but there isn't a heck of a lot of selling beyond that. This could change if many index fund investors bail out when the market enters a prolonged slump. Should this happen, a fund might be forced to sell some stocks to pay off departing shareholders. Normally, however, these funds don't generate a lot of capital gains. Fewer capital gains, which must be passed on to all shareholders, means you pay less each year at tax time. With the recent tax-law changes, this can be a real boon to tax-averse investors. When Congress tinkered with the capital-gains rules, short-term profits took a real hit. If an investment is held for a year or less, an investor must pay at a rate equivalent to his tax bracket for his gains. But if stocks are held more than 18 months, the capital gains tax is just 20 percent, and it's even less for those in the lowest tax bracket.

Shortcut #1: index investing strategies

If you are just getting started and only have enough money for one investment, an S&P 500 Index fund is a great beginner fund. You buy yourself exposure to America's largest and most stable corporations. Another way to use indexing is as a core fund.

You can go elsewhere for exposure to areas that indexes don't cover. For instance, some investors will want to pick an equity income fund that invests heavily in companies with above-average dividend

Watch Out!
If you notice that an index fund's return has soared beyond the others in its peer group, investigate closely. It's probably not a true index fund. What you've found is an *enhanced* index fund. These funds try to tweak the return by investing in such things as futures and options. Needless to say, they can be more volatile and their track record is mixed.

yields. You'd also look beyond indexing for funds that specialize in aggressive growth; junk bonds; municipal bonds; and single sectors such as technology, healthcare, the financial industry, utilities, and retailing. Even the folks at Vanguard don't think you should put everything in index funds. How much is enough? They recommend keeping 60 percent to 70 percent of your money in index funds.

Shortcut #2: dollar cost averaging

Do you waste a lot of time agonizing about when you should invest your money? The market just dropped 200 points, maybe I should hold off putting any more money in. Wall Street just soared to its all-time high. Surely this isn't a smart time, either. Does this sound familiar? If so, you're the perfect candidate for dollar cost averaging. For starters, with dollar cost averaging, you don't fret about when to invest, you just do it—automatically, a little bit at a time. It's not only easy, but it's quick and hassle-free.

The strategy is remarkably simple. You invest a certain amount of money each month or each quarter. The trick to making this method work is wearing blinders. If the market loses 20 percent of its value today, and it is your day to make that monthly investment, you're not going to chicken out. Here's an example of how this strategy can work. Let's imagine you inherit $25,000 from a distant relative. You can sink it all today into a company like Intel or Boeing. Or maybe you will put it all into one mutual fund. Of course, if Intel discovers a glitch in its latest semiconductor chip or Boeing loses a contract to build a fleet of European jets, the stocks could skid. Disgusted, you might never again fool with the stock market. The same thing could happen to your mutual fund if Wall Street collapses. Ultimately, you might decide that the only way to stop stewing about this windfall is to invest it chunk by chunk. You might buy $5,000 worth of shares in the Vanguard index fund and arrange to put an additional $2,000 a month into the account until the money is fully invested.

Frankly, economists do not like dollar cost averaging. In fact, they think it's a joke. It's not that they view dollar cost averaging as wimpy, it's just that this approach won't lock in the highest possible returns. Countless academic studies have shown that investing your entire enchilada in the stock market at one time will, in the long run, make you richer. At this point, you might be finding this hard to swallow. "Yeh, right," you're saying. "What about the poor slob who invests 24 hours before the market crashes? Surely he'd lose out big time!" But no, the economists insist. Even assuming the worst, gloomiest scenarios, the experts swear that we'd all do better investing in a one-lump sum. Of course, that's because of the stock market's long-term upward bias.

But these guys in the ivory tower don't necessarily appreciate human nature. There are plenty of reasons why dollar cost averaging makes sense. Here are a few.

Dollar cost averaging gives you the courage to invest in crazy markets.

If the stock market is getting battered, it's only natural to want to avoid the mayhem. Yet far too many people yank their money out of the market at the first sign of trouble. Of course, this is the wrong thing to do, because neither you nor I can predict when the market will rebound. If you dollar cost average, you'll still hate those paper losses, but you'll have a great consolation prize. With your ongoing monthly investments, you'll be able to buy at cheaper prices while the market is down.

Dollar-cost averaging can make it easier for rookies to take that first step.

The prospects of stock investing can be terrifying for anybody who has his money tied up in a passbook savings account. Dollar cost averaging can give folks like that the courage to get off the sidelines.

You can afford exclusive mutual funds.

Many funds won't take your money if you don't have at least $2,500 or $3,000 to get started. If you don't have that much, you can jump over that barrier with dollar cost averaging. Lots of funds waive their minimum requirements if you promise to invest a set amount each month.

Dollar cost averaging makes you more disciplined.

We all excel at frittering away our money, but dollar cost averaging takes away the temptation. Obviously, you can't spend the money you invest each month someplace else. The best way to force yourself to save is with an automatic withdrawal program.

Dollar cost averaging buys you time.

Let's say you've just left your job and have to decide how to invest your 401(k) money. It might take you a while to figure out what to do with all the money. In the meantime, you can put all of it in a money market and gradually shift it into a mutual fund while you're finishing your research.

Shortcut #3: one-stop fund shopping

Imagine what it would be like if you could buy milk at one store, but not peanut butter. Another store carries carrots, but not ice cream. And still another sells you cheese, but you have to go elsewhere for cereal. Hardly convenient, but that's what the mutual fund industry was like until not too long ago. If you wanted shares in the Janus Overseas Fund, you had to call the Denver fund family. If you also liked the Strong Opportunity Fund, you had to contact the Milwaukee operation. If the Hotchkis & Wiley International Fund in Los Angeles piqued your interest, once again, you needed to make another call. No mutual fund company could sell you more than their own investments. I can tell you, as one of the millions of investors who has held shares in more than three or four different fund families, the paperwork this generates can require its own filing cabinet. With so many different pieces of paper jammed into various manila folders, it can be tough at tax time.

But that's all behind us. Now you can shop for no-load funds the way you shop for food at a grocery store. You can buy them all in one place. With one phone call, you can request all the information you need about hundreds of funds. When you are ready to buy or sell funds, you can also accomplish this with one phone call. During the same conversation, you can transfer money between one mutual fund and another. Even better, all your fund holdings can be summed up on one piece of paper. How is this possible? You can thank fund supermarkets.

Within fund supermarkets, you can find an over-whelming assortment of hundreds of funds offered by fund families scattered from Boston to San Francisco. Fund supermarkets, of course, aren't really like the stores that bag your groceries. Most people never actually set foot in one. You'll find these fund supermarkets at all the leading discount

Unofficially...
According to the American Association of Individual Investors, 24 of these one-stop fund super-markets now exist. That's up from 15 just two years ago.

Unofficially...
Jack White, a discount broker-age firm based in San Diego, invented the supermarket fund concept in the mid-1980s. Back then, investors had to pay a fee for the privilege of this conve-nience. Charles Schwab, another discount broker, weighed in next with its own supermarket plan. Beginning in 1992, investors could buy many funds through discount brokerages with-out paying any fees at all.

brokerage firms. Some of the biggest fund families, such as T. Rowe Price, Vanguard, and Fidelity, also sell you competing funds through their own broker-age arms.

These supermarkets are actually located in the vast customer service rooms that sprawl from floor to floor at these brokerage firms. In cubicles across giant rooms, customer service reps wearing headsets take mutual fund orders from customers all across the country. If you want to buy the Fremont U.S. Micro-Cap Fund, no problem. During the same call, if you'd like information on the Strong Government Securities Fund, your rep makes sure it's dropped in today's mail. When you become disgusted with a fund, whoever answers the phone at the brokerage firm gets rid of that perennial loser for you, too.

If you like the idea of one-stop shopping, here's a list of financial institutions that can help you estab-lish an account:

AccuTrade	(800) 494-8939
American Express	(800) 297-8800
Charles Schwab	(800) 435-4000
Discover	(800) 688-3462
Dreyfus	(800) 843-5466
E*Trade	(800) ETRADE-1
Fidelity	(800) 544-9697
Fidelity Investments	(800) 544-9697
Jack White	(800) 233-3411
Muriel Siebert	(800) 872-0666
Scudder	(800) 700-0820
T. Rowe Price	(800) 638-5660
Vanguard Group	(800) 635-1511
Waterhouse Securities	(800) 934-4443

You'll probably recognize the names of some of the fund families sold through supermarkets. Here is just a short list: American Century, Invesco, Strong, PBHG, Neuberger & Berman, Oakmark, Dreyfus, Gabelli, Berger, Hotchkis & Wiley, Janus, Robertson Stephens, Stein Roe, and Warburg Pincus. You'll also find the little boutique funds that most investors don't even know exist, like Firsthand Technology Value Fund. This itty-bitty fund, which recently had a three-year annualized return of 41 percent, has earned raves from the financial press, but it's still not big enough to be listed in the *Wall Street Journal* or many other newspapers.

By now you might be asking yourself, *Where's the catch?* I know I did at first. I wondered what this convenience was going to cost me. Surely it wasn't free. When the fund supermarkets first opened their doors, customers were indeed charged a transaction fee. But happily that doesn't often happen anymore. Usually you aren't hit with a fee—at least not directly. Rather, these discount brokers make their money off the fund families themselves. Fund companies typically must pay the discount brokers operating these supermarkets $24 to $35 for every $10,000 in assets they sell.

Not surprisingly, Americans love this latest investing shortcut. Shoppers are flooding into these supermarkets. Here's just one example. Customers sank $1.8 billion into Charles Schwab's OneSource program during the first year of its operation in 1992. By the end of 1997, OneSource contained $56.6 billion, which represents an amazing jump of 34 percent just from the previous year.

Still unsure about what one-stop shopping can do for you? Here's why the aisles of these fund supermarkets are so crowded.

Watch Out!
Fund companies pass the costs for participating in these supermarkets on to all their customers by increasing the yearly expenses all of us pay. The Securities and Exchange Commission has been examining whether fund companies could be paying too much.

Keeping your money fully invested is much easier.

Let's say you want to pull $5,000 out of one fund and use it to buy into a fund located thousands of miles away. And let's pretend you want to do this without one of these one-stop middlemen. If you are lucky, the fund company will let you cash out your holdings with a phone call. But some companies insist that you make your request in writing. Some companies even require that you get a signature guarantee from a bank, which can be a real pain. A signature guarantee, which simply means your signature is authenticated by a third party, must be obtained at a bank or a New York Stock Exchange brokerage firm. Silly as it might seem, a notary public cannot provide a signature guarantee. Once you've accomplished all that, you have to wait for the company to receive your bailout notice in the mail. Then you have to wait a few *more* days until your mail carrier delivers your redemption check.

In the meantime, you need to contact the new fund company and request an application. Once you cash your redemption check, you need to wait for it to be credited to your account. Finally, you'll be able to write your own check and mail it to start your new account. Sound exhausting? Definitely. It can also be infuriating if the price of the fund that you want skyrockets while you get bogged down with all this paper rigamarole.

How would this scenario be different using a supermarket fund? Here's what would happen: You call your discount broker and instruct the telephone rep to sell shares in mutual fund A. Then you ask him to deposit the proceeds into mutual fund B. You're off the phone in less than five minutes. No muss. No fuss.

These one-stop shopping programs allow you to buy from among thousands of different mutual funds.
You'll find funds of every variety—from the safest short-term bond funds to the most heart-stopping emerging market funds and everything in between. And the shelves at these supermarkets are getting more crowded by the day.

Researching funds can be easier.
The discounters appreciate that many of their customers are going to be paralyzed by all their fund choices. So they try to make it as easy as possible for investors to make the best choices. They also help customers with their homework. For instance, Fidelity publishes a quarterly fund-screening guide that provides information on stock and bond funds that have received four- or five-star ratings from Morningstar. These funds must also enjoy high three-year annual returns. Meanwhile, Schwab provides anybody with its own quarterly all-star list for domestic, foreign, international, and asset allocation/balanced funds. You don't have to be a customer to receive these handouts, as well as the publications that list all of a network's fund offerings. It's also possible to research funds through some of the discount brokerage firms' Web sites.

It's not all nirvana

But supermarkets are not perfect. You will discover a few irritating disadvantages, and if you are prone to making impulsive investing decisions, these networks might not be for you. Here's one drawback: You might not find the fund you want. Some brokerages stock their shelves better than others. Through Charles Schwab, a giant in the field, you can invest in 1,400 different funds. Jack White, the

Timesaver
You generate a lot less paperwork with fund networks. Instead of receiving regular account statements from a variety of different funds, you file just one. You can check on the performance of all your funds by just scrutinizing one or two pieces of paper. And all tax data you need for your yearly federal and state taxes is summarized, too.

supermarket granddaddy, offers roughly 1,250 funds from 200 mutual fund companies. Some discount brokers, however, only carry a fraction of that number. Before you commit yourself, find out what funds each of these discounters offer. To do that, just call the toll-free number for each brokerage firm and ask for their no-fee supermarket literature. It will be sent to you free.

Alas, noticeably missing from this trend toward convenience shopping are three heavyweight holdouts. Vanguard, T. Rowe Price, and Fidelity, all no-load giants, have refused to play by the rules. All three have balked at paying fees to the discounters to peddle their funds. They all make the same argument against participating. If Vanguard, for instance, had to pay Charles Schwab a transaction fee every time the discount broker sold a fund on its behalf, the expense would become far too great to absorb. Consequently, Vanguard would have to bump up the yearly fees it charges all its customers, even those that never use a fund supermarket. If you prefer to buy a fund from this trio through a discount broker, you still can, but it will cost you more. Since the discounters aren't getting compensated by Vanguard and the other holdouts, you have to pay a transaction fee. At Charles Schwab, for instance, the basic charge is $39. You can whittle down this price by placing your order electronically or by using a touch-tone phone. The price also falls if you place a sizable order.

The privileges in these networks aren't always free. Discounters get irritated with antsy investors who love to flit in and out of funds. They have directed their ire at market timers, who are treated about as warmly as rattlesnakes. The discount brokers are doing all they can to chase these guys away. For instance, Schwab investors who sell shares within six months have to pay a typical redemption fee of $39. When somebody does this 15 times in one year, they are bounced from the program. Fidelity and others have cracked down as well.

Fund networks can lead to bad habits since the convenience can be mesmerizing. Because there's no paperwork or other hassles involved in trading through these one-stop fund sources, some investors buy and sell all too quickly. You have to remember to keep your eyes focused on your long-term investing goals.

Making the switch to a fund supermarket

Investing through a supermarket might sound good to you, but there could still be one nagging problem. What if your money is already scattered in mutual funds from Milwaukee to New York to Denver? Actually, it's possible to get all or most of your funds into a program like Fidelity's Funds Network or Schwab's OneSource. You have to fill out paperwork, but it could ultimately be worth it. Just place a call to the discount broker you want to establish an account with. The firm sends you an application, as well as a transfer form. On the form, you list the names of your fund, the account numbers, and the amount of shares you want transferred. The broker takes on the responsibility of contacting all your fund companies and notifying them of your request.

Of course, a firm like Schwab will only accept funds that it already carries in its inventory. If you own shares in proprietary Merrill Lynch or

Unofficially...
Distressed that so many people are buying funds through supermarket programs, fund companies are fighting back by setting up their own discount brokerage services. An increasing number of companies, including American Century, Lindner, Dreyfus, and Scudder, are hoping customers will stick with them since they now also offer funds from their competitors.

PaineWebber funds or any others sponsored by full-service brokers, you won't be able to transfer them. If you want that money in Schwab, you have to sell those shares.

Just the facts

- Shortcuts can make investing less painful.
- Don't believe those index-fund myths.
- Dollar cost averaging can give you the courage to invest.
- Fund supermarkets can make mutual fund investing a breeze.

GET THE SCOOP ON...
Tips for a cozy retirement ▪ His and her
401(k)s: how to coordinate them ▪
College investing strategies for your little
genius ▪ Never saved for college? Places to get
cash in a hurry ▪ Financial pitfalls during
divorce and remarriage

Strategies for Financial Success

Chapter 12

The team that annihilates the losers in the Super Bowl each year always starts the game with a strategy. You'd never dream of approaching your boss about a raise unless you had a strategy in mind. Even kids who hound their parents for a puppy have some kind of scheme in mind before they open their mouths. Strategies are an inevitable part of life. And they are absolutely essential if you expect to pay for some of the biggest-ticket items you will ever face. In the next few pages, you should get a better idea of how to face these looming challenges.

If you've already formulated some sort of financial blueprint in your brain, loaded it onto your computer's hard drive, or scribbled it on a yellow legal pad, that's great. Go to the head of the class, but don't necessarily go straight to the next chapter. You still might learn something in the next few pages that could help fine-tune your strategies for retirement, college savings, and even the cataclysmic event none of us likes to contemplate—no, I'm not talking about death. Try divorce. In this chapter, you'll learn tips about saving for retirement, and you can bone up on 401(k)s and IRAs as well. You'll also find out how you should bulk up on big bucks for college. And there's even some practical advice for the guilt-stricken parents who wait until Johnny has taken his SAT *(Scholastic Aptitude Test)* before they focus for the first time on the King Kong–size tab that awaits them. Finally, I'll provide some money tips for divorcing couples—so their split won't leave only their lawyers enriched.

Retirement strategies—better now than later

If you live long enough, one thing is certain—you will retire someday. Sure, there are probably a few 90-year-olds who haven't cleaned out their desks, but it's highly unlikely that you or I will be one of them. Since retirement is an inevitable part of most of our lives, it shouldn't have to sneak up on us. And the sooner we plan for the inevitable, the better off we'll be.

Entire books have been written about retirement planning, but all those millions of words of advice can be boiled down to a few key points. Here are the most important tips you'll ever read:

- Start saving for retirement now.

- Put the maximum amount allowed into your workplace's retirement plan. If you can't swing that, at least contribute enough to capture your employer's cash match.

- Contribute $2,000 each year to an IRA.

- Don't assume you can live on your future Social Security checks.

- Don't rely exclusively on bonds in your retirement portfolio.

- Review your investment strategy annually.

- Make sure your retirement investments are well diversified.

- Be consistent. Don't let any wild market gyrations spook you into halting your savings plan.

And here's another one to add to the list:

- Don't start banking Social Security checks until you're 65. (For some of us, that age will be 67.) You'll receive fatter checks if you wait longer. Here's something to ponder: 61 percent of retirees in a recent Gallup poll said they'd like to go back to work at some point.

Of course, one of the biggest questions on everyone's mind is how much is enough to save. If you start stashing money into your retirement accounts while you're in your twenties or thirties, you should be fine setting aside 10 percent of your pretax income every year. But that won't be the case with procrastinators. Somebody who waits until she's middle-aged could very well need to save 15 percent to 20 percent of her pretax income if she expects to be financially secure later on.

Anybody who wants to retire early has an even higher hurdle to jump. By one estimate, you can retire before you're 60 if you've faithfully saved 20 percent of your pretax salary for 25 years. (How many people do you know who have the discipline to pull this off?) This remarkable savings program should allow you to maintain your standard of living unless the Social Security system caves in. But if Social Security falls apart, even these superhuman savers could be in trouble.

Unofficially...
Revolutionary War journalist Thomas Paine lobbied for America's first retirement system. He thought the nation should provide £10 each year to every person who was lucky enough to live to the age of 50. This money was to "guard against poverty in old age." The plan went nowhere, but it just shows that our preoccupation with retirement is nothing new.

The reasons why you're better off starting early can all be traced to the power of tax-deferred compounding. All that interest paid on your retirement contributions has many, many years to grow and multiply. Here's one example: If you contribute just $57 a month when you're 25, you could amass nearly $200,000 by the time you retire at 65. (This assumes your investments grow at an annual 8 percent a year.) But if you don't start until you're 55, you have to contribute $1,093 a month to save the same amount in 10 years.

How much will you need when you retire? Most financial experts suggest that you'll require anywhere from 60 to 80 percent of your preretirement income to live comfortably. If you're used to leasing new cars every two years and wearing the latest fashions, or planning to spend a lot of time on winter cruise ships, you could need more. Your expenses also will be higher if your parents are still alive and dependent on you. Also expect to chip in a lot more in health-care costs. Sure, you'll be eligible for Medicare when you reach 65, but Medicare usually pays less than half of a retiree's medical bills. How much you'll need will also depend on geography. If you own an expensive co-op in Manhattan and plan to sell it and move to Florida for the sunshine, you won't need as much in your retirement assets. This would be true in any state, like California, where people approaching retirement are living in homes with values rivaling small gold-mining operations.

Of course the big wild card in retirement planning is Social Security. Just ponder this: In 1945, there were 43 workers for every Social Security recipient. In 1992, there were three workers for every person on the receiving end. By 2020, the

> **"**
> Don't beat yourself up if you haven't saved enough. Starting now is better than not starting at all. With the markets so wonderfully cooperative, you'd be surprised how well you could do even if you're starting in your late forties or fifties. This will put you in good stead when you're in your seventies and eighties.
> —Bambi Holzer, senior vice president, PaineWebber
> **"**

ratio could very well be 2 to 1. Who knows what will happen when the Baby Boomers start attending their own retirement parties? But we all know that the chances of the politicians fixing this mess while keeping everyone happy are pretty remote.

As it is, Social Security accounts for less than 25 percent of the typical retiree's income. This will no doubt be a jolt to many people who daydream about living happily ever after with their government checks. The percentage is even lower for more affluent workers. Social Security only replaces 19 to 25 percent of the income of a couple who earned $80,000 before retirement, and just 10 percent or less of a couple who earned $200,000.

As you approach retirement, you'll need hard figures so you can calculate just how much money you can expect after you quit your last job. Your first task is to ask your Social Security office for a copy of your *Personal Earnings and Benefit Estimate Statement.* You'll learn what you've paid in Social Security taxes during your lifetime, as well as how much you've earned. You'll also get a rough estimate of how much your Social Security payments will be if you retire at ages 62, 65, or 70. The statement is free; just contact your local Social Security office or call (800) 772-1213. If you have a computer, you can request the statement through the Social Security Administration's Web site at www.ssa.gov.

While you're at it, check out your traditional workplace retirement plan. Ask your employer for a summary plan description. This document, which outlines how your company's pension system works, explains how pension calculations are made. You'll also need your individual benefit statement. This pinpoints what your pension benefits are currently

Watch Out!
Staying 24 years at one company should generate a higher pension than spending 12 years at one place and 12 years at another. Making a mid-career move could sharply reduce your pension, since your ultimate payout is typically based on your years of service, age, and salary prior to retirement.

worth and how many years you've been enrolled in your employer's plan. The statement might project what your monthly checks will be when you retire. And if you contribute to a 401(k) plan, don't forget to keep track of that money, too.

Of course, saving more can make you less reliant on whatever crumbs are left of the Social Security pie by the time you retire. But another excellent strategy is to put your portfolio on steroids with stocks. This probably sounds like a dreadful idea to all those conservative retirees who are much more comfortable receiving steady income from their bonds. Sticking exclusively with bonds was a sensible approach when the average life expectancy was 60 years of age, but today it's pushing 80. Putting all your money into bonds and certificates of deposit won't keep you ahead of inflation. And if you think inflation is no longer a threat, think again. Even at the rather anemic long-term inflation rate of 3.7 percent, $1,000 loses half its purchasing value by the ninetieth year.

Need a concrete example? Let's take a look at what might happen to Brian, a 66-year-old retired engineer, who could be a poster boy for fixed-income investing. He figures he needs $3,500 a month or $42,000 a year, before taxes, to maintain his current standard of living. He's not sweating this at all. He's getting $1,072 a month from Social Security and another $1,000 from his company pension plan. For the remaining $1,428, he taps into his $300,000 nest egg. Brian hates taking financial risks, so he has that money tied up in certificates of deposit, money markets, and U.S. Treasuries. His portfolio is earning 5 percent a year.

Brian doesn't realize it, but his 5 percent return will leave him in the lurch if he lives long enough.

His $300,000 nest egg will vanish by the time he's 81 years old. But if Brian keeps half his portfolio in stocks, he might never face this cash crunch. If his investments earn 9 percent a year instead of 5 percent, his money will last another eight years.

Of course, many people feel uncomfortable investing in the stock market. Here are some good guidelines for anybody who loves or hates risks, or falls somewhere in between. If you can stick with any of these model allocations, you'll be doing better than a lot of investors.

RECOMMENDED PORTFOLIOS FOR CONSERVATIVE, MODERATE, AND AGGRESSIVE INVESTORS

Preretirement Savings

Conservative	Moderate	Aggressive
50% stocks	65% stocks	80% stocks
50% bonds	35% bonds	20% bonds

Postretirement Allocations

Conservative	Moderate	Aggressive
35% stocks	50% stocks	65% stocks
65% bonds	50% bonds	35% bonds

One of the exasperating aspects of retirement planning is that no one right way exists. Nor is there a magic amount of money that everyone needs to aim for. Someone who has accumulated $500,000 might be able to retire tomorrow, while another person who is the exact same age might have to work for another 10 years to ensure that he won't run out of money. Why? The early bird perhaps has already torn up his mortgage, and he's written his last check for his kids' college bills. Maybe his wife will continue to work, which means he won't have to pay for his own health insurance, which can be a prohibitive expense. He might live in a state with low income taxes or no sales taxes.

Because generalities are only so helpful, it's all the more important for each person to look at her own figures. Make it an annual habit to see what you have in your retirement portfolio and whether you're heading in the right direction. Are you feeding the retirement beast enough? If not, how much more cash should you toss in to satisfy its hunger?

Timesaver
If you aren't sure how much income your nest egg will generate, here are a couple of rough figures. A $400,000 portfolio growing at 8 percent a year generates $32,000 a year. With $300,000 in a retirement account, the owner can expect $24,000, and a $1 million nest egg would provide $80,000 annually.

Of course, you can get these kinds of answers from a financial planner, but don't assume that it's impossible to run your own numbers. There are plenty of free or cheap sources to turn to for worksheets, interactive calculators, and software programs. For the computer literate, many mutual fund Web sites maintain built-in retirement calculators. You don't have to know any mathematical formulas—just punch in the numbers the calculator asks for. You can find these helpful gadgets at the Vanguard Group's Web site (www.vanguard.com), which maintains a wealth of materials on retirement planning. You might also want to order the *Vanguard Guide to Planning for Retirement* ($13) by calling (800) 950-1971. T. Rowe Price, (800) 638-5660, will send you its retirement planning kit for free, or if you prefer the software to do the calculations, it costs $19.95. If you hate computers and don't own a calculator, you still have an option. Ask for a free cardboard calculator from the Scudder mutual fund family, (800) SCUDDER, to calculate your retirement needs.

Don't pass up those retirement tax perks

Regardless of how you juggle stocks and bonds, where you keep your retirement money is critically important. Your first priority should be to put as much money as legally possible into your workplace retirement plan—often called a 401(k)—and an *Individual Retirement Account* (IRA). As an incentive to save for retirement, Uncle Sam has given you great tax perks. No matter what you do, you should not pass these up. If you are strapped for cash and can't fund both during any given year, make the 401(k) your first priority if your employer kicks in a match for your own contribution. That, after all, is free money.

Here's the scoop on both of these options.

IRAs

Want to ruin a party? Start chatting about IRAs. It's hard to imagine discussing anything more tedious. Would anybody really disagree that contributing to an IRA is a lot like brushing teeth? It's good for you, but nobody really likes doing it.

Of course, over the years, you've probably heard some of the reasons why IRAs are so good for our financial health. IRAs are really self-funded little pension plans. Every year, the federal government allows you to squirrel away $2,000 into one of these special accounts that you set up for yourself. You might establish your IRA in a mutual fund, a stock brokerage account, or your bank or credit union.

The beauty of an IRA is that it grows without the shackles of yearly taxes. You pay no federal or state taxes on your earnings until you begin withdrawing the money. And now, thanks to monumental changes in IRA regulations, you might never have to pay taxes when you start pulling money out of these accounts. In 1997, Congress gutted the old IRA regulations and created a new turbocharged Roth IRA that it hopes will get all of us excited about saving for our old age. Once you learn how you can save a bundle on taxes with one of these new IRAs, you could find it irresistible. (You'll learn whether the new IRA makes sense for you in Chapter 13, "Taxes and Investing—What You Should Know.")

Congress also decided to be less stingy with its IRA privileges. In the past, a homemaker could only kick in $250 a year to an IRA, bringing a couple's total contribution to $2,250. Yet if the husband and wife held down paying jobs, they could each contribute $2,000, for a total of $4,000. Now somebody who stays home with the kids can put in $2,000 as well. As you can tell from the example, this change can make a dramatic difference for a couple.

A comparison of savings with old and new IRA limits. Source: Fidelity Investments

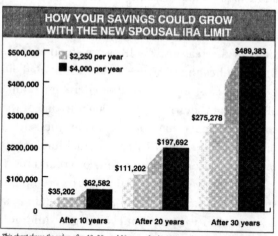

HOW YOUR SAVINGS COULD GROW
WITH THE NEW SPOUSAL IRA LIMIT

$2,250 per year
$4,000 per year

	After 10 years	After 20 years	After 30 years
$2,250 per year	$35,202	$111,202	$275,278
$4,000 per year	$62,582	$197,692	$489,383

This chart shows the value after 10, 20, and 30 years of a $2,250 or a $4,000 annual investment made at the beginning of each year, with an 8% hypothetical annual rate of return and earnings reinvested. It does not reflect the effect of taxes or a possible 10% penalty for early withdrawals. Not intended to represent the actual performance of any investment product. Please note: no more than $2,000 can be contributed to an IRA for any tax year. The above chart shows the effects of combined contributions to a married couple's regular and Spousal IRAs. New $4,000 combined limit effective for the 1997 tax year. Fidelity Distributors Corporation.

The government hopes that the new IRA will tempt a lot more Americans who have resoundingly ignored IRAs in the past. If you are among the many millions who have never considered funding an IRA until now, here are answers to some nuts-and-bolts questions.

What's the deadline for contributing to an IRA?

You have up until April 15 to fund an IRA for the previous tax year. For instance, you can wait until April 15, 1999, to put money into an IRA in time for your 1998 tax return.

When is the best time to fund an IRA?

To get the most bang for your buck, you should contribute as early in the tax year as possible. The first day you can contribute to your 1999 IRA, for instance, is January 1, 1999; the cutoff is April 15, 2000.

What if I don't have $2,000?

No problem. Set aside what you can throughout the year. Many mutual fund companies, for instance, allow you to mail in periodic checks as low as $50 designated for your IRA. If you get a bonus at work or a paycheck with lots of overtime, consider using the extra cash to fund the IRA. There is no requirement that you put in the full $2,000 every year— contribute whatever you can manage.

How do I set up an IRA?

It's very easy. In fact, you don't even have to get up out of your chair. Just call a brokerage firm, bank, or mutual fund company for an application. You can send it back through the mail.

Can I have more than one IRA?

Sure. There's no limit to how many accounts you can have. But don't let your IRA accounts pile up like mismatched socks. If you have a lot of IRAs scattered among, say, a brokerage house, a couple of mutual fund companies, and a bank, it'll be harder for you to keep track of them all. What's more, you'll be required to pay yearly maintenance fees. Consolidating accounts can save you money.

Once I establish an IRA, do I have to contribute to it every year?

No. You can skip as many years as you want.

Can I move my money from one IRA to another?

Yes. In fact, it's very easy to do. Here's one scenario: You have money in the Fidelity Emerging Markets mutual fund and want to move it to a better-performing fund with foreign exposure. You choose the Janus Worldwide Fund. When you call Janus for a prospectus on its foreign fund, also ask for an IRA rollover transfer form. You fill out the transfer form, mail it back, and Janus takes care of the rest. Janus sends you a letter after the transfer is completed. You don't have to pay any taxes when you make these direct transfers.

Are some investments inappropriate for IRAs?

Yes. It makes absolutely no sense to include municipal bonds or muni bond funds in an IRA. People in upper tax brackets gravitate to these bonds, because the income they spin off is sheltered from federal taxes. Well, the income generated by all investments within an IRA is also tax-free. So putting muni bonds in an IRA would be like using an umbrella in the house when it's raining outside. You'll get absolutely no benefit from doing this. For the same sort of reason, it's also not a good idea to plunk a variable annuity into your IRA. For more on variable annuities, see Chapter 13.

401(k) plans—can't be beat

While IRAs have been snubbed for years, another nifty tax deferral, the 401(k) plan, has become as popular as beer and hot dogs at a baseball game. With fewer companies offering traditional-style pension plans, 401(k) plans are filling the void. In fact, the number of people siphoning money into these plans has doubled in the past decade. Now one out of every five workers punching a time clock is enrolled in a 401(k) plan. More than a quarter million companies now offer 401(k)s, which you might see referred to as *qualified plans*. Amazingly, money is gushing into 401(k) plans at a rate of about $1.5 billion a week.

Named after an obscure section of the IRS code, the 401(k) is surely the Cadillac of retirement plans. Here's how one works: When you sign up for your company's 401(k) plan, your contributions are automatically taken out of your payroll checks before they can be taxed. You avoid federal, state, local, and even Social Security taxes on this chunk of money. This retirement money is not even reported as income on your tax return. It's quite a deal. Your 401(k) is classified as a tax-deferred account, because you can postpone paying any taxes on the money for decades. You won't owe anything until you retire and start pulling the money out.

There is a limit to how much you can protect from the IRS's reach in these plans. In 1998, a worker's maximum contribution can't exceed $10,000. (If you work for a state or local government or a not-for-profit institution, the latest ceiling is $8,000.) Even if this is doable, not everyone will qualify to kick in that much money. Your Human Resources department can tell you how big your

Unofficially...
The employer-sponsored retirement program for people who work for tax-exempt institutions, such as schools and some hospitals, is called a 403(b) plan. Government workers contribute to a 457 plan. Both are quite similar to the 401(k) program.

contribution could be. Keeping Uncle Sam at bay, however, isn't the only perk. Even better, about 70 percent of these employers offer their workers some sort of match. For example, if you contribute 10 percent of your pretax salary to a 401(k), your employer might kick in an extra 3, 5, or even 10 percent. If you're wondering if your employer's match is in line with others, here's the prevailing standard: The typical employer matches 50 cents of every dollar that a worker contributes, up to 6 percent of her salary. Let's say you make $50,000 and you set aside 6 percent of your salary, which is $3,000. Your company will deposit $1,500 into your account.

Unlike a traditional company pension, which is often called a *defined benefit plan,* you get to decide how the money is invested. Often, a company gives you a choice among stock, bond, and money market funds, as well as corporate stock. Frequently you will recognize the names of funds offered in your 401(k) plans. Big fund players like Vanguard, Fidelity, Franklin Templeton, Invesco, and IDS are often the ones managing these corporate 401(k) mutual funds. Don't assume that once you select funds, you are stuck with your choices. Companies typically maintain toll-free numbers you can call to find out your account balances and make changes in your investment holdings.

Figuring out how to divvy up your 401(k) money doesn't have to be as difficult as assembling a tricycle on Christmas Eve. Workplaces typically hold information seminars for 401(k) novices, and they supply you with all sorts of handouts. Read them. But companies, which often hire outside financial firms to conduct 401(k) seminars, aren't always anxious to explain too much to their workers. For instance, a financial advisor hired by a union to explain the 401(k) benefits was sent a menacing letter from corporate headquarters after she told workers that the program fees were high. It's quite possible, even when a company's intentions are honorable, to read all the materials and attend a seminar and still not know what's important.

Actually, you should scrutinize your 401(k) plan the same way that you do your other investments. Evaluating funds shouldn't be as hard as it might seem. Your workplace can provide you with historical performance figures on the funds. Check on the experience of the fund managers, as well as how long they have been on the job. Pay the closest attention to the three- and five-year performance records. While a fund might have a great year, this is far less important than the long-term track record. (For more tips on evaluating mutual funds, check back to Chapter 7, "Research—The Investing Advantage.")

It's been estimated that only a quarter of all the money sloshing around in 401(k) plans is invested in stocks. To put it bluntly, this is not good. Think about it for a minute. You're not going to use the money to buy a new car next month or to pay for a Caribbean vacation. The money has the luxury of working hard for you for many years. And with such a lengthy time horizon, you can afford investments that are riskier but historically more lucrative. Of course, I'm talking about stocks.

It's also generally a bad idea to choose company stock as an investment option in a 401(k). That's especially true if your employer matches your 401(k) contributions with more company stock. And yet, investing in employers' stock is wildly

Sex education and 401(k) education have a lot in common: No one can agree on how much students should be told.
—article in the *Wall Street Journal*

Watch Out!
Not long ago,
the U.S.
Department of
Labor reported
that roughly 300
companies—
most of them
small—had been
siphoning off
their employees'
401(k) contribu-
tions to bolster
their own cash
flows. While the
chances of this
happening to
you are remote,
it pays to exam-
ine your quar-
terly or yearly
statements
closely. Contact
your Human
Resources
department with
any concerns.

popular. According to one survey, company stock—in plans where it's offered as an option—represented 30 percent of workers' portfolios. Since your livelihood depends on the health of the company, it's best not to link your entire financial future to the company as well.

With these do-it-yourself workplace retirement plans so popular, it's more and more likely that a husband and wife will have his-and-her 401(k)s. When that happens, you need to keep the big picture in mind. Look at the strengths and weaknesses of your spouse's plan before you make any decisions. If you can swing it, both of you should contribute as much pretax money as your employers allow. But if that's a financial pipe dream, scrutinizing both plans can really pay off. You should consider contributing the most money to whichever 401(k) offers the best employer match. If a husband's workplace offers a 50 percent match for his contributions, while the wife's stingy employer offers no match, funding his 401(k) should be the higher priority. What happens if both plans offer matches? Aim for at least capturing the employer match in each one.

A couple also shouldn't select its 401(k) investment options without considering what choices each plan offers. Don't pick and choose in a vacuum. For starters, examine the quality and variety of the mutual fund choices in each plan. Let's suppose that the husband has lots of great stock fund choices, while his wife has a couple of excellent bond funds. If their goal is to structure a balanced portfolio of stocks and bonds, the decision could be an easy one. The wife could put all or most of her contributions into fixed-income funds, while her husband sticks with the stock funds.

Finally, never make 401(k) decisions without looking at your entire holdings—assets held in taxable accounts, IRAs, your children's college funds, and elsewhere. It's good to review just how all your assets are allocated before making your selections or contemplating changes.

Saving for college—no need to panic

Saving for college is no picnic. It can be downright numbing just thinking about it when you're also stuck with 300 more mortgage payments, a minivan that spends too much time with your mechanic, and children who nickel and dime you with their dance lessons, summer camps, and Little League fees.

The only thing scarier than trying to figure out where the money will come from is knowing what the tab will be. If your child enrolls today at a four-year private college, the College Board estimates that you'll pay more than $13,600 in tuition. In comparison, a state university looks downright cheap at roughly $3,100. However, after you finish writing checks for such things as dorms, meals, and books, your price can easily jump to about $10,000 for a public school and $20,000 for a private one.

With college costs multiplying faster than fruit flies—one study says tuition has jumped an average of 7.3 percent a year for almost four decades—what's really spooky are the numbers that lie ahead. Let's say your oldest child will be ready for college in 10 years. She wants to attend an average-priced private university—the one that today costs $13,600. Assuming 7 percent annual tuition inflation, the four-year tab could easily cost you $118,800. And that doesn't include books, room and board, and personal expenses. Got your heart set on your baby being accepted into Harvard? With Harvard's latest

Bright Idea
It's easy to calculate how much money you'll need to save for college if you have access to the Internet. The Web sites sponsored by the National Association of Student Financial Aid Administrators (www.finaid.org) and the Student Loan Corporation (www.salliemae. com) both provide interactive calculators.

tuition priced at $21,342, it could cost you, in 18 years, more than $320,000 in tuition alone. When you add in such costs as the dorm, student services, and health fees, the tab could reach close to $500,000.

Granted, numbers like these can give you a headache. But knowing what you're up against is the first line of defense. And the sooner you start preparing, the better. Luckily, parents today are blessed with more options than ever before. Through free booklets and workbooks, mutual funds recommend model portfolios for college savings and pinpoint how much money you'll need. In addition, the federal government is now giving parents new savings incentives with the Education IRA and some education tax credits. And for those who don't want to be bothered with the nitty-gritty details of investing, more and more states are offering no-brainer prepaid tuition plans that allow you to pay for college tuition years in advance at a lower price.

Before deciding where to invest, you need to avoid the temptation to panic. Many parents get so discouraged by the sticker shock that they don't even attempt to save. In fact, you're probably better off assuming that you won't stash enough away to pay the entire bill. That's the advice, anyway, of Raymond Loewe, president of College Money, a financial planning firm in Marlton, New Jersey, which has advised about 40,000 parents. Out of that group, Loewe figures he's met three or four who had saved enough to write a check for four years of tuition and expenses.

The trick is not letting the expenditures overwhelm you. Kicking yourself for not saving enough is like getting discouraged because you can't purchase a home outright. Paying for college up front would be comparable to buying a house in cash, and we all know that very few people do that. The best you can hope for is to save a big down payment for those college years. So scrimp the best you can, and then you'll compete with all the other parents for scholarship money and financial aid. Last year alone, students received more than $55 billion in college financial aid.

Luckily, there are more ways to save for college than ever before. Here's a rundown of your various options.

Mutual funds

Financial experts overwhelmingly agree that the best way to tackle this huge expense is to bulk up on mutual funds. Mutual funds essentially allow you to play the stock market without sweating through your own stock selections. Mutual funds can be risky, but if your children are young, it's far riskier to sock your money away in a bank.

If your child is still in diapers or in grade school, your best bet is with a growth or aggressive growth mutual fund. There is no need to put any of her college money in bond funds. You can afford to be a bolder investor at this stage, because you have many years to recover and rebound financially if the stock market takes one of its periodic dives.

If your children are in junior high, however, you can't be invested in the most volatile funds. At this stage, you must protect your gains because your 12- or 13-year-old will be graduating from high school soon. You should stick with more conservative mutual funds. Your best bet could be growth-and-income or equity-and-income funds, which typically invest in larger, more mature companies that generate dividends, such as Proctor & Gamble

> 66
> It's appalling when you look at the projections. With my three kids, I see the figures and think I'm looking at the federal budget deficit. It's that outrageous.
> —Jonathan D. Pond, personal finance expert and commentator on public television's *Nightly Business Report*
> 99

and American Express. Another alternative is to choose a balanced fund, which simply means that it includes a mix of stocks and bonds.

Zero coupon bonds

Another popular choice among parents is the U.S. Treasury's zero coupon bonds. In bond lingo, *zero coupon* simply means *no interest*. You receive no interest from this type of bond until it matures. Because of this feature, the bond can be sold at a deep discount, which is what appeals to many investors. I could have bought a 10-year zero recently for as little as 57 cents on the dollar. That breaks down to a 5.8 percent annual yield for the 10 years.

If you purchase a zero coupon and hold on to it until maturity, there can be no nasty surprises. You'll know exactly how much money you can expect at the end. That's not true, however, if you get antsy and sell early. The price of zero coupons can be extremely volatile based on changes in interest rates, so it's best not to buy if you might not hold onto them.

Zero coupons, however, can't provide the *umph* you need in your savings plan. They are not a smart idea when your children are young, but relying on zero coupons can be a great investment strategy once they enter high school. Why? At this point, you can no longer take chances with a potentially volatile stock market. The beauty of zero coupons at this stage is that you can time the bond's maturity to your children's college years. You can do this by shifting your money into short-term zero coupons that come due in each of the years your child is in college. If she starts school in 2010, for instance, divide the money up into bonds that mature in 2010, 2011, 2012, and 2013.

Prepaid tuition—a solution for the financially timid

What if you're allergic to personal finance matters? Maybe you'd rather concentrate on getting Junior academically prepared for UCLA while you let someone else worry about how you'll pay for it. If that's so, you should consider a prepaid tuition plan. These plans offer parents a simple way to save for a child's education at a state university and be guaranteed that the investment will cover the tuition when freshman year starts. The motto of these plans could be *Pay Now, Learn Later.* While every plan has its own nuances, basically you prepay your child's college tuition at today's rate rather than its actual future cost. The state takes your money and invests it with the aim of making it grow enough to meet Junior's tuition costs years later. With a prepaid tuition plan, the state sweats out the investment decisions, not you. A state government must invest your money wisely, or it will have to kick in its own contribution to pay your child's college tuition bills if the earnings fall short.

Here's how Florida's prepaid plan worked wonderfully for Chris, a librarian and single mom, who used it to pay the tuition for her daughter, Kim, in advance. When her child entered the University of Central Florida, Chris was thrilled that the expense of college was behind her. "It's really been a win-win situation for me," says Chris, who concluded after a divorce that a prepaid plan was the least-painful way to save for college.

Through the state of Florida's tuition payment plan, Chris paid $85 a month until she had contributed the required $4,677, which will cover all her daughter's tuition payments. At $58 a credit hour, four years at Central Florida recently cost $6,960. By planning ahead, she figures she saved herself at least $2,283.

The number of states participating in these programs is increasing all the time. Here is the latest lineup of states that offer the programs:

Alabama	Ohio
Alaska	Oregon (begins in 2000)
Florida	Pennsylvania
Illinois	South Carolina
Maine	Tennessee
Maryland	Texas
Massachusetts	Virginia
Michigan	Washington
Mississippi	West Virginia
Nevada	Wisconsin

Don't be completely discouraged if you don't see your state on the list. Many other states have established what are called *savings trusts*. They aren't, however, quite as good a deal. Unlike the prepaid plans, these trusts don't guarantee parents that their money will keep up with tuition inflation. States that offer these trusts include Connecticut, Delaware, Iowa, Kentucky, Minnesota, New Jersey, New Mexico, New York, North Carolina, and Utah.

While prepaid tuition plans are almost exclusively offered by states, a pioneer of these plans is in the private sector. The College Savings Bank of Princeton, New Jersey, offers federally insured certificates of deposit linked to the college inflation rate. Participants buy CDs that are indexed to the annual increases in private college costs and are guaranteed to cover tuition, fees, and room and board in the future. The money saved through the College Savings Bank can be used at any private or public university.

Before you sign up for any of these programs, you should know about the warts. Here's the ugliest one: Investing wisely in the stock market on your own should bring you a much greater return than what any state can offer. The states are investing your money quite conservatively, so the returns are modest. But that argument assumes that moms and dads will take the initiative to invest appropriately on their own. A survey of parents participating in Alabama's prepayment plan suggests otherwise. If the tuition program wasn't available, 52 percent said they would have put the money in a savings account. Another 17 percent would have invested in savings bonds, and only 6 percent would have chosen stocks. So if your inclination is to stick your kid's college fund in a CD or savings bonds for the long haul, a prepaid plan is a better bet.

Critics also charge that the plans aren't flexible and could force a child to attend a state school that he doesn't want to attend after all. What happens if a Michigan family using the state's prepayment plan moves to Pennsylvania? A report by the U.S. General Accounting Office suggests the criticism is not warranted. Its survey of state plans indicates that parents generally may apply the value of their prepaid benefits to private schools or out-of-state universities. In Michigan, for instance, 18 percent of students chose to attend schools outside the scope of the state's prepaid plan. They simply arranged for Michigan to send the dollar value of their contracts to their chosen school. Nonetheless, parents can

Timesaver
Want to learn more about prepaid plans in a hurry? Visit the Internet home of the College Savings Plans Network (www.collegesavings.org). The group provides links to state prepaid plans and telephone numbers. Or you can call (606) 244-8175.

take a financial hit if their kids stray out of state. Nonresident tuition at state schools is higher, and if your brainy son gets accepted into Stanford University or some other budget-busting private school, the money that would have been adequate to pay for four years at an in-state public university will look ridiculously inadequate under the circumstances.

Series EE savings bonds

Here's another safe alternative. If you're like most parents, you probably have savings bonds stashed in a desk drawer or safe deposit box. A savings bond is a thoughtful gift to bring to a baby shower, and grandparents love to buy them. What's nice about these bonds is that they aren't budget-busters. For just $25, you can buy a $50 bond—the purchase price is always 50 percent of its face value.

But don't make savings bonds a major source of college funding. Once again, the returns percolating from these bonds just can't keep up with the torrid pace of college costs. That said, savings bonds do offer one tantalizing feature. While you never have to pay state or local tax on these bonds, you will owe the Internal Revenue Service when the bonds are redeemed. However, if the bonds are used for a child's college tuition, the federal tax is waived, provided you meet the income requirements at the time of redemption. A married couple filing a joint income tax return can skip the tax if their adjusted gross income doesn't exceed $78,350. The tax break phases out entirely if your adjusted income surpasses $108,350.

Timesaver
If you have questions about savings bonds, you can call the Savings Bond Customer Service Unit at the Federal Reserve Bank of Kansas City at (800) 333-2919.

Education IRA

Congress recently dreamed up this new IRA. The name is misleading, because you're not supposed to let it sit around until you retire. Each year, you, a grandparent, or anyone else for that matter can put up to $500 in one of these for any child under the age of 18. If the money is used for college expenses, the earnings are tax-free. Sounds simple enough, but it isn't.

There are a lot of nitpicky rules about these Education IRAs that could drive you batty. For instance, any year that you contribute to a prepaid state tuition plan, you won't be able to fund an Education IRA. What's more, you can't tap into an Education IRA during the same year that you claim one of the new education tax credits—the Hope Scholarships and the Lifetime Learning Credit. Under the Hope Scholarship, you receive a tax credit up to $1,500 per student for each of the first two years of college. With the Lifetime Learning Credit, you can take a credit of $1,000 per year for qualified college expenses, and this one can be claimed for an unlimited number of years. The tax credit will increase to $2,000 by 2003. Here's another zinger—the Education IRA may be considered the child's asset, which could reduce the amount of financial aid she is qualified to receive.

But quite frankly, these niggling rules wouldn't be so exasperating if a parent could sock a lot of money away in one of the new IRAs. But quite frankly, you have to put up with a lot of grief for a relatively small amount of money. And your investment gains can very well be eroded by fees. The logical choice, after all, would be to sink that annual $500 into a mutual fund. But guess what? The mutual fund is probably going to charge you $10 to $15 a year for expenses. And if you put the money in a load fund (this is not recommended), your investment shrivels even more.

Not everyone will qualify for the Education IRA. Your contribution is phased out for a single taxpayer with an adjusted gross income between $95,000 and $110,000 and for couples with combined incomes of $150,000 to $160,000. But if parents make too much money, that won't prevent grandparents or other relatives or friends from opening the accounts.

Custodial accounts—pros and cons

When you start saving for college, you'll have to decide whether to establish an account in your child's name. While it's a popular practice, creating a "kiddie" account might interfere later with your child's chance at grant and scholarship money. According to the guidelines, students are expected to spend 35 percent of their savings each year for college. Under this equation, parents only have to part with 6 percent of their assets. If you think none of this matters because you'd never qualify for financial aid, don't be so sure. A lot of your income won't necessarily be considered by colleges. For instance, money stashed away in your 401(k) and IRAs isn't included in the calculations.

A big reason why so many parents embrace custodial accounts is for the tax advantage. If your child is under 14, the first $650 of annual investment earnings is tax-free. The next $650 is taxed at 15 percent. Because the money is in the child's name, only annual gains above $1,300 are taxed at your rate. Some parents also like custodial accounts because they know that money will only be used for college. If dad's car needs a new transmission or the furnace gives out in the dead of winter, there is less temptation to raid the education fund.

On the other hand, custodial accounts can become a disaster if your "A" student decides to skip college and take up glassblowing instead. When your children become adults—in many states, that age is 18—the money in a custodial account is technically theirs. If your daughter withdraws her windfall to travel around the world, buy a sports car, or enrich a cult leader, you legally can't stop her.

Your child's fair share

Those scary tables that detail college costs leave out an important factor: your child's contribution. If you're lucky, your kids will qualify for scholarships or accumulate college credits through advanced high school courses. In what could be a trend, more and more teenagers are zipping through college in three or three-and-a-half years, which can go a long way toward easing your financial burden.

There's nothing wrong with expecting your kids to pay part of the bill. Instilling in your child the need to save for this big expense can start as soon as your little ones begin receiving allowances. By the time your child is working the takeout window at McDonald's, she can be turning over part of her paychecks. One place to keep a teenager's future college money is in a Roth IRA. As long as your child makes at least $2,000 annually, she can contribute the maximum $2,000 to the account. When she starts college, she can withdraw her contributions tax-free.

And it doesn't hurt to let your children know that you're doing your part. When my daughter was four, I told Caitlin that her dad and I were saving money for her in a mutual fund. I gave her lots of stickers and let her decorate a file folder for her financial papers. When her statements arrive, she gets to open the mail. Sometimes she'll get out her purple calculator to find out what she's "worth."

Bright Idea
What if you change your mind about a custodial account you've already established? Don't panic. In the future, simply put money you've earmarked for college into one of your own accounts. You can't, however, erase your mistake by transferring money from a kiddie account into your own. Federal law requires that the money only be used for the benefit of the child.

She's now eight, and every couple of months she'll walk up to me and say, "Hey mom, how are my mutual funds doing?"

Short of money? Don't despair.

Despite people like me haranguing parents to start saving early for college, most don't until their kids are suddenly teenagers. If this sounds familiar, don't beat up on yourself, you'll just have to be more creative. There are all sorts of scholarships available from sources you might not have ever dreamed about. And financial aid, which is now awarded to more students than ever before, is always a possibility.

If you need an inspirational story to convince you, Chris Vuturo can provide it. As a teenager growing up in Louisville, Kentucky, Vuturo realized that his parents couldn't afford to write four years' worth of tuition checks. He spent months researching scholarships and applying for any that he thought worthwhile. After stuffing countless envelopes, Vuturo ended up with $885,782 worth of scholarship money. Ultimately, he accepted an award of $68,000 to attend Harvard. If you think your kid can't duplicate what Vuturo did, think again. Just hand him Vuturo's book, *The Scholarship Advisor*, which explains how he managed to hit the jackpot.

Kids also can find scholarships through scholarship search sites on the Internet. At FastWeb (www.fastweb.com), you can fill out a standard application, and every time you log on, you are updated with scholarships you might qualify for. Another scholarship site to visit belongs to Princeton Review (www.review.com).

If scholarship money still leaves you short, there's always financial aid. The biggest source is the federal government, followed by state governments, colleges, and private organizations. Here are some of the major types of financial aid available:

- **Federal grants and loans:** Two huge sources of grants, which do not have to be repaid, are the Pell Grant and the *Federal Supplemental Educational Opportunity Grant* (FSEOG). Only the neediest students get these.

- **Federal Stafford loans:** These come with a low interest rate and are issued to college students if they meet the requirements of a financial aid formula. The federal government pays the interest on these loans while students are in school. Students can also obtain unsubsidized Stafford loans regardless of family income, but they are responsible for the interest payments while still enrolled. If they choose to postpone paying the interest, the amount is tacked onto the loan principal after graduation.

- **Federal PLUS loans:** These loans allow parents, who don't have to be financially needy, to borrow up to the full cost of their child's education. The borrowers must start making payments within 60 days of receiving the loan.

Here are some places to look for financial aid:

- **Financial aid administrator's office:** Contact the office at the universities you are interested in. The staff will provide you with information about federal financial assistance and other aid programs.

- **Guidance counselor's office:** Your child's high school guidance counselor's office is another good place to find scholarship possibilities, as well as information on federal, local, and state programs.

Bright Idea
Need help with college costs? You can get started by asking your student's high school guidance counseling office for the *Free Application for Federal Student Aid* (FAFSA). You can also get the form by calling (800) 4-FED-AID. Submit the form as soon as possible after January 1. Aid is generally awarded on a first-come, first-served basis.

- **Local private sources:** Money for scholarships or grants could be available in your area based on your child's religious affiliation, ethnicity, achievements, hobbies, and special talents. Places to contact include your church, local foundations, civic groups, and workplace.

- **Federal education awards program:** High school graduates can earn education awards through a new federal program by working before, during, or after college graduation. To get more information, call (800) 942-2677.

Starting over: divorce and your finances

Many of us make incredibly elaborate plans when we get married. We arrange everything from the champagne served for the best man's toast to the airline used for the honeymoon getaway. But no one really plans to get divorced. It just sort of happens for many couples. It is obviously a period of great crisis, but unfortunately, it's also a time when you must try to remain level-headed. Sticking with a strategy can save you a great deal of financial grief later on.

I have friends who have let their legal separations drag on because they are afraid of what will happen to them if they take the final step. Will they lose their house? Will the child support be enough? The fear of the unknown has paralyzed them. Yet there is less likelihood of a divorce settlement turning sour if they know what to expect up front and what kinds of resources are available to help.

One of your first tasks is to see if you can walk away from the marriage without incurring outrageous legal bills. Money that gets sucked up by the divorce process is money you'll never get to spend for a child's education or a comfortable retirement.

You'll pay more for a contested divorce with major attorney bills on both sides. An alternative is to enlist the help of a mediator, who will charge a lot less per hour than a lawyer representing you in a contentious court battle. Mediation is often used to get past the emotional issues, such as confusion, anger, and mistrust, that draw out legal proceedings. Do you really want to sob on your lawyer's shoulder about what a jerk your husband is when she's charging you $200 an hour? If both sides are open to mediation, it can reduce your attorney and court costs down the line, as well as other expenses.

If you think you'd rather have an attorney handle the entire matter, consider this: A two-day court hearing, with the depositions, discovery, court motions, court reporter, and pretrial settlements, could cost $25,000. In contrast, a full week of mediation might cost $5,000. And the outcome might not be any different.

You can find a list of mediators in your area by contacting the Academy of Family Mediators, 4 Militia Dr., Lexington, MA 02173 (www.mediators.org). To belong to the academy, a mediator must complete a minimum of 60 hours of family mediation training, two hours of domestic violence–awareness training, as well as ongoing training. The mediator must also have logged at least 100 hours of family mediation in at least 10 different cases. Mediators can be lawyers, therapists, ministers, or psychologists.

Your focus, however, shouldn't be exclusively on saving money. Hiring a tax attorney, a certified public accountant, or a certified financial planner can ultimately save you a great deal of money. Professionals who appreciate the tax consequences

Minimize your divorce expenses as much as possible. Do as much negotiating as you can with your spouse and try mediation before going into a full-blown war.
—Ginita Wall, certified financial planner and author of *Your Next Fifty Years*

"

of your decisions can steer you clear of making common and irrevocable mistakes.

CPAs can assess the value of such things as a spouse's stock options, partnership agreements, pension benefits, and increased worth of an inheritance. To find a CPA experienced in divorce cases, contact the American Institute of CPAs at (800) 862-4272. Ask for a list of experts in your area. Another resource is the Institute of Business Appraisers at (407) 732-3202. For suggestions on finding a financial planner, see Chapter 3, "Financial Planners and Brokers—The Best of the Bunch."

Falling out of love will seem relatively easy compared to what must happen next. Here are some thorny issues to consider when a divorce is looming.

Alimony and child support

As far as the IRS is concerned, alimony and child support payments are two different animals. If you pay alimony, your checks are tax-deductible, but your ex-spouse has to pay income tax on the amount. This is just the opposite with child support—the person receiving the checks doesn't have to pay taxes on the money. Obviously, if you are the one writing the checks, you prefer to get a tax write-off. Consequently, many people are tempted to disguise child support payments as alimony to get that tax break. This is a bad idea. The IRS often detects this ruse. If child support and alimony are not differentiated, that is if they are lumped together in payments, the entire amount is taxable. That's because the IRS doesn't want to get involved in deciding what portion is tax-deductible.

Filing taxes

Divorcing couples need to decide how they will be filing their taxes while they are still legally married.

These are their options: married filing jointly, married filing separately, or filing as head of household. To qualify as head of household, a person must have provided a home for her child for more than six months, and her husband cannot have lived in the house for the last six months of the year. As a general rule, someone filing as head of household is better off than if she files separately as a married women. Choosing the head-of-household option can also be preferable to filing jointly if both spouses earn income. Before you decide which way to file, it's important to consult a tax professional. See Chapter 3 for tips on picking an expert.

Filing jointly can create problems for both people later on if one person gets entangled with the IRS. If you are legally separated, but you suspect that your spouse won't be completely truthful at tax time, it could be wise not to file together.

You can save money by timing your divorce. Ask a tax professional whether it makes sense for you to file before the end of the year or wait until January. There is no one pat answer.

Making decisions about the family home

Often, one spouse wants desperately to hang onto the house, perhaps so the children won't be disrupted. The mother who remains in the house might surrender her share of her ex-spouse's pension benefits or other valuable assets in return. Yet that isn't always a good idea. The house, which after all doesn't produce any income, can be quite costly to maintain with mortgage payments, property tax bills, and repairs.

Often it's better to sell the house and split the proceeds. However, dividing property can be booby trapped with tax implications, so once again, don't do anything without professional advice.

Bright Idea
For Internet divorce resources, here are three Web sites to visit: Divorce Online (www. divorce-online .com), DivorceNet (www.divorcenet.c om), and Divorce Helpline (www. divorcehelp.com). These sites maintain articles about common divorce issues, family law information, bulletin boards, recommended books, and relevant Internet links.

The dilemma of whether to keep the house in the settlement can often hinge on the person's age. Let's say the husband of a 50-year-old woman is pressuring her to surrender her share of his future pension benefits in exchange for their home. This would not be a good swap because the woman, who has no pension benefits of her own, would not have enough years left to build up an adequate retirement nest egg for herself. For that very reason, Ginita Wall, a San Diego certified financial planner who has written extensively on divorce, says she often discourages women from relinquishing their claim on pension benefits in exchange for the house if they are 45 years of age or older. Of course, if a woman is expected to receive an inheritance or has enough money for retirement, this wouldn't be a problem.

Pension calculations

Future benefits in a couple's retirement plans can be an important part of any settlement. The simplest way to divide up the retirement money is for each spouse to keep what's in his or her own name. But this won't be equitable if one person will enjoy a much more generous pension plan. To keep a portion of your ex-spouse's retirement plan, you'll need a judge to issue something called a *Qualified Domestic Relations Order* (QDRO). A QDRO can prevent a spouse from pulling out all the money in his retirement nest egg and leaving his former partner in a financial crisis. Don't ever relinquish your claim on a pension until you've had it valued by a professional. People are often surprised at how much they are worth.

A common financial mistake that divorced couples fall into is not spending time reflecting on how their money is invested. Are the investments made when a couple was happily married still the right ones after they divorce? Often the answer is no. Let's look at the case of a woman who was married to a wealthy real estate developer who had sheltered a great deal of his income from taxes with municipal bonds. During the divorce settlement, a lot of these tax-free bonds ended up with the ex-wife. Since she considered her ex-husband a savvy investor, it didn't occur to her to question whether all these bonds were appropriate for her. Actually, the last thing she needed was income-tax protection—her income-tax bracket had plummeted during the divorce. What she needed was a portfolio with a healthy amount of stocks so her investments could grow fast enough to guarantee her a retirement free of financial woes.

Remarriage and money

Getting married again can be trickier than the first time you took your vows. Kids, alimony, separate financial accounts, and warring investment philosophies can make melding two households together exasperating. But it doesn't have to be impossible. There are ways to make the union financially easier.

At the start, you need to share all your financial information. Don't hold back. Keeping secrets now can blow up in your face later. Also share your feelings about your new financial situation, but don't let any discussion become confrontational. If you marry a guy with a huge credit card debt, tell him how you feel about this new burden. If your new partner has spoiled his children with the latest clothes, frequent trips to Toys ' Я ' Us, and generous allowances, you need to discuss whether this will work in the future. Remember, your marriage will be a happier one if both partners feel they have an equal say in how the money is spent and invested.

Bright Idea
The Stepfamily Association of America provides educational tapes, books, videos, and a quarterly newsletter for members. Contact them at 650 J St., Suite 205, Lincoln, NE 68508, or call (800) 735-0329. Another resource is the Stepfamily Foundation at (212) 799-7837.

Establishing a budget that takes into account such things as child support and alimony could also be a good way to start anew. You also have to decide how to divvy up the money. Some couples put everything they own in joint accounts. Others opt for his-and-her pots—one for the husband, one for the wife. People who prefer this way might be affluent or have a tough time letting others control their money. A third option is using three pots. Each partner stashes some money into an individual account, but each makes contributions to the household fund for food, cars, schooling, and other expenses. There is no right way to proceed, but both persons need to feel good about the decision.

When the honeymoon is over, here are some other steps you should take:

- Evaluate your health, life, car, and disability insurance coverage. What worked in your old marriage could very well not be appropriate in the new one.

- Change the beneficiaries listed on your insurance policies, mutual fund accounts, pensions, and 401(k) plans.

- Review your dental and medical coverage. If there is overlapping coverage, take the appropriate steps.

- Revise your W-4 tax forms at work.

- Review the new combined investment portfolio. Once again, there could be overlaps that require some tinkering.

Here are some other resources on divorce, as well as remarriage, that you might find helpful:

- *The Unofficial Guide to Divorce,* by Sharon Naylor. You'll find this divorce volume helpful, easy to use, and up-to-date.

- *How to Do Your Own Divorce,* by Charles Sherman (California and Texas editions), contains all the forms and explanations for getting divorced without an attorney.

- *Divorce and Money: How to Make the Best Financial Decisions During Divorce,* by Violet Woodhouse and Victoria F. Collins, with M.C. Blakeman, offers advice on how to divide property and agree on alimony and child support.

- *Money Advice for Your Successful Remarriage,* by Patricia Schiff Estess, offers practical advice for bringing two families together financially.

Just the facts

- As a general rule, you need 60 to 80 percent of your preretirement income to live comfortably.

- Putting as much money as you can into a 401(k) is an excellent strategy.

- If your children are young, aim for growth in their college savings funds.

- If you didn't save enough, there are plenty of scholarships and financial aid available.

- Keeping divorce expenses down is one key to landing on your feet financially.

GET THE SCOOP ON...
Understanding the landmark tax laws ▪ Stocks—
the capital gains winner ▪ The ins and outs of
IRAs ▪ Roth IRAs—to convert or not? ▪ Variable
annuities—are they really worthwhile?

Chapter 13

Taxes and Investing—
What You Should Know

Have any idea what happened on August 5, 1997? Maybe you were getting a tan at the beach, buying the last air conditioner left at Sears, or watching your baseball team drop out of World Series contention. Perhaps only a certified public accountant would know why this was such a landmark occasion. On a hot, muggy day, President Bill Clinton signed into law what are arguably the most sweeping tax changes to hit this country in 10 years. You, I, and just about anybody else who has a little money tucked away will be affected. And for once, we don't have to grumble about those darn politicians. Overall, the legislation, called the *Taxpayer Relief Act of 1997,* is a wonderful development for many investors.

Of course, all the tax goodies aren't immediately apparent. Many of the rules are so complicated—you can't possibly explain any of this in a 30-second sound bite—that they will keep CPAs and other tax experts drinking caffeine late into the night for a very long time. But in this chapter, I'll dispel some of the confusion. You'll see what this landmark legislation will mean to you, and I'll make some suggestions on how you might want to tinker with your portfolio to take full advantage of it. You'll learn what the new capital gains laws are—sorry, bond lovers, the news isn't pretty, but stock investors can generally rejoice. You'll also understand why so many people are making a fuss over the new *Individual Retirement Account* (IRA), which is named after a decidedly unflamboyant U.S. Senator from Delaware. You'll finish the chapter with a better idea of whether you want to open a Roth IRA or move your other retirement money into one. Lastly, I'll fill you in on one of the biggest casualties of the 1997 legislation—variable annuities. Championed by full-service brokers, the reasons to buy a variable annuity, which were never all that compelling for most people, have dwindled even more.

The new tax lineup

So what's the hoopla all about? Here's a snapshot of some of the biggest changes.

Capital gains taxes, long the bane of investors, were replaced with much lower rates and new holding periods. These changes are a big boon for long-term stockholders, but they offer bond lovers, who earn taxable interest, nothing to cheer about. More people are eligible for a tax deduction when they invest in an IRA, but the really big news is the brand-new Roth IRA. (Both of these big changes are covered in depth later in the chapter.)

Home-sellers' relief

The 1997 legislation could have just as easily been called the Home Seller Tax Relief Act. Couples can now sell their principal house and keep as much as

$500,000 in profit without being taxed at all. You and your spouse can buy your house for $75,000 and sell it for $575,000 years later for a $500,000 profit, and you owe the IRS absolutely nothing! A single owner can enjoy a profit up to $250,000 before he's liable for capital gains taxes.

In the past, home sellers often dodged taxes on the sale of their home by spending their profit on another home. The catch was that the next house had to cost at least as much as the previous one, and the purchase had to be completed within two years of the sale. Home sellers who were 55 years of age or older enjoyed a better deal. They didn't have to roll their profit into another home if they didn't want to. Instead, they could claim a one-time exemption of $125,000 in capital gains. With the new law, you don't have to be a senior citizen to use the exemption. To qualify for this tax break, however, you must have owned and lived in the house for at least two of the previous five years.

Quite simply, this law change is a boon to homeowners and represents just one more great incentive to own a house. Those who will benefit the most are folks who want to stop the spiral of continually trading up in houses to avoid the capital gains tax. It's a perfect solution, for instance, for a couple who no longer has kids living with them. They can cash out of their house and trade down to a cheaper condo or even move into an apartment without paying a stiff tax bill.

Education IRAs

Education IRAs also have debuted with the new tax laws. I'm not sure how this one got its name. It's actually an educational savings account for kids. Don't expect to send your little genius to Harvard

Watch Out!
The capital gains break on home sales won't be good news if you want to unload a fixer-upper in a ZIP code like Aspen or Grosse Pointe. If your profits soar past the exemptions, you'll generally be subject to a maximum tax of 20 percent. Home sellers who pocket these monster capital gains will no longer be able to shelter the money by rolling it over into even tonier property.

with this money. If you put in the maximum $500 a year, you'll have $9,000 (plus earnings) available to withdraw tax-free by the time your contributions must end when the child turns 18. And that's the major knock against these Education IRAs. With the cost of college skyrocketing, annual $500 contributions for an infant who moves into a dorm in 2016 will be laughable. Here's a breakdown on what you'd have available by then if your annual $500 investments earned 8 percent a year.

Age	Value	Contributions
Birth	$500	$500
5	$3,668	$3,000
10	$8,323	$5,500
15	$15,162	$8,000
18	$20,723	$9,500

Source: American Association of Individual Investors

Timesaver
Adjusted gross income refers to your total income minus a few deductions you may take on your federal tax form. These deductions can include an IRA deduction, alimony paid, moving expenses, and half of any self-employment taxes. Look on your latest tax form, and you'll see your adjusted gross income on line 16 on the 1040A tax form and line 4 on the 1040EZ.

The miserly contributions aren't the only problem. These IRAs also will interfere if you expect to use one of the new education tax credits or a prepaid tuition plan. See more on this potential snafu in the section "Prepaid tuition—a solution for the financially timid" in Chapter 12.

If you do fund an Education IRA for each of your children, it isn't tax-deductible. And these IRAs aren't available to wealthier parents. The option is phased out for a single taxpayer with an adjusted gross income of between $95,000 and $110,000, and for couples with incomes of $150,000 to $160,000. If you don't qualify, however, it won't prevent grandparents from pitching in $500 a year.

Estate tax exemption

The tax legislation is also good news for anybody who expects an inheritance or plans to leave one.

Someone who intends to pass along a lot of money to loved ones can keep more of it away from Uncle Sam. In the past, $600,000 was shielded by something called the *unified estate and gift tax credit* when a person died. This might have seemed generous when it took effect in 1987, but people had been clamoring for the ceiling to be lifted. And now it has. Under the new law, the estate tax exemption has been raised to $625,000 ($1.3 million for family-owned businesses and farms) in 1998. The threshold for individuals will continue increasing until it reaches $1 million in 2006. Ultimately, this will mean that a married couple can pass $2 million onto their heirs without getting hit with estate or gift taxes.

Capital gains rules made simple

At the risk of sounding like a CPA, I won't share every nuance of the new law. Instead, let's focus on two of the more attention-getting provisions—capital gains and IRAs. Suffice it to say, you should consult a professional with any tax questions you may have. And you could have plenty.

Slogging through the new capital gains rules can give the most stoic taxpayer a headache. But before plunging into the numbers, let's review the bottom line. Here's what you really need to remember: The capital gains changes could very well alter the way you invest your money. Particularly for wealthier investors, bonds and other fixed-income securities will not be as appealing anymore.

Why? It's simple. The new capital gains rates are much lower than the taxes you'll typically get hit with for dividends and other interest income. This income will be taxed at your regular income tax rate. For taxpayers in the upper tax brackets, the capital gains rate was always lower, but now the gulf is even wider. Here's an example: Let's say you're in the top tax bracket (39.6 percent), and you sell your stake in Intel for a profit of $5,000. Having held the stock for two years, your tax rate for the capital gain is 20 percent. (In the old days, the long-term capital gains rate for everybody, except those in the lowest 15 percent bracket, was 28 percent.) You'd owe $1,000. Now let's suppose you own bonds that generated $5,000 of income. Alas, this income is going to be taxed at your own personal tax bracket—39.6 percent. You'd owe $1,980. Ouch!

The way to avoid paying Uncle Sam at your own tax rate is to sink more of your money into stocks. That's because most of the boost you'll enjoy with stocks comes through price appreciation or capital gains. You'll also dodge more taxes by holding stocks that pay little or no dividends. Mutual fund fans might prefer stock funds over bond funds for the same reason. While taxable bonds can produce capital gains, they are much more likely to yield interest that is taxed at your regular income tax rate, thereby eliminating any capital gains break. That is, the interest your bonds generate will be taxed at a higher level.

Now, on to the nitty-gritty. The new capital gains laws will tax your profits at different rates, depending on how long you keep your investment. There are four holding periods:

- **Short-term capital gains rates:** Assets held 12 months or less.

- **Mid-term rates:** Assets held more than one year but not longer than 18 months.

- **Long-term rates:** Assets held more than 18 months.

Bright Idea
Keep in mind that avoiding taxes should never be your sole motivation when making investment decisions. What's most important is keeping your portfolio well-balanced and within your tolerance for risk. If you feel more comfortable with bonds, don't buy stocks just because the tax burden will be lighter.

- **Super long-term rates:** Generally assets bought after 2000 and held more than five years.

The government is definitely rewarding buy-and-hold investors. As you'll see, the longer you keep your investments, the lower your tax bill will be later on.

- **Short-term gains:** You could get clobbered. You will owe taxes at your personal income tax rate. If you are in the 31 percent tax bracket, for instance, your capital gains are taxed at a rate of 31 percent. By the way, federal tax brackets range from 15 percent to 39.6 percent.

- **Mid-term gains:** You pay 28 percent if you sold your assets after July 28, 1997, unless you're in the lowest bracket—then you pay 15 percent. However, if you sold your assets between May 7 and July 28, 1997, you only pay 20 percent. Once again, there is an exception for those in the lowest bracket. Those individuals pay 10 percent.

- **Long-term gains:** Everybody owes 20 percent except for those at the bottom of the tax ladder. Anybody in the 15 percent bracket owes just 10 percent.

- **Super long-term gains:** Most investors pay 18 percent in capital gains taxes. Those in the 15 percent bracket owe a mere 8 percent and can begin taking advantage of this rate in 2002. Everybody else has to wait until 2006.

Okay, now that you know the latest wrinkles in the capital gains tax laws, you are probably wondering what investing strategies exist to keep your tax burden lower. Here are some suggestions.

Watch Out!
Don't expect any tax break for the killing you made selling your Beanie Baby collection. If you pocket a bundle from selling coins, stamps, antiques, art, or any other collectibles, you still have to pay the old 28 percent capital gains tax rate.

Resist being impatient. If you purchase stock or mutual fund shares but change your mind, your tax liability could soar. Remember, investments that aren't kept for more than 18 months are taxed at your individual tax bracket. By contrast, the investments held more than 18 months are only taxed at 20 percent or lower. To avoid the IRS radar, a buy-and-hold strategy is your best bet.

If you are a hard-core mutual fund investor, look for funds with a record of low stock turnover—that is, the managers don't acquire many stocks and then sell them in the same year. In the more tax-efficient funds, what's referred to as the *portfolio turnover rate* will be low. Why does a manager's proclivity to hold onto stocks affect your tax bill? Once again, if the fund generates a lot of short-term gains, they will be taxed at a higher level. And it's all the shareholders who will proportionately pay this tax obligation every year.

How do you find these tax-averse funds? Well, index funds, by their very nature, certainly fit this description. (For more about index funds, see Chapter 11, "Investing on the Run: Sure-Fire Shortcuts.") An index fund often contains all the stocks that track whatever benchmark it's trying to match, such as the Standard & Poor's 500. In the classic index fund, stocks are rarely sold, because the whole point is to mimic the benchmark. Consequently, an index manager would never be tempted to sell stock of a company experiencing hard times, such as McDonald's, which has been locked in a bruising ground-beef war with Burger King. In 1997, the turnover rate for the country's most popular index fund, Vanguard Index Trust 500 Portfolio, was a mere 5 percent.

You aren't limited to the index universe if you want tax-efficient funds. Some funds actually specialize in avoiding taxes for shareholders without sacrificing returns. Vanguard, for instance, offers a Tax Managed Capital Appreciation Portfolio, Tax Managed Growth & Income Portfolio, and Vanguard Tax Managed Balanced Portfolio. If you are a fan of Vanguard's Index Trust 500, you might want to consider the fund family's Tax Managed Growth & Income. Its tax-adjusted return in 1997 was 32.6 percent, which was .4 percent better than the huge index fund. The three-year-old fund slightly beat out the index fund for the other two years of its existence as well.

Timesaver
You can find out what a mutual fund's past portfolio turnover rates were by reading its annual report. But the quickest way is to simply call the fund company's toll-free number and just ask.

And here's another idea. A study done by *Mutual Funds Magazine* in 1997 suggests that the top-performing fund families are usually the most tax-efficient as well. In this computer search, the fund families that did the best job of shielding customers from taxes were Vanguard, T. Rowe Price, Fidelity, Putnam, MFS, AIM, and Oppenheimer. Then again, other experts suggest finding smaller fund shops where managers are very conscious of the tax ramifications of their trading because they have a great deal of their own money sunk into their funds. Funds that fit into that category include Mairs & Power Growth and Torray funds, both growth funds; Muhlenkamp Fund, a growth and income fund; and Weitz Series Hickory Portfolio, a small cap fund.

If you are adamant about keeping your tax burden down, you should avoid many aggressive growth funds. You'd need a scorecard to keep track of the stocks flying in and out of some of these portfolios. And there is a reason for this. Managers at the helm of these flashy funds tend to buy stocks that they

perceive are ready to soar. When the managers suspect these stocks are starting to sputter, they abandon them and look for the next highfliers. There is
little stock loyalty among this breed of managers.
Among these funds, it's easy to find portfolios with
turnovers of 150 to 200 percent and even higher.
(I've even spotted one out there with a turnover rate
of more than 1,000 percent.) That said, there is
some danger in making generalities. Some aggressive growth managers actually do an admirable job
of keeping down taxes. How's this possible? When
they sell winning stocks, they try to offset the taxes
by unloading losers at the same time.

What if you love aggressive growth funds or like
to make short-term stock trades on your own? You
won't get clobbered with taxes if you limit this
kind of investing to your IRA or other tax-sheltered
retirement accounts. Remember, you can shuffle
your money among stocks, bonds, and mutual funds
all you want in these accounts without having to
worry about any tax consequences. Of course, keep
in mind that excessive trading is never a good idea.

I know that I'm much more inclined to fine-tune
my own retirement accounts because I realize Uncle
Sam won't be standing there with his outstretched
hand. I tend to be a little more cautious and patient
if an investment in my taxable brokerage account
isn't doing as well. Here's one example. My daughter's grandparents bought her $2,500 worth of the
Janus Fund back in 1989. Janus Fund, which is one
of the biggest stock funds in the nation, is a solid
one, but its returns have trailed the typical growth
fund's average during the past five years. Janus
Fund, for example, ranked number 448th out of 690
funds during the most recent three-year period,
according to CDA/Wiesenberger. That's not the

kind of record that Janus will be highlighting in its ads. No doubt, one reason for the lackluster performance is because the fund's long-time manager has a conservative bent. During turbulent times, he is known to keep a stockpile of cash just in case the market crashes. If that happens, Janus's drop won't be as alarming as some of the more aggressive funds. That's all well and good, and many of his shareholders probably appreciate this strategy. However, this cautiousness doesn't really do my daughter any good. She has 9 years before she even takes her SAT exam. Whether to hold on or switch to another fund is really a close judgment call. But since I know my husband and I would have to pay a large chunk in capital gains for Caitlin's Janus stake, which has grown considerably in eight years, we've decided to do nothing. We stopped putting any more money in the fund, however, and are putting money elsewhere for her instead. The decision would have been different if Janus Fund had been in my IRA account. I would have sold it by now since there would be no taxes to pay.

The new IRAs—the one that's best for you

Why did Congress tinker with the IRA regulations? Well, politicians love to get calls from happy voters. But here's an even better reason. The old IRA program just wasn't working. Taxpayers began ignoring IRAs when Congress—tinkering as it's prone to do—erased the IRA's tax-deductibility feature for the more affluent in 1987. A quick look at the figures shows how quickly the IRA's popularity fizzled. In 1985, a record 16.2 million taxpayers claimed an IRA tax deduction. But two years later, only 7.3 million taxpayers bothered. By 1993, the number of taxpayers declaring an IRA deduction had withered to about 4 million. The IRA was well on its way to oblivion.

Taxpayers now can choose between the old IRA, which has undergone a face-lift, and a new variety called the Roth IRA. Whether this major development will stir any excitement remains to be seen, but I take it as a good sign that people are at least starting to talk. At a dinner party not long ago, I got my first "Roth IRA" question. The hostess, who had perfected the art of breadmaking, is also no slouch when it comes to investing. But the Roth IRA had her perplexed. She read one article by Jane Bryant Quinn, the doyenne of personal finance journalists, that seemed to urge her to transfer all her eligible retirement money into a Roth IRA as soon as she could. The next week, she read a column by another personal finance writer who seemed to be advising just the opposite. Dipping a ladle into a soup tureen, she paused and lamented, "I have no idea what I should be doing."

Join the crowd. Many people are confused about just what the Roth IRA is. Most probably haven't even heard about it yet. But trust me, they will. The Roth IRA is just too good a deal for too many people to ignore all the tax goodies it can offer the most devout taxaphobes. And without a doubt, the Roth version is the best choice for most people who want to fund an IRA.

But simply, the Roth IRA offers big incentives for anybody disciplined enough to stash away cash for retirement. As with the old kind of IRA, you can put $2,000 a year into a Roth tax-free account. (If you're married, your spouse can also kick in $2,000.) As the

Unofficially...
Why is it called the Roth IRA? The new IRA's namesake is U.S. Senator William V. Roth, Jr. (R), a gray-haired septuagenarian from Delaware who happens to be chair of the Senate Finance Committee. He has been doggedly working in the trenches for many years to make the IRA more attractive. Congress finally listened.

years pass by, you won't have to pay a cent in taxes for all the capital gains and other earnings that your workhorse IRA generates. And the best part of this new Roth IRA is that you will never ever have to pay the IRS again. That's right—never!

Now this certainly is revolutionary. We all pay taxes every day, from a puny 30 cents or so for a Big Mac lunch to thousands for a new Ford Expedition. But we won't have to pay anybody when we tap into our private retirement reserve. There is, however, a trade-off—I'd argue that it's minor—for setting up your own tax-free oasis. You can't deduct your yearly contribution to a Roth IRA on your tax return. That option, however, is still available with the traditional IRA. (This is the main attraction for those who still want to use an old IRA.) In the past, married couples making more than $40,000 generally couldn't fully deduct their IRA contribution and neither could single taxpayers who made more than $25,000. The eligibility ceilings, however, have now been lifted for the traditional IRA. For the 1998 tax year, married couples who earned less than $50,000 could qualify for a deductible IRA, while single persons could earn under $30,000. These limits will continue rising until the year 2007, when married couples filing jointly can make $80,000 and singles can earn $50,000 and still qualify for the tax deduction. (See the following table for the eligibility breakdown.) You should also know that a married couple or a single person making any amount of money can qualify for the full IRA deduction if they are not covered by a retirement plan at their workplace.

TAX-DEDUCTIBLE CONTRIBUTIONS
TO A TRADITIONAL IRA

Tax Year	Single Taxpayer	Married Filing Jointly
1998	$30,000	$50,000
1999	$31,000	$51,000
2000	$32,000	$52,000
2001	$33,000	$53,000
2002	$34,000	$54,000
2003	$40,000	$60,000
2004	$45,000	$65,000
2005	$50,000	$70,000
2006	$50,000	$75,000
2007	$50,000	$80,000

Note: To qualify for a tax-deductible IRA, your adjusted gross income must not exceed these figures.

Unofficially...
Fidelity Investments estimates that most Americans— 145 million— are eligible to contribute to a Roth IRA.

Even without a tax deduction, you'll find most tax experts agreeing that the Roth IRA is a better deal for most people. With a traditional IRA, after all, your immediate payoff is minimal. Let's say you're in the 15 percent tax bracket and you contribute the maximum $2,000. By using the traditional IRA's tax deduction, you pocket just $300. I'd say $300 is not a compelling reason to reject the Roth IRA. Especially if you're just going to blow your extra cash on a new CD player or a weekend trip. Need more convincing? Consider this scenario: Let's say you contribute $2,000 for 30 years in a Roth IRA and it grows at a steady 10 percent a year. When you retire, you'll have $328,988.

Lucky you! It's all yours to spend tax-free. Your neighbor, who is in the 28 percent tax bracket, sticks with the traditional IRA and also kicks in $2,000 for each of the next 30 years. (He doesn't bother to invest his modest IRA tax deduction each year.) But guess what happens to his identical windfall? He has to pay $92,116 in taxes, leaving him just $236,872.

Most Americans will qualify for a Roth IRA. A married couple who files a joint tax return can make a full contribution as long as their income does not exceed $150,000 a year. The benefit disappears for couples making $160,000. For a single taxpayer, the phaseout is from $95,000 to $110,000.

Congress is letting freelancers, consultants, and anybody else who works for themselves jump on the Roth bandwagon. Self-employed taxpayers won't be forced to choose between a Roth IRA and a SEP-IRA, which is a popular tax-deductible retirement option for them. Because the federal government realizes that self-employed workers won't enjoy a company pension, it allows people like me to set aside more than $2,000 a year in one of these special IRAs. The SEP-IRA permits someone to contribute up to $24,000 or 15 percent of her income, whichever is less. I can now continue contributing to a SEP-IRA and kick in $2,000 a year to a Roth IRA as well.

Both IRAs offer you more than just different tax breaks. Congress also tackled one of the other big reasons why IRAs historically haven't spurred much interest: sticky fingers. My friend Sue has hesitated putting money into a retirement account because she figured she wouldn't be able to touch it for 20 to 25 years. Worried about her rocky marriage and contemplating returning to school, Sue didn't think that tying up money she might need during a divorce made much sense. In the past, she would have been right. Up until the 1998 tax year, if you withdrew money from an IRA, even if you needed it to stave off foreclosure, the IRS slapped you with a

10 percent penalty unless you were at least 59½ years old. On top of that, you had to pay whatever income taxes you owed on the money. (There were narrowly written ways to sidestep the penalty. For instance, you could use the money to pay health insurance premiums if you were unemployed, and you could dip into the IRA for medical expenses, but the bills had to be astronomical—surpassing 7.5 percent of a family's adjusted gross income.)

The new IRAs come equipped with an escape hatch for people like Sue. You can withdraw the actual contributions from a Roth IRA any time—tax- and penalty-free. There is, however, one exception to this arrangement. You can't take the contributions out of a Roth IRA that has been converted from a regular IRA. More on converting IRAs later in this chapter.

Watch Out!
If you withdraw money from your IRA to buy a home, you must use it within 120 days. If the sale gets delayed for any reason, you'll have to deposit the money back in your IRA before the 121st day to avoid paying taxes on it.

You also won't owe any taxes on the earnings if you keep the Roth for at least five years and you're over age 59½. You can also use a Roth IRA to pay for college without incurring the traditional 10 percent penalty for early withdrawals. The bills that are covered include tuition, fees, books, supplies, room and board, and equipment. You will, however, be liable for the income taxes. As long as you've had the Roth IRA for five years, the IRS also will let you use up to $10,000 of that money if you are a first-time home buyer. But the rules are even more flexible than that. A taxpayer can dip into his IRA to help buy a home for his child, grandchild, and certain other relatives. You won't have to pay income taxes, and the 10 percent penalty is once again waived.

The Roth IRA, while it has many excellent features, makes it easy to squander money earmarked for retirement on other expenses. While pulling your money out of an IRA can be easy, you need to remain disciplined. You should try to avoid using your retirement money, for instance, to pay for your children's college education. After all, you can usually borrow to meet educational expenses but not your own retirement needs.

Since the IRS is hardly a poster child for the plain-English movement, sometimes you (or your CPA) will need to delve behind the regulations to know exactly where you stand. That's certainly the case with the new home-buying exemption. You and I might assume that when the IRS says it won't penalize first-time home buyers who dip into their IRAs that they are referring to people who have never bought a house. Silly us. Actually, more people than you might think could qualify. The IRS, in its infinite wisdom, defines a first-time home buyer as someone who hasn't owned a house during the two years prior to the upcoming purchase.

The new IRA rules also reward people like my dad, who hates touching his IRA. He's 72 years old, which means he's legally required to dip into his IRA. According to the old IRS rules, once a person reached the age of $70\frac{1}{2}$, he or she had to make mandatory annual IRA withdrawals. Anybody who didn't faced a really nasty financial penalty. My dad grudgingly withdrew from his IRA, even though he didn't need the money. With a Roth IRA, somebody like my dad would never have to touch his money. (The traditional IRA still requires yearly withdrawals after the age of $70\frac{1}{2}$.) What's more, he could continue contributing $2,000 a year into a Roth IRA as long as he continues to work as a consultant. And even better, my mom could contribute $2,000 as well. Once again, you can't do this with the traditional IRA.

Bright Idea
If you crave in-depth tax news (the breaking developments from Washington), The *Kiplinger Tax Letter* is for you. Published since 1925, this biweekly news-letter, which tries to filter out legal jargon, contains the latest on IRS rulings, court decisions, and new tax laws. It's read by tax professionals and ordinary folks as well and can be helpful to small business owners.

There's another reason why some retirees like these new IRAs. Unlike traditional IRAs, the Roth money can be passed on to heirs tax-free. That could be quite a bit of money if retirees transfer all the assets in their existing IRAs into the Roth version. Of course, there can be a huge tax liability up front when they do this.

The Roth IRA sounds great, but you might hesitate if your cash flow is really more like a trickle. A natural question, under the circumstance, would be this one: If you can't afford both, which is better—putting money into a Roth IRA or a 401(k) plan? If your employer offers a 401(k) match, your first priority should be to meet the match. For instance, let's say your employer kicks in 50 percent of whatever you contribute up to 6 percent of your salary. If you earn $60,000, you should try to kick in $3,600 to capture your company's no-strings offer of $1,800. But what if your plan allows you to invest 10 percent of your salary? Should you contribute the other $1,800 to the 401(k) or choose the Roth IRA? Here's one reason to consider siding with the Roth. Your employer isn't going to match the $1,800, and with the Roth IRA, you never have to pay taxes on the money again.

What do you do with your old IRAs?

So far so good, but here comes the hard part. You have one more decision to make if you already have money stashed in traditional IRAs or an IRA rollover. You typically establish an IRA rollover account when your leave your company and take any pension or 401(k) with you. When you put your money into the rollover account, you continue to protect it from the tax man. Your money continues to grow in this new account just as it would if it had remained with your old employer. Anyway, you'll have to determine whether you want to move any of your regular IRA or IRA rollover money into a Roth IRA. If you transfer the cash, you won't have to pay taxes on this bundle when you retire. But there is one catch that has paralyzed some otherwise gung-ho investors. If you make the switch, you'll need to pay income taxes up front on the money you move. (You aren't required to transfer all of it.) If you have a sizable chunk in IRAs already, this could be a huge tax bill. The federal government, however, gives you four years to pay your tax obligation if you make the move in 1998.

Okay, so is this a good idea? How's this for a wimpy answer: It depends. It makes sense for some and not for others. And not everyone needs to wrestle with this choice. You only qualify if your adjusted gross income is under $100,000 a year. For some inexplicable reason, the ceiling is the same for single taxpayers and couples alike. But a word of warning for any taxpayers hovering near that magic cutoff. If you earn a nickel more than $100,000, beware. You'll be forced to withdraw the money from the Roth IRA and put it in a taxable account. So don't start converting until you're sure you won't cross that magic threshold.

Here are some scenarios where converting to a Roth IRA could make sense:

- You don't expect to need the money in your traditional IRA when you retire. Remember, only the Roth IRA won't force you to make yearly withdrawals after you're 70½ years old. If you intend to leave your IRA money to heirs, this could be a better vehicle.

- You expect to be in the same tax bracket or higher when you retire.

Bright Idea
You don't have to convert all your IRA money into the Roth version. You can move over whatever amount you'd like.

- Your traditional IRA is fairly new, and most or all of your contributions have been nondeductible.

- Your retirement is many years away, and you expect a high rate of return because your portfolio is heavily invested in stocks. The more you accumulate in earnings, the more valuable the advantage of withdrawing the money tax-free later.

Here are some situations where a Roth conversion might not be smart:

- You'll be retiring soon. As a rule of thumb, the older you are, the less sense it makes to do the conversion. There won't be sufficient time to allow the Roth to accumulate enough tax-free earnings to outweigh the cost of the taxes.

  There is one notable exception to this scenario. An older IRA holder might want to covert for estate-planning reasons. As you know, unlike regular IRAs, you never have to make yearly withdrawals from a Roth IRA. Consequently, this could be an ideal place to park money that you have every intention of leaving to heirs. Your beneficiaries won't have to pay any income taxes on the money they receive from your Roth IRA.

- You believe you will be in a lower tax bracket during retirement than you are now.

- In order to pay the taxes for a Roth conversion, you'd have to take money out of your current IRAs. If you do this, your portfolio loses momentum. The money you pull out for taxes never has the ability to steadily compound in value. What's more, if you are younger than 59½ years of age, you are hit with a 10 percent penalty. You also pay a penalty if you pay the tax bill out of your spanking-new Roth IRA.

To convert or not to convert? Rather than ago-nize, consider consulting a certified financial plan-ner, a CPA, or a tax attorney. Meanwhile, if you think you can figure this out on your own, there are plenty of free sources of help. Just about any bro-kerage firm or mutual fund company will be able to provide materials to help you decide whether a con-version makes sense for you. For instance, T. Rowe Price, the mutual fund family at (800) 333-0740, will send you a free detailed worksheet that helps you with those tough IRA decisions. T. Rowe Price also offers a software program, IRA Analyzer, that does the calculations for you. Call (800) 332-6407.

Many people who are converting IRA money into the Roth versions no doubt think they can out-smart the IRS. Let's assume for instance, that you have $100,000 stashed away in your IRA accounts. Of that amount, $25,000 can be traced back to nondeductible IRAs. You were one of those rare birds who contributed money into IRAs even when the tax deduction was eliminated. The remaining $75,000 is in an IRA rollover account that you estab-lished when you quit your job and took your 401(k) money with you. This is pretax money, which means the IRS is still waiting for you to ante up on this nest egg. *Ah,* you think to yourself, *I'll just convert the $25,000 since I've already paid my taxes on that years ago. And I won't convert the $75,000 since that would trigger a tax bill.* Not so fast. The IRS won't let you do that. Unfortunately, you'll still owe a proportional amount of taxes. In this example, $25,000 repre-sents 25 percent of your IRA money. So you'd have to calculate your taxes based on 75 percent of $25,000.

Unfortunately, a calculator can't help you with one other crucial consideration before you convert.

Timesaver
Converting an IRA into a Roth isn't hard. If you have your IRA money invested in mutual funds, just call the investment firm holding your shares and ask for the conver-sion paperwork. It should take you no more than 10 minutes to fill out.

Can you trust the federal government? The reason why this is important is quite simple. We must base our decision, which could trigger an astronomical tax bill in the short term, on the federal tax code as it's printed today. But Congress has never hesitated to muck around with the IRS regulations when the political winds shift. The politicians on Capitol Hill could change the laws one day, making the Roth IRAs look much less appealing. There is no guarantee that the Roth IRAs will still exist when we're ready for those senior discount movie tickets. We might find out years later that scotching our vacation plans for a couple of years to pay for this conversion was a dumb idea.

Making millions with kiddie IRAs

IRAs aren't just for adults anymore. Actually, they never have been, but most people never realized that. If a child, no matter what her age, makes money, she can qualify to open a kiddie IRA. Actually, an adult will have to do it for her, but it will be in her name. You can choose a Roth or a traditional IRA, but the Roth would be the best bet for your pint-sized investor.

Not all kids can qualify for one of these. The key factor here is whether the money in your kid's piggy bank is earned income. You can't take a child's allowance money and open an IRA. However, it is kosher if the child uses money he earned around the house by shoveling snow, cutting the lawn, ironing clothes, or other chores. If you go this route, it's best to keep records just in case the IRS later asks questions. Keep track of what you pay for what work and what comparable work costs if paid to outside help. While the IRA maximum is $2,000, a child can't contribute more than what he earned in a single year.

Practically speaking, it will be the teenagers who can really take advantage of this opportunity. Obviously, a teen won't be thinking about what a nursing home bed might cost her in 2055 when she's working the takeout window at Burger King. But there are ways to focus on long-term investments with a little financial prodding on your part. For instance, you might consider contributing 50 cents or one dollar every time your child contributes $1 to an IRA. Actually, an IRA should be more attractive to kids today, since the Roth will allow her to use the money for a home or for college.

I can't imagine anybody arguing with this—IRAs are the surest and cheapest path for kids to become millionaires. Here's an example from *Mutual Funds Magazine*. Suppose your child contributes $1,000 a year for 10 years, starting when she's 10 years old. If she resists the temptation to touch the $10,000, it could be worth close to $1.3 million when she turns 65 (assuming the account earns 10 percent annually).

Unfortunately, not all financial institutions offer the kiddie IRA option. Here's a list of some that do.

LARGE MUTUAL FUND SOURCES THAT OFFER KIDDIE IRAS

American Funds	(800) 421-8511
Janus	(800) 525-3713
Oppenheimer	(800) 525-7048
Pioneer	(800) 225-6292
T. Rowe Price	(800) 225-5132
Prudential	(800) 843-7625
Vanguard	(800) 635-1511
Merrill Lynch	Check your local phone book listing.

> ❝
> Reinforcing savings for kids is a great idea. Kiddie IRAs helps kids learn something they don't get in school. It's a practical hands-on experience and it can help get them started on longer-term goals.
> —Joel M. Dickson, senior investment analyst, The Vanguard Group
>

Variable annuities—not your first choice

One thing is certain about the new tax changes: Congress sure didn't help the bustling variable annuity industry. In recent times, variable annuities have become an increasingly popular option for retirement savings. In fact, sales quadrupled between 1991 and 1996. By one estimate, there is about $600 billion invested in them. People have flocked to variable annuities, because they offer one of the same benefits of the old-style IRA: A contribution into a variable annuity is not tax-deductible, but once your money is in one, Uncle Sam can't touch it. Your money can happily compound for many years while you postpone paying taxes until the cash is withdrawn. Sounds pretty good, but the fine print, as you'll see in a minute, has always been troubling.

A variable annuity can best be described as a financial hybrid. It's part insurance policy and part mutual fund. Within an insurance wrapper, policyholders park their money in mutual funds that are referred to as *subaccounts*. The annuity is called *variable* because the return depends on how the underlying mutual funds perform. The insurance component guarantees that if you die, your heirs at least get the amount of money that you initially put in. Suppose someone invests $100,000 in one and then the stock market crashes. The investor dies a short time later when his annuity is only worth $90,000. Thanks to the insurance, however, his survivors pocket the $100,000.

Annuities also offer customers a chance to spread monthly distribution checks over a lifetime. For instance, if you start collecting payments when you are 65 and you're still alive 30 years later, the insurance company continues to mail those checks, even if your original investment vanished long ago. This type is called a *life annuity*. The insurer, using actuarial charts, bases your payments on how long you are likely to live. Most people, however, avoid this lifetime stream of checks in favor of a lump sum or some other type of payment. Why? For the majority of people, it's too big a gamble. Let's say you invest $100,000 in an annuity and you opt for those lifetime payments to begin at age 65. If you die at the age of 66, tough luck. Your heirs can't collect anything. The insurance company pockets all your remaining annuity money. Of course, that wouldn't have happened if you had pulled out all your annuity money at one time.

Annuities aren't as attractive anymore, thanks to the new lower capital gains rates. Here's why: When you withdraw money from a variable annuity, it is taxed at your highest marginal personal tax rate. So if you're in the 31 percent bracket, that's what you pay. If you're in the top 39.6 percent bracket, the tax bill hurts even more. Yet if you had invested in stocks or stock mutual funds outside an annuity and held them for more than 18 months, you'd only have to pay a 20 percent capital gains tax or less. Obviously, with the highest tax bracket, the disparity between the two rates is even more stunning.

So which sounds better to you—investing in stocks within an annuity, where you can defer the tax for many years, or in a regular mutual fund account, which carries a yearly tax obligation? In a side-by-side comparison, mutual funds actually are the clear winner. With the combined whammy of the eventually significant tax liability and high costs,

Watch Out!
Once you've been receiving annuity checks under a specific payout method, you can't change your mind and switch to a different payout alternative.

you have to hold onto a tax-deferred variable annuity for many, many years before your ultimate return could even equal the one enjoyed by the typical mutual fund. Patrick Reinkemeyer, Morningstar's variable annuity expert, says an investor would have to hold onto an annuity for 16 to 18 years before the investment would match the return of a taxable mutual fund. It would take even longer than that before a variable annuity would pull out ahead in a horserace. Of course, it's not realistic to expect somebody to hold onto any investment for 18 years.

The annuity also has a hard time looking good next to a Roth IRA. Like the Roth IRA, taxpayers who choose an annuity don't get a tax deduction for their contributions. But with a Roth IRA, you don't have to pay tax when it's time to withdraw money. And we know that's not the case with annuity customers. But annuity executives say they aren't worried about Roth IRAs encroaching on their turf. That's because you can only add $2,000 a year to an IRA, but you can contribute an unlimited amount to an annuity. A recent survey of 49 annuity companies indicated that the average customer plunks down $35,000 in a new annuity.

Before you ever consider shopping for a variable annuity, ask yourself these two questions:

- Am I already contributing the maximum amount each year to my IRA?

- Am I doing the same with my 401(k) plan or other workplace retirement plan?

If the answer is no, forget all about a variable annuity. The features of these other two retirement savings programs are so superior that it makes no sense to look elsewhere first.

Moneysaver
Some discount brokerages, including Fidelity Investments, offer handy worksheets that can help you decide whether annuities are a proper investment for you. Call (800) 544-4702 for more information, or visit Fidelity's Web site at www.fidelity.com.

If you are still interested in annuities, you should know what some of that fine print says. For starters, variable annuities are price hogs—they charge high annual fees that can dramatically cut into your profits. The typical expense ratio for a variable annuity is 2.17 percent. There is also an annual insurance contract charge that could range from $25 to $50. Meanwhile, if you want to bail out of a lousy annuity, watch out—you could be gouged. Imagine paying a 7 percent surrender fee. Many people do. The insurer typically zaps you with a stiff penalty if you pull out your money within the first six to ten years. This cold-feet penalty usually declines each year and eventually disappears for the long-term investor.

Why do variable annuities get away with charging fees that dwarf the ones assessed by the mutual fund industry? Because they can. Many customers, puzzled by this complicated product, do not comparison shop. Unlike no-load mutual fund buyers, they usually depend on salespersons who steer them to products with fat commissions. Also, some folks are so determined to shelter their money from current taxes that they never think to focus on the real cost of the annuity.

If you do buy an annuity, try to stick with one that comes with low annual expenses and no surrender charge—they are sometimes referred to as *no-load variable annuities.* You can find an assortment through these no-load mutual fund companies: Vanguard, Fidelity, Scudder, Janus, T.Rowe Price, and USAA, as well as the discount broker Charles Schwab.

Annuities also aren't as flexible as investing in regular mutual funds. If you want to dump a losing mutual fund, you can transfer your cash to any mutual fund you want. But if you get fed up with the investments in your annuity, you can only transfer the money into other subaccounts offered within the same annuity policy. Unless, of course, you don't mind getting hit with a surrender fee. Because a variable annuity requires such a long-term commitment, you need to pay attention to the fund choices you'll find within one. The average variable annuity offers about 11 different choices. Make sure there is a wide range of funds available, including growth, small cap, foreign, and bond offerings. If you're buying an annuity when you're 38, you might not think you'll need any bond choices, but remember that you'll be growing old with this investment. By the time you're 58, you'll probably be glad there are bonds to fall back on.

Variable annuities do provide some flexibility that you don't receive with regular mutual funds. You can transfer money among any fund choices within the annuity without getting slammed with taxes. This isn't the case if you want to shuffle your money in and out of taxable mutual funds. For instance, if you call up the Vanguard Funds and instruct the phone rep to take all your money out of Vanguard Windsor II and put it into a Vanguard index fund, you have to pay taxes for any price appreciation or earnings that you enjoyed with your former fund over the years. This is often quite a tax shock for investors who don't realize that switching from one choice to another, even within the same fund family, can trigger taxes.

If you think comparing apples and oranges is tough, wait until you try comparison shopping for variable annuities. Information on variable annuities is still in the Dark Ages. Luckily, however, there are ways to reduce your chances of picking a bad one.

Most information comes from the companies themselves. Before making any decision, carefully read through the prospectus of at least a half dozen annuities. To obtain the literature, call a company's toll-free number. After you receive it, make sure that the annuity isn't padded with high fees. Excessive fees, after all, are the quickest way to knock the air out of a high-flying annuity. Consider buying one directly from a no-load mutual fund company or discount broker. And pay close attention to the subaccounts' three and five-year track records—to weed out the poor performers.

Chances are a financial planner or a broker will sell you a variable annuity, so make him provide the independent research. Before you endorse his suggestion, ask him for Morningstar's assessment of the annuity. Morningstar, (800) 735-0700, publishes two monthly reports on variable annuities—one is in CD-ROM form. At a subscription price of $495 a year, these reports aren't practical for an individual, but they are used by financial professionals to evaluate the hundreds of variable annuities on the market.

For further information on variable annuities, try these resources:

> The Monday edition of the *Wall Street Journal.* The *WSJ* features stories on annuities and provides a listing of them along with their performance returns. In addition, *Barron's,* the weekly financial newspaper that is also owned by Dow Jones & Company, publishes a table of annuity information in each issue.

> *Mutual Funds Magazine* also covers the variable annuity industry—you can read past stories at its Web site at www.mfmag.com.

The National Association for Variable Annuities, an industry trade group in Reston, Virginia, can provide free educational materials. Call (703) 620-0674.

Just the facts

- Thanks to changes in the capital gains law, you should reexamine your portfolio.

- The new tax rules reward buy-and-hold investors.

- For many Americans, the Roth IRA makes more sense than the traditional IRA.

- You might want to seek professional advice before you convert an IRA to a Roth rollover.

- Variable annuities are an unfavorable investment for many taxpayers.

Protecting What You Have

PART V

GET THE SCOOP ON...
Buying insurance can be less painful than a
root canal ▪ Term life insurance—simple and
cheap ▪ Cash value life insurance—
sorting through your option ▪ Protect your
livelihood with disability insurance ▪ Long-term
care insurance

Insuring Your Investing Future

My friend bought a life insurance policy because she couldn't get an agent off her living room couch. Jane didn't want to meet with the guy, but he was married to her best friend and... well, it would have been awkward to turn him down. And yet Jane, who is an architect, seriously questioned why she'd need life insurance! What was there to protect? At 28, she was single. Her only dependent was a pampered dog named Berkeley (her alma mater).

The agent arrived promptly for the appointment. Jane had an inkling it might be a long night when she watched him empty the contents of his bulging brief case: glossy charts, computer-generated illustrations, a complimentary folder for Jane that was stuffed with promotional materials, two sharp pencils, and a yellow legal pad. The man was on a mission. Four cups of coffee and a plate of chocolate chip cookies later, the agent showed no sign of leaving. Jane's frequent glances at her watch and some well-timed yawns did not budge the man from the couch.

Moneysaver
If you immediately regret buying a life insurance policy, relax. You can change your mind. Many insurers allow you a grace period of about 10 days, during which time you can get your money back.

If an insurance agent has ever made you squirm in your own house, you know how Jane felt. During times like these, there are no escape routes. Navigating through white water in a rowboat would be easier than just standing up and saying, "Look, I'm confused and I'm not prepared to buy any insurance right now." Instead, maybe you've opted for plan B. That's what Jane did. She bought a darn policy just so he'd go away.

You don't need this book to tell you that buying insurance to please a stranger is worse than a bad idea. But scenes like these are played out in living rooms and around dining room tables every day. That's because many of us have never taken the time to learn some insurance basics. You'll be surprised how you can make better decisions if you are armed with a little knowledge. Reading the next few pages should help. I can make your job easier by explaining your options and directing you to places where you can obtain even more detailed information so you can make thoughtful choices. In this chapter, you'll find out why term life insurance is the best and cheapest option for most people. I'll also explain where you can find the most reasonably priced cash value life insurance. You'll be amazed at how much you could save by following my advice. I'll also acquaint you with disability and long-term care insurance, which is unfortunately ignored all too often. At the risk of sounding like a shill for the insurance industry, millions of people who should probably be buying these policies are not. Failing to do so can ultimately make your life a lot harder than it is already. Being unprotected can suck the money out of investment accounts and, of course, ultimately make your heirs unhappy campers.

The ABCs of life insurance

Sorting out the nuances of life insurance policies can make untangling wet spaghetti noodles look easy. But bear with me, and we can get through this. The first question you'll need to answer is this: How much is enough?

Life insurance worksheet.

First, how much money does your family need each year to continue living the way they do now?

Calculate your current living expenses	$	a
(including food, clothing, rent/mortgage payments, taxes, utilities, entertainment, etc.)		
Child Care..	$	b
(anticipated cost if one person dies)		
Ongoing parent/grandparent care...	$	c
Total Annual Expense...a + b + c =	$	d
Income of surviving spouse...	$	e
Social Security Benefit...	$	f
Total Annual Shortfall...e + f =	$	g
Expected Income		
Annual Expense - Annual Shortfall................,.....d - g =	$	h

Second, lump sum needed.

Other debts you would want to pay	$	i
(automobile, credit card balance, etc.)		
Estimated funeral and administrative expenses	$	j
Uninsured medical expenses	$	k
Children's future educational needs	$	l
Subtotal of Final Expenses......................i + j + k + l =	$	m
Annual Expense Shortfall previously calculated (h)_____ x 10 yrs.......... =	$	n
TOTAL OF FINAL AND FUTURE EXPENSES ....m + n =	$	o

Third, add up the sources of income which would be available to your surviving dependents.

Existing life insurance	$	p
Income producing assets	$	q
(Stocks bonds, rental income, etc.)		
Cash and savings accounts	$	r
Social Security benefits	$	s
TOTAL ASSETS ....p + q + r + s =	$	t
Now subtract:		
TOTAL ASSETS..t	$	
minus		
TOTAL OF FINAL AND FUTURE EXPENSES....................................o	$	
TOTAL INSURANCE NEED .... o - t =	**$**	

Now that you've assessed your family's financial situation, and estimated your need for life insurance, call or FAX the Wholesale Insurance Network. The insurance policies available through WIN are offered by leading companies committed to excellent customer service, each with a record of keeping promises to policyholders. The Wholesale Insurance Network works for you -- the consumer who knows what they want.

Some insurance advisors suggest that you need coverage that provides anywhere from 5 to 10 times your yearly income. Generalities, however, won't pinpoint what you should do. But a worksheet devised by the *Wholesale Insurance Network* (WIN), an insurance referral service, can help you calculate how much life insurance coverage you need. Filling it out won't take much time, and it will be well worth the effort.

Once you determine what coverage you need, you should explore what types are available. We'll review term life insurance and three types of *cash value* policies—whole life, universal life, and variable life.

Term life insurance: the simplest way to go

This is the life insurance industry's striped-down version of a new car that comes without any extras. With a term policy, you buy insurance that pays a benefit to your survivors if you die. And that's it. Term insurance offers no investment component. You pay a premium based on your age, health, and other factors. The older you are, the more a policy costs.

Term insurance is the most straightforward and easy to understand of all life insurance on the market. It is also undoubtedly the cheapest. And for the vast majority of people, it's all they really need. But don't expect your insurance agent to ever recommend a term policy. Sales of these policies generate small commissions, so many agents prefer to steer people toward cash value policies.

While these policies are fairly straightforward, there are a few decisions you have to make. Here are the biggies:

■ How long do I want the insurance to last?

You can insure your life for various amounts of time—1 year, 5 years, 10 years, even 20 years.

■ Do I want a policy with a level premium that stays the same until the policy expires or one that has a lower teaser rate?

With the latter kind of policy, your premium increases as you get older. If you stick with your policy until the end, the level premium policy costs you less money.

However I've always selected the teaser-rate policies. Why? I don't want to pay more at the start, because I could very well switch policies down the road. The competition among term life insurers is so fierce that prices continue to drop. Therefore it doesn't make sense to be stuck with a more expensive policy when cheaper policies are coming out all the time.

Here's an illustration that demonstrates just how prices have been disintegrating. This is based on what healthy 35-year-olds would have paid over the last several years if they wanted a 20-year premium level policy worth $250,000.

■ Do I want to buy term insurance through an insurance agent or through an insurance quote service?

Insurance agencies are easy to find, but you might not have heard about quote services. They work this way: You call a toll-free number and

Moneysaver
Before you determine how much coverage you need, check with your workplace's Human Resources department. Companies often provide a limited amount of life insurance in their employee benefits packages. Figure this into your calculations when determining how much insurance you need.

Women's Yearly Rates

1994	$347
1995	$295
1996	$195
1997	$200
1998	$190

Men's Rate

1994	$365
1995	$278
1996	$240
1997	$230
1998	$212

Source: Wholesale Insurance Network

explain how much coverage you want, as well as the length of the policy. While on the phone, you provide a cursory background of such things as your medical history, age, height, weight, and whether you smoke. The quote service tries to find the cheapest policies available and provides a list with prices from a variety of insurance companies. These referrals are free. If you buy a policy, the firm receives a commission from the insurer.

Some quote services survey many insurers for you. Others check only a handful. It makes sense then to get quotes from more than one of the services. You can also obtain quotes over the Internet. At some of these insurance Web sites, you'll find calculators to help you determine how much coverage you might need.

While some people assume that they'll get a cheaper price with a quote service, that's not generally true. The firm pockets the commission just as an agent would if you bought a term policy through

CONTACTING QUOTE SERVICES

Quote Service	Phone Number	Web Site
AccuQuote	(800) 442-9899	www.accuquote.com
Direct Quote	(800) 845-3853	www.directquote.com
InsuranceQuote Services	(800) 972-1104	www.insurancequote.net
Quick Quote	(800) 867-2404	www.quickquote.com
Quicken InsureMarket	(800) 695-0011	www.insuremarket.com
Quotesmith	(800) 431-1147	www.quotesmith.com
Select Quote	(800) 343-1985	www.selectquote.com
TermQuote	(800) 444-8376	www.term-quote.com
Wholesale Insurance Network	(800) 808-5810	www.ge.com/capital/ insurance/ci5.htm
RightQuote		www.rightquote.com
QuoteShopper	(800) 367-8044	www.quoteshopper.com
NetQuote		www.netquote.com

him. Consequently, if you feel you need advice before you make your selection, you might as well consult an agent. Just make sure that he has access to the quotes of many insurance companies. On the other hand, if you hate dealing with agents and like the convenience of finding insurance after one or two short phone calls, stick with the quote services.

My husband and I have always bought our term policies through these direct quote services. We've never had any complaints. The price we're quoted is never more than what we pay after the entire screening process is over. But when I mentioned this to Peter Katt, a West Bloomfield, Michigan, fee-only insurance advisor quoted widely by the national media, he just laughed. "Let me guess," he snorted. "You have low blood pressure, low cholesterol, you're not overweight, you don't smoke, and your parents haven't died." How did he know?

If you're not careful with quote services, Katt maintains, you can get caught up in a bait-and-switch scenario. You're quoted one price, but ultimately you are asked to pay a lot more when the bill arrives.

Qualifying for the best rates

Let's see what happened to Cheri after she calls for her quotes. Not long afterward, she receives a list of reasonably priced insurance policies in the mail. After looking at her choices, Cheri, who is a college professor with two small children, picks the cheapest policy. For $500,000 worth of coverage, it will cost her $475. So far, so good. Next, the insurer sends one of its representatives to Cheri's house to obtain her medical history and a sample of her blood and urine. The rep even brings a scale to get her accurate weight. She's a little surprised when her visitor pulls out a tape to get some measurements. Cheri also has to answer a lot of questions about her medical background, as well as that of her siblings and parents. Her mother died of breast cancer when she was 59. A nonsmoker, Cheri is healthy, she exercises regularly, and she is blessed with an ideal blood pressure.

Cheri remembers thinking to herself that she's glad she won't have to go through this ordeal again. A couple of weeks later, however, she receives bad news. The insurer says something like this: "Sorry, but we now realize that you don't qualify for our bargain-basement policy. That policy is reserved for preferred applicants who pose the lowest risk. But we are prepared to insure you for $900."

At this point, Cheri might be tempted to pay almost double the price rather than repeat the process. One way to make sure the price you are quoted is accurate is to be very specific on the phone. If you are aware of anything in your background that would prevent you from getting the best rate, say so. That should increase the odds that your quote will match whatever risk category underwriters decide you're in. In Cheri's case, she was legitimately disqualified from the cheapest policy because her mom died at a relatively early age.

Here are the qualifications you must typically meet to snag the best rates:

- Not overweight
- Low cholesterol level
- No heart disease or cancer deaths in parents or siblings before age 60
- Blood pressure below 140/90 without medication
- No more than three moving traffic violations during the past three years
- No drunk driving convictions
- No serious illnesses
- Do not travel in private planes

The whole story behind cash value policies

Unfortunately, cash value policies are more complicated than the cut-and-dry term policies. That's because these policies provide more than just a simple death benefit. They also double as a tax-deferred investment as well. Part of your annual premium pays for the death benefit, and the rest—after expenses and commission are deducted—goes into the investment side of your policy.

Older persons lucky enough to be enjoying sizable estates typically use cash value policies as a

Unofficially...
Unlike term insurance, the premium for whole life insurance stays the same, no matter how many years a policyholder lives. If you should be so lucky to reach the age of 100, your policy will usually expire. Then look for your check in the mail.

way to pay the death taxes so their heirs won't be forced to sell off assets when they die. Some people who already have maximized other tax-deferred investment plans also use cash value policies as a way to shelter even more money. The interest generated by this cash stockpile grows tax-free through the duration of a policy. Family businesses also rely on these policies to preserve the company after one of the partners dies. The proceeds of a policy can be used to buy out a deceased partner's share of a business. This is an effective way of spinning off a portion of the company's wealth to heirs who have zero interest in its operations.

As a general rule, there is little reason for people who are not approaching retirement age to sign up for one of these traditional cash value policies. Common sense, however, has never dissuaded persistent insurance agents from pressuring customers in their twenties, thirties, and forties from buying them. What's the rationale? Agents insist it's a fool-proof way of forcing people to save despite any spendthrift tendencies. But these conservative investments, which can charge mind-boggling commissions (more on that later) are rarely a smart move. Further complicating matters, there is more than one type of cash value policy. The three major types are whole life, universal life, and variable life policies. Here's a summary of each kind.

Whole life

Whole life is the oldest type of cash value policy on the market today. If you buy a whole life policy, you won't be surprised by your future premiums. They typically stay the same throughout the lifetime of the policy. Since your payments remain level even as your life expectancy shrinks, insurers charge you more than the actual cost of the insurance in the early years of a policy. This surplus is invested so there will be sufficient money when a policyholder dies and a big check is cut. When someone dies, the beneficiary receives the policy's face amount.

There is nothing risky about how your cash is invested in one of these policies. The insurance company puts your money into fixed-income securities, such as corporate bonds and mortgages. Usually the insurer guarantees a minimum return on your money, such as 4 percent. Unlike term insurance, you don't have to die to enjoy the benefits of whole life insurance. You can, for instance, take out a loan against the money you've already accumulated in your policy. If the loan remains unpaid when you die, the insurer subtracts that amount from your heir's payout. You can also use the cash built up in your policy to cover your premiums.

Universal life insurance

In some respects, universal life insurance acts like its whole life brethren—a portion of the premiums is directed toward the death benefit, while the rest is stashed in the investment side. Universal life policies, however, are more flexible than the whole life ones. And that's what attracts many people. You can adjust the amount of the annual premium, withdraw cash, and increase or reduce the death benefit. (Fattening the death benefit usually requires that you undergo another medical exam.) You could conceivably pay a reduced premium or none at all on occasion and kick in additional money at other times.

As with whole life, you can use money from the policy's cash account to pay the premium. The

Watch Out!
Before you purchase any cash value policy, ask yourself if you can afford it. Many people experience buyer's regret or decide they can no longer manage the cost of the premium. One in four people let their policies lapse during the first three years and recover little if any of their investment. Nearly half of all customers drop their policies during the first 10 years.

yields on the policies can be higher than the whole life offerings. And you are told up front what the guaranteed return rate will be. It'll usually be low, 4 percent or so, but there is potential for the return to be much greater.

Variable life insurance

This kind of cash value policy isn't as staid as universal or whole life. If you think the stock market is as risky as a spin of the roulette wheel, then this kind of policy is not going to be for you. The rate of return depends on how well the underlying investments do. You get to decide where you want your money to go. You can typically choose from among stock, bond, and money market mutual fund accounts. Sometimes a minimum death benefit is guaranteed no matter how badly the stock market performs, but you won't hear the same kind of assurances about your cash investment.

If your policy's stock and bond holdings don't do well, you might receive less money than if you had put it all into a whole life or universal life policy. You also might be forced to increase the premium payments to protect your insurance coverage. Unlike the other types of cash value policies, you receive a prospectus before you sign any papers. Take advantage of this and read it carefully. Variable, as well as universal life policies, can generate higher fees than the simpler whole life alternative.

Getting the help you need

Whether you are buying a new cash value policy or shopping for a replacement, it is extremely difficult to evaluate different policies. There are no meaningful tools to evaluate whether the policy your former college roommate is pressuring you to buy from him is any better than the one your Uncle Jack wants you to choose. There is no unit cost pricing of cash value life insurance, no *annual percentage rate* (APR) to scrutinize. In fact, it's because of the gobbledygook factor that there are still hundreds of insurers in this country—the lousy ones can hide behind the confusion.

If you aren't an accountant, your best bet when trying to make sense of an agent's computer illustrations is to call the Consumer Federation of America. The not-for-profit organization has developed an effective way to evaluate all types of cash value policies and even compare one to another. An insurance consultant with the federation determines the value of a policy's death benefit, as well as the rate of return on the savings portion.

The federation estimates the true investment returns on any policy and compares that to the alternative of buying a term policy and investing the money you'd save in a bank account or mutual fund. The cost of the analysis is $40 for the first policy and $30 for each additional one. You can contact the federation at 1424 16th St. NW, Washington, D.C. 20036; (202) 387-6121.

The federation's research also might help you decide whether you want to buy a policy through an agent—and pay a stiff sales commission—or buy what's called a *low-load* policy instead. Low-load policies are sold directly by insurance companies that do not employ agents. Because these companies have cut out the middleman, low-load policies are not shackled by commissions. During that first year, these low-load policies charge 2 or 3 percent of the premium. For one-stop shopping for a low-load policy, call Wholesale Insurance Network, which can provide quotes for most of the low-load insurers, at (800) 808-5810. However, you have to call USAA, a prominent low-load player, directly for its prices at (800) 531-8000.

In one comprehensive analysis, the federation examined the average annual rates of return for 57 different cash value policies for periods of 5, 10, 15, and 20 years. In this example, the policies were offered by such companies as TransAmerica, John Hancock, Mass Mutual, New York Life, and Guardian. At the same time, the federation examined low-load policies offered by USAA and Ameritas, another major low-load insurer. The results bolstered the federation's contention that a commission-based cash value policy must be held at least 15 years to get a decent return. To achieve even better numbers, the policy must be kept for 20 years.

CASH VALUE POLICIES: LOAD VERSUS LOW-LOAD POLICIES SOLD BY AGENTS

LOAD POLICIES

Years Policy Held	Annual Average Rate of Return
5	-14.5%
10	2.3%
15	5.1%
20	6.1%

LOW-LOAD POLICIES

Years Policy Held	Annual Average Rate of Return
5	6.7%
10	6.9%
15	7.2%
20	7.2%

Why do low-load policies soundly beat the policies that agents sell? It's simple—blame it on the exorbitant commissions. It's not rare for your entire first-year premium to be swallowed by the commission. So if your premium is $3,000 the first year, your assets 12 months later will be zero. As if this isn't bad enough, your second year's premium could get gobbled up by commissions as well.

Here's a shocking example of what happened when a wealthy sports figure, who will remain anonymous, went shopping for cash value insurance. He wanted tens of millions of dollars in coverage. Admittedly, most of us will never need that kind of protection, but it's a good way to illustrate just how devastating commissions can be. After the star's financial advisor obtained three different quotes from well-regarded insurers, he faxed them to Ray Del Cueto, a certified financial planner at Fee for Service, Inc., which provides low-load insurance quotes for investment advisors and insurance agents. (Fee for Service's consumer arm is Whole Insurance Network.) Del Cueto was stunned by what he saw when he scrutinized the figures. The pro athlete's premiums would range from $70,000 to $85,000 a year. But that wasn't the outrageous part. After paying these steep premiums for several years, the athlete would have next to nothing to show for it. For instance, with one policy, he would have written checks totaling $369,000, but if he decided to cancel the policy after five years, guess how much cash he could withdraw from his policy? Just $9,993!

Making the switch—a dumb idea?

If you already own a cash value policy, don't expect persistent insurance agents to leave you alone. Why?

Watch Out!
Never cancel your current life insurance policy before you purchase a new one. Typically, you have to undergo the medical screening process again before you receive another policy. If the new insurer turns you down, you don't want to be stranded without protection.

Because they can make another juicy commission if you agree to switch policies. Most of the time, replacing one cash value policy with another is a major financial mistake. That's because if you switch policies, you incur those exorbitant up-front sales charges all over again. Let's say you buy a $500,000 whole life policy that comes with an annual $3,500 premium. The first year, your investment is worth nothing because the entire premium goes toward the commission. Two years later, an agent convinces you that a universal life policy is offering more generous terms. You agree and drop your old policy. Once again, however, your first year's premium gets gobbled up by the commission. So far, you've paid $7,000 and have nothing to show for it.

One argument you will hear from agents is that your type of cash value policy no longer makes the most sense financially. And that very well could be. When economic conditions change, for instance, when interest rates go up or down, the attractiveness of your policy might diminish. In the 1980s, for example, universal life policies were popular because high interest rates allowed them to offer better returns. But a lot of people who rushed to sign up were later disappointed with their returns when interest rates slumped. Trading in a policy every time economic conditions change only makes your insurance agent a wealthy person. That said, there are times when abandoning a policy in favor of another makes sense.

Here are three major reasons to bail out:

■ Your insurer is in danger of going out of business.

■ If you're more affluent, there can be solid estate-planning reasons to necessitate a change.

- Your policy is dramatically overpriced, and you're considering a low-load policy.

The Consumer Federation of America says that universal life policies are excellent candidates for replacement if interest rates are below 6 percent and the owner will not be hit with a surrender charge. The CFA says these policies should be replaced with the low-load variety.

Here are some questions you should ask an agent if he is pushing you to replace your policy:

- If I replace my current policy, how soon will I have access to the same amount of cash value that I currently have?

- What is the difference in guaranteed values between the two policies?

- Can the payment of a death claim be challenged if I die within two years of buying the new policy?

    If a policy is at least two years old, the insurance company has less right to snoop around in the private life of a dead customer. The insurer must pay, absent any fraud. If the policy is a newer one, however, the insurer has the right to deny a claim or reduce the benefits if it determines that the deceased customer fibbed in any way on the application. What's more, if the policyholder commits suicide within the first two years, the beneficiaries don't receive the death benefit.

- If interest rates go down, how will the proposed policy perform? How would my existing policy perform?

- Are there any tax consequences when considering a replacement?

Timesaver
The American Society of Chartered Life Underwriters & Chartered Financial Consultants will send you a detailed questionnaire that your agent should fill out and show you before you decide whether to replace your cash value policy. You can call the organization at (800) 3922-6900.

Bright Idea
If an agent is pressuring you to swap your current cash value policy for a new one, check back with the person who sold you the original policy. It wouldn't hurt to run by the new figures with him and hear his opinion.

There could be. When a cash value policy is surrendered, a calculation must be made to determine if there was a taxable gain. There also might be a loss of other income-tax benefits, such as the deductibility of interest payments and "grandfathered" benefits that newer policies can't offer.

- Are there features in my policy that would be lost if I replaced it?

Your old policy might have a low, fixed loan rate, while the new one might have a variable loan rate that can conceivably become prohibitively expensive. Also, some policies sold in the 1980s have an interest-rate guarantee as high as 6.5 percent, while today's policies might only guarantee 4 or 4.5 percent. A new policy might not be underwritten on as favorable a basis as the old one.

Disability insurance—often overlooked

I bet you don't need me to tell you how important it is to insure your life, your home, your health, and those cars you have parked in the garage. But I'm pretty sure that you haven't given much thought—if any—to insuring your very ability to earn a living.

Disability income insurance is just as important as the other kinds of policies you have tucked away in file folders. It is definitely not a frill. Just look at the odds: If you are 40 years old, the likelihood of becoming disabled for at least 90 days is a staggering 67 percent. If you just turned 30 years old, the chances of becoming incapacitated for at least three months is 70 percent. (These statistics take into account all sorts of occupations, including the most dangerous, so if you work behind a desk, your chances of becoming disabled aren't necessarily so high.)

Essentially, a disability policy bails you out if you can't perform your job because of a temporary illness or a permanent one. The reasons why somebody might need one of these policies are limitless. Back surgery might keep a carpenter off the job for several months. A nagging carpal tunnel problem in the wrist might sideline a telephone operator. A serious car accident with a drunken driver might leave an innocent passenger critically injured for the rest of her life. Some people have relied on their disability policy when a sudden heart problem forced them to curtail their hours at work.

Take a minute to ponder this: Could you survive without your salary for a year, two years, maybe longer? What would happen if your spouse couldn't work? If you could handle this financial nightmare without trouble, then you don't need this insurance. But for everybody else, read on.

Alas, picking out a disability policy can be tricky. But here's a checklist that should make the task easier.

Bright Idea
Do you typically receive a sizable amount of your compensation each year in commissions and bonuses? If so, check to see if your company's disability policy covers more than your salary.

- **Contact your employer first.** If you work for a large or medium-size company, your chances of already having some kind of freebie coverage are excellent. Be sure to learn what the policy covers. Usually, a corporate policy only helps you out for one year. If that's the case, you need to buy more coverage.

- **Learn the insurance lingo.** When shopping for a policy, insurers will ask how long of an *elimination period* you want. This is essentially your deductible. The elimination period refers to the length of time it takes before you start receiving disability checks. Elimination periods range from 30 days to as long as two years. Not surprisingly, your policy costs more if you don't want a long wait. Most policyholders choose a disability period of 60 to 90 days. And you should, too. Need convincing? You can often cut 20 percent off the price of the policy if you pick a 60-day rather than a 30-day elimination period.

You'll also hear insurance agents talking about a *benefit period*. This refers to the length of time your policy pays once you make your claim. The benefits can last for as little as a year, while on the other extreme, they can continue until you die, however long that might be. Most people ask for a policy that stops when they reach 65, to coincide with retirement. This, after all, is usually when people start receiving Social Security and pension benefits.

■ **Make sure you and the insurer are on the same wavelength.** Know what an insurer's definition of disability is. When somebody complains bitterly about his policy, it's usually about this definition. There are three definitions:

Own occupation: This is the Cadillac of policies that kicks in if you can't perform your specific job, even if you could make the same amount in a different one. Imagine what would happen if an orthopedic surgeon loses several fingers in a car accident. Since he can no longer work in an operating room, he starts teaching at a medical school and also works as a medical consultant. No matter, with this policy, he's still entitled to disability checks since he can no longer perform surgery.

Any occupation: Under this definition, you don't qualify for disability payments if you can still work at a job that is appropriate for your level of education and training. In this scenario, the surgeon couldn't expect any checks.

Income replacement: This is the cheapest of the three policies. It guarantees your old salary level if your disability forces you to work at a lower-paying job.

Which policy should you buy? I'd forget about an own-occupation policy. They are getting increasingly difficult to find, and the cost is prohibitive. Some policies, especially the ones you can obtain through professional organizations, use an own-occupation definition for several years but then stop payments if you can hold onto a job that fits the any-occupation category. That seems quite acceptable. Income replacement could be your best bet since it does guarantee your old salary.

You need to determine what kind of benefits you'll require if you're disabled. Most often, insurers only provide coverage for 60 to 70 percent of your gross earned income. Realistically, you're not going to be able to find coverage better than this. And actually, this makes sense. Insurers don't want you to be living as well as you did before your setback, because then there'd be zero incentive to ever return to the workaday world.

When calculating what you'd need to cover all your monthly bills, keep in mind that—unlike your regular salary—you won't owe taxes on your disability payments. But there is one big exception. If your employer paid for your premium, then you'll owe Uncle Sam.

Watch Out!
Don't buy a policy that refuses to cover somebody as long as he can work somewhere. Suppose that you used to be a software engineer, but if the only job you can now hold is working the milkshake machine at McDonald's, your insurer will tell you, "Tough luck!"

If you're a woman, expect to pay a little more for your coverage. As any insurance actuary can tell you, that's because women file more disability claims. No one is certain quite why. Here's just one example of how gender can inflate the premium. UNUM, a major disability player in Portland, Maine, was asked to provide a quote for a man and a woman, who are both 40 years old. Their policies would replace 60 percent of their income until the age of 65. The elimination period would end in 90 days. UNUM would pay if the policyholders could not perform their own jobs for two years and then would continue only if they could not find work that matched their occupation, training, and education. For this coverage, the woman would pay $1,535. The man's identical policy would be $1,143.

Long-term care insurance—nursing home protection

A lot of misconceptions exist about long-term care insurance, but the biggest is the one I heard from somebody the other day: "I don't need one of those policies. If I end up in a nursing home, Medicare will handle my bills."

Guess again. Medicare won't pay for a long stay in a nursing home, and neither will Medi-Gap insurance. And to qualify for Medicaid, the federal-state welfare program, you have to be nearly impoverished. You can keep a car, a small amount of cash, your home, a prepaid funeral, and some jewelry (you won't have to sell your wedding ring), but just about everything else must go. When you die, you can't even be assured that your heirs will hang onto the family home—the state can seize it to pay your old bills. Rather than become impoverished, plenty of people have shifted anything of value to their children or other relatives. But even that trick is becoming harder to pull off. If you transfer your estate to others, Medicaid can make you wait three to five years before it begins picking up your nursing home tab.

To avoid that financial nightmare, you should seriously consider buying long-term care insurance if you are nearing retirement. Find a policy that covers not only a nursing home stay, but also home healthcare costs. That way, if you want to stay in your house but need some assistance, the policy can kick in. These policies aren't cheap, so you might be wondering if it's worth playing the odds that you'd ever need one. A study in the *New England Journal of Medicine* estimated that close to half of all Americans who reach the age of 65 will spend time in a nursing home.

Here's a worksheet from the National Association of Insurance Commissioners that provides questions you should ask prospective long-term care insurers.

Are you rich or barely surviving? If so, you can skip this section—you won't need one of these policies. If your retirement nest egg could barely feed a hummingbird, it doesn't make sense to buy a policy, since Medicaid will come to your rescue fairly quickly. On the other end of the spectrum, a millionaire should be able to foot his or her own nursing home bill. This kind of policy is best-suited for the middle class and upper middle class, who have accumulated a significant amount in assets during their lifetime.

Like any other kind of insurance, the rates can vary quite a bit, depending on such factors as your age, health, and whether you want a fancy policy. Your premium will be steeper if you demand

> " Long-term care on either end of the spectrum doesn't make sense. If you have a million dollars or more in assets, you can afford to pay for your own nursing home care. If you have few assets, you probably are going to end up on Medicaid anyway, so it's not worth it.
> —Janet Bamford, author of *Smarter Insurance Solutions* "

A long-term care
worksheet.
*Source: National
Association of
Insurance
Commissioners.*

A Shopper's Guide To Long-Term Care Insurance

Worksheet 2: Information About Long-Term Care Insurance Policies

Fill in the information below so that you will be able to compare the policies. Most of the information you need is in the outline of coverage and the policy. However, some information you will need to calculate or obtain by talking to the agent or company.

Topics	Policy 1	Policy 2	Policy 3
Company Information			
Name			
Telephone Number			
Agent Name			
Is Company Licensed?			
Rating Agency Name			
Rating			
Rating Agency Name			
Rating			
Review what levels of care are covered by the policy.			
Does the policy provide benefits for these levels of care:			
Nursing care?			
Personal care?			
Does it pay for any nursing home stay regardless of the level of care you receive?			
If not, what levels are excluded?			
Review where you can receive care covered under the policy.			
Does the policy pay for care in any licensed facility?			
If not, what are the restrictions on where you can obtain care?			
Does the policy provide home care benefits for:			
Skilled care?			
Care given by home-health aides?			
Homemaker services?			
Does the policy pay for care received in:			
Adult day care centers?			
Community centers?			
Other settings? (list)			

coverage that kicks in only 20 to 30 days after you need help. The length of your coverage also matters. A policy with lifetime coverage, for instance, costs a lot more than one that only lasts four years. Four years is how long the typical person stays in a nursing home.

The price tag of a long-term care policy depends on a lot of factors. Here's a quick look at average premiums for policyholders at different ages. The policies in this chart all last four years.

Before you invest in a policy, you should know what the going rates are in your community. After

A Shopper's Guide To Long-Term Care Insurance

Questions	Policy 1	Policy 2	Policy 3
Ask how long are benefits provided and what amounts are covered.			
What is the maximum daily benefit amount for:			
Nursing home care?			
Home care?			
Are there limits on the number of days (or visits) per year for which benefits will be paid?			
If so, what are the limits for:			
Nursing home care?			
Home care? (days or visits)			
What is the length of the benefit period you are considering?			
Are there limits on the amounts the policy will pay during your lifetime?			
If so, what are those limits for:			
Nursing home care?			
Home care?			
Total lifetime limit?			
Ask if the policy has inflation protection.			
Are the benefits adjusted for inflation?			
Are you allowed to buy additional increments of coverage?			
If so:			
When can you buy additional coverage?			
How much can you buy?			
When can you no longer buy additional coverage?			
Are benefits increased automatically?			
If so, what is the amount of the increase?			
Is this a simple or compound increase?			
When do automatic increases stop?			

all, you don't want a policy that provides for $100 coverage if the nursing home down the block only charges $80 a day. (You'd lose that $20 a day.) Actually, pinpointing nursing home costs really isn't tricky. Your local agency on aging can provide these numbers.

Careful number crunching won't be as necessary if you pick a *pool-of-money* policy. These flexible policies are becoming very popular, and it's not hard to see why. Let's say you buy a four-year policy that will pay $100 a day in a nursing home. That equals $146,000. If the nursing home only charges $75 a day, the policy will stretch beyond the four

A Shopper's Guide To Long-Term Care Insurance

Questions	Policy 1	Policy 2	Policy 3
If you buy inflation coverage, what daily benefit would you receive for:			
Nursing care			
5 years from now?			
10 years from now?			
Home care			
5 years from now?			
10 years from now?			
After the limits have been reached for inflation adjustments, what is the maximum benefit you will receive for:			
Nursing care?			
Home care?			
Ask if other provisions are covered under the policy.			
Is there a waiver of premium provision?			
If so, how long do you have to be in a nursing home before it begins?			
Does the policy have a nonforfeiture benefit?			
What kind?			
Does the policy have a return of premium benefit?			
Does the policy have a death benefit?			
If so, are there any restrictions before the benefit is paid?			
Ask when benefits begin.			
How long is the elimination or waiting period before benefits begin for:			
Nursing home care?			
Home health care?			
How long will it be before you are covered for a pre-existing condition?			
How long will the company look back in your medical history to determine a pre-existing condition?			

years. The policy would work the same way for home health-care coverage.

No matter what kind of policy you buy, I strongly suggest paying extra for inflation protection. We've all heard those spooky warnings about how inflation can rip the best-laid retirement plans to shreds. Well, consider this scenario: A 50-year-old man buys a policy that provides for $45,000 worth of coverage a year. He doesn't need the policy until he's 80 years old and he breaks a hip. A year in a nursing home, however, now costs $235,000. (This assumes a 5.8 percent inflation rate, which is realistic for this industry.) Obviously his policy will only cover a

AVERAGE ANNUAL PREMIUMS
FOR LONG-TERM CARE INSURANCE

**Coverage Amount: $80-a-Day Nursing Home Care,
$40-a-Day Home Healthcare**

Age	Premium	Premium with 5% Compounded Inflation Protection
50	$310	$651
65	$817	$1,481
79	$3,353	$4,579

**Coverage Amount: $100-a-Day Nursing Home Care,
$50-a-Day Home Healthcare**

Age	Premium	Premium with 5% Compounded Inflation Protection
50	$378	$798
65	$1,010	$1,881
79	$4,148	$5,889

Source: Health Insurance Association of America

Bright Idea
Before you buy
any health-
related insur-
ance, be sure the
companies are
financially solid.
You can learn
this by calling
any of the fol-
lowing indepen-
dent rating ser-
vices: A.M. Best:
(800) 424-BEST,
(900) 555-BEST;
Duff & Phelps:
(312) 368-3198;
Moody's: (212)
553-0377;
Standard &
Poor's: (212)
208-1527.

fraction of his costs. Insurers calculate inflation protection two ways: by a *simple* or *compounded* method.
If you can afford it, select the compounded inflation protection.

Well over one hundred insurance companies
would love to sell you a long-term policy. Of these, a
dozen companies sell the vast majority of policies.
I'd stick with a company that has a track record in
this relatively new field. Three insurers you might
want to consider are CNA, Travelers, and UNUM.
You shouldn't pick the companies that are significantly cheaper than the rest. They could go out of
business or might have to increase their rates significantly to survive.

If you think you're too young for long-term care
insurance, you might want to consider what could

Bright Idea
An increasing number of employers are now offering, as a benefit, long-term care insurance for employees' parents.

happen to your parents or in-laws. Some insurers suggest that you spring for the premium so you won't have to subsidize their costly care later. Obviously agents want to sell a ton of these policies so they can win a trip to Hawaii, but they have a point. Coverage for older parents can be especially important for middle-aged women. Let's face it, it's the moms of the world who will be expected to sacrifice their careers when Aunt Marge is diagnosed as senile. In one study published in the *Journal of Gerontology,* 23 percent of middle-aged female caregivers left their jobs, while 43 percent cut back their hours to care for aging relatives.

Taxes

There's one more thing you need to keep in mind—taxes. You might remember back in 1996 when Congress held lots of hearings at which folks like you and I griped about the big bad health insurance industry. In response, Congress passed the Health Insurance Portability and Accountability Act of 1996. Thanks to the politicians, you can now take your insurance with you as you hop from job to job. What the press pretty much ignored was a more obscure section of the act that divided long-term care policies into tax-qualified and non–tax-qualified policies.

If you purchase a tax-qualified policy, you pay no taxes on your benefits. Based on your age, you also can deduct all or part of your premium. But here's the catch: You can't use this policy if you only need a nursing home or assistance in your home for less than 90 days. (This could happen, for instance, if you suffer a stroke and need help for two months while you recover.) The other kind of policy doesn't impose the same 90-day restriction, but no one is sure whether this kind of policy will be tax deductible. The IRS has remained stonily silent on this question.

Some consumer advocates have complained that Congress's tinkering with long-term care rules didn't do the elderly any favors. They maintain that the new rules will make it tougher to take advantage of a tax-qualified policy in other ways, too. Under a tax-advantaged plan, for instance, somebody would have to be in worse shape to qualify for coverage than a frail senior who buys the other kind. A tax-qualified policyholder would have to be unable to perform two out of five or six so-called "daily living activities." These include eating, bathing, dressing, going to the bathroom, and transferring from a bed to a chair. Many nonqualified policies have less onerous hoops to jump through before benefits kick in. For instance, many insurers pick up the tab if a doctor certifies that a person can no longer take care of himself.

The federal government is feeling pressure to dispel the uncertainties clouding these policies. What should you do until the mystery is cleared up? Before you decide, you might want to determine what your tax bite could be if you chose the non–tax-qualified plan. Let's say your policy will pay $40,000 a year for nursing home costs, and you are in the 28 percent tax bracket. Your tax bill for one year would be $11,200. If you can afford to absorb that tax, you might want to take a chance. To hedge your bet, you could buy a policy from an insurer that promises to convert all nonqualified plans if the federal government rules unfavorably against them.

Before selecting a policy, it's best to learn as much as you can about long-term care insurance. Here are some resources:

Unofficially...
If you bought a policy before January 1, 1998, your policy automatically enjoys tax-favored status. Be careful, though. Its tax protection could be jeopardized if you make certain changes to your policy, including raising or lowering the benefit level. Before making any alterations, ask your insurer what this could do to your policy's tax status.

- *A Shopper's Guide to Long-Term Care Insurance.* National Association of Insurance Commissioners, 120 W. 12th St., Suite 1100, Kansas City, MO 64105-1925. (816) 842-3600; www.naic.org.

- *Long-Term Care Planning: A Dollar and Sense Guide.* Published by the not-for-profit United Seniors Health Cooperative, 1331 H St., NW, Suite 500, Washington, D.C. 20005-4706. (202) 393-6222.

- *Long-Term Care Planning Guide,* by Phyllis Shelton, an insurance agent and consultant. LTC Consultant, P.O. Box 17526, Nashville, TN 37217. (800) 587-0473.

- Eldercare Locator provides the telephone numbers of state or local agencies on aging anywhere in the country. (800) 677-1116.

- Order a reprint of a lengthy long-term disability insurance article that was published in *Consumer Reports* in October 1997. You can contact the magazine at Consumer Reports Reprints, 101 Truman Ave., Yonkers, NY 10703-1075. (914) 378-2000.

- *Smarter Insurance Solutions,* by Janet Bamford. Bloomberg Press.

- *How to Insure Your Income,* by Merritt Publishing.

No room for little white lies

No matter what kind of medical insurance you are applying for, don't fib on your application. Little white lies or half-truths can only backfire. Policy coverage can be denied or reduced if an insurance company determines you were fudging the truth.

How would an insurer know? You'd be surprised how little medical privacy you really have. If you've ever applied for health-related insurance before, your medical profile could be in the hands of a Massachusetts outfit called the *Medical Information Bureau* (MIB). How did the MIB become such a medical depository? Remember the waivers you sign that allow your physicians to bill your insurer? Those pieces of paper typically give your insurer the right to pore through your records and share them with other insurers through the MIB.

Thanks to that waiver, insurance companies ship tons of sensitive medical secrets to the industry's clearinghouse, which maintains files on more than 15 million Americans. The drinking problem you thought you had whispered in confidence to your internist could very well end up here. Did you scribble in your medical history questionnaire that your mother and grandmother had breast cancer? Did your doctor fib in your chart that you had a bad back just so you could get free massages? This type of information could be used against you and has been for countless people who are applying for life, disability, and individual health insurance policies. The MIB is one of the first places insurers look when they process your application.

Just as it's important to periodically check your credit report to make sure it contains no errors, it's also critical to review what the MIB is saying about you. Insurers have denied thousands of Americans coverage because of what they've learned from the MIB. To see if the MIB has a file on you and that it's accurate, contact the organization by calling (617) 426-3660. It's also a good idea to read your medical

Video rental records are afforded more federal protection than are medical records.
—Sheri Alpert, privacy expert and member of Computer Professionals for Social Responsibility

records and make sure they're correct. Damaging mistakes can haunt you when you apply for insurance.

Just the facts

- Don't be pressured into signing a life insurance contract you don't want.

- For most people, term life insurance is the best bet.

- You'll save a great deal of money by using low-load policies.

- Consult an unbiased source to evaluate cash value insurance policies.

- Know what the insurer means by *disability* before you by a disability policy.

- If you aren't rich or poor, you might need to buy long-term insurance.

Chapter 15

Our $452-billion shopping spree ▪ Strategies for
avoiding more debt ▪ Credit card consolidation
options ▪ What's in your credit report could
shock you ▪ Slamming the door on pesky
creditors ▪ The pros and cons of bankruptcy

When You're in Financial Trouble

Look around next time you're at the mall, and
you'll see an awful lot of people who owe
$7,000 on their credit cards. Why $7,000?
That's the average balance facing about 60 million
households who never seem to be able to pay off
their monthly credit card bills. Add that all up, and
we're talking about a stratospheric $452 billion,
surely enough to buy all the shopping malls in
America.

The typical American family owns about 14
credit cards, which is probably 12 too many. And
remember many are paying an outrageous 18 percent interest rate or higher for the privilege of carrying this addictive plastic.

How deadly is debt? Consider this example from
Gerri Detweiler, a prominent consumer advocate
who is on a personal mission to get us all to live
within our means. Let's suppose you owe $10,000 on
a VISA that carries a 17 percent interest rate. The

minimum required payment is $200 a month. If you only pay the minimum each month, it will take you 50 years to get rid of the balance. That's right, five decades. In the process, you will pay $33,447. Essentially, you'll spend $167 for every $50 purchase. That's quite a steep penalty for the convenience of carrying plastic.

If you are in trouble, perhaps you can take some comfort knowing that you are not alone. Millions of people are in your same predicament, but at least you want to do something about it. Keep reading to find out what your options are if your debts are seriously endangering your financial health and sanity. In this chapter, you'll learn how to avoid common credit card traps. I'll also provide you with two dozen ways to save money. And I'll discuss what could booby-trap your well-intentioned plans for consolidating your debts. I'll also explain why even somebody who has never once made a late bill payment should examine her own credit report. I'll also offer strategies for anybody who desperately wants to repair a poor credit history, as well as provide a backgrounder on bankruptcy options.

For starters, here are your seven best credit card strategies:

- **Limit your plastic.** Keep a MasterCard and a VISA or one of those along with a gasoline card. Funny as it might seem, creditors get suspicious if you only carry one card. The folks with the money want to make sure you can handle more than one card at a time. Another option is to choose American Express as one of your cards, which is what I do. The nice thing about American Express is that it imposes discipline. You must pay the balance every month.

Unofficially...
Even celebrities can end up in debt. When entertainer Sammy Davis died in 1990 of throat cancer, he owed millions in back taxes. His attorney blamed this sad affair on "bad investments." Davis's widow had to sell the couple's Beverly Hill's mansion, along with memorabilia and jewelry to pay the IRS.

If, realistically, you know you're going to keep a balance, put all that debt on the card with the very lowest interest rate. Find a no-fee or rebate card for all the purchases you know you'll pay off when your bill arrives.

- **Limit your total credit lines** to no more than 20 percent of your annual income. This way, you'll put a ceiling on your debt load.

- **Tear up those blank checks.** Card companies love to bombard people with invitations to charge, charge, charge. A favorite ploy is to mail you blank checks that are tied to your plastic. (These unrequested checks often land in mailboxes during tax season.) What's the harm in using just one? Maybe for a weekend in Palm Springs or to splurge on a new suit? For starters, you can be dinged 2 percent of the total just for the privilege of using the check. Then of course, you're stuck paying the interest, which can be astronomical.

- **Skip the heavy metal cards.** You'll enjoy a higher credit limit with a gold or platinum card. A gold card also might offer disability or life insurance and extended warranties on card purchases. Still, there are fewer and fewer reasons to own one of these. Many of the gold card's features are already offered by the plain old cards. And it's also arguable whether some of these perks are even necessary. For instance, American Express Platinum cardholders can access 24-hour-a-day travel and concierge services and room upgrades at hundreds of hotels. But is it worth paying an annual $300 fee? Often, the heftier fees for status-symbol cards don't make financial sense. After all, do you

Timesaver
Hunting for a better credit card? You can obtain a list of the best low-rate, gold, secured, rebate, and no-fee cards from CardTrak. For the latest list, send $5 to CardTrak at P.O. Box 1700, Frederick, MD 21702; (800) 344-7714. Or visit CardTrak's Web site (www.cardtrak. com).

Unofficially...
The platinum cards are the ultimate, right? Guess again. One of the country's major credit card issuers has unveiled a titanium card. First USA, which is a unit of Banc One, is offering a card with a 9.99 percent annual rate and no annual fee. The credit line can go up to $100,000. Whether this titanium card will catch on with other issuers, not to mention consumers, remains to be seen.

really want to pay a stiff annual fee just so you can impress a clerk at a cash register?

Even the merchandise warranty on items purchased with a credit card isn't necessarily worth the trouble. "People get a warm and fuzzy feeling because they think they can call a toll-free number and get their money back within days. In most cases, that won't happen," suggests Sarah Campbell, senior vice president of Bank Rate Monitor, which tracks the credit card industry. She knows from personal experience. As she was taking an expensive ceramic shower head she had purchased out of the box, it fell and broke. When she contacted her gold-card issuer, she had to fill out an incredible amount of paperwork, make quite a few calls, and provide her homeowner's insurance policy and the receipt. It took 90 days before she received a check.

- **Renegotiate your card's interest rate.** People know they can haggle with a car salesman, but not many realize they can ask their card issuer for a lower interest rate. Actually, it makes sense. If you carry a balance, the bank issuing your card certainly doesn't want you to look elsewhere for a cheaper one. Keeping you happy is important. Call your card's toll-free number—you might be surprised at the rate you get.

- **Cut up department store plastic,** at the very least. If you thought the interest rate on your MasterCard is ridiculous, have you checked what your favorite department store is gouging you for? You might be paying rates as high as 24 percent. Since major department stores accept other plastic, there's no reason to use these cards.

Simply cutting up your Macy's card, however, won't do. To get your accounts closed down, you must call each retailer. While you're on the phone, ask the store to send you a letter that states that it was your idea to end the relationship. Why is this important? You can use these letters as ammunition if all the card cancellations are mistakenly interpreted the wrong way by the credit-reporting agencies. Imagine what would happen if you were turned down for a car loan because the car dealer, reviewing your credit report, read that four department stores had terminated your cards. Actually, there is less chance of this snafu happening than there was in the past, since the Fair Credit Reporting Act was strengthened in 1997. Congress insisted that the credit bureaus improve their record keeping so an account closed by you won't be confused with one a store terminates.

- **Consider using a debit card** if you tend to lose self-control within five minutes of entering a mall. One of these cards can look like the typical MasterCard, but it's not. It is actually an ATM card issued by MasterCard or Visa. When you buy something, you punch in your secret code on the keypad, and the money is instantly sucked out of your checking, savings, or brokerage account. Some debit cards act more like plastic checks—it could take a couple of days before your purchase clears. Before you sign up for one, be sure to ask about fees—especially any fees you have to pay every time you use the card.

Timesaver
If you don't want to be tempted by all those preapproved credit card offers, turn off the spigot. Call any one of the three major credit bureaus, and your name will be purged from future pre-screened credit offers. Your name will stay off the lists for two years. If you never want to be bothered again, you'll have to make the request in writing.

Money-saving tips for tight budgets

Of course, there's another surefire way to reduce your debt load. Just don't spend as much money. Here are a few tips to help you do just that. You can find others in Chapter 2, "Organizing Your Finances from A to Z."

- Don't pay more than 5 percent above your new car's invoice. You can find those prices in new-car buying guides at your local library.

- Raise your automobile insurance deductible. If you bump up your deductible from $200 to $500, you can save 15 to 30 percent off your collision and comprehensive premium.

- In quite a few states, you can find the cheapest auto insurance by calling Consumer Reports Auto Insurance Price Service at (800) 807-8050.

- Take advantage of the telephone wars. Ask your carrier for the cheapest calling plan possible. And then comparison shop with other telephone carriers. For a handy long-distance comparison guide, contact the not-for-profit Telecommunications Research & Action Center at P.O. Box 27279, Washington, D.C. 20005. Enclose a self-addressed envelope (with 55 cents postage) and $5.

- Bring a brown bag for lunch.

- Stop buying lottery tickets.

- Refinance your mortgage with a no-points loan if interest rates are down.

- Swap baby-sitting duties with friends rather than hiring a teenager.

- Pay off credit cards with the highest interest rates first.

- Avoid vacation time-shares—they are financial losers.

- If you still have student loans, see if you can consolidate them into a lower-rate loan. Call (800) 4FED-AID for details.

- Put your household on a budget.

- Don't watch the shopping channel.

- Don't buy on impulse. Go home and think about it for a day.

- Wait until movies come out on video.

- Request auto insurance discounts. Having air bags, antilock brakes, antitheft devices, a safe driving record, or any one of these can cut the price.

- Bargain for a cheaper hotel price. Don't just accept a quote from a chain's toll-free number—call the hotel directly, too. And ask for any discounts you might be entitled to for such things as AAA and AARP memberships, as well as military service.

- When leasing a car, bargain as if you are going to buy it outright. When the price is down, then announce that you want to lease it.

- When selling your house, don't pay the agent's standard 6 percent commission. Offer 5 percent or less.

- Shop for items off-season. For instance, buy heavy clothes at the end of winter, swimsuits in September, and furnaces in the summer. And try to vacation off-season when airfares and hotels offer better deals.

Unofficially...
Bad spending habits begin early. Almost 60 percent of college students use at least one credit card. One in every five coeds carries four cards.

- When shopping for appliances or electronics, look for closeouts or last year's models. The discounts are often 10 to 25 percent.

- Save on your energy bill by lowering the setting on your hot-water heater to 120 degrees rather than 140 to 145 degrees.

- Scrutinize your itemized hospital bill. Studies have shown that 95 percent or more of the bills contain errors favorable to the hospital.

- Consider banking at a credit union—the fees are often fewer and lower.

Still not sure where you can realistically cut back? A national survey funded by Fidelity Investments might give you some ideas. When asked where they could cut spending in their own lives, here's what the typical American said:

Eat out less	60%
Buy less extras for the kids	53%
Grocery shop more carefully	49%
Buy fewer clothes	36%
Cut back on travel	32%
See movies less often	28%
Spend less on hair salons and beauty-care products	25%

The pros and cons of debt consolidation

Budget-trimming suggestions are fine, but what if you already have enough bills sitting on your desk to fill a recycling bin? As moderator of an America Online forum on credit and debt, Gerri Deitweiler has spent hundreds of hours listening to people who are asking this very question. And you know what many of these folks are most eager to learn about—debt consolidation. The idea is simple. Instead of having a dozen or more creditors pestering you for your payments, you transfer all your debts to one place. Then you have one bill every month. This could give you a psychic boost, but you'll obviously need a better payoff to make it worthwhile. Merging all your bills can work if you can manage to refinance the debt at a lower interest rate. If you do try debt consolidation, aim to repay your debt in three to five years. When you crunch the numbers, the financial reasons can be compelling.

Let's look at how much Benjamin, a store manager, could save with debt consolidation. Benjamin ended up relying on his credit cards when he was laid off for several months. Now he's stuck with a $10,000 balance on cards that are charging an average of 19 percent interest. Each month, he's paying the bare minimum. Eager to shrink those payments, he moves all his debt to a new credit card that only charges 13 percent. When he mails off his last payment three years from now, Benjamin can celebrate. He'll save $34,468 over what he would have owed if he had stuck with those minimum payments.

Before you explore your consolidation options, do some soul-searching. All too often, squeezing your debt into one payment fails. Somebody with all these great intentions will end up as deep in debt as always. Why? Because debt consolidation won't work for anybody who continues to spend more than he earns. And the consequences could be dire. For instance, if you tap into all your equity when you obtain a loan against your house, you could lose the house if you fall behind in your payments.

There are several ways to consolidate your debt. Here are your main options.

> " Debt consolidation can be very helpful at reducing your costs and getting a handle on the problem, but it's not the whole solution. The default rates for people with home equity loans for debt consolidation are very high. The reason is people aren't addressing how they are going to increase their income or reduce their debt.
> —Gerri Detweiler, author, *The Ultimate Credit Handbook* "

Watch Out!
When you get preapproved credit card offers in the mail, tear them up. A crook, fishing the offer out of your trash, could accept the card on your behalf and simply change the address where the card will be sent. You won't know about it until a bill collector starts bothering you.

Credit cards

Credit card companies are always urging customers to move all their debt onto their cards. Find one that offers a low rate, preferably for a long time. A lot of the card offers that clog your mailbox come with an introductory teaser rate. When your teaser rate is about to expire, you can switch to another card with another lower introductory rate, but this can get tiring. Your best bet is to contact current card issuers and explain that you want to consolidate your debts on its card. Ask each card issuer if they will lower the rate so this can be financially feasible. If this doesn't work, contact the card issuers with the cheapest rates, which you can find through the CardTrak list. In Appendix E, you'll also find a list of the best credit card deals. If you do transfer your balance to a better card, cut up the original card and close out the account.

Home equity loans

Home equity loans are a big hit with consumers who need help paying their bills. And banks love them. If you're like me, you probably get junk mail every week from lenders who want you to tap into your home's equity. Of course, you have to stop and wonder why lending institutions are so eager to thrust money in our faces. The answer is simple. The banks aren't really risking anything. Since you'll use your home as collateral, the banks can legally confiscate your house if you can't make the payments. For this reason, you have to consider the consequences before you make this move.

That said, there are reasons why home equity loans are enticing. Unlike many other types of loans, the interest you pay is still tax-deductible. Remember, however, that you only enjoy this tax break if you file a tax return that itemizes deductions.

With a home equity loan or a line of credit (I'll explain the difference shortly), you borrow against whatever equity you have in your house. *Equity* is the portion of the home that you actually own. For instance, if your house is worth $175,000 and there's a $100,000 balance on the mortgage, your equity is $75,000. Banks will often loan you 80 percent of your equity, which in this case is $60,000. Some financial institutions will approve a loan that equals 100 percent of your equity and sometimes even 125 percent.

The traditional home equity loan works like a traditional second mortgage. You borrow for a set number of years, and the loan is usually offered at a fixed rate. You repay little by little every month for a preset number of years. Your other option is a *home equity line of credit,* which is sometimes referred to as a HELOC. This type of loan works a lot like a credit card. A bank approves you for a certain amount of credit up to a ceiling. You don't have to use that money all at once or ever, but it's there if you need it. Let's say you have a $50,000 line of credit, but you only use $30,000. You're still entitled to borrow the remaining $20,000 anytime you want. As you repay what you owe, the amount available to borrow increases.

Home equity lines of credit are usually offered with variable interest rates. The rate is tied to the prime rate—the rate the best corporate customers receive—or some other index. Lenders often generate business by offering teaser rates—a ridiculously low rate that may vanish in six months. Don't be snookered by these offers. Ask what will happen

Moneysaver
HSH Associates, a prominent publisher of mortgages and other consumer loans, offers a booklet, *Home Equity: A Consumer's Guide to Loans and Lines*. Contact HSH at 1200 Route 23, Butler, NJ 07405; (800) 873-2837. Or visit HSH's Web site at www.hsh.com. You can also buy lists of the best credit card deals. And HSH is a good resource for borrowers with a spotty credit history.

to the interest rate after the introductory offer expires.

When you're determining whether one of these loans makes financial sense, don't forget to include in your calculations what you'll have to pay in fees for such things as credit and title reports and your home's appraisal. But don't assume you must agree to all these costs. With the industry so competitive, many lenders are willing to shave some fees and eliminate closing costs. Also find out if you'll get hit with a yearly fee for your loan—many lenders charge $25 to $50.

If you do shop for home equity loans, watch out for unscrupulous lenders. To be safe, I'd stay away from any lender you have never heard of—like those that send the irritating junk mail. They could try to entice you into signing papers for a high-cost loan that could ultimately become a financial nightmare. While you might not fall for these slick come-ons, perhaps your mom or dad or a grandparent would. These shady companies typically prey on homeowners who are elderly, as well as those who are experiencing credit problems.

In 1998, the Federal Trade Commission issued a consumer alert on these home equity scams. Here are some unethical practices to look for:

- **Equity stripping:** The lender issues a loan based on the equity of your home, not on your ability to pay. If you can't make the payments, you could lose the house.

- **Loan flipping:** You are urged to refinance over and over again. Each time you refinance, you pay extra fees and interest points that only increase your debt.

- **Bait and switch:** The lender offers you one set of loan terms when you apply and then pressures you to accept higher charges when you sign the final papers.

- **Credit insurance packing:** The lender adds credit insurance to your loan that you might not need.

- **Deceptive loan servicing:** You never get accurate or complete account statements. That makes it almost impossible to determine how much you've paid or how much you still owe. You might pay more than you should.

Turning to family or friends

Never borrow from relatives—there are probably good reasons why this adage has survived so many years, but in some cases, turning to a rich uncle, your parents, or a friend might be worthwhile. Ask yourself if there will be strings attached or if you can emotionally handle a loan from someone so close. Also consider whether the person willing to bail you out should be loaning money at all. If he or she is on a fixed income, think twice about taking the money.

A relative might be willing to lend you money if you make the deal more attractive. Making a loan with a 7 percent interest rate could be more attractive to your dad than keeping it in a certificate of deposit offering 5 percent.

Tapping into your 401(k) plan

If you have money squirreled away in a corporate 401(k) plan, the chances are very good that your employer will let you borrow against it. By law, you can borrow no more than 50 percent of your 401(k) assets up to a maximum of $50,000. Typically, you are expected to pay off the loan within five years

> **"**
> Using an equity loan to pay for a vacation makes no sense. You'll be paying that off for the next 15 to 30 years. By the time it's paid for, you'll have long forgotten where you went, and possibly, even who you went with.
> —Rex Bentley, portfolio manager, SAFECO's Value and Balanced funds **"**

unless it was used to buy a house. In that case, the terms are longer.

Can you get a better deal if you are essentially the lender? In some cases. The interest rate you pay often is one or two points above the prime interest rate, which is what banks charge their best corporate customers. Your employer is prohibited from offering you a rate that is below the prevailing market interest rates. As you repay the loan, the interest you are charged is added to your 401(k) account.

If you choose this option, proceed carefully. When the money is temporarily withdrawn from the plan, your retirement nest egg can't grow. Imagine, for instance, if you borrowed $20,000 early in 1997, a year in which the Standard & Poor's 500 Index finished up 31 percent. You would have missed that wonderful ride. You'll also have to pay the entire loan all at once if you leave the company for any reason. If you can't come up with the money, you will have to pay income taxes on the amount, as well as a 10 percent IRS penalty.

Facing your creditors with confidence

When you're feeling overwhelmed by your bills, another strategy is to negotiate with your creditors. Usually 9 out of 10 creditors will let you reduce your payments temporarily if you just ask. You should do this by the time you've received a couple of letters from a company asking why you are delinquent. You'll probably feel awkward calling a credit card issuer to ask for this favor, but remember they take calls like this all day, every day. Know what you're going to say before you dial the number. Be prepared to discuss what payments you'd like to make, as well as how long you want the reduced payments to continue. Get the name of the person whom you talked with and take notes during the conversation. Follow up by sending a letter explaining why you are requesting the leniency and what you are proposing.

Even if your uncollected debt gets shipped to a collection agency, you still have an opportunity to negotiate. Sometimes you will be able to pay 50 to 80 percent of what you owe simply by paying a lump sum. If that's out of the question, see if the creditor will take the past-due notation off your credit report if you start paying monthly installments again.

There is no reason why you should battle with creditors on your own. The *Consumer Credit Counseling Service* can be a great ally. The CCCS is a not-for-profit organization that assists people in getting debt off their back. These offices are funded by creditors, such as card issuers and department stores, as well as the United Way and state and local governments. Depending on what you can afford, the service is free or dirt-cheap. There are more than 1,100 offices scattered across the United States and Canada. Contact them at (800) 388-CCCS.

While dealing directly with your creditors, a counselor evaluates how you are spending your money and recommends changes to get you out of the red. She can help devise a repayment program to keep the creditors happy. A counselor might also be able to get wage garnishments stopped.

Unofficially...
Just about two million people consult the Consumer Credit Counseling Service each year. To handle the demand, the CCCS annually opens nearly 100 new offices.

Examining your credit report

Whether you enjoy sterling credit or your financial life is in a shambles, you should know what's in your credit report. You might be amazed at what you find. The last time I checked, everything was correct, but that hasn't always been the case. In past credit reports, I've had cards listed that weren't mine. It didn't seem to hurt my credit standing, but obviously, you don't want strangers sharing your credit history. To play it safe, you should check your credit report every year. And it's crucial to obtain copies if you are contemplating a major purchase such as a house, a condominium, or a car. You don't want to discover that your credit report is pock-marked with inaccuracies after you've applied for a home loan. A snafu like that could jeopardize your moving date.

Here are some potential problems to watch out for:

- Inaccurate or incomplete name, as well as wrong address, Social Security number, and marital status
- Closed accounts that still look open
- Closed bankruptcies older than 10 years
- Credit cards you never owned
- Lawsuits you have never heard of
- Accounts that you closed that don't have the notation "closed by consumer"
- Paid-off accounts that still report a balance due
- Erroneous late payments

Each credit bureau has a file on just about every American adult. That adds up to 180 million people and 540 million files. Here's how you can reach the big three:

Equifax: (800) 685-1111

Experian (formerly TRW): (800) 392-1122

Trans Union: (800) 851-2674

By federal law, you won't have to pay more than $8 for your credit report. And if you live in one of the following six states, you can receive a free annual copy: Colorado, Georgia, Massachusetts, Maryland, New Jersey, and Vermont. Meanwhile, if you've been rejected for credit (it could be for a credit card, a mortgage, or a car loan), you are entitled to a free report. You must, however, ask for it within two months of the rejection. Credit bureaus must investigate a complaint within 30 days.

Not long ago, spotting an error in a credit report was easy compared to getting it erased. Fortunately, federal legislation has made the process easier. If you find a mistake, simply write to the agency and ask that this error be removed. The agency must investigate your complaint and share what it has learned within one month. If you need this done quickly because of a pending car or home loan, the agency should be able to speed up the process. If you are right or the creditor has no records of the disputed item, the bureau is obligated to erase it.

Of course, if all those black marks on your report are accurate, your job is tougher. Wiping all those smudges off your past spending history won't be fun, but it is possible.

There are proven ways to rehabilitate yourself. Here are four tips:

■ **Try damage control.** If there are understandable reasons why your credit is fouled up, explain them. By law, you are entitled to attach a letter, no longer than 100 words, to your credit report. In the note, you should explain— to any potential creditors—why your credit history looks bad. Be as direct and concise as possible. If you were conscientious about paying your bills up until a divorce, a job layoff, or a hospitalization set you back, be sure to mention that.

Unofficially...
Credit-reporting agencies bitterly complain that they are unfairly portrayed as the bad guys. They like to tout a 1992 study that suggested that 97 percent of the records are accurate. Of course, the credit bureaus paid for the study. They might be getting a bad rap, but that doesn't explain the hundreds of thousands of complaints they get every month.

Bright Idea
The Debt Counselors of America (www.dca.org) is a not-for-profit group that provides plenty of downloadable materials on such things as budgeting, credit cards, and strategies for erasing debt. It also maintains a forum where you can discuss your own financial predicament.

- **Make sure you receive credit for any good news.** If your credit report fails to include accounts that you pay on time, try to get that information mentioned. To do that, you should write a letter to the credit bureaus and attach a copy of a couple of recent statements that show your payment.

- **If despite your financial troubles, you've managed to hold onto credit cards, keep only a couple.** Then do everything in your power to make sure your payments are timely. Losing these cards could make your troubles even worse. To play it safe, try to write a check the day your bill arrives.

- **If you feel resolve to live within your means slipping, consider joining Debtors Anonymous.** Just like Alcoholics Anonymous, this support organization uses a 12-step recovery program. If you suspect you are a compulsive spender, you might want to consider joining. There are branches throughout the country. For more information, contact the group at Debtors Anonymous, General Services Board, P.O. Box 400, New York, NY 10163-0400; (212) 642-8220.

Building your credit back from scratch

Once you have your debt under control (perhaps due to the intervention of credit counselors), it can be time to start using credit cards again. Ironically, the only way creditors will respect you again is if you show you can use plastic responsibly. But the problem can be getting the chance. If you lost your cards during financial troubles, you can try obtaining one through a local department store or a gasoline station chain. These issuers often have more lenient requirements for their cardholders. Once you have established a good repayment record, you can aim for a MasterCard or VISA.

If you get turned down for a gas or department store card, the only way to redemption might be through a secured credit card. These are credit cards with training wheels. Bank card issuers take a chance on you because the risk for them is minimal. To qualify, you must deposit an agreed-on amount of money into a certificate of deposit or a savings account with the bank. If you fail to pay your bills, the bank can use your money to cover the debt.

Expect to pay more for these second-chance cards. Typically, the annual fee and the interest rates are higher. And you also might be dinged for an application fee that can run as high as $79. Luckily, however, more and more banks seem to be dropping these application fees, which they wouldn't dare try to charge for their regular credit cards. One way to avoid the stiffest fees is to shop for a card at a credit union first. Credit unions generally offer more reasonable terms for their plastic.

Secured cards are a true niche for the banking industry—many financial institutions don't bother with them. Bank Rate Monitor, which tracks thousands of credit cards, does maintain a list of secured credit card issuers it considers competitive (see the following table). You can find more details on these cards at its Web site (www.bankrate.com), as well as the best rates for all sorts of other credit cards. What's more, you can research the best buys for home equity lines of credit on the Web site. Not plugged into the Internet? Here's another option. You can obtain a copy of Consumer Action's recent survey of top secured cards by sending a self-addressed envelope to Consumer Action

"
Although secured cards tend to have higher interest rates and annual fees, they provide a valuable stepping stone. Many people find they can graduate to an unsecured credit card within a year or 18 months.
—Linda Sherry, editorial director, Consumer Action (a California consumer group)
"

BANKS THAT ISSUE SECURED CREDIT CARDS

Institution	Interest Rate	Deposit Required
American Pacific Bank Aumsville, OR (800) 610-1201	17.4%	$400–$15,000
Bank of Hoven Hoven, SD (800) 777-7735	19.8%	$300–$5,000
Bank One Tempe, AZ (800) 544-4110	19.99%	$500–$5,000
Citizens Bank Riverside, RI (800) 438-9222	15.65%	$300–$10,000
Community Bank Parker, CO (800) 779-8472	15.9%	$300–$4,000
Cross Country Bank New Castle, DE (800) 322-3210	21.24%	$200–$5,000
Federal Savings Bank Rogers, AR (800) 290-9060	9.72%	$250–$10,000
First Consumers Natl. Bank Beaverton, OR (800) 876-3262	18.9%	$250–$10,000
First National Bank of Brookings Brookings, SD (800) 658-3660	18.9%	$250–$5,000

First National Bank of Marin San Rafael, CA (702) 269-1100	18.4%	$300–$2,500
First Premier Bank Sioux Falls, SD (800) 987-5521	18.9%	$400–$10,000
Household Bank/Union Plus Salinas, CA (800) 622-2580	18%	$250–$5,000
Key Bank & Trust Havre de Grace, MD (800) 539-5398	19.4%	$350–$2,000
Marine Midland Bank Buffalo, NY (800) 850-3144	21.9%	$300–$2,000
Orchard Bank Beaverton, OR (800) 873-7303	15.5%	$200–$15,000
People's Bank Bridgeport, CT (800) 262-4442	16.9%	$500–$1,500
Sanwa Bank San Francisco, CA (800) 237-2692	15.9%	$625–$5,750
Sterling Bank & Trust Southfield, MI (800) 767-0923	22%	$200–$5,000

Source: Bank Rate Monitor

(secured cards), 717 Market St., Suite 310, San Francisco, CA 94103.

Looking at this list, you might think your task is a simple one. The banks advertising the lowest interest rates no doubt have caught your eye. Yet you could get frustrated if you expect that the bank with the best deal will cut you a card. Secured card issuers all have their own peculiar requirements. For instance, Sanwa Bank won't issue a card to anyone who has a bankruptcy listed on her credit report. The Community Bank rejects anybody whose bill payments have been delinquent during the prior six months. The Colorado bank also won't consider you if you have a federal tax lien or haven't held a job for one year.

What you should do as you rebuild your credit is avoid credit repair clinics. These outfits promise to polish your tarnished credit reputation, but beware. You could very well end up paying $500 to $1,000 or much more and be no better off. The tactics many of these outfits use on your behalf are questionable at best. For instance, they might flood credit bureaus with countless letters refuting the black marks on your credit report. By overwhelming a credit bureau, the clinic hopes that some of the negative entries will be erased at least temporarily. Some of these companies even suggest that their clients assume another identity to escape their bad credit history.

The Federal Trade Commission has been cracking down on credit repair clinics. Under federal law, for instance, these outfits are prohibited from accepting any money from a customer until it has fulfilled its contract. That means a clinic is breaking the law if it demands money upfront. Even if a clinic follows the rules, there is no reason to use one. Everything one of these companies can legally do, you can accomplish yourself. For instance, a clinic might give you a list of banks issuing secured credit cards, but you already have plenty of names from this book. You can also contact credit bureaus about mistakes on your credit report.

Protecting yourself from irritating bill collectors

Bill collectors are famous for being rude, sneaky, and bullheaded. They might be the only workers in America who are rewarded for acting like jerks. But believe it or not, debt collectors legally aren't supposed to behave like that. If they do, you have the right to tell them to get lost. And by law, they are supposed to do exactly that—leave you alone.

You have more leverage if your tormentor works for a collection agency. A collection agency is essentially a hired gun. When a creditor, lets say a local department store, can't get someone to pay his bill, it often pays an outside agency to retrieve the money. If the collector who is hounding you is an employee of the department store, you have less recourse.

Thanks to federal law, collectors can't threaten to break your legs or any other parts of your body. (This isn't a joke.) And they can't let curse words slip into the conversation. Calling too early or too late is also unacceptable—calls must be made between 8 a.m. and 9 p.m. These guys can't pretend to be your long-lost uncle or an old college chum when they contact friends and acquaintances to dig up dirt on you. In fact, they aren't supposed to call anybody else, other than your lawyer, unless it's to

Moneysaver
If you sign a contract with a credit repair agency and regret it the next day, don't worry. You can cancel the contract within three days of signing it.

Bright Idea
If you want to complain about a collection agency that is hounding you, contact the Federal Trade Commission at (202) 326-2222 or www.ftc.gov. The FTC will send you a complaint form to fill out. You also should consider contacting your state's consumer protection office. It might help to send a letter listing your complaints to the original creditor.

simply locate where you are living. When they call you, they must always identify themselves as bill collectors. And they can't telephone you repeatedly.

If a collection agency has broken these rules, you can simply write a letter to it saying you don't want to be contacted again. By law, the debt collector must honor your request. Your decision, however, won't prevent the agency or the original creditor from suing you to recoup the money. But you will have every right to sue the agency yourself if it has flagrantly harassed you. The low-cost way is to file in small claims court.

Bankruptcy—a last resort

For some people, the only way out of debt could be bankruptcy court. A milestone was reached in 1997 when more than one million Americans filed for personal bankruptcy. While declaring bankruptcy is a drastic step, it can ultimately help you dig out from under a mountain of debt and start fresh. But you should know that bankruptcy won't necessarily be a cure for your financial problems. In fact, declaring bankruptcy isn't even advisable for everyone being pestered by creditors.

If you are considering bankruptcy as an option, there are two ways to proceed. You can file a Chapter 7, which is the most popular method, or a Chapter 13 petition.

A Chapter 7 petition, which gets its name from—surprise, surprise—Chapter 7 of the Federal Bankruptcy Code, can wipe out all or most of your debts. But in exchange, you won't necessarily be able to keep all your possessions. Whether you file a Chapter 7 petition could depend on whether you'd have to surrender a lot of your assets. You often can keep a car, household furnishings, appliances, pensions, a certain amount of jewelry, clothing, and what's called a person's *tools of the trade*. If you are a writer, for instance, you could hold onto a computer, and a musician could keep a piano.

You might also be able to save your home. Under federal guidelines, a person can protect $15,000 in home equity, but laws in some states don't allow this much to be shielded. On the other hand, the homestead provision in other states is far more generous. You'll have to check with your own state to see what rules apply. Some states, such as Massachusetts, New Jersey, Pennsylvania, Texas, and Wisconsin, allow you to choose whether you want to use the federal or your own state's exemptions. Here's how exemptions work. Let's say you live in a state with a $2,500 car exemption. If your automobile is only worth $2,500, you get to keep it. But if it's valued at $10,000, the car could be sold to pay off creditors. You'd only be entitled to $2,500 from the proceeds.

Creditors can usually confiscate stocks, bonds, or other investments you have; any other vehicles; stamp or coin collections; and a second home.

This is a no-muss, no-fuss bankruptcy. With any luck, you'll only have to visit the courtroom once. The whole process could be finished in several months.

Chapter 7, however, isn't a solution for everybody. For instance, there are some debts the judge can't erase. The following obligations can't be wiped away:

- Alimony payments or child support
- Student loans that came due less than seven years ago
- Your income tax bill if it's less than three years old

Unofficially...
Some states are considered so-called *debtor's paradises* because they allow bankruptcy filers to shelter mansions, as well as millions of dollars in wages, pensions, and annuities. States with pro-debtor laws include Florida, Texas, Kansas, Iowa, and South Dakota.

Unofficially...
A bankruptcy filing can remain on a person's credit history for up to ten years after it's discharged. Most credit bureaus, however, will erase the notation after seven years for Chapter 13 filers. And many creditors won't hold a bankruptcy filing against somebody if five years have passed without further money problems.

- Condominium dues

- Certain court judgments

- Debts incurred from a drunk-driving conviction

The attorneys at Nolo Press, which publishes a huge selection of books on bankruptcy and other consumer law issues, offer this advice: If you can't get more than half of your debts erased through Chapter 7, it's not worth filing the petition.

Your other choice is a Chapter 13 petition, which can also take the heat off your money problems. When you seek this kind of bankruptcy petition, you are asking for more time to pay your creditors back. You can expect to be making the court-approved payments for three to five years. Just how much you have to kick in depends on each court. Some judges pressure you to pay as close to 100 percent of your debt as possible, while others are a lot more lenient.

You might be asking yourself, *Isn't this a no brainer? Why not get all or most of my debts wiped out through Chapter 7 after perhaps just one relatively painless court visit?* For starters, you might feel a strong obligation to pay those whom you owe. You also might owe federal taxes and or other debts that you can't necessarily dodge with a Chapter 7 petition. If you filed Chapter 7 recently, you also can't come back too soon. Without Chapter 13, you probably won't be able to keep a lot of assets, such as family heirlooms or perhaps even your house. And filing a straight bankruptcy could make life hellish for any co-debtor. Let's say you rack up $30,000 on two credit cards that your dad co-signed when you graduated from college. If you file for bankruptcy, guess who the credit card company is going to bug to pay your debts? That's right. Dear old dad.

The bankruptcy court would prefer not to see you again after your Chapter 7 case is closed. But if you get into more financial difficulties, you must legally wait at least six years from the date of your original filing before you can seek bankruptcy protection again. You won't have the same waiting period for Chapter 13.

Additional resources for credit woes

Anybody who needs further advice on credit rebuilding, bankruptcy, and surviving money troubles might want to check out the following books. You can also learn quite a bit for free by visiting Nolo Press's self-help law center at **www.nolo.com**.

- *The Ultimate Credit Handbook,* by Gerri Detweiler.

- *Invest in Yourself: Six Secrets to a Rich Life,* by Marc Eisenson, Gerri Detweiler, and Nancy Castleman.

- *How to File for Bankruptcy,* by Stephen Elias, Albin Renauer, and Robin Leonard.

- *Chapter 13 Bankruptcy; Repay Your Debts,* by Robin Leonard.

- *Take Control of Your Student Loans,* by Robin Leonard and Shae Irving.

- *Surviving Debt: A Guide for Consumers,* 2nd edition, by Jonathan Sheldon and Gary Klein.

- *Nolo's Law Form Kit: Personal Bankruptcy,* by Stephen Elias, Albin Renauer, Robin Leonard, and Lisa Goldoftas.

- *Credit Repair: Clean Up Your Credit Report,* by Robin Leonard.

- *Money Troubles: Legal Strategies to Cope with Your Debts,* by Robin Leonard.

Just the facts

- You can reduce your debt by following smart credit card strategies.

- There are plenty of proven ways to reduce that nagging debt.

- Without motivation, debt consolidation often backfires.

- You shouldn't let debt collectors push you around.

- Even if your credit is immaculate, order a credit report.

- You need to study your choices before filing for bankruptcy.

GET THE SCOOP ON...
Money makes us crazy—one way or another ▪
Discovering your own money quirks ▪
Wall Street daredevils, money worriers, and
more ▪ Couples' money therapy ▪ Kids and
money hangups

Money and Your Psyche

Chapter 16

Has money ever made you feel jealous, guilty, depressed, or anxious? It's okay to confess. You're not alone. The money in our wallets, in our bank accounts, and even in our pipe dreams does funny things to our psyches. Most of us think about money every day, and yet it's still a dark taboo. The chatty guests on tabloid talk shows divulge the most embarrassing and intimate secrets, but you never see any of them spreading out their financial records for all to see.

If you think your only problem with money is not having enough, think again. In fact, a little soul-searching might be in order. Our attitudes about money are as distinct as our fingerprints, and they start taking shape when we're still playing on swing sets. For that reason, a growing number of therapists believe that our money troubles really begin in our minds. Are you a compulsive spender? You might be compensating for low self-esteem. Or perhaps you're a money hoarder who is terrified to risk even $1,000 in a mutual fund. Maybe you absorbed the money fears of your Depression-era parents. On the flip side, you might be somebody who fritters away your money on risky stock options or initial public offerings. This kind of person doesn't need Las Vegas when he has Wall Street. Scratch below the surface, and you'd discover yet another type of psychological hangup.

If you have your own money quirks, there's no need to panic. In most cases, you can change your unhealthy attitudes about money without spilling your guts to a therapist. (Believe it or not, there are quite a few therapists out there who specialize in financial disorders, and their ranks are growing.) Of course, I'm sure there are people reading this book right now who are thinking to themselves, *This is all a bunch of mumbo jumbo!* I know it might sound a little odd, and I admit I do live in Southern California, but bear with me. There are all sorts of legitimate reasons to explore this issue. All those financially dysfunctional attitudes we harbor about money can prevent us from becoming confident investors, savvy savers, and prudent consumers. In fact, researching stocks or selecting the right mutual funds might not get you as far ahead as you might think. Not if your money hangups prompt you to sabotage your financial strategies.

Unfortunately, we don't have the luxury of shrugging off whatever financial dysfunctions we might have. That's because we're living in a time when we're expected to make the most of our own money decisions. Not too long ago, the workplace took care of our future financial needs. Companies invested their employees' pension money, and we didn't have to worry our little heads about it. Nobody used to agonize about what mutual funds to pick for a 401(k) plan, because there was no 401(k) plan. When somebody retired, she'd leave knowing

> " More and more financial advisors are realizing that the best-laid financial plans will go astray if a person is not emotionally healthy.
> —Victoria Felton-Collins, certified financial planner and national lecturer on the psychology of money "

that she'd be guaranteed a steady stream of checks for the rest of her life. Back then, all that was required of workers was staying employed. Yet these private pension plans are disappearing as companies decide workers must do more to fund their own retirements through 401(k) plans.

Unfortunately, financial plans can blow up in our faces because, let's face it, money for a lot of us isn't just loose change and dollar bills. Ideally, money should just be a medium to pay for things. We use it to splurge a little, pay bills, invest for retirement, donate to charity, and the rest of the time we shouldn't think much about it. Money should not be an emotionally charged issue that looms larger than Mount Rushmore. But unfortunately, many people confuse money with power, independence, love, or self-esteem. And that's when we get in trouble.

Do you recognize your money personality?

If you aren't sure what your money demons are, here is the lowdown on some of the more common personality types. While some might be obvious, others are trickier to detect. See if you can recognize yourself in any of the categories. If you do, read the action plan for tips on how to prevent yourself from mentally sabotaging your own financial future.

No matter what your own money demons might be, it makes sense to pause for a little self-reflection at the start. You need to think about where your attitudes about money came from. One of the best ways is to reflect on what kind of relationship your own parents had with money. In this section, you'll find a sample of the kinds of questions you should ask yourself. And by all means, include your partner in this question-and-answer session. Chances are excellent that his or her attitudes about money aren't completely healthy either.

This doesn't have to be a completely serious exercise. It can be fun to laugh at what our parents did that they thought was so smart. When I was a kid, for instance, my mom wouldn't let me make any cake that called for more than three eggs. This, she argued, would be entirely too extravagant.

- How did your parents deal with money?
- Did your parents obsess about money?
- How did it affect you?
- Did you ever feel ashamed or guilty about how much money your family had?
- Do you have any traumatic memories about money?
- Were you able to receive most or all of what you needed as a child?
- Did your parents argue about money?
- Are your attitudes about money similar to one of your parents'?
- Was money used as a threat in your family?

> " None of us were raised with sane, rational models of how to deal with money. We imitate our parents' irrational ways or we make vows to never be like our parents so we become the opposite. In neither case are we free to have a relationship with money.
> —Olivia Mellan, New York psychotherapist specializing in money conflicts "

Thrill seekers

You'll find some professionals with more than your average amount of disposable income fitting into this category. They get their kicks by earning big returns and showing off their wealth. They are driven to collect badges of success. That could be a Lexus, a Rolex, or a very fat portfolio.

They have a real drive to win because they often are scared to death that others will think they're incompetent. So what's the big problem? They take too many crazy chances. Instead of bungee-jumping, skydiving, or motorcycling, they take big risks with their portfolio. They might dabble in futures, commodities, or the tiniest small cap stocks, all of which can blow up.

Brokerage houses and mutual funds are all too familiar with these highfliers who try to push the envelope. Some investors get so caught up in trading that they can't stop even when they've lost tons of money. With trading available 24 hours, reckless investors can get into serious trouble. Strange as it sounds, some compulsive investors have won lawsuits against brokerage houses that they insist didn't stop them from recklessly trading. The founder of Jack White & Co. recently talked to a reporter I know about how his brokerage firm shuts down some customers' accounts when they persist in irrational Wall Street gambling. He observes,

> If a person is constantly losing money on short-term trading, we call it to his attention, and we ask him to give us details on his suitability to invest, given his risk tolerance and available cash. If we're not comfortable, we will ask him to move on.

An action plan for thrill seekers

There are ways to muzzle a thrill seeker. When you invest, avoid getting swept up by the excitement of a potential trade. If you hear someone on a financial television program gush about a stock, do not rush to place an order. Try not to make a costly decision until you've thought about it for a couple of days and thoroughly researched your pick. If a company was a wise choice yesterday, it should still be one in two or three days. Here's another tactic: See if you can find pleasure in other things besides investing.

Keep this in mind, as well: Some researchers have concluded that people who are generally positive about life are usually less likely to take crazy

Moneysaver
If you're tempted to spend more than you should, try a little cash therapy. For an entire week, only buy things with cash—preferably with single dollar bills. Do not venture near the mall unless you have a legitimate need to be there. The same admonition applies to the Home Shopping Network!

chances in the stock market. And try to evaluate your portfolio objectively. Put a modest amount of money into speculative investments—maybe micro-cap stocks, futures, whatever makes you happy. Then you can feel content leaving the bulk of your money in blue chip stocks and other less-risky possibilities.

Compulsive spenders

I have a friend who is a classic shopaholic. To keep her husband from realizing how much money she is blowing, Molly has credit card bills sent to a post office box. When her plastic debt reached $15,000, her husband began asking questions. In a panic, she borrowed money from a wealthy neighbor to pay off the cards. While she's paying off that loan, she's still using credit cards like Las Vegas poker chips. The funny thing is, Molly doesn't even use all the stuff she buys, but she throws the best garage sales. When her purchases start piling up, she gets rid of almost new merchandise at cut-rate prices. I always insist that she let me know when she's having a sale.

Admirably, my friend realizes she needs to start an IRA for herself. But for more than a year, an application to open a mutual fund account has sat on her desk. "As soon as I can get ahead financially, I'm going to mail it in," she keeps promising.

What motivates people like my friend? It could be a poor self-image. Children who grow up in sta-ble, loving homes generally end up with healthier attitudes toward money than do kids who spend a lot of time dodging fists or insults.

Admittedly, it can be tricky figuring out if you are a money binger or someone who simply likes fine things. Here are some questions to ask yourself:

- Do you have clothes with the price tags still on that have never been worn?

- Do you daydream a lot about shopping?

- Do you pay for others or lend money as a way to make friends?

- Do you buy things you don't need but talk yourself into thinking you will some day?

An action plan for compulsive spenders

If you're a shopaholic, the first really big step is acknowledging that you have a problem. If you automatically dismiss your spouse's accusations that you are hauling way too many shopping bags home from the mall, you won't break out of your destructive behavior.

Try to reflect on why you binge on shopping. You might think it's because the malls are stocked with incredible goodies, but that can't be the reason. Often, people turn to shopping to fill some hidden emotional need. Someone who could use another quart of self-esteem goes to the mall to fill up the tank. Other people might hit the malls to momentarily chase away depression.

Consider diverting your attention from shopping by exercising or spending more time with family and friends. And it could be worthwhile attending Debtors Anonymous meetings. You might want to consider making an appointment with the nearest Consumer Credit Counseling Service. You also can't spend it if you save it. Have the credit union at your company automatically deduct money from your weekly paycheck and deposit it into a savings account. Once you have enough saved, open a mutual fund account. Lastly, put money into a retirement plan—you'll be less tempted to pull it out prematurely, because you'll have to pay taxes and penalties.

Unofficially...
Yes, people can actually be clinically diagnosed with a financial phobia. Here are some taken from the *Encyclopedia of Phobias, Fears and Anxieties*: *atephobia*—fear of ruin or being ruined, can refer to financial ruin; *aurophobia*—fear of gold; *chrematophobia*—fear of money; *decidophobia*—fear of making decisions; *harpaxophobia*—fear of becoming a victim of robbers; *peniaphobia*—fear of poverty.

Avoiders

Are you petrified whenever you need to make a financial decision? You could be a money avoider. People fitting this description typically need tax extensions from the IRS because they're too uncomfortable dealing with dollars and cents. They get the shakes when they contemplate balancing their checkbooks.

Sometimes avoiders postpone financial decisions because they are terrified of making a mistake. Take Patrick, for instance. Patrick received a $1 million inheritance from his grandfather, but he's got the money stashed in a savings account. Why? He feels guilty about not earning all this money—a common feeling—and he's also petrified of investing it badly. Subconsciously, he's worried that he'll hear the voice of his critical grandfather rising from the grave. A psychiatrist who specializes in helping investors with their money hangups finally convinced Patrick to put some of the money into an index fund. Since the index fund would simply track the market, the ghost of Patrick's grandfather couldn't criticize him from the grave for lousy stock picks.

Money aversions can pose major problems, because the avoiders won't devote the time necessary to devise sensible financial strategies. Avoiders who do have money stashed in the stock market might face another critical problem. Let's see how Vince deals with financial decisions. One day he gets a phone call from his broker, who says, "The foreign emerging markets fund that you bought two years ago has done nothing but hemorrhage money, and the manager is in way over his head. I think you should sell your shares." Vince thanks his broker and promises to make a decision soon. But it's too painful to think about selling for a loss, so he doesn't. He never calls his broker back, and Vince continues to lose money on the fund.

What are the psychological reasons for avoiding money matters? A fragile ego can be responsible for some of it. A money therapist once shared a story with me about a young couple who had asked a lawyer to draw up an estate plan. After seeing their net worth, the attorney said, "I guess we could pull together a bare-bones estate plan." The couple was so mortified they refused to go back.

Actually, some people shrink from consulting a broker or financial planner because they're petrified of being snickered at. Granted, these fears aren't always crazy. Someone once complained to me about the treatment he received when he called up a mutual fund about setting up a new retirement account. He didn't have a lot of money to start, so he planned on opening the account with the lowest contribution allowed. "I was treated with disdain by a salesperson when I said 'minimum.' He didn't drive me away though, I'm a tough old codger. What I did do, though, was switch to a different salesperson."

An action plan for avoiders

If you procrastinate paying bills, try to get to them as soon as they arrive. Set a deadline for doing financial tasks such as balancing your checkbook or organizing your receipts for tax time. For hard-core avoiders, find a money manager you can trust to help you invest your money. If you're too intimidated to make that call, educate yourself first. You can find plenty of basic financial primers at your library or bookstore.

Bright Idea
Want to know more about your own money profile? Read Olivia Mellan's *Money Harmony: Resolving Money Conflicts in Your Life and Relationships.*

Hoarders

You're probably thinking that a hoarder is one of those crazy people who not only pinches pennies, but keeps 40 years' worth of mildewed *National Geographic* magazines in the garage. Actually, financial pack rats can be a lot harder to detect. On the surface, their actions seem harmless or even admirable. They might clip coupons, collect those little sugar and ketchup packets, and order tap water at a restaurant rather than spend $1.50 on an iced tea. For some, frugality is necessary to stretch a tight budget. But hoarding becomes a problem when you can't enjoy any of your money because you agonize every time you pull out your wallet. Spendaphobes, for instance, will endure a 16-hour bus trip to visit their grandchildren, even though they have plenty of money for the two-hour plane trip.

Most hoarders do not hide their money under a Serta Sleeper, but they might stash it in a savings and loan where returns can't keep up with inflation. These people sit on money like hens sit on eggs. By holding on tight to their money, they hope to feel secure in this cold and crazy world.

An action plan for hoarders

Find ways to enjoy your money. Nobody is suggesting that you splurge on a new car, but try buying small items that you've always wanted but considered too frivolous. If all your money is stashed away in certificates of deposit or in a passbook account, ask yourself why. Push yourself to consider shifting some of it to potentially higher return investments like mutual funds.

Worriers

All of us worry about money at one time or another. It makes perfect sense to worry about your retirement if it's 10 years away and all you've got to rely on is Social Security. In that case, a healthy amount of worry is a good thing if it motivates someone to get serious about saving. Some worrying is also healthy when you invest in the stock market. Being a little anxious can keep you alert and more mindful about what is happening to your money. You'll also be less inclined to risk too much when you invest.

But some people get carried away. You could call worriers magical thinkers. It's as if they believe that crunching their financial numbers over and over in their minds will somehow make them richer. A woman who sought help with one financial planner was so anxious about money that she couldn't bear being reminded of what she had paid for things. She'd take the price tags off everything, even ketchup bottles. She came from an impoverished family, but she wasn't poor anymore. Yet she couldn't shake that poverty mind-set.

Often worriers do grow up poor or come from families where the parents act as if they were just one paycheck away from the streets. A father, for instance, might frequently complain at the dinner table that the stock market was wiping him out. He could simply be exaggerating, but his children don't understand that.

An action plan for worriers

Set aside 15 to 30 minutes each day to worry about money. You might spend that time writing about your money anxieties in a journal. Or try to worry only on alternate days. The rest of the time, try to avoid thinking about money. Ask yourself what you gain from obsessing about money. What bad things would happen if you eliminated the anxiety? What is making you worry so much? What would your life be like without the worry?

Manipulators

Typically manipulators use money to punish or reward others. "If you lose 20 pounds, I'll buy you a diamond ring," a manipulating husband might promise. A grandfather pulls aside his carefree granddaughter and says, "If you get a law degree, I'll leave much of my inheritance to you." Ironically, people who seem to have no control over money can also be manipulators. Among this group are the money martyrs.

Here's a classic example. A homemaker feels utterly powerless financially, and yet she pretty much decides where her family's money is spent. Her chief complaint is that she spends all her money on her children, and there is nothing left for her. Her voice quivers with resentment when she recounts the expensive name-brand clothes and toys she buys her children. Are her kids happy? Hardly. They feel guilty and depressed. In this case, the mom is using money to buy approval and yes, even love, from her children, but it isn't working.

In the investment world, manipulators, just like hoarders, can encounter trouble making the wisest investment decisions. Under the surface, they fear losing money. They lose control in a sense by putting money into something that isn't safe, government insured, and guaranteed.

An action plan for manipulators

Explore why you use money as a carrot to change other people's behavior. Anyone who identifies with the angry homemaker should consider establishing a budget that sets aside some money just for her. The children should also be given some financial freedom with allowances. Also explore the reasons why controlling money is so important. And try to find a financial advisor you can trust to help you make sound financial decisions.

Exploring money issues together

Of course, no matter what financial ghosts are haunting you, your money hangups, unless you are single, are bound to affect your partner. There is probably no marriage on the planet that is free from money tensions. Imagine what it's like for a spender to be married to a money hoarder. Or a thrill seeker hooked up with an avoider. Hurt feelings and resentment are sure to exist. Sharing your own money messages with your partner can help as long as the discussion doesn't seem threatening. The worst thing you can do is criticize your partner about his financial peculiarities. This will only provoke him. Here are some questions the two of you can answer to get the discussion started:

- How do I feel about money? Are these feelings realistic?

- How much is enough money? Will I ever be realistically happy with the amount I have?

- How do I feel about charitable giving?

- How do I feel about my spouse's money habits?

- What ways can we compromise to reduce our money conflicts?

- What are realistic short-term and long-term financial goals? Are we somehow sabotaging these goals?

- How have we behaved during past financial hard times? Is there a better way to handle the rough periods?

Bright Idea
The best way to know what kind of investor you are is to see what kind you've been in the past. Examine your past investment behavior. Look at what you've bought and sold in the past and why you made those trades. Pay close attention to how you reacted when the stock market took some hits.

Remember that managing a household's finances takes teamwork. Chances are, the closer you work together, the more likely you'll be to reach your goals.

Kids and money

And while you're working on your own financial psyche, think about what kinds of attitudes you are telegraphing to your own children. No doubt, your kids are blotting up your attitudes about money like a paper towel. Of course, it's easier to develop healthy money habits or change habits when you're young.

Perhaps the best way for parents to teach their children of any age about the value of saving is by example. Think about it. How much success can a chain smoker expect from warning his kids not to smoke? Badgering a child not to waste his money on the latest Nintendo game or $150 tennis shoes will have little effect if a parent's second home is at the mall.

Parents should also try dispelling children's misperceptions about money. For instance, children no longer think money grows on trees, they think automatic teller machines spit it out magically. It's the same story with credit cards. Your children see you handing plastic to a clerk and carrying home anything you want. Kids start thinking about money when they are four or five, when they are more open to suggestions. You really need to start early before bad habits and manipulating are finely tuned.

Preschoolers aren't ready to understand the nuances of mutual funds, but children who are old enough to brush their teeth are ready to start learning some basics. These tips, some of which come from the National Center for Financial Education in San Diego, can help get you get started:

Bright Idea
The National Center for Financial Education maintains a treasure-trove of educational materials on children and money. For a catalog, send $2 to the NCFE at P.O. Box WWW-34070, San Diego, CA 92163-4070. Or visit the NCFE's Web site at www.ncfe.org.

- **When a child knows how to count, introduce him to money.** Make it fun by asking him if he wants a dime or nine pennies. A quarter or two dimes. Put a pile of change on the table and see if he can pick out the correct amount of his allowance.

- **Help your children set financial goals for toys they want.** If a child is in love with the latest Barbie doll, she'll be more inclined to save up enough money. Making kids save for toys rather than writing a check at Toys 'R' Us on a whim should help instill the value of saving.

- **Hand out money in denominations to children that will encourage saving.** Instead of giving your child a $5 bill for cleaning out the garage, pass out five ones.

- **Open up a kiddie account with your child at a neighborhood bank.** Don't always talk your kids out of withdrawing money from the account, because it will discourage them from ever wanting to save.

- **Teach your child about the value of compounding.** Consider paying your child interest on the money she's managed to save. I borrow money from my eight-year-old and pay interest just so she appreciates how she can earn money simply by not spending it. At this early age, Caitlin has already concluded that it's a much better deal to lend money than to borrow.

- **Explain the virtues of stock investing.** If you have a mutual fund established for your child, show her how to calculate what it's worth by using the figures on the account statements. Talk to her about what kind of return she might expect from a stock mutual fund versus a low–interest bearing savings account.

- **Teach your children to be smart shoppers,** since about a third of our take-home pay is gobbled up by groceries and other household expenses. Talk to them about using coupons, comparison shopping, and determining which is the better deal by using unit pricing.

- **Use everyday transactions as learning opportunities.** For example, when paying a restaurant bill by credit card, explain how the tip is calculated and show your child how you can verify if the bill is correct.

- **Allow your older kids to make spending decisions,** both good and bad, but encourage them to talk about the pros and cons of the purchase ahead of time. Teach kids how to shop for the best value. That could mean helping them to evaluate ads on TV and magazines—does the toy really perform the way it looks on TV?

- **Order a subscription to** *Zillions,* a *Consumer Reports* money magazine for kids aged 10 to 14. Call (800) 234-2078. The address is P.O. Box 54861, Boulder, CO 80322-4861.

Just the facts

- A money phobia could be jeopardizing your investment returns.

- Your attitudes toward money can be traced back to your childhood.

- Strategies exist to help stamp out bad money habits.

- Financial teamwork is a necessity for couples.

- Make sure your kids don't develop bad money habits—start them off right.

GET THE SCOOP ON...
How to avoid troubles ▪ Arbitration—the last
resort ▪ Scams, scams, and more scams ▪ Watch
your step in cyberspace

Chapter 17

Troubleshooting

Investing in today's financial markets is no won-
derland. The experience can often feel more
like an excursion into the twilight zone. Where
there is money, there are crooks and the kind of
unethical people your mother used to warn you
about. But these bad guys don't wear ski masks, and
you won't see their mugs on the FBI's most wanted
lists. They might dress in $1,000 suits and keep pho-
tographs of their kid's Little League team on their
desk. These folks can look like you and me. When a
burglar visits your home, you know you've been
robbed. But if you've been swindled in a financial
deal, you might not even realize it, especially since
the markets have been roaring to new annual highs.
And that's where the danger lies.

Of course, some of the scams are as old as the
brokerage firms themselves. We've all heard the stories. A widow who doesn't know the difference
between a zero coupon bond and a grocery store
coupon depends on her stockbroker to put her
money in a Teflon-coated portfolio stuffed with safe

investments with a capital S. The stockbroker, who in this tale, is always portrayed as a fast-talking cad, assures the grandmother that she needn't worry. But her seat in the broker's tastefully decorated office is barely cold before he starts investing her money into casino junk bonds, penny stocks, and other highly risky investments that generate fat commissions for him. The widow, of course, loses money.

But in the 1990s, there are new sophisticated twists to this woeful tale. Shifty stock promoters, as well as unethical financial publications and Web sites, are bribed to hawk stocks that belong to shell corporations that have nothing behind them except the name and stock ticker symbol. Investors are unwittingly duped into buying stocks that are hyped on the Internet, and with the skyrocketing popularity of electronic stocktrading, many people are losing big bucks by impulsively gambling on companies with little if any track record. Even the most conservative among us aren't necessarily safe if we keep our money in banks. Federal regulators have been cracking down on rogue financial institutions that select the name of a prestigious bank like Citicorp, slightly alter it to, say, Citicorp Financial Services, and hope customers are fooled.

While no one can accurately pinpoint how successful these flimflam operators are, the projections are disturbing. The *North American Securities Administrators Association* (NASAA), which represents state securities watchdog agencies, estimates that financial fraud is costing investors about $1 million an hour. The Council of Better Business Bureaus has noticed an uptick in financial hankypanky. The council has reported a 46 percent increase in investment-related complaints that its own field offices have handled. It's not hard to understand why so many people are being duped. With the stock market enjoying phenomenal returns in recent years, the wild claims made by scam artists don't seem so outrageous anymore.

Don't assume that financial disasters like these only haunt the elderly or the novice. Almost anyone with enough spare cash to invest is vulnerable. Having a lot of money, a fancy title, or an advanced degree or two won't protect you from the financial barracudas. But this chapter might. If you're wondering whether your stockbroker is a great guy or a leech, keep reading. I'll present the telltale signs of a bad stockbroker. I'll also explain how you can reduce your chances of getting stuck with a loser to begin with. Happily, you've got new ammunition. With little fanfare, the regulatory body that keeps track of stockbrokers recently decided to release more of its records to the public.

This chapter also explains in detail what your options are if you do encounter troubles. After reading the next few pages, you might marvel at the ingenuity of white-collar criminals to rip off unsuspecting targets. And I'm not just talking about ostrich-farm schemes here. I'll describe a few for you. Lastly, you'll look at some of the dangers you can encounter when you plug into the Internet. I'll tell you where you can find a list of some of the bad boys of the financial industry that was compiled by a persistent watchdog group called the Stock Detective.

The telltale signs of a bad stockbroker

Of course, most brokers are neither greedy nor incompetent, but you probably won't know for sure until you experience a problem. Unfortunately, the

> 66
> I firmly believe that conditions are ripe for a bull market in fraud. We have many first-time investors in the market and they have very unrealistic expectations. They have never even seen a bear market.
> —Denise Voigt Crawford, Texas Securities Commissioners and NASAA president
> 99

Bright Idea

To avoid making some of the mistakes you'll learn about in this chapter, try reading *How to be an Informed Investor,* a book that is available through your local Better Business Bureau as well as bookstores. It was written as a joint effort of the NASAA and the Council of Better Business Bureaus.

heady days of the surging bull market have only increased the chances of investors getting into trouble.

With roughly 20,000 companies being traded on America's financial markets and trillions of dollars in play, it's inevitable that some brokers will be tempted to tweak the rules. Unfortunately, all too many people dazzled by the fortunes of others and eager to cash in themselves are pouring money into the market without giving much thought to who will be baby-sitting it.

Luckily, there are ways to protect yourself from dishonest brokers. You'll minimize your risks of encountering any problems if you spend time carefully selecting a broker. For some tips on how to do that, check back to Chapter 3, "Financial Planners and Brokers—The Best of the Bunch." And here's your second line of defense: Spot any problems with your account quickly. To do that, you should know what the most common complaints are. Here are the biggies:

- **Trading without permission:** Imagine looking at your monthly brokerage statement and noticing that you bought 500 shares in a company you've never heard of. You are astounded. When your broker bought that stock, it was an unauthorized trade, which is prohibited. Sometimes a broker tries to cover his tracks by calling the customer after the trade. This still doesn't make the trade legal.

- **A guaranteed sure winner:** Your broker is on the phone just bubbling with good news. He's promising that the stock he wants you to buy is a guaranteed winner. Caught up with his enthusiasm, you approve the deal. If you regret your decision later, you might have grounds to recoup your money. While seasoned investors should know that no stock can be a certified moneymaker, a less-sophisticated investor might not understand that an aggressive broker's claim is outlandish. If your broker promises that a stock will soar 30 percent in the next year, 15 percent within 60 days, or some similar boast, he's lying. No one knows for certain what the price of any stock will do in the future.

- **Churning:** Does this sound fishy to you? Your broker buys shares in a mutual fund that comes with a 4.5 percent load. He, of course, pockets a commission for the sale. Two months later, the broker dumps the mutual fund and buys shares in a different one that could be its twin sister. The two funds invest in the same type of stocks. Once again, your broker enjoys a generous commission. Emboldened, he picks up the pace. He buys shares in Coke and then dumps it for Pepsico stock. Then he picks up shares in Merck, the pharmaceutical giant, but he sells them quickly to buy a position in Pfizer, another drug company kingpin. For every transaction, he collects a commission. What he's been doing is a big no-no. Even if he calls you before every trade, it's still not acceptable because he's churning your account to make himself richer. In other words, he's making trades simply to generate commissions for himself. This example actually illustrates another type of prohibited behavior. A broker is not supposed to switch you from one mutual fund or other type of investment to another, very similar one when there is no legitimate reason for the switch.

- **Ignoring your wishes:** You are a conservative investor and your broker understands that. But he isn't going to let your wishes get in the way of his trading. For example, recommending a limited partnership, which is a risky, very long-term investment, wouldn't be appropriate for an 80-year-old widow. Making investments that are unsuitable for a client's comfort level is not kosher.

- **Stupidity:** There are some brokers who shouldn't even be in the business. They might have trouble following your instructions, executing trades, and providing competent advice. If a broker can't demonstrate a minimal amount of competency, he might be guilty of broker malpractice.

- **Margin abuse:** A customer can also get into trouble when a broker creates a margin account for his client. With this type of account, you use money borrowed from your brokerage house to put more cash into play. This sort of leveraged account, however, is only appropriate for sophisticated investors who thoroughly understand the risks. While a customer might complain that he never authorized a margin account, most of the time people did give their okay. They just didn't understand what they were agreeing to.

- **Outright theft:** This one is easy enough to understand. In extreme cases, a broker might steal money out of your account.

- **Selling too soon:** Boy, you'll hear this complaint a lot. Your broker recommends a stock, and then it jumps up. It's what we all dream will happen. Eventually, he calls and urges you to get rid of it for a modest profit. You agree. But then you notice that the stock keeps soaring. In fact, it doubles not long after you authorized the sale. Sorry, but you won't get much sympathy if you complain that your broker is an idiot. In hindsight, your broker made the wrong call, but bad judgments happen every day in the markets.

What you should be aware of is whether your broker consistently advises you to dump securities after less than a year. A buy-and-hold investor could legitimately wonder if a broker is really performing his job if he's recommending stocks that can't be held in a portfolio for years. Of course, there can be a cynical explanation for all this. The stockbroker might be only interested in locking in short-term gains, because he won't continue to make commissions if you sit on a stock forever.

Avoiding a lousy broker

If you've just discovered that your broker is behaving badly, your first instincts might be to sue. But think again. The brokerage industry, concerned about its own bottom line, has made it extremely difficult for anybody to sue them. When you open up an account, you might not make it through all the fine print, which looks as intelligible as mouse tracks. But the brokerage houses' legal beagles were no doubt paid a fine sum to insert a provision that states that any customer signing this application will agree to arbitration if any disputes arise.

There are several places you can turn if you want to pursue a grievance, but first, let's see how you can avoid these problems in the first place.

Don't ever hire a broker who dials your number out of the blue.

The broker, who could be hundreds of miles away at an obscure firm, can make a great living reeling in

Unofficially... Americans love to sue, but they very rarely can sue their stockbroker. You can blame this legal no man's land on the 1987 U.S. Supreme Court case *Shearson v. McMahan*. The justices said a client who signs a contract with a brokerage house that requires all disputes to be handled through arbitration is out of luck.

investors with a confident, friendly demeanor. You, however, are just asking for trouble if you agree to turn over your money to a telephone caller. This isn't to say that all the brokers dialing for dollars are up to no good. It's a rite of passage for greenhorns at all the big brokerage houses to make cold calls to build up their client lists. But regardless of who is on the other end of the phone, you should never sink money into anything without seeing written documents about a security.

Do your own background check.

The broker who manages your money could be one of the more important persons in your life, but do you know anything about him? Most people don't. And until the spring of 1998, the financial industry was doing its part to pretty much keep us in the dark. But now investors will be able to find out exactly what dirt, if any, has stuck to their prospective broker. The information can be found in a massive databank—the Central Registration Depository—that keeps tabs on all the nation's brokers. The databank is operated jointly by the *National Association of Securities Dealers* (NASD), the brokerage industry's self-regulating body, and the NASAA.

The databank was never as tight as a vault. The NASAA, with its roots in state governance, was always more willing to give callers better access to the files. But with the NASD, it was a different story. Up until recently, a caller could have found out if her broker had ever been convicted of a crime, slapped with a civil judgment, or sanctioned by the NASD. Sounds good until you hear what was left out. You wouldn't have heard, for instance, if your broker was facing a backlog of complaints against him, and you'd never know if the broker had paid off defrauded investors in settlements.

Here are some of the things you can now expect to hear about:

- Pending arbitration hearings and civil proceedings involving a stockbroker's actions

- All arbitration hearings that a broker lost

- Written customer complaints alleging forgery, theft, or misappropriation of funds or securities during the past two years

- Formal investigations involving criminal or regulatory matters

- Outstanding liens or judgments

- Customer complaints alleging unethical sales practices

- Bankruptcies

- Ten years of employment history

- Bonding company denials, payouts, or revocations

You'll also be able to find out whether a brokerage firm has been in trouble. This could be invaluable information for anybody using an obscure brokerage firm.

Here's what you'll learn:

- Criminal felony charges and convictions, along with certain misdemeanor charges and convictions

- Actions taken by a regulatory body, such as the New York Stock Exchange or the NASD, due to investment-related wrongdoing

- Bankruptcies or liquidations during the past 10 years

- Outstanding liens and judgments
- Bonding company denials, payouts, or revocations

You can receive this information by calling the NASD's public disclosure line at (800) 289-9999 (www.nasdr.com/2000/htm) or the NASAA at (202) 737-0900. The list that follows lists the locations of all the local NASD offices.

NASD DISTRICT OFFICES

District 1

525 Market St., Suite 300
San Francisco, CA 94105-2711
(415) 882-1200

300 Grand Ave., Suite 1600
Los Angeles, CA 90071
(213) 627-2122

District 3

Republic Office Building
370 17th St., Suite 2900
Denver, CO 80202-5629
(303) 446-3100

Two Union Square
601 Union St., Suite 1616
Seattle, WA 98101-2327
(206) 624-0790

District 4

12 Wyandotte Plaza
120 W. 12th St., Suite 900
Kansas City, MO 64105
(816) 421-5700

District 5

1100 Poydras St., Suite 850
Energy Centre
New Orleans, LA 70163
(504) 522-6527

District 6

12801 N. Central Expressway, Suite 1050
Dallas, TX 75243
(972) 701-8554

District 7

One Securities Centre, Suite 500
3490 Piedmont Rd., NE
Atlanta, GA 30305
(404) 239-6100

District 8

10 S. LaSalle St., 20th Floor
Chicago, IL 60603-1002
(312) 899-4400

Renaissance on Playhouse Square
1350 Euclid Ave., Suite 650
Cleveland, OH 44115
(216) 694-4545

District 9

11 Penn Center
1835 Market St., 19th Floor
Philadelphia, PA 19103
(215) 665-1180

District 10

33 Whitehall St.
New York, NY 10004-2193
(212) 858-4000

District 11

260 Franklin St., 16th Floor
Boston, MA 02110
(617) 261-0800

Carefully read your monthly statements.

The statement will usually tip you off if there's something fishy about your account. Pay special attention to the opening value of your account and its ending value. The opening balance is how much your portfolio was worth last month. The ending balance is what it was worth 30 days later. If your account has suddenly gained or lost a great deal of money, make sure you check the statement to see why.

You'll also find in your statement a description of each investment, its quantity, and its value on the

Timesaver
Monthly brokerage account statements are not known for being user-friendly, but most brokerage firms have booklets that explain how to interpret them. If that doesn't work, ask your broker for an explanation.

monthly closing date. By comparing your holdings with previous statements, you can see which investments did well and which might be lagging. Lastly, you'll see what activity your account generated for the month. If you bought or sold securities, received dividends, or transferred money from one mutual fund to another, all those moves will be listed. If you notice a strange transaction, this could be a tip-off that something is wrong. For instance, a broker might have picked up shares in a stock that you never authorized.

One way to double check on your account activity is to file all transaction slips you receive in the mail. When a trade is made on your behalf, the brokerage sends you a piece of paper that lists the name of the investment, sale price, number of shares bought or sold, and date of the transaction. It also lists just how much your broker made through his commission.

Don't assume that if you work with a discount broker you won't have to do this. Just because you don't have a personal broker doesn't mean you're immune to glitches. A few years ago, for instance, I instructed my broker, Fidelity Investments, to transfer some of my IRA money into a mutual fund with the Invesco fund family. When my next statement arrived, I noticed that Fidelity had not transferred the full amount, and what's worse, the price of the Invesco fund had been inching up. By the time the rest of the money could be transferred, the shares were more expensive. I called Fidelity and followed up with a letter explaining the problem and asking to be reimbursed for the additional cost of the Invesco shares. Fidelity readily admitted its mistake and sent me a check for the amount I had requested.

Bright Idea
Put everything in writing. When you talk to your broker, keep a telephone log of the conversations. When you instruct your broker to make any changes in your portfolio, follow up with a letter detailing what you said on the phone. All these documents could be invaluable if problems develop later.

Save all the documents you receive from your brokerage. If you're embroiled in a dispute in the future, you'll never know what you'll need to fight back.

When trouble strikes—fight back

Despite taking precautions, problems will occur. If they do, here are the steps you should take:

1. **Call your broker and discuss the problem.** Be ready to explain how you'd like the matter to be resolved. Send a follow-up letter to the broker that includes all your grievances.

2. **Contact the branch manager** if the broker doesn't help. With any luck, your problems will end there. But watch out if the supervisor sends you a "comfort" letter. This letter will make you want to scream. Rather than addressing your complaints, the writer will note that you are satisfied with the trading done in your name. Don't ignore this goofy letter, since the motivation could be to provide legal ammunition for later on.

3. **Call and write to the compliance division of the brokerage firm,** going up the chain of the command. Once again, state what your grievance is and how you'd like it to be resolved.

4. **Consider sending a copy of all the correspondence to your state securities agency.** If you don't know where to locate it, call the NASAA for the contact number and address in your state.

Bringing in an arbitrator

If nothing works, you might want to consider arbitration—thousands of cases are filed by angry

Watch Out!
If you spot a problem with your brokerage account, act quickly. The clock could already be ticking, since there can be time limits to taking action. A brokerage firm could use any procrastination to insist that you really didn't have any problem with the disputed trading.

investors across the country each year. Your first step is to dig out the form you signed when you opened your account. The brokerage house could have designated the arbitration forum that it favors. Contact that forum and request an arbitration packet. The materials will explain how to get the process started.

Bright Idea
It is possible to fight a brokerage firm through the courts. A well-known class action involving thousands of investors was aimed at Prudential Securities, which sold customers billions of dollars in limited partnerships in the 1980s. Most often, however, these lawsuits are aimed at companies that the plaintiffs invested in rather than the brokerage firms that sold the shares.

MAJOR ARBITRATION ALTERNATIVES

National Association of Securities Dealers
125 Broad St., 36th Floor
New York, NY 10004
(212) 858-4400

New York Stock Exchange
20 Broad St., 5th Floor
New York, NY 10005
(212) 656-2772

American Stock Exchange
86 Trinity Place
New York, NY 10006
(212) 306-1000

American Arbitration Association
140 W. 51st St.
New York, NY 10020
(212) 484-4000

Arbitration is not free. Just how much it will cost depends in part on how much money you want to recoup. For instance, if you claim you've lost $10,000 to $30,000, the filing fee at the NASD will be $100. You'll also have to pay a deposit of $300 or $400, depending on whether you are requesting one, three, or a panel of arbitrators. Of course, you'll be writing more checks if you hire an attorney or feel you need an expert witness to testify at the arbitration hearing. Some attorneys might agree to take the case on a contingency-fee basis, which means you won't have to pay them up front. Instead, they'll take their cut from any money you are awarded. It might be difficult, however, to find an attorney to represent you if the disputed amount is less than $100,000.

If you want a lawyer to lead the charge, consider calling your state or local bar association and asking for the names of attorneys who specialize in this area of the law. See Appendix B, "Resource Guide," for a list of state bars.

Is arbitration worth the effort? A report from the federal General Accounting Office in the early 1990s suggests that it could be. The report found that investors won in nearly 60 percent of the cases. The typical investor received 64 percent of what he wanted when the arbitration was handled through the NASD, while the average person walked away with a little over half of what he sought through the New York Stock Exchange.

While arbitrators are chosen differently, typically the panel that hears your complaint will be composed of one to three people. If the amount in dispute is under $10,000 through the NASD, there won't be any hearing at all. In this case, a single arbitrator reviews all the paperwork without any of the parties present and makes a decision. The arbitrators, who have all been trained to do this specialized work, aren't all picked from the financial industry. In fact, you are shown the names in advance and have an opportunity to reject someone.

This isn't like the People's Court. You won't know the verdict by the end of the day. It could take months before you hear anything. You'll receive the verdict in the mail. What's more, with the system overloaded, you'll have to wait a long time just for your day in court. At the NASD, which carries the heaviest workload, it will take 12 to 18 months before you face an arbitration panel.

Watch Out!
If you decide to arbitrate, keep one thing in mind. Once you choose arbitration, there is no turning back. You must agree to accept whatever the outcome. If the panel sides with your broker, you are out of luck.

A scam a minute

Lousy brokers aren't the only hazards you might encounter in your investing career. Con men and scam artists are thriving as Americans ignore their common sense and chase after promises of great riches. Remember, if a deal sounds too good to be true, it probably is. One way to avoid problems is to resist get-rich-quick investments. Here are a few of the common investment scams you want to stay away from.

Limited partnerships

This is one of the most abused investments you could possibly stumble into. Brokers love them because they provide juicy, ongoing commissions and they are packaged with plenty of expenses and fees. After all those costs are deducted, you could very well end up with just 67 to 80 percent of your money actually devoted to the limited partnership. They are usually sold for a minimum investment of $5,000. Many limited partnerships are involved in real estate, equipment leasing, and oil and gas. These ventures are usually made up of a general partner who manages the project and the limited partners who invest money but aren't involved in the daily management. Typically, these investors receive a share of capital gains, income, and tax benefits. If you need to bail out of one, you'll find few takers. Consequently, you might only be able to unload it at a fire-sale price.

Beyond the expenses, a common rap against limited partnerships is that you can't follow them by simply opening up the daily newspaper. Unlike stocks and mutual funds, limited partnerships are frequently not listed on any of the stock exchanges.

Investors rely on their brokers to keep them informed about how the limited partnership is faring. After assurances over the years that an investment is doing well, an investor can learn that his limited partnership is worth a fraction of the original price or maybe worth nothing at all. Your natural instinct might be to retaliate legally, but you might have to contend with statute of limitations issues. As with all investment complaints, it's best to act quickly.

Precious metals

You'll hear great promises of how the price of gold, silver, or platinum will soon skyrocket. Don't believe it.

Ponzi schemes

These are one of the oldest investment frauds around. In these pyramid schemes, people are promised fabulous returns on investments in real estate, gold mines, and anything else you can imagine. Early investors are paid off with the money from people lured into the scheme later. When the rush of new victims slows, the money dries up and the Ponzi collapses. In this scenario, many investors lose their money.

Oil and gas

Beware of the scam artists who use fake drilling equipment set on worthless land. Promoters also might try to sell you a cut of a huge new oil field that no one previously knew existed. You could be told that a reputable oil company is already operating nearby or that the operator has hit oil or gas every time he has drilled. Check the outfit's reputation with the Better Business Bureau, the U.S. Postal Inspection Service, and your state attorney general's

Bright Idea
A cybersource on broker malfeasance is the Investor Protection Trust at www. investorprotection.org. You'll find advice on how to spot bad brokers and what you can do if your broker is ripping you off.

consumer protection office. Better yet, avoid these investments altogether.

Penny stock fraud

The price of these stocks can seem cheap—often you can pick up shares for less than $5 apiece. But they can belong to tiny outfits with a brief, erratic, or even nonexistent history of sales and earnings. To play it safe, most investors should avoid these stocks. Here's one good reason why: During one recent year, securities regulators estimate that Americans lost about $6 billion investing in penny stock companies. While some of these companies are legitimate, others are not, and it is hard for many to tell them apart.

Promoters for an unethical company work hard to lure people like you into their web. Scam artists assure their would-be shareholders that they are about to buy into the next Microsoft or Coca-Cola on the ground floor. But if you stop and think about it, some of their claims will sound absolutely ridiculous. You might hear that a tiny company is on the verge of making fossil fuel obsolete or developing a sure-fire cure for cancer. But wouldn't you suppose that advances of this dimension would be trumpeted on the front pages of the *New York Times* or the *Wall Street Journal*?

Here's how small-stock scams can work: Swindlers take over a small company and fill its key positions. If the company isn't already publicly traded, they arrange for that through an initial public offering. The swindlers hire outside people, such as a public relations firm, a stock analyst, a financial radio show host, or some Internet financial sites, to hype the stock. When the price of the stock jumps up, the con artists, who paid little or nothing for

> **"**
> Penny stocks are for people who can afford to lose money. I call it speculating. There is a place for it, but it's not for most people. The potential for gain is much greater than with established stocks, but there is a much greater potential for losing.
> —Kevin Lichtman, founder of Stock Detective (www. stockdetective. com)
> **"**

their shares, bail out and make a tidy sum. The stock inevitably deflates, leaving the unaware investors with potentially big losses. This kind of scam is called a *pump and dump*. The stock is pumped up, and then all the players quickly cash in their shares.

You'll find thousands of penny stocks trading on the OTC (*Over-The-Counter*) Bulletin Board, which unfortunately a lot of people confuse with the NASDAQ. Investors believe these penny stocks carry the imprimatur of the NASDAQ, so the companies must be on the up and up, but the assumption is wrong. The OTC Bulletin Board is not part of the NASDAQ stock market. In fact, it's often the stocks that can't manage to qualify for inclusion on the NASDAQ that end up here on the Bulletin Board. Unlike NASDAQ stocks, OTC stocks don't have to meet rigorous financial requirements, nor do they have to file annual or quarterly updates (10-Ks or 10-Qs) with the Securities and Exchange Commission. Penny stock promoters sometimes take advantage of this misconception and claim that a stock is traded on the NASDAQ.

If you want to immerse yourself in the netherworld of slimy penny stocks, visiting the Stock Detective Web site (www.stockdetective.com) is a must. There are enough frightening tales at this site to make you think twice before trading beyond the established exchanges. One of the Stock Detective's most popular warnings is called "Stock Scams, Schemes and Scums," which gives you some idea of the sort of fare you'll be served here. At Stock Detective, you'll also find a list of direct mail producers, financial radio shows, Internet sites, and financial newsletters that might benefit financially from the penny stocks they rave about.

Even if you hang up on telephone solicitors and you never troll the Internet, you won't necessarily be completely safe from financial shysters. You can be victimized at your own church or synagogue, as well as at professional and cultural organizations. Con artists join groups just so they can acquire legitimacy. Wouldn't you be more comfortable with a pitchman if he belonged to your own political club or church group? People who have fallen for scams include political conservatives in Southern California; Chinese-American business owners in San Francisco; physicians in Utah; affluent Indian and Polish immigrants in New York; and Catholic parishioners, along with their priest, in Rockford, Illinois. The popularity of affinity fraud has grown so dramatically that the NASAA has included it on its list of the nation's top 10 types of frauds.

Strange as it may seem, you even need to be suspicious of some banking institutions. Think twice before you deposit any money into a bank that has a familiar-sounding name. It could be a rogue bank that's not licensed by federal or state regulators. These banks purposely trade on the names of prominent financial institutions to lure in customers. The federal Office of the Comptroller of the Currency knows of at least 50 institutions that it suspects are operating without any regulatory authorization.

Morgan Guaranty Trust sure sounds like it must be affiliated with the well-known Morgan Guaranty Trust Company of New York. But it isn't. It's the same story with Citicorp Financial Services in Beverly Hills, California. It has no connection with Citicorp in New York at all. Chase Manhattan Bank in New York has obtained a court order forbidding Chase Bank of Las Vegas from using its trademark.

What can you do to protect yourself?

- Apply for a loan at local banks and credit unions. It's easier to resolve problems.

- Get written documentation of any contracts or transactions.

- Make certain the bank you're dealing with is licensed. You can find out by contacting your state banking or finance department.

- Find out if an institution is covered by FDIC insurance.

- Be even more vigorous in researching a bank that's operating on the Internet.

- Steer clear of any financial services company that charges up-front fees for promising to repair a consumer's bad credit rating. This is illegal.

The federal Bureau of the Public Debt is also warning about other scams that have fooled conservative, fixed-income investors. Crooks are offering to rent or lease U.S. Treasury securities, and they are using two official U.S. Treasury forms to make the deals look real. The scam artists who want to lease these securities obviously can't produce them if you ask. They might tell you they are scattered in banks around the world, or they'll claim that they belong to a wealthy philanthropist who wants to remain anonymous. You also need to avoid Treasuries that are advertised as "fresh-cut" Treasury bills, limited-edition Treasuries, U.S. dollar bonds, or de-facto Treasuries. They are all as phony as a three-dollar bill. Avoid getting entangled

> 66
> People should be on the lookout for any offer of financial services from a company if they don't know anything about it. It's one thing to have an offer from Fidelity Investments. It's another thing to get something from Colonial Financial Services.
> —Collot Guerard, Federal Trade Commission attorney
> 99

in these sorts of messes by purchasing Treasuries directly from the federal government or through a brokerage firm.

Cyberfraud knows no bounds

Pssst. I've got this great investment I want to share with you. I'm allowing you in at the beginning—not many will get the same chance. What's this opportunity of a lifetime? Well, let me start off by asking if you know anything about ethanol. It's going to be the fuel of the future when we no longer can stand choking on that nasty automobile exhaust. Well, at this very minute, an ethanol plant is being constructed in the Dominican Republic. We need investors to complete the project. I know, I know. You're thinking it sounds pretty risky, this being out of the country and all. Well, we are willing to compensate you handsomely. We promise a return of 50 percent or more.

Of course this is a rip-off. A scam right out of the actual case files of the Securities and Exchange Commission. The SEC cracked down on this venture after scrutinizing its sales literature, which was littered with lies.

Investors who were sucked into the Dominican venture learned about it through the Internet, which is the hottest new area where hucksters congregate. Alas, the potential for shenanigans on the World Wide Web appears as boundless as eternity. It's not hard to see why. For a scam artist, conning innocent people used to be incredibly time-consuming. He often needed to pay people to make telephone calls to hundreds and hundreds of potential victims. He'd also have to rent a space big enough to fit all these telephone solicitors. Interrupting people with cold calls when they were eating dinner didn't help business. It was even more tedious if the shysters walked door to door looking for hapless victims. But with a computer equipped with a high-speed modem, a crook can send his pitch to thousands of people almost instantaneously.

The ethanol plant is just one of an untold number of scams that unwitting investors will run across in cyberspace. Want other examples? Somebody else was prowling the Internet for suckers who would invest in a proposed eel farm. Those interested were promised a 20 percent return for the farm, which was promoted as "low risk." Then there was the guy who was raising money for a couple of Costa Rican companies that produce coconut chips. These chips were so tasty that a major supermarket chain had promised to buy every last bag. The promoter insisted that the investment was as safe as a certificate of deposit. Not! The SEC caught up with both of these operations.

Maybe these investments sound so outrageous that you think you'd never be trapped by slick scam artists. But not all the fraudulent deals on the Internet look so patently exotic and bogus. For instance, would you have been able to figure out what was wrong with a scheme that offered "prime bank" securities? Investors pumped $3.5 million into the securities after receiving assurances that they would double their money in four months. There was a clue that something was amiss. There is no such thing as a prime bank security. Astronomical profits also were promised to online users through a worldwide telephone lottery. More than $2 million of unregistered securities were sold

Watch Out!
Older Americans are the most vulnerable to scam artists. Crooks love to target senior citizens because they are most likely to be sitting on a pile of money. By one FBI estimate, seniors account for 30 percent of all scam victims, while they only represent 12 percent of the population.

to 20,000 people, who were encouraged to recruit other investors on the Internet. And then there was the online promoter who promised bystanders that they could turn $5 into $60,000 in just three to six weeks. In reality, this was just an electronic version of a classic pyramid scheme.

Telltale signs of scams

Luckily, there are ways to protect yourself from clever con men. Most often, you will hear about these dubious investments by phone. Consequently, your best protection is to hang up on anybody who tries to sell you anything that way. But whether you are approached by phone, on the Internet, or elsewhere, here are clues that something is amiss:

- You are promised an astronomical rate of return for your money.

- You are pressured to make an immediate decision or one within a short period of time, because other people are signing up quickly.

- The promoter promises that it's impossible for you to lose money on this deal. Claims that the investment is risk-free are a sure sign of trouble. No financial investment is risk-free, and a high rate of return will mean greater risk.

- Be wary of anyone offering to share "inside information," and watch for buzzwords like "limited offer," "safe as a certificate of deposit," and "IRA-approved."

- The opportunity is located in another country. When you send your money abroad and something goes wrong, it's difficult to determine what happened, much less get your money back.

- Watch out for Internet promoters who use aliases. Pseudonyms are common online, and some salespeople hide their true identity.

Even if an investment seems tantalizing, never agree to anything until you receive written documentation. Ask for an organization's prospectus, a financial statement, and any other documents that are available. Show the materials to a broker, lawyer, or accountant and ask for her opinion.

Also ask your state securities regulation office if it has more information on the company and the people behind it. The agency can tell you whether the company or individual has broken any securities regulations in the past and whether they are authorized to do business in your state. It's also a good idea to contact your local Better Business Bureau to see if any complaints have been logged.

Lastly, check with the SEC. The federal agency doesn't require companies that are raising less than $1 million to register with it, but these small outfits must file a Form D. Form D is a short document that includes the names and addresses of owners and promoters. If a Form D wasn't filed, call the SEC's Office of Investor Education & Assistance at (202) 942-7040.

You can contact the SEC in several ways besides the telephone number listed earlier. By e-mail, you can reach the SEC's Office of Investor Education & Assistance at www.help@sec.gov or the Division of Enforcement at www.enforcement@sec.gov. You can also write to the SEC's Investor Education Office at 450 Fifth St., NW, Mail Stop 11-2, Washington, D.C. 20549.

Just the facts

- To avoid getting hurt, know the signs of a bad broker.

- It's easy to run a background check on a prospective broker.

- Arbitration will probably be your only option if your broker misbehaves.

- If an investment seems too good to be true, walk away.

- Watch out for cyberscams: They can be cleverly disguised as legitimate.

Glossary

10-K   A corporation's yearly financial report, which must be filed with the Securities and Exchange Commission.

10-Q   A company's quarterly financial report, which must be filed with the Securities and Exchange Commission.

12b-1   A fee that allows a mutual fund to pass along to its shareholders the costs of its promotional materials.

52-week high   A stock's highest price for a one-year period.

401(k)   An employer-sponsored retirement plan, which is named after a section of the Internal Revenue Code. Workers contribute pretax money, which can grow tax-deferred until withdrawn.

403(b)   An employer-sponsored retirement plan for persons who work for tax-exempt organizations, such as schools and health-care facilities. Workers contribute pretax money, which can grow tax-deferred until withdrawn.

ADR   See *American Depositary Receipt.*

aggressive growth fund   A mutual fund that invests in small companies or fast-growing companies. These are among the riskiest funds you can own.

American Depositary Receipt (ADR)   Instead of buying stock of a foreign company in an overseas market, Americans can purchase stock in the form of a receipt. The shares are held in the vault of a U.S. bank. ADRs are traded on the stock exchanges here.

American Stock Exchange (AMEX)   A stock exchange located in downtown Manhattan. The Exchange will soon become a subsidiary of the NASDAQ.

analyst   An expert who evaluates companies and makes conclusions about whether a stock is in the buy or sell range. Most analysts specialize in a particular industry, like aerospace, banking, or health care. Many analysts work for brokerage houses, investment advisors, or mutual funds.

annual report   A corporation's yearly accounting of its financial status. The Securities and Exchange Commission requires publicly traded companies to issue these.

asset   Anything you own that has a monetary value, such as stocks, bonds, real estate, cars, and jewelry.

asset allocation fund   A fund that maintains a mix of stocks, bonds, and cash in an attempt to balance risk. Some funds keep the balance fairly constant, while others tinker with the mix when economic conditions change.

automatic investment plan   Typically a person makes arrangements with a mutual fund to regularly invest money through payroll deductions or automatic transfers from a checking account.

back-end load   A sales commission charged when an investor sells mutual fund shares. May also be referred to as a *redemption fee*.

balanced fund   A type of mutual fund that attempts to provide current income and long-term growth with a combination of stocks, bonds, and cash in its portfolio.

bankruptcy   When a person is unable to pay his debts, bankruptcy is an option. Through federal bankruptcy court, an individual can reorganize his debts and even get financial obligations erased by court order. An individual can file for Chapter 7 or 13 bankruptcy.

basis   A security's purchase price (plus commission or other expenses), which is needed to calculate what taxes, if any, are owed when it's sold.

bear market   A sustained declining stock market of 20 percent or more.

benefit period   With a disability insurance policy, this refers to the length of time your policy will pay once you make your claim.

beta   Measures a stock's volatility in relation to the overall stock market. Here's one way beta is used: The beta of a particular stock is 1.5 when compared to the Standard & Poor's 500 Index. If the S&P 500 goes down 1 percent, this stock drops 1.5 percent. If the index goes up 1 percent, the stock increases 1.5 percent.

bid   The price a buyer is willing to pay for a stock.

bid-offer spread   The difference in the buy and sell prices of securities.

big board   Nickname for the New York Stock Exchange.

blue chip stock   Common stock of nationally known companies that possess a long record of growth and dividend payments. The term comes from the blue chips used in poker, which are always the most valuable. Examples include McDonald's, General Electric, and DuPont.

bond   A debt security that generally pays interest at regular intervals for a set period of time and repays your principal at maturity.

bond rating   A letter grade given to a bond signifying the amount of credit risk on the bond. A high rating indicates that rating services believe there is an excellent chance that the bond issuer will pay off the debt as promised. American bond-rating agencies include Duff & Phelps, Moody's, and Standard & Poor's.

book value   The difference between a company's assets and liabilities. Book value is a tool investors use when contemplating buying shares in a company.

book value per share   Book value is calculated by dividing net assets available for common stock by the number of shares outstanding. See also *book value.*

broker   Someone who charges a fee or commission for buying and selling stocks, bonds, and other securities.

brokerage commission   Fees paid to a broker for executing a security transaction.

bull market   Describes the stock market when prices have risen for an extended period of time.

buy and hold   A long-term investing strategy of investors who purchase stocks or mutual funds and keep them despite ups and downs in the financial markets.

callable bond   Bonds that the issuer has a right to redeem (or call) prior to maturity at a specified price.

capital gain The profit you make when selling assets like stocks, bonds, or real estate for more than you paid.

capital gains tax The tax on profits from the sale of securities. New capital-gains schedules, which are more favorable to stock investors, were recently approved by Congress.

capital loss The loss you suffer in selling assets like stocks, bonds, and real estate for less than you paid.

capitalization The value of a corporation, which is determined by multiplying the price per share of its stock by the number of shares outstanding.

cash value policies Different types of life insurance policies that provide an investment component. Term life insurance policies have no cash value.

CD See *certificate of deposit.*

certificate of deposit Debt securities issued by banks. CDs pay a stated amount of interest and mature on a specific date. Maturities can range from a few weeks to several years.

certified financial planner (CFP) A financial advisor who possesses a wide knowledge of a variety of personal finance issues. A CFP has passed rigorous exams administered by the Certified Financial Planner Board of Standards in Denver.

certified public accountant (CPA) An individual who specializes in accounting, auditing, and preparing tax returns for individuals and corporations. They must pass certain exams.

CFP See *certified financial planner.*

churning Excessive trading by dishonest brokers to generate more commissions from their clients.

closed-end fund Mutual funds that trade like stocks. Shares are bought and sold on the stock market rather than redeemed by a mutual fund company.

commission   The fee you pay a broker for completing a trade for such securities as stocks, bonds, and mutual funds. The fee is based on the dollar amount of the trade or the number of shares involved. See also *brokerage commission.*

common stock   One class of stock in a company. Sometimes corporations only issue common stock, sometimes they also issue preferred stocks, which carry with them certain special rights for investors.

compounding   The growth that results from investment income and gains on the original investment as long as the reinvested income and capital gains are left in the investment account.

confirmation   A written acknowledgment from a broker that a trade has been completed. It contains the number of shares bought or sold, price per share, fees, date, and commission.

Consumer Price Index (CPI)   The index, calculated by the U.S. Bureau of Labor Statistics, measures the cost of buying a fixed bundle of goods (such as housing, food, and transportation costs), which is supposed to represent realistic purchases of Americans. Pensions are often tied to changes in the CPI.

corporate bond   These taxable bonds are issued by private companies. The corporate bonds that are issued by less financially secure companies are called *junk bonds* or *high-yield corporate bonds.*

CPA   See *certified public accountant.*

crash   A dramatic drop in the stock market, such as the 1929 crash that triggered the Great Depression.

creditor   A business or person that is owed money. The creditor may be the actual person or business, or a bill collector acting on their behalf.

cyclical   Refers to industries, such as oil and manufacturing stocks, whose fate is closely tied to the country's economic conditions.

day order   An order to buy or sell that expires—if not completed—at the end of one trading day.

death taxes   Taxes levied on the estate of someone who has died. Federal death taxes are called *estate taxes*. State taxes go by various names, including *inheritance taxes*.

debit card   *Automatic teller machine* (ATM) cards issued by MasterCard or VISA. When you buy something at a store, you punch in your secret code on a keypad, and the money is instantly sucked out of your checking, savings, or brokerage account.

debt consolidation   Persons who have many creditors pestering them sometimes transfer all their bills into one place. Some people use a credit card, a home equity line of credit, or a loan from a relative to accomplish this consolidation. They then have one bill every month to pay instead of many.

debtor   A person who owes money.

disability insurance   Provides a policyholder with regular payments if he cannot perform his job because of temporary or long-term illness.

discount broker   A no-frills brokerage house that trades securities at commission rates that are cheaper than full-service brokers.

diversification   The process of owning different types of investments in a portfolio to reduce its risk.

dividend   A distribution of earnings to investors who own stocks or mutual fund shares.

dividend-reinvestment plan (DRIP)   DRIPs allow you to reinvest dividends that are generated by stocks you own.

Dogs of the Dow   A stockpicking strategy that works this way: You buy shares in the 10 highest dividend-yielding stocks from the Dow Jones Industrial Average. You hold them for one year, then sell any that are no longer among the top 10 and replace them with those that are. These stocks are called *dogs* because typically they have been the Dow's underperformers.

dollar cost averaging A systematic method of investing a set amount of money each month or quarter. With this strategy, you try to reduce the risk of investing a large amount of money all at once.

double tax-free Municipal bonds that allow the purchaser to avoid paying federal and state taxes on the interest income.

Dow Jones Industrial Average (DJIA) An index of 30 major U.S. corporations listed on the New York Stock Exchange. It is the oldest and most widely quoted stock index.

early withdrawal penalty A bank can charge you a penalty if you cash out your certificate of deposit early.

earned income Any money you earn in making a living, including salary, wages, and self-employment income.

earnings per share A key way to evaluate a stock's prospects. If a company's profit is $1 million, and 500,000 shares are outstanding, the earnings per share is $2 ($1 million ÷ 500,000 = $2).

EDGAR (Electronic Data Gathering Analysis and Retrieval) The electronic depository for all the public filings a corporation must provide to the Securities and Exchange Commission. EDGAR (**www.sec.gov/edgarhp.htm**) is a great research tool for stock investors.

Education Individual Retirement Account (IRA) Each year, up to $500 can be invested in one of these for a child's college years. The earnings are tax-free.

elimination period This is essentially a disability insurance policy's deductible. It refers to the length of time it will take before you can start receiving disability checks. The average waiting period is 60 to 90 days.

emerging market fund Invests in the stocks of companies in less-developed countries.

enrolled agent A professional tax preparer who must generally undergo a rigorous two-day test administered by the Internal Revenue Service. About 30,000 enrolled agents are practicing across the country.

equity The value in something you own after deducting all liabilities related to the asset. For example, if you own a house valued at $225,000, and your mortgage is $100,000, then you have $125,000 in equity.

estate planning The preparation of a plan to carry out how you want your property to be handled before or after your death. An estate plan can include a will, a power of attorney, and trusts.

expense ratio What you pay a mutual fund to invest your money. The expense ratio includes management fees, administrative fees, and 12b-1 fees.

FDIC See *Federal Deposit Insurance Corporation.*

Federal Deposit Insurance Corporation (FDIC) A federal agency that guarantees that a customer's money in a bank will be protected—up to a certain ceiling—if the institution fails financially.

Federal Reserve banks The 12 banks, along with their branches, that make up the Federal Reserve System.

Federal Reserve Board The governing board of the Federal Reserve System. Its members are appointed by the president of the United States and confirmed by the U.S. Senate.

Federal Reserve System Established in 1913 to regulate the country's monetary and banking network.

fee-based planner A financial planner who is compensated through a combination of fees and commissions.

fee-only planner A financial advisor who isn't compensated through commissions. Some charge by the hour or for a complete financial plan.

financial advisor A generic term used broadly by many professionals, including financial planners, money managers, insurance agents, and brokers.

front-end load A sales commission, or load, that is paid when shares in a mutual fund are purchased.

fund families Organizations that operate a group of mutual funds. Prominent fund families include Fidelity, Vanguard, Strong, and Franklin Templeton.

global fund A mutual fund that can invest in foreign companies as well as ones in the United States.

good-till-canceled order An order to buy or sell stock that remains in effect until the trade is completed or the request is canceled. This is also referred to as an *open order*.

growth and income fund A fund that invests in corporations that expand at a decent clip and also generate dividends.

growth fund A mutual fund that invests in companies that have the potential to grow handsomely over time and provide juicy returns.

high-yield corporate bond fund A fancy term for a junk bond fund. These funds invest in the bonds of riskier corporations that do not enjoy sterling financial reputations.

home equity loan The traditional home equity loan is the classic second mortgage. You borrow for a set number of years, and the loan is usually offered with a fixed interest rate. You repay in monthly installments. The other kind is a home equity line of credit, and the interest rate will vary just like those adjustable rate mortgages. You won't be borrowing a fixed amount—it's like a credit card in that way. You borrow what you need—up to a cap.

Hope Scholarship Meant to make college more affordable, parents can receive a federal tax credit up to $1,500 per student for each of the first two years of college.

income statement A financial statement that reports the financial results of a company's operations, usually for one year. It's also referred to as an *earnings report* or *statement of earnings*.

index fund A mutual fund that seeks to nearly match the returns of whatever stock or bond benchmark (index) it is tied to. The most popular index funds are linked to the Standard & Poor's 500.

Individual Retirement Account (IRA) A retirement savings vehicle sanctioned by the government. Every year, you are allowed to squirrel away $2,000 in one of these special accounts. You can establish an IRA in a mutual fund, a stock brokerage account, or a bank or credit union.

inflation The rate at which the price of consumer products and services increases.

inflation index bond A relatively new bond offering from the U.S. Treasury that is linked to the Consumer Price Index. The bond's principal rises if inflation does. For instance, if inflation jumps 4 percent one year, the $1,000 face value of the bond is $1,040. The Treasury Department uses that figure—not $1,000—to determine what the annual interest payment will be.

initial public offering (IPO) A new issue of stock available to the public.

international mutual fund   A fund that invests in foreign corporations.

investment club   A group of people who pool their money to buy and trade stocks. Many investment clubs belong to a not-for-profit umbrella organization called the *National Association of Investors Corp.,* in Madison Heights, Michigan.

Investor Relations Department   The division of a company that answers stockholder questions and sends them regular updates about the company's performance.

IPO   See *initial public offering.*

IRA   See *Individual Retirement Account.*

junk bond   High-yield corporate bonds that are rated below investment grade.

Keogh plan   A retirement savings program for small-business owners or the self-employed.

lifetime learning credit   You can claim a $1,000 tax credit per year for qualified college expenses. The credit, which will be increased to $2,000 by 2003, can be claimed for an unlimited number of years.

limit order   An order to buy or sell stock at a specific price or better. There is no guarantee that this kind of trade will be completed.

limited partnership   One of the most abused investments you can find. Brokers love them because they provide juicy, ongoing commissions. Many limited partnerships are involved in real estate, equipment leasing, and oil and gas. These ventures are usually made up of a general partner who manages the project and the limited partners who invest money. Typically, these investors receive a share of capital gains, income, and tax benefits.

load fund   This simply means that the fund comes with a sales charge. This fee pays a stockbroker's or a financial advisor's commission.

long-term care insurance   A policy that will pay for nursing home or at-home care expenses if you can no longer care for yourself.

low-load fund   Usually sold directly by a mutual fund group, low-load funds typically charge an up-front fee of 2 to 3 percent.

low-load insurance   Life insurance policies sold directly by insurance companies that do not pay commissions. These policies are cheaper than ones sold by insurance agents receiving commissions.

management fee   The fee all mutual funds charge investors each year to pay salaries, rent, and other management and overhead expenses.

market order   An order to buy or sell a stock at the best-available price. Most orders executed on the stock exchanges are market orders.

market timing   An investment strategy used by people who think they can outsmart the market. They try to anticipate trends—buying when they think the market is on the verge of advancing and selling before they expect a market downturn.

market value   The price at which an individual buys or sells a security at any given time.

maturity   The date on which a bond matures. When this happens, the bondholder gets back the face value of the bond.

Medical Information Bureau (MIB)   A depository in Massachusetts that maintains files on the medical history of millions of Americans. The MIB provides this information to insurance companies when they are investigating customers who have applied for health, disability, or life insurance policies.

Medicare   The federal health insurance program for persons 65 years of age or older and some disabled individuals. Part A of Medicare covers hospital costs. Part B covers physician bills and other medical costs.

mid-cap (capitalization) stocks Stocks belonging to medium-sized companies. The definition of a medium-sized company depends on who you ask. The capitalization can range anywhere from $1 billion to $5 billion.

money market fund A mutual fund that invests in very liquid short-term securities. Money markets seek to provide current income while maintaining a stable $1 per share.

Morgan Stanley EAFE (Europe, Australasia and Far East) Index This index tracks the performance of stocks in developed markets overseas.

Morningstar A well-known mutual fund ratings outfit in Chicago. Morningstar is best known for its five-star designation for the nation's best mutual funds. You can usually find Morningstar's mutual fund publication in libraries.

municipal bonds Debts of municipal governments, essentially IOUs, that are issued by state and local governments to fund capital projects.

mutual fund A mutual fund pools the money of thousands of shareholders and invests the money in stocks, bonds, or cash. As a shareholder, you can own a tiny piece of dozens or hundreds of individual stocks or bonds just by holding a few shares of the mutual fund.

NASD See *National Association of Securities Dealers*.

NASDAQ The acronym for a stock exchange called the *National Association of Securities Dealers Automated Quotation system*.

National Association of Investors Corp. (NAIC) The not-for-profit investment club organization that has helped thousands of investment clubs around the country get started. The NAIC is based in Madison Heights, Michigan.

National Association of Securities Dealers (NASD) Brokerage firms belong to this not-for-profit organization, which operates the NASDAQ. It also sets ethical guidelines for the industry and investigates violations of its rules.

NAV See *net asset value.*

net asset value (NAV) The value of one share of a mutual fund's investments. The NAV is adjusted daily and is reported every day in a newspaper's financial pages.

net income A corporation's total earnings after the costs of doing business are subtracted. It's also referred to as *net earnings* or *net profit.*

net profit See *net income.*

net worth The result of a person's or company's assets minus his or her debts or liabilities.

New York Stock Exchange (NYSE) Begun in 1792, it's the oldest stock exchange in the country.

Nikkei index An index of 225 leading blue chip stocks on the Tokyo Stock Exchange.

no-load fund A mutual fund that does not impose a sales charge.

noncallable bond A bond that cannot be redeemed by the issuer prior to maturity.

NYSE See *New York Stock Exchange.*

odd lots Shares of stock that are not bought in multiples of 100. Stocks traded in units of 100 are known as *round lots.*

open order An order to buy or sell a stock that remains in effect until you cancel the order or the trade is completed.

option The right to buy or sell at a specified price during a certain time period.

OTC   See *over-the-counter.*

over-the-counter   Securities trading done in settings other than the New York or American Stock Exchange.

P/E ratio   See *price-to-earnings ratio.*

par value   The face value of a bond. When the bond matures, the issuer must pay back the bond's par value.

penny stocks   Sometimes sold for less than $1 a share. Issued by companies with a short or erratic history of sales and earnings. Extremely speculative and best avoided.

pension plan   A qualified retirement plan established by an employer for its employees.

personal finance specialist   Designation used by certified public accountants who specialize in personal financial planning.

Ponzi scheme   One of the oldest investment frauds around. In such a scheme, people are promised great returns on investments such as real estate, gold mines, and anything else you can imagine. Early investors are paid off with money obtained from people lured into the scheme later. When the influx of new victims slows, the money dries up and the Ponzi collapses. Named for Charles Ponzi, a con artist who set up shop in Boston in 1919. He promised investors a 50 percent return on their investment in 45 days. His scheme collapsed six months later when he couldn't pay up.

portfolio   All the securities held by an individual.

portfolio manager   The person who manages an investment portfolio, such as a mutual fund's assets.

prepaid tuition plan   A college savings program typically offered by state governments. You prepay your child's future tuition at a state university or college, paying less today than you would in the future. The state decides how to invest your money.

price-to-earnings ratio (P/E ratio) The current market price of a share divided by the company's annual earnings per share. A *trailing P/E* is obtained by dividing the current price by the latest year's reported earnings. This is the P/E printed in newspapers. A *forward P/E* is based on analysts' forecasts of next year's earnings.

prime rate The interest rate that banks charge their most creditworthy customers.

principal The amount of money you originally put into an investment.

profit-sharing plan A defined contribution plan in which contributions, based on each participant's compensation, can be varied and no minimum contribution is required.

prospectus A legal document containing important information about a mutual fund, including its risks, costs, and past performance.

proxy Written authorization by a shareholder to give someone else authority to vote at a shareholder meeting.

qualified domestic relations order (QDRO) In a divorce case, a QDRO gives a former spouse the right to receive all or part of the benefits of the ex-partner's retirement benefits.

R&D See *research and development*.

real return The actual return on an investment after factoring in the rate of inflation. If an investment returns 8 percent and inflation is 3 percent, the real return is 5 percent.

redemption fee A fee charged by some mutual funds when investors sell or redeem shares.

registered representative An employee of a brokerage house who has acquired a background in the securities business and has passed a series of tests.

research and development (R&D) The section of a corporation that is devoted to creating new products and services.

return on equity A percentage obtained by dividing a company's earnings per share by its book value.

return on investment Profit from an investment that is usually expressed as an annual percentage rate.

risk The potential of losing money or not making an expected rate of return on an investment.

rollover A tax-free transfer of assets from one retirement plan to another.

Roth IRA Named after a senator from Delaware, this is the latest IRA offered by the federal government. You can invest up to $2,000 in a Roth IRA. You can't deduct your contribution from your taxes, but you won't have to pay any taxes on this nest egg when you retire.

Russell 2000 This stock market index is made up of 2,000 companies that are considered small.

S&P 500 See *Standard & Poor's 500 Index*.

sales load A commission charged by some mutual funds on new purchases of shares. The average commission, or load, is about 4 percent.

SEC See *Securities and Exchange Commission*.

sector fund A mutual fund that only buys stocks in a particular industry, such as health care, banking, or computers.

secured credit card A credit card with training wheels. Banks will typically issue these cards to persons with troubled credit histories. The cardholder must agree to deposit money into a bank account as collateral. The money will be used by the bank to cover the card debt if necessary.

securities A catch-all name for stocks, bonds, and other types of investments.

Securities and Exchange Commission (SEC) A federal agency, created in 1934, that oversees the securities industry. A chief aim is to protect the investing public from abuses in the industry.

Securities Investor Protection Corp. (SIPC) A not-for-profit corporation created by Congress to provide financial protection to clients who lose money when their brokerage firms declare bankruptcy.

share price The price of one share of stock.

shareholder An individual who owns shares of stock in a corporation.

simple interest Interest that is calculated on the original amount of money invested. It is not compounded over time.

small cap (capitalization) stock Stock in companies whose market value is less than $1 billion. Small cap companies as a group have historically grown faster than large companies, but they are also more volatile and fail more often.

spousal IRA An Individual Retirement Account for a nonworking spouse. Not long ago, the federal government raised the maximum contribution from $250 to $2,000 a year.

spread The difference between a stock's bid and asked price.

Standard & Poor's 500 Index (S&P 500) An index of the stocks of 500 very large American corporations. The index is widely regarded as a barometer of the overall health of the U.S. stock market.

Standard & Poor's MidCap 400 Index Created in 1991 to monitor the investment performance of medium-sized companies. Today the average market capitalization of one of these index stocks is $1.9 billion.

Standard & Poor's SmallCap 600 Index   Created in 1995, this index includes 600 small companies that have an average market value of about $581 million, which is tiny by Wall Street standards. Familiar companies in this index include Chiquita Brands International, the Toro Co., and Swiss Army Brands.

stock   Shares of ownership in a corporation.

stock split   An increase in a company's shares of stock. Splitting a stock's price (often in half) without affecting its value is a popular way to make individual shares less expensive. In a 2-for-1 split, a $100 stock would now cost $50, but an individual would hold two shares of the $50 stock.

stock tables   Listings found in newspapers of companies and their current share prices.

stop order   An order to sell a stock when its price falls to a certain level. This order is intended to limit an investor's losses.

Student Loan Marketing Association (Sallie Mae) A large financial services company that provides funds for education loans as well as operational support for lenders and colleges.

takeover   One corporation taking control of another, either through a friendly acquisition or through what's called a *hostile takeover*.

tax deferral   Any earnings on a tax-deferred investment remain untaxed until you make a withdrawal.

tax-free bonds   Another name for *municipal bonds*. These tax-exempt bonds are free from federal income tax and might be free of state and local taxes as well.

term life insurance   Life insurance that provides a cash benefit to your survivors if you die. There is no investment component to this insurance.

ticker symbol   Letters that identify a company for trading purposes; these symbols can be found in a newspaper's stock tables.

total return   A measure of an asset's performance—it includes the income an investment has generated as well as any capital appreciation.

transfer agent   A bank or trust company charged with keeping a record of a company's stockholders and canceling and issuing certificates as shares are bought and sold.

Treasury bill   Also called a *T-bill,* this is a short-term discounted security issued by the federal government, with a maturity that doesn't exceed one year.

Treasury bond   A federal government obligation that matures more than 10 years after it's issued.

Treasury note   A federal government obligation that matures from 2 to 10 years after it's issued.

turnover   How often a mutual fund portfolio manager buys and sells stock.

uniform resource locator (URL)   A Web site's address. For example, the address of the Securities and Exchange Commission's Web site is www.sec.gov.

unit investment trust   A fixed bundle of investments that usually includes either stocks or bonds. Someone who buys into a unit investment trust buys units or shares. Unlike mutual funds, securities in a unit investment trust generally can't be sold, no matter what happens, until the unit trust is disbanded.

universal life insurance   A cash value life insurance policy that provides a death benefit as well as an investment component.

U.S. savings bonds   Savings bonds issued by the federal government at face values that range from

$50 to $10,000. Issued at a discount, they are redeemed for face value at maturity.

Value Line   An independent stock-evaluation service that is popular with individual investors. Value Line packs a great deal of statistics into its one-page evaluations of individual stocks.

value stocks   Stocks that have a low market price relative to their earnings. On the flip side are *growth stocks,* which have a high price-to-earnings ratio due to anticipated expansion opportunities.

variable annuity   A variable annuity is part insurance policy and part mutual fund. Within an insurance wrapper, policyholders invest their money in mutual funds. The annuity is called *variable* because the return depends on how the mutual funds perform. The insurance guarantees that if you die, your heirs will at least get the amount of money that you initially put in.

variable life insurance   This type of policy provides a death benefit but also serves as a tax-deferred investment vehicle. The rate of return on your investment depends on what underlying securities you choose.

venture capital   A source of money for start-up companies.

volume   The number of shares of a company's stock that are traded during a day.

Wall Street   The financial district at the lower end of Manhattan in New York City. Many brokerage firms, as well as the New York and American stock exchanges, are located here.

Web site   The location of a business or other entity on the Internet. A Web site's welcome mat—that is, the first thing you see when you arrive—is called the *home page.*

whole life insurance   A life insurance policy that provides a death benefit to the survivors, as well as a tax-deferred investment. Part of the annual premium pays for the death benefit, while the rest is invested for you.

Wilshire 5000 Index   The broadest stock market index. It tracks the prices of more than 6,000 American companies traded on the New York and American exchanges, as well as the NASDAQ.

yield   Income received from investments, usually expressed as a percentage of the market price of the investment.

yield to call   Yield on a bond, assuming that the bond will be redeemed by the issuer at the first possible opportunity.

yield to maturity   The yield an investor will receive if a bond is held until its maturity date.

zero coupon bond   A bond sold at a deep discount of its face value. It can be extremely volatile unless it's held to maturity.

Resource Guide

American Depositary Receipts (ADRs)

Bank of New York
Global Buy Direct
Shareholder Relations Department
P.O. Box 11258
Church Street Station
New York, N.Y. 10286-1258
(800) 943-9715
www.bankofny.com/adr

J.P. Morgan Guaranty Trust
Shareholder Services
P.O. Box 8205
Boston, MA 02266-8205
(800) 749-1687

Appraisers

American Society of Appraisers
P.O. Box 17265
Washington, D.C. 20041
(703) 478-2228

Institute of Business Appraisers
P.O. Box 1447
Boynton Beach, FL 33425
(561) 732-3202

Bonds

Bonds Online
www.bonds-online.com
Includes a feature called Bond Professor and
provides links to other bond sites.

Moody's Bond Record
Moody's Investors Service
99 Church St.
New York, NY 10007
(800) 342-5647

Standard & Poor's Bond Guide
Standard & Poor's Corp.
65 Broadway, 8th Floor
New York, NY 10006
(800) 221-5277

U.S. Bureau of Public Debt
Savings Bonds Department
Parkersburg, WV 26106-1328
(304) 480-6112
www.publicdebt.treas.gov andwww.savingsbonds.gov

Federal reserve branches (for buying U.S. Treasuries directly)

Atlanta	(404) 521-8653
Baltimore	(410) 576-3300
Birmingham	(205) 731-8708
Boston	(617) 973-3810
Buffalo	(716) 849-5000
Charlotte	(704) 358-2410
Chicago	(312) 322-5369
Cincinnati	(513) 721-4794

Cleveland	(216) 579-2000
Dallas	(214) 922-6770
Denver	(303) 572-2473
Detroit	(313) 964-6157
El Paso	(915) 521-8272
Houston	(713) 659-4433
Jacksonville	(904) 632-1179
Kansas City	(816) 881-2883
Little Rock	(501) 324-8272
Los Angeles	(213) 624-7398
Louisville	(502) 568-9238
Memphis	(901) 523-7171
Miami	(305) 471-6497
Minneapolis	(612) 340-2075
Nashville	(615) 251-7100
New Orleans	(504) 593-3200
New York City	(212) 720-6619
Oklahoma City	(405) 270-8652
Omaha	(402) 221-5636
Philadelphia	(215) 574-6680
Pittsburgh	(412) 261-7802
Portland	(503) 221-5932
Richmond	(804) 697-8372
Salt Lake City	(801) 322-7844
San Antonio	(210) 978-1305
San Francisco	(415) 974-2330
Seattle	(206) 343-3605
St. Louis	(314) 444-8703
Washington, D.C.	(202) 874-4000

Brokers

Check your Yellow Pages for numbers of the nearest full-service brokers.

Prominent discount brokers

AccuTrade	(800) 494-8939
Charles Schwab	(800) 435-4000
E*Trade Securities	(800) 786-2575
Fidelity Brokerage Services	(800) 544-8666
Jack White & Co.	(800) 494-8946
Kennedy Cabot & Co.	(800) 252-0090
Muriel Siebert	(800) 872-0711
Quick & Reilly	(800) 672-7220
Scottsdale Securities	(800) 619-7283
T. Rowe Price Discount	(800) 638-5660
Waterhouse Securities	(800) 934-4410

Certificates of deposit

Bank Rate Monitor
P.O. Box 088888
11811 U.S. Highway One, Suite 200
N. Palm Beach, FL 33408
(800) 327-7717
www.bankrate.com

Children and money

Jump Start Coalition for Personal Financial Literacy
919 18th St. NW
Washington, DC 20006
(888) 400-2233

National Center for Financial Education
P.O. Box 34070
San Diego, CA 92163
(619) 232-8811
www.ncfe.org

Closed-end mutual funds

Morningstar
225 W. Wacker Dr.
Chicago, IL, 60606
(800) 735-0700
www.morningstar.net

Mutual Funds Magazine
(800) 442-9000
www.mfmag.com
The *Wall Street Journal* and *Barron's* weekly listings of closed-end mutual funds

College planning

College Savings Plans Network
2760 Research Park Dr.
Lexington, KY 40511
(606) 244-8175
www.collegesavings.org

FastWeb
(online college scholarship search service)
www.fastweb.com

Federal Student Aid Information Center
(800) 4-FED-AID

National Association of Student Financial Aid Administrators
1920 L St. NW, Suite 200
Washington, D.C. 20036-5020
(202) 785-0453
www.finaid.org

Princeton Review
www.review.com

Student Loan Marketing Association (Sallie Mae)
1050 Thomas Jefferson St. NW
Washington, D.C. 20007-3871
(202) 333-8000
www.salliemae.com

Consumer organizations

Consumer Action
717 Market St., Suite 310
San Francisco, CA 94103
(415) 777-9648

Consumer Action's Southern California Office
523 W. Sixth St., Suite 1105
Los Angeles, CA 90014
(213) 624-4631

Consumer Federation of America
1424 16th St., NW, Suite 604
Washington, D.C. 20036
(202) 387-6121

Credit bureaus

Equifax
(800) 685-1111

Experian (formerly TRW)
(800) 392-1122
Trans Union
(800) 851-2674

Credit, debt, and bankruptcy

Bank Rate Monitor
P.O. Box 088888
11811 U.S. Highway One, Suite 200
North Palm Beach, FL 33408
www.bankrate.com

CardTrak
(publishes lists of best credit cards)
P.O. Box 1700
Frederick, MD 21702
www.cardtrak.com

Debt Counselors of America
(nonprofit online resource)
www.dca.org
(800) 680-3328

Debtors Anonymous
General Services Board
P.O. Box 400
New York, NY 10163-0400
(212) 642-8220

HSH Associates
(publishes lists of mortgage, home equity, and car
loan rates from around the nation)
1200 Route 23
Butler, NJ 077405
(800) 873-2837
www.hsh.com

National Center for Financial Education
P.O. Box 34070
San Diego, CA 92163
(619) 232-8811
www.ncfe.org

National Foundation for Consumer Credit
8611 Second Ave., Suite 100
Silver Springs, MD 20852
(800) 388-2227

Nolo Press
(provides a wealth of legal information on dozens of
topics)
www.nolo.com

Dividend-reinvestment plans

*The Individual Investor's Guide to Dividend
Reinvestment Plan*
American Association of Individual Investors
625 N. Michigan Ave., Suite 1900
Chicago, IL 60611
(800) 428-2244

The Moneypaper's Guide to Dividend Reinvestment Plans
1010 Mamaroneck Ave.
Mamaroneck, NY 10543
(800) 388-9993

Standard & Poor's Directory of Dividend Reinvestment Plans
65 Broadway
New York, NY 10006
(800) 221-5277

Divorce and remarriage

The American Academy of Matrimonial Lawyers
(312) 263-6477

Stepfamily Association of America
650 J St., Suite 205
Lincoln, NE 68508
(800) 735-0329

Stepfamily Foundation
(212) 799-7837

The following divorce Web sites maintain articles about common divorce issues, family law information, bulletin boards, recommended reading, and links to other relevant Internet sites:

Divorce Central
www.divorcecentral.com

Divorce Helpline
www.divorcehelp.com

Divorce Online
www.divorce-online.com

DivorceNet
www.divorcenet.com

Financial planners

American Institute of Certified Public Accountants
Personal Financial Planning Division
1211 Avenue of the Americas
New York, NY 10036
(888) 999-9256
www.aicpa.org

American Society of CLU & ChFC
270 S. Bryn Mawr Ave.
Bryn Mawr, PA 19010
(888) ChFC-CLU
www.agents-online.com/ASCLU/index.html

Certified Financial Planner Board of Standards
1700 Broadway, Suite 2100
Denver, CO 80290
(888) CFP-MARK
www.cfp-board.org

The Institute of Certified Financial Planners
Consumer Division
3801 E. Florida Ave., Suite 708
Denver, CO 80210
(800) 282-7526
www.icfp.org

International Association for Financial Planning
5775 Glenridge Dr., NE, Suite B-300
Atlanta, GA 30328
(888) 806-PLAN
www.iafp.org

LINC, Inc.
(Licensed Independent Network of CPA Financial Planners)
404 James Robertson Parkway, Suite 1200
Nashville, TN 37219
(800) 737-2727

The National Association of Personal Financial
Advisors
1130 Lake Cook Rd., Suite 150
Buffalo Grove, IL 60089
(800) 366-2732
www.napfa.org

Financial trade organizations
Investment Company Institute
1401 H St. NW
Washington, D.C. 20005-2148
(202) 326-5800
www.ici.org

Mutual Fund Alliance
100 NW Englewood, Suite 130
Kansas City, MO 64118
(816) 454-9422
www.mfea.com

Securities Industry Association
120 Broadway
New York, NY 10271
(212) 608-1500

Government agencies and financial regulators
American Arbitration Association
140 W. 51st St.
New York, NY 10020
(212) 484-4000

American Stock Exchange
86 Trinity Place
New York, NY 10006
(212) 306-1000

Federal Reserve Bank-New York
(publications office for consumer materials)
33 Liberty St.
New York, NY 100045
(212) 720-6134

Investor Protection Trust
www.investorprotection.org
(provides advice on how to spot a bad broker and
what you can do if your broker is ripping you off)

NASD's Public Disclosure Program
P.O. Box 9401
Gaithersburg, MD 20898-9401
Public Disclosure Hotline: (800) 289-9999

National Association of Securities Dealers (NASD)
125 Broad St., 36th Floor
New York, NY 10004
(212) 858-4400
www.investor.nasd.com and www.nasdr.com

NASD DISTRICT OFFICES

District 1

525 Market St., Suite 300

San Francisco, CA 94105-2711

(415) 882-1200

300 Grand Ave., Suite 1600

Los Angeles, CA 90071

(213) 627-2122

District 3

Republic Office Building

370 17th St., Suite 2900

Denver, CO 80202-5629

(303) 446-3100

Two Union Square

601 Union St., Suite 1616

Seattle, WA 98101-2327

(206) 624-0790

District 4

12 Wyandotte Plaza

120 W. 12th St., Suite 900

Kansas City, MO 64105

(816) 421-5700

District 5

1100 Poydras St., Suite 850

Energy Centre

New Orleans, LA 70163

(504) 522-6527

District 6

12801 N. Central Expressway, Suite 1050

Dallas, TX 75243

(972) 701-8554

District 7

One Securities Centre, Suite 500

3490 Piedmont Rd., NE

Atlanta, GA 30305

(404) 239-6100

District 8

10 S. LaSalle St., 20th Floor

Chicago, IL 60603-1002

(312) 899-4400

Renaissance on Playhouse Square

1350 Euclid Ave., Suite 650

Cleveland, OH 44115

(216) 694-4545

District 9

11 Penn Center

1835 Market St., 19th Floor

Philadelphia, PA 19103

(215) 665-1180

District 10

33 Whitehall St.

New York, NY 10004-2193

(212) 858-4000

District 11

260 Franklin St., 16th Floor

Boston, MA 02110

(617) 261-0800

New York Stock Exchange
20 Broad St, 5th Floor
New York, NY 10005
(212) 656-2772

North American Securities Administrators
Association
10 G St., NE, Suite 710
Washington, D.C. 20002
(202) 737-0900
www.nasaa.org

Securities and Exchange Commission (SEC)
450 Fifth St. NW, Mail Stop 11-2
Washington, D.C. 20549
(202) 942-4108
SEC's EDGAR
www.sec.gov/edgarhp.htm

SEC's Office of Investor Education and Assistance
(202) 942-7040

SEC'S REGIONAL OFFICES

Midwest

Citicorp Center

500 W. Madison St., Suite 1400

Chicago, IL 60661-2511

(312) 353-7390

Northeast

7 World Trade Center, Suite 1300

New York, NY 10048

(212) 748-8000

Rocky Mountain

1801 California St., Suite 4800

Denver, CO 80202-2648

(303) 844-1000

Southeast

1401 Brickell Ave., Suite 200

Miami, FL 33131

(305) 536-4700

West Coast

5670 Wilshire Blvd., 11th Floor

Los Angeles, CA 90036-3648

(213) 965-3998

Insurance

American Society of Chartered Life Underwriters &
Chartered Financial Consultants
270 S. Bryn Mawr Ave.
Bryn Mawr, PA 19010-2195
(800) 392-6900

Consumer Federation of America
1424 16th St. NW
Washington, D.C. 20036
(202) 387-6121

Eldercare Locator
(800) 677-1116

Federal Deposit Insurance Corp.
(800) 934-3342
www.fdic.gov

Medical Information Bureau
P.O. Box 105
Essex Station
Boston, MA 02112
(617) 426-3660

National Association of Area Agencies on Aging
1112 16th St. NW, Suite 100
Washington, D.C. 20036-4823
(202) 296-8130

National Association of Insurance Commissioners
120 W. 12th St., Suite 1100
Kansas City, MO 64105-1925
(816) 842-3600
www.naic.org

United Seniors Health Cooperative
1331 H St. NW, Suite 500
Washington, D.C. 20005-4706
(202) 393-6222

Insurance company rating services

A.M. Best
(800) 424-BEST
(900) 555-BEST

Duff & Phelps
(312) 368-3198

Moody's
(212) 553-0377

Standard & Poor's
(212) 208-1527

Weiss Ratings
(800) 289-9222

Insurance quote services

AccuQuote
(800) 442-9899
www.accuquote.com

Direct Quote
(800) 845-3853
www.directquote.com

InsuranceQuote Services
(800) 972-1104
www.insurancequote.net

NetQuote
www.netquote.com

Quick Quote
(800) 867-2404
www.quickquote.com

Quicken InsureMarket
(800) 695-0011
www.insuremarket.com

Quoteshopper
(800) 367-8044
www.quoteshopper.com

Quotesmith
(800) 431-1147
www.quotesmith.com

RightQuote
www.rightquote.com

Select Quote
(800) 343-1985
www.selectquote.com

TermQuote
(800) 444-8376
www.term-quote.com

Wholesale Insurance Network
(800) 808-5810
www.ge.com/capital/insurance/ci5.htm

Investor education

American Association of Individual Investors
626 N. Michigan Ave.
Chicago, IL 60611
(800) 428-2244

www.aaii.com
The National Association of Investment Clubs
711 W. 13 Mile Rd.
Madison Heights, MI 48071
(248) 583-NAIC
www.better-investing.org

Legal resources

Academy of Family Mediators
4 Militia Dr.
Lexington, MA 02173
(617) 674-2663

American Academy of Matrimonial Lawyers
(312) 263-6477

American Bar Association
750 N. Lake Shore Dr.
Chicago, IL 60611
(312) 988-5000
www.abanet.org

STATE BAR WEB SITES

Alaska	www.alaska.net
Arkansas	www.arkbar.com
California	www.calbar.org
Canadian	www.algonquinc.on.ca
Colorado	www.usa.net
District of Columbia	www.dcbar.org
Florida	www.pwr.com
Georgia	www.kuesterlaw.com
Illinois	www.illinoisbar.org
Indiana	www.iquest.net
Kansas	www.ink.org
Kentucky	www.ink.org
Maryland	www.msba.org
Michigan	www.sbmnet.org
Missouri	www.mobar.org
Native American	free.website.com

Nebraska	www.nol.org
New Hampshire	www.nh.com
New Jersey	www.njsba.com
New York	www.nysba.com
North Carolina	www.barlinc.org
Oklahoma	pwr.com
Pennsylvania	www.pbi.com
South Carolina	www.scbar.org
Tennessee	www.tba.org
Utah	www.utahbar.org
Washington	www.wsba.org
Wisconsin	www.wisbar.org

National Academy of Elder Law Attorneys
(520) 881-4005

Nolo Press
(provides a wealth of legal information on dozens of
topics)
www.nolo.com

Mutual funds

CDA/Wiesenberger Mutual Funds Update
1355 Piccard Dr., Suite 220
Rockville MD 20850
(800) 232-2285

Morningstar
225 W. Wacker Dr.
Chicago, IL 60606
(800) 735-0700
www.morningstar.net

Value Line Mutual Fund Survey
220 East 42nd St.
New York, NY 10017-5891
(800) 833-0046

Pensions

National Center for Employee Ownership (NCEO)
1201 Martin Luther King Dr. Way, 2nd Floor
Oakland, CA 94612
(510) 272-9461
www.nceo.org

Pension and Welfare Benefits Administration
U.S. Department of Labor
200 Constitution Ave. NW
Washington, D.C. 20210
(202) 219-8233
www.dol.gov/dol/pwba

Pension Rights Center
918 16th St. NW, Suite 704
Washington, D.C. 20036
(202) 296-3776

Social investing

Co-op America
1612 K St. NW
Washington, D.C. 20006
(202) 872-5307
www.coopamerica.org

Council on Economic Priorities
30 Irving Place, 9th Floor
New York, NY 10003
(212) 420-1133

The GreenMoney Journal
608 W. Glass Ave.
Spokane, WA 99205
(800) 318-5725
www.greenmoney.org

Social security

Social Security Administration
Call your local office or (800) 772-1213
www.ssa.gov

Stock investing

Moody's Investors Service
(produces numerous stock publications)
99 Church St.
New York, NY 10007
(800) 342-5647

NASDAQ Fact Book and Company Directory
P.O. Box 9403
Gaithersburg, MD 20898-9403
(301) 590-6142

Public Registers Annual Report Service
(mails callers free corporate annual reports)
(800)-4-ANNUAL

Red Chip Review
(publication that analyzes hundreds of small cap stocks)
(800)-RED-CHIP
www.redchip.com

Standard & Poor's Corp.
(releases many stock publications)
65 Broadway, 8th Floor
New York, NY 10006
(800) 221-5277

STOCK INVESTING WEB SITES

American Stock Exchange	www.amex.com
Dogs of the Dow	www.dogsofthedow.com
FreeEDGAR	www.freeedgar.com
Hoover's Inc.	www.hoovers.com
Invest-O-Rama!	www.investorama.com

IPO Central	www.ipocentral.com
IPO Intelligence Online	www.ipo-fund.com
IPO Maven	www.ipomaven.com
J.P. Morgan	www.jpmorgan.com
Microsoft Investor	www.investor.msn.com
NASDAQ	www.nasdaq.com
New York Stock Exchange	www.nyse.com
Russell Index	www.russell.com
Silicon Investor	www.techstocks.com
SmallCap Investor	www.smallcapivestor.com
Standard & Poor's	www.stockinfo.standardpoor.com
Wilshire Associates	www.wilshire.com
Yahoo! Finance	www.quote.yahoo.com

Taxes

Coopers & Lybrand
www.taxnews.com

Deloitte & Touche
dtonline.com/taxguide97/cover.htm

Drake Software
www.1040.com

Internal Revenue Service
Guide to Free Tax Services and other publications
(800) 829-3676

IRSwww.irs.ustreas.gov
IRS Check Refund Status phone line
(800) 829-4477

IRS Tax Fax
(fax service for the 100 most requested tax forms)
(703) 321-8020

Dial from fax machine, then follow instructions. Forms will be faxed back.

National Association of Enrolled Agents
200 Orchard Ridge Dr., Suite 302
Gaithersburg, MD 20878
(800) 424-4339

Free materials you can get from the IRS

Pub. 550, *Investment Income and Expenses*
Covers investment income such as dividends and interest, expenses related to investments, and the sale and trade of investment property, including capital gains and losses.

Pub. 552, *Recordkeeping for Individuals*
A reference guide for general record keeping for individual income tax filings.

Pub. 554, *Older Americans' Tax Guide*
Explains tax matters that affect senior citizens.

Pub. 559, *Survivors, Executors, and Administrators*
Provides helpful information for reporting and paying federal income tax if you are responsible for a deceased person's estate. Answers many questions that a spouse or other survivor faces when a person dies.

Pub. 560, *Retirement Plans for Small Business*
Explains tax considerations relevant to small businesses and the self-employed. Includes simplified employee pensions (SEPs), Keoghs, and simple retirement plans.

Pub. 561, *Determining the Value of Donated Property*
Defines what fair market value is and helps you determine the value of property you donate to a charity.

Pub. 564, *Mutual Fund Distributions*
Explains tax treatment of distributions and how to figure gains or losses on the sale of mutual fund shares.

Pub. 575, *Pension and Annuity Income*
Explains how to report pension and annuity income from retirement plans. Also covers taxes for lump-sum distributions from pensions, stock bonuses, profit-sharing plans, and IRA rollovers.

Pub. 1518, *Free Tax-Tip Calendar*

Variable annuities

Barron's
(publishes a table of annuity information in each issue)

Morningstar Variable Annuity Life Performance Report
(monthly)
225 W. Wacker Dr.
Chicago, IL 60606
(800) 735-0700

National Association for Variable Annuities
12030 Sunrise Valley Dr., Suite 110
Reston, VA 20191
(703) 620-0674

The Wall Street Journal
(publishes information on annuities every Monday)

Recommended Reading List

Bonds

Faerber, Esme. *All About Bonds From the Inside Out.* Probus Publishing Co.

Children and money

Godfrey, Neale S. and Carolina Edwards. *Money Doesn't Grow on Trees: A Parent's Guide to Raising Financially Responsible Children.* Simon & Schuster.

Zillions (children's magazine from *Consumer Reports*), P.O. Box 54861, Boulder, CO 80322-4861; (800) 234-2078.

Closed-end mutual funds

Fredman, Albert J. and George Cole Scott. *Investing in Closed-End Funds: Finding Value and Building Growth.* Simon & Schuster.

College planning

Chany, Kalman A. with Geoff Martz. *Princeton Review Student Advantage Guide to Paying for College.* Random House.

Drumm, Alice and Richard Kneedler. *Funding a College Education.* Harvard Business School Press.

Solorzano, Lucia. *Barron's Best Buys in College Education,* 4th ed. Barron's Educational Series.

Vuturo, Chris. *The Scholarship Advisor.* Random House/Princeton Review Books.

Credit problems

Detweiler, Gerri. *Debt Consolidation 101: Strategies for Saving Money & Paying Off Your Debts Faster.* Good Advice Press. Booklet can be obtained calling (800) 255-0899.

————. *The Ultimate Credit Handbook.* Plume Books.

Eisenson, Marc, Gerri Detweiler, and Nancy Castleman. *Invest in Yourself: Six Secrets to a Rich Life.* John Wiley & Sons.

Elias, Stephen, Albin Renauer, and Robin Leonard. *How to File for Bankruptcy.* Nolo Press.

Elias, Stephen, Albin Renauer, Robin Leonard, and Lisa Goldoftas. *Nolo's Law Form Kit: Personal Bankruptcy.* Nolo Press.

Leonard, Robin. *Chapter 13 Bankruptcy; Repay Your Debts.* Nolo Press.

————. *Credit Repair: Clean Up Your Credit Report.* Nolo Press.

————. *Money Troubles: Legal Strategies to Cope with Your Debts.* Nolo Press.

Leonard, Robin and Shae Irving. *Take Control of Your Student Loans.* Nolo Press.

Divorce, remarriage, and finances

Naylor, Sharon. *The Unofficial Guide to Divorce.* Macmillan Publishing.

Schiff Estess, Patricia. *Money Advice for Your Successful Remarriage.* F&W Publications.

Sherman, Charles. *How to Do Your Own Divorce* (California and Texas eds). Nolo Press.

Woodhouse, Violet and Victoria F. Collins, with M.C. Blakeman. *Divorce and Money: How to Make the Best Financial Decisions During Divorce.* Nolo Press.

Financial advisors

Allen, John Lawrence. *Investor Beware! How to Protect Your Money from Wall Street's Dirty Tricks.* John Wiley & Sons.

Brenner, Lynn. *Smart Questions to Ask Your Financial Advisors.* Bloomberg Press.

Financial primers

Downes, John and Jordan Elliot Goodman. *Barron's Finance & Investment Handbook,* 4th ed. Barron's Educational Series.

Friedlob, George T. and Franklin Plewa, Jr. *Financial and Business Statements.* Barron's Business Library.

Lynch, Peter. *Learn to Earn: A Beginner's Guide to Basics of Investing and Business.* John Wiley & Sons.

Morris, Kenneth M. and Alan M. Siegel. *The Wall Street Journal Guide to Understanding Money & Investing.* Simon & Schuster.

————. *The Wall Street Journal Guide to Understanding Personal Finance.* Simon & Schuster.

Morris, Kenneth M., Alan M. Siegel, and Virginia B. Morris. *The Wall Street Journal Guide to Planning Your Financial Future*. Simon & Schuster.

Szurovy, Geza and S.B. Costales. *The Guide to Understanding Financial Statements*. McGraw-Hill.

Financial strategies

Bryant Quinn, Jane. *Making the Most of Your Money: Smart Ways to Create Wealth and Plan Your Finances in the '90s*. Simon & Schuster.

Clements, Jonathan. *Twenty Five Myths You've Got to Avoid If You Want to Manage Your Money Right*. Warner Books.

Kobliner, Beth. *Get a Financial Life: Personal Finance in Your Twenties and Thirties*. Simon & Schuster.

Wall, Ginita and Victoria F. Collins. *Your Next Fifty Years*. Henry Holt & Co.

The Wall Street Journal Lifetime Guide to Money. Hyperion.

Foreign investing

Dow Jones Guide to the World Stock Market. Prentice Hall Business Group, Order Processing Center, P.O. Box 11071, Des Moines, IA 50336-1071; (800) 947-7700.

Hoover's Handbook of World Business. Hoover's Inc., 1033 La Posada Dr., Suite 250, Austin, TX 78752; (800) 486-8666.

Prestbo, John A. and Douglas R. Sease. *The Wall Street Journal Book of International Investing: Everything You Need to Know About Investing in Foreign Markets*. Hyperion.

Insurance

Bamford, Janet. *Smarter Insurance Solutions*. Bloomberg Press.

How to Insure Your Income. Merritt Publishing.

Katt, Peter C. *The Life Insurance Fiasco: How to Avoid It*. Dolphin Publishing.

"Long-Term Disability Insurance," *Consumer Reports* (Oct. 1997). To order a reprint, contact 101 Truman Ave., Yonkers, NY 10703-1075; (914) 378-2000.

Shelton, Phyllis. *Long-Term Care Planning Guide*. LTC Consultant, P.O. Box 17526, Nashville, TN 37217; (800) 587-0473.

Internet investing

Brown, David L. and Kassandra Bentley. *Wall Street City: Your Guide to Investing on the Web*. John Wiley & Sons.

Farrell, Paul. *Mutual Fund Investing on the Net: Making Money Online*. John Wiley & Sons.

Gerlach, Douglas. *Investor's Web Guide: Tools and Strategies for Building Your Portfolio*. Lycos Press.

Goldstein, Douglas and Joyce Flory. *The Online Guide to Personal Finance & Investing*. Irwin Professional Publishing.

Investment clubs

O'Hara, Thomas E. and Kenneth S. Janke, Sr. *Starting and Running a Profitable Investment Club*. Times Business, Random House.

Magazines and newspapers

Barron's
(800) 544-0422
www.barrons.com

Investor's Business Daily
(800) 831-2525
www.investors.com

Bloomberg Personal
(888) 432-5820
www.bloomberg.com

Kiplinger's Personal Finance
(800) 544-0155
www.kiplinger.com

Business Week
(800) 635-1200
www.businessweek.com

Mutual Funds Magazine
(800) 442-9000
www.mfmag.com

Forbes
(800) 888-9896
www.forbes.com

SmartMoney
(800) 444-4204
www.smartmoney.com

Fortune
(800) 621-8000
www.pathfinder.com

Wall Street Journal
(800) 568-7625
www.wsj.com

Individual Investor
(800) 383-5901
www.iionline.com

Worth Magazine
(800) 727-9098
www.worth.com

Mutual funds

Bogle, John C. *Bogle on Mutual Funds.* Irwin.

Clements, Jonathan. *Funding Your Future: The Only Guide to Mutual Funds You'll Ever Need.* Warner Books.

Rowland, Mary. *A Commonsense Guide to Mutual Funds.* Bloomberg Press.

Stocks

Buffett, Mary and David Clark. *Buffetology: The Previously Unexplained Techniques That Have Made Warren Buffett the World's Most Famous Investor.* Scribner.

Graja, Christopher and Elizabeth Ungar. *Investing in Small-Cap Stocks*. Bloomberg Press.

Hall, Alvin D. *Getting Started in Stocks,* 3rd ed. John Wiley, Inc.

Lowe, Janet C. *Value Investing Made Easy*. McGraw-Hill.

Lynch, Peter. *Beating the Street*. Fireside Publications.

Malkiel, Burton G. *A Random Walk Down Wall Street*. W.W. Norton & Co.

Murphy, Michael. *Every Investor's Guide to High-Tech Stocks & Mutual Funds*. Broadway Books.

O'Shaughnessy, James. *How to Retire Rich*.

Important Documents

Here are some documents that you will find elsewhere in the book that might come in handy.

INTERNAL REVENUE TAX RATE SCHEDULES FOR 1998

Schedule X: Single Individuals

Taxable Income	Tax Bracket
$0–$25,350	15%
$25,351–$61,400	28%
$61,401–$128,100	31%
$128,101–$278,450	36%
$278,451 and up	39.6%

Schedule Y-1: Married Filing Jointly and Surviving Spouses

Taxable Income	Tax Bracket
$0–$42,350	15%
$42,351–$102,300	28%
$102,301–$155,950	31%
$155,951–$278,450	36%
$278,451 and up	39.6%

Schedule Y-2: Married Individuals Filing Separately

Taxable Income	Tax Bracket
$0–$21,175	15%
$21,176–$51,150	28%
$51,151–$77,975	31%
$77,976–$139,225	36%
$139,226 and up	39.6%

YOUR NET WORTH WORKSHEET

Assets

1. Cash

   Checking account _____

   Money markets _____

   Certificates of deposit _____

2. Investments

   Stocks _____

   Bonds _____

   Mutual funds _____

   Life insurance (cash value) _____

3. Fixed assets

   Home _____

   Other real estate _____

4. Retirement assets

   Vested interest in company pension
   or profit-sharing plan _____

   Annuities (cash value) _____

   401(k) plan _____

   Other retirement plans _____

   Future Social Security
   benefits _____

5. Personal assets
   (fair market or replacement value)

   Cars _____

   Computers _____

   Jewelry _____

   Art and antiques _____

6. Money loaned to others
   (if repayment is expected) _____

7. Other assets _____

Total assets _____

Debt

1. Home mortgage _____

2. Mortgage on real estate _____

3. Vehicle loans _____

4. Bank loans _____

5. Credit card balances _____

6. Student loans _____

7. Outstanding judgments _____

8. Income taxes due _____

9. Loans on 401(k) plan _____

   10. Loans on life
       insurance policies _____

   11. Other liabilities _____

Total debt _____

Net worth

**Subtract total debt from
total assets** _____

INCOME STATEMENT

Yearly Cash Income

1. Salary _____

2. Commissions, bonuses, and
   profit sharing _____

3. Dividends and interest _____

4. Proceeds from sale of
   investments _____

5. Alimony or child support
   received _____

6. Pension _____

7. Social Security _____

8. Annuity and life insurance
   income _____

9. Cash gifts _____

10. Other income _____

Total Income _____

Yearly Cash Expenses

1. Housing

   Rent or mortgage _____

   Utilities _____

   Insurance _____

   Property taxes _____

   Repairs _____

   Improvements _____

2. Food _____

3. Clothing (include dry
   cleaning) _____

4. Telephone _____

   5. Automobile

   Gas and repairs _____

   Car loan(s) _____

   Car lease _____

   Insurance _____

   6. Medical

   Physicians _____

   Dentist _____

   Medicines _____

   Health insurance _____

   7. Child-care expenses _____

   8. Tuition _____

   9. Alimony/child support _____

   10. Charity _____

   11. Entertainment _____

   12. Vacations _____

   13. Gifts _____

   14. Life insurance
       premiums _____

   15. Union dues and professional
       expenses _____

   16. Income and Social Security
       taxes _____

Total annual living expenses _____

Surplus or shortfall _____

Subtract expenses from income _____

Value Line's one-page analysis of corporations contains a great deal of information that you can use to analyze stocks.

Value Line stock analysis of Intel.
Source: Value Line

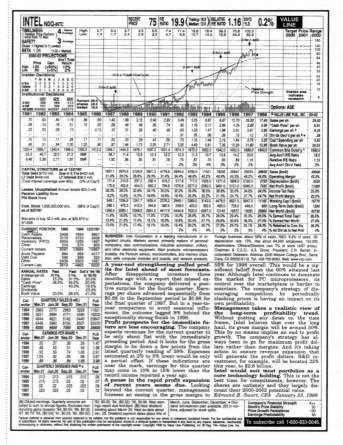

When evaluating mutual funds, you might want to use the research offered by Morningstar and Value Line.

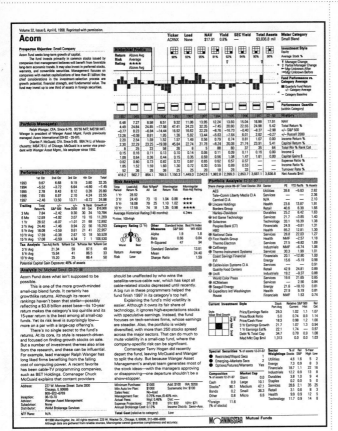

Typical Morningstar fund analysis. *Source: Morningstar*

Typical Value Line
fund analysis.
Source: Value Line

The National Association of Investors Corp., the
umbrella group for thousands of investment clubs,
provides worksheets to help analyze stocks.

NATIONAL ASSOCIATION OF INVESTORS CORPORATION

NAIC ®
INVESTMENT EDUCATION
FOR INDIVIDUALS AND CLUBS
SINCE 1951

Stock Check List ®
for Beginning Investors

Company _____

Prepared by _____

Date_____

See Chapter 7 of the NAIC Official Guide.

While Investors are learning to use NAIC's Stock Selection Guide, it is suggested the following Check List be used for each stock considered for investment.

1 PAST SALES RECORD

Sales for most recent year were .... (1) $ _____

Sales for next most recent year were .... (2) $ _____

Total of above (1 + 2) .... (3) $ _____

Figure above divided by 2 .... (4) $ _____

Sales 5 years ago were .... (5) $ _____

Sales 6 years ago were .... (6) $ _____

Total of above (5 + 6) .... (7) $ _____

Figure above divided by 2 .... (8) $ _____

Increase in sales in above period (8 from 4) .... (9) $ _____

Percentage increase in sales (9 divided by 8) .... (10) _____ %

CONVERSION TABLE

This % increase in Sales Gives →	27	33	46	61	76	93	112	129	148	205	271
This % Compounded Annual Growth Rate →	5	6	8	10	12	14	16	18	20	25	30

Look for the percent increase that meets the objective you have set.

COMPOUND ANNUAL RATE OF SALES GROWTH WAS _____ %

2 PAST EARNINGS PER SHARE RECORD

Earnings Per Share for most recent year were .... (1) $ _____

Earnings Per Share for next most recent year were .... (2) $ _____

Total of above (1 + 2) .... (3) $ _____

Figure above divided by 2 .... (4) $ _____

Earnings Per Share 5 years ago were .... (5) $ _____

Earnings Per Share 6 years ago were .... (6) $ _____

Total of above (5 + 6) .... (7) $ _____

Figure above divided by 2 .... (8) $ _____

Increase in Earnings Per Share in above period (8 from 4) .... (9) $ _____

Percentage increase in earnings (9 divided by 8) .... (10) _____ %

See **Conversion Table** above to determine ➤

Earnings Per Share have increased _____ than sales in this period.
(more)   (less)

COMPOUND ANNUAL RATE OF EARNINGS PER SHARE GROWTH WAS _____ %

Explain Apparent Reason for Difference in Sales and Earnings Per Share Growth: _____

_____

© 1996. National Association of Investors Corporation; 711 West Thirteen Mile Road, Madison Hgts., Michigan 48071

Front and back page of the NAIC stock check list. *Source: National Association of Investors Corp.*

Discuss Possible Reasons for Past Growth:
A new product was very successful_____.
A cyclical business that experienced recovery_____ .
A research program has produced several new products or uses for older products_____.
Purchase another company_____ .
Has taken larger share of business in its field _____ .
Skill of management _____ .

Will Factors Which Produced Past Growth Continue Effective
for the next five years _____ yes, _____ yes, but less effective, _____ no.

3 PRICE RECORD OF THE STOCK

Present Price $ _____ . Present Earnings Per Share_____ .

List Last 5 Years	High Price Each Year (A)	Low Price Each Year (B)	Earnings Per Share (C)	Price Earnings Ratio at High (A ÷ C)	at Low (B ÷ C)
Totals					
Averages					

Average of High and Low Price Earnings Averages for the past five years.

Present Price is ———— (higher) (lower) ———— than high price five years ago.

Present Price is _____% higher than the high price 5 years ago. Compare this figure with the percent sales increase in 1 (10) and percent earnings per share increase in 2 (10).
The price change compares with sales growth and earnings per share growth ———— (favorably or unfavorably) ———— .

This stock has sold as high as the current price in _____ of the last 5 years.
In the past five years the stock ———— (has) (has not) ———— sold at unusually ———— (high) (low) ———— price earnings ratios.
The Present price earnings ratio is _____ .
In relation to past price earnings ratios the stock is currently
_____ selling at a higher ratio
_____ selling about the same
_____ selling lower
The average price earnings ratios of the past might be expected to continue _____ ,
or should be adjusted to_____ high, _____ low.

4 CONCLUSION

1. The past sales growth rate _____ (does) (does not) _____ meet our objective.
2. The past earnings per share growth rate _____ (does) (does not) _____ meet our objective.
3. Our conclusion has been that possible earnings per share growth rate_____ (will) (will not) _____ meet our objective in the coming five years.
4. The price of the stock is currently _____ (acceptable) (too high) _____ .

This form is not meant to give you an adequate analysis of the stock, but is meant to help the beginner ask questions to indicate whether the company is likely to become more valuable and if it can be purchased reasonably. As Investors gain practice, a more thorough study of the stock is suggested using NAIC's Stock Selection Guide and Report as a guide.

ST-1040

Front and back page of the NAIC stock selection guide. *Source: National Association of Investors Corp.*

2 EVALUATING MANAGEMENT Company _____ xyz corp _____   8/6/95

													LAST 5 YEAR AVE.	TREND UP	DOWN
A	% Pre-tax Profit on Sales (Net Before Taxes ÷ Sales)															
B	% Earned on Invested Capital (E/S ÷ Book Value)															

3 PRICE-EARNINGS HISTORY as an indicator of the future

		PRESENT PRICE			HIGH THIS YEAR _____		LOW THIS YEAR _____		
	Year	A PRICE HIGH	B PRICE LOW	C Earnings Per Share	D Price Earnings Ratio HIGH A ÷ C	E Price Earnings Ratio LOW B ÷ C	F Dividend Per Share	G % Payout F ÷ C X 100	H % High Yield F ÷ B X 100
1									
2									
3									
4									
5									
6	TOTAL								
7	AVERAGE								
8	AVERAGE PRICE EARNINGS RATIO					9 CURRENT PRICE EARNINGS RATIO			

4 EVALUATING RISK and REWARD over the next 5 years

A HIGH PRICE - NEXT 5 YEARS
Avg. High P/E _____ x Estimated High Earnings/Share _____ = Forecast High Price B-1 $ _____
(3D7)   (4A1)

B LOW PRICE - NEXT 5 YEARS
(a) Avg. Low P/E _____ x Estimated Low E/Share _____ = $ _____
(3E7)
(b) Avg. Low Price of Last 5 Years = _____
(3B7)
(c) Recent Severe Market Low Price = _____
(d) Price Dividend Will Support $\frac{\text{Present Divd.}}{\text{High Yield (H)}}$ = _____ = _____
Selected Estimated Low Price _____   B-2 $ _____
(4B1)

C ZONING
$\frac{(4A1)}{\text{Lower }^1/_3}$ = _____ High Forecast Price Minus _____ Low Forecast Price Equals _____ Range. $^1/_3$ of Range = _____
(4B1)   (C)   (4CD)
Middle $^1/_3$ = _____ To _____ (Buy) (4C2)
(4B1)
Upper $^1/_3$ = _____ To _____ (Maybe) (4C3)
(4A1)
Present Market Price of _____ (Sell) (4C4)
is in the _____ (4C5) Range

D UP-SIDE DOWN-SIDE RATIO (Potential Gain vs. Risk of Loss)
$\frac{\text{High Price}}{\text{Present Price}}$ $\frac{\text{(4A1)}}{\text{}}$ Minus Present Price _____ = _____ =To 1
Present Price _____ Minus Low Price _____ (4D)
(4B1)

5 5-YR POTENTIAL

A Present Full Year's Dividend $_____
_____ = _____ x100 = _____ Present Yield or % Returned on Purchase Price
Present Price of Stock $_____

B AVERAGE YIELD OVER THE NEXT 5 YEARS
Avg. Earn. Per Share Next 5 Years _____ x Avg % Payout _____ = _____ %
(3G7)
Present Price $_____

1/5/98 1:07 PM

You can buy U.S. Treasuries without a middleman.
Here is the form to use.

Form for buying
U.S. Treasuries
direct.

PD F 5381
Department of the Treasury
Bureau of the Public Debt

OMB No. 1535-0069

TREASURY DIRECT®

TREASURY BILL, NOTE & BOND TENDER

For Tender Instructions, See PD F 5382

TYPE OR PRINT IN INK ONLY – TENDERS WILL NOT BE ACCEPTED WITH ALTERATIONS OR CORRECTIONS

DEPARTMENT USE

1. BID INFORMATION Tender amount must meet or exceed the minimum for the term selected below. *(Must Be Completed)*

Par Amount: **Bid Type:** *(Fill in One)*

○ Noncompetitive

○ Competitive at |___|___|.|___|___|___| %
(Bid bids must end in 0 or 5.)

$_____

TENDER NO.

RECEIVED BY/DATE

ENTERED BY

2. TREASURY DIRECT ACCOUNT NUMBER
(If NOT furnished, a new account will be opened.)

|___|___|___|___|___|___| - |___|___|___|___|___|

3. TAXPAYER ID NUMBER *(Must Be Completed)*

|___|___|___| - |___| - |___|___|___|___| OR |___|___| - |___|___|___|___|___|___|___|
Social Security Number (First-Named Owner)   Employer ID Number

APPROVED BY

4. TERM SELECTION *(Fill in One)*
(Must Be Completed)

Treasury Bill   Circle the Number of
$10,000 Minimum   Reinvestments

○ 13-Week........0   1   2   3   4
             5   6   7   8

○ 26-Week........0   1   2   3   4

○ 52-Week........0   1   2

Treasury Note/Bond
$5,000 Minimum

○ 2-Year Note

○ 3-Year Note

- - - - - - - - - - - - - - - - - - -
$1,000 Minimum

○ 5-Year Note

○ 10-Year Note

○ 30-Year Bond

○ Inflation-Indexed _____
               Term

5. ACCOUNT NAME Please Type or Print! *(Must Be Completed)*

6. ADDRESS *(For new account or if changed.)*   ○ New Address?

_____
City   State   ZIP Code

ISSUE DATE

CUSIP 912794-

CUSIP 912827-

CUSIP 912810-

FOREIGN ☐

BACKUP ☐

REVIEW ☐

7. TELEPHONE NUMBERS *(For new account or if changed.)* ○ New Phone Number?

Work ( ) -   Home ( ) -

8. DIRECT DEPOSIT INFORMATION *(For new account only.)* Changes? Submit PD F 5178.

Routing Number |___|___|___|___|___|___|___|___|___|

Financial Institution Name _____

Account Number |___|___|___|___|___|___|___|___|___|___|___|___|___|___|___|___|___|

Name on Account _____

Account Type: *(Fill in One)* ○ Checking   ○ Savings

9. PURCHASE METHOD
(Must Be Completed)

○ *Automatic Withdrawal*
(Existing Treasury Direct Account Only)

○ Cash: $_____

○ Checks: $_____

         $_____

○ Securities: $_____

Total Payment
Attached: $_____

CHECKS ARE DEPOSITED IMMEDIATELY

CHECK #

10. AUTHORIZATION *(Must Be Completed – Original Signature Required)*
Tender Submission: I submit this tender pursuant to the provisions of Department of the Treasury Circulars, Public Debt Series Nos. 2-86 (31 CFR Part 357) and 1-93 (31 CFR Part 356), and the applicable offering announcement. As the first-named owner and under penalties of perjury, I certify that the number shown on this form is my correct taxpayer identification number and that I am not subject to backup withholding because (1) I have not been notified that I am subject to backup withholding as a result of a failure to report all interest or dividends, or (2) the Internal Revenue Service has notified me that I am no longer subject to backup withholding. I further certify that all other information provided on this form is true, correct and complete.

Automatic Withdrawal: (If using this purchase method.) I authorize a debit to my account at the financial institution I designated in TREASURY DIRECT to pay for this security. I understand that the purchase price will be charged to my account on or after the settlement date. I also understand that if this transaction cannot be successfully completed, my tender can be rejected and the transaction canceled. If there is a dispute, a copy of this authorization may be provided to my financial institution.

_____   _____
Signature(s)   Date

SEE BACK FOR PRIVACY ACT AND PAPERWORK REDUCTION ACT NOTICE

If you are wondering how much life insurance coverage to purchase, here is a worksheet provided by *Wholesale Insurance Network* (WIN).

First, how much money does your family need each year to continue living the way they do now?

Calculate your current living expenses	$_____	a
(including food, clothing, rent/mortgate payments, taxes, utilities, entertainment, etc.)		
Child Care..	$_____	b
(anticipated cost if one person dies)		
Ongoing parent/grandparent care..	$_____	c
Total Annual Expense..a + b + c =	$_____	d
Income of surviving spouse...	$_____	e
Social Security Benefit...	$_____	f
Total Annual Shortfall...e + f =	$_____	g
Expected Income		
Annual Expense - Annual Shortfall.................,...d - g =	$_____	h

Second, lump sum needed.

Other debts you would want to pay	$_____	i
(automobile, credit card balance, etc.)		
Estimated funeral and administrative expenses	$_____	j
Uninsured medical expenses	$_____	k
Children's future educational needs	$_____	l
Subtotal of Final Expenses....................i + j + k + l =	$_____	m
Annual Expense Shortfall previously calculated (h)_____ x 10 yrs.......... =	$_____	n
TOTAL OF FINAL AND FUTURE EXPENSES ....m + n =	$_____	o

Third, add up the sources of income which would be available to your surviving dependents.

Existing life insurance	$_____	p
Income producing assets	$_____	q
(Stocks bonds, rental income, etc.)		
Cash and savings accounts	$_____	r
Social Security benefits	$_____	s
TOTAL ASSETS ....p + q + r + s =	$_____	t
Now subtract:		
TOTAL ASSETS..t	$_____	
minus		
TOTAL OF FINAL AND FUTURE EXPENSES.....................................o	$_____	

TOTAL INSURANCE NEED .... o - t   = $_____

Now that you've assessed your family's financial situation, and estimated your need for life insurance, call or FAX the Wholesale Insurance Network. The insurance policies available through WIN are offered by leading companies committed to excellent customer service, each with a record of keeping promises to policyholders. The Wholesale Insurance Network works for you -- the consumer who knows what they want.

Important Statistics

STATISTICS

	Annualized Return			
	1 Yr.	**3 Yr.**	**5 Yr.**	**10 Yr.**
Consumer Price Index	1.7%	2.3%	2.5%	3.3%
Dow Jones Industrials	23.5%	28.4%	23.1%	19.3%
Standard & Poor's 500	30.7%	29.5%	22.2%	18.6%
Russell 2000	27.2%	22.7%	17.3%	14.9%
Wilshire 5000	30.2%	28%	20.8%	17.8%
NASDAQ Composite	27.9%	27.9%	21.4%	18.1%
Morgan Stanley Cap. Intl. EAFE	11.4%	10.1%	9.8%	6.7%
Lehman Bros. Long Government Bonds	19.3%	10%	9.3%	11.5%
Lehman Brothers Municipals	9.4%	7.4%	6.7%	8.4%
U.S. 30-day Treasury bills	4.8%	4.8%	4.3%	5.0%

Percentages based on returns through May 31, 1998. Source: CDA/Wiesenberger

Appendix E

TEN LARGEST CAPITALIZATION STOCKS ON THE NEW YORK STOCK EXCHANGE (IN BILLIONS OF DOLLARS)

1. General Electric	$273.9
2. Coca-Cola	$214.9
3. Exxon	$182
4. Merck	$140.3
5. Philip Morris	$122.1
6. Proctor & Gamble	$113.5
7. IBM	$112.8
8. Bristol Myer Squibb	$105.7
9. Pfizer	$100.3
10. Johnson & Johnson	$96.6

Source: New York Stock Exchange

TOP 10 MOST ACTIVELY TRADED NASDAQ STOCKS

1. Intel
2. Cisco Systems
3. 3 Com Corp.
4. Microsoft
5. Oracle
6. Ascend Communications
7. Dell Computer
8. Applied Materials
9. WorldCom
10. Sun Microsystems

Source: NASDAQ

Before buying a bond, you should understand what impact interest rates will have on it. The longer the bond's maturity, the more volatile it can be. As you can see from the next two tables, even a slight movement in interest rates can affect a bond's price. For purposes of the illustration, the face value of the hypothetical bond in the next two tables is $1,000 with a 7 percent coupon.

PRINCIPAL VOLATILITY OF BONDS

Bond Maturity (Years)	Value of $1,000 Bond If Interest Rates Increase By				
	.5%	1%	1.5%	2%	2.5%
2	$991	$982	$973	$964	$955
5	$979	$959	$940	$921	$902
10	$965	$932	$900	$870	$841
20	$946	$901	$857	$816	$778

PRINCIPAL VOLATILITY OF BONDS

Bond Maturity (Years)	Value of $1,000 Bond If Interest Rates Decline By				
	.5%	1%	1.5%	2%	2.5%
2	$1,009	$1,019	$1,028	$1,038	$1,047
5	$1,021	$1,043	$1,065	$1,088	$1,111
10	$1,036	$1,074	$1,114	$1,156	$1,200
20	$1,056	$1,116	$1,181	$1,251	$1,327

Municipal bonds aren't appropriate for all taxpayers. That's because a muni bond's yield is discounted due to the built-in tax break. If you're in the lowest 15 percent tax bracket, your tax savings in a muni would be so puny that you'd be better off with a taxable bond offering a higher yield. In contrast, the people in the highest federal tax bracket—39.6 percent—reap the best tax break.

The following chart shows quite clearly that it's the higher-income taxpayers who have the most to gain from muni bonds. Here's how someone in the 28 percent tax bracket can use the table to decide whether munis are appropriate for him. In this example, the investor has a chance to buy a high-quality corporate bond yielding 7.5 percent or a muni bond yielding 6 percent. Using the table, you can see that the muni bond looks like a better deal. The taxable equivalent yield of the 6 percent muni is 8.33 percent.

TAXABLE EQUIVALENT YIELD TABLE

Marginal Income Tax Bracket	If the Tax-Exempt Yield Is		
	4%	5%	6%
	The Taxable Equivalent Yield (Percentage) Is		
15%	4.71	5.88	7.06
28%	5.56	6.94	8.33
31%	5.80	7.25	8.70
36%	6.25	7.81	9.38

Source: American Association of Individual Investors

TOP 10 MUTUAL FUNDS BASED ON THE HIGHEST 5-YEAR ANNUALIZED RETURNS (NOTICE THAT ALL OF THEM ARE SECTOR FUNDS)

1.	Fidelity Select Electronics	35.68%
2.	Fidelity Select Home Finance	33.30%
3.	Seligman Communications	31.23%
4.	Fidelity Select Energy Service	30.93%
5.	J. Hancock Regional Bank, A	30.20%
6.	Fidelity Select Computer	29.52%
7.	J. Hancock Regional Bank, B	29.35%
8.	Pilgrim Am. Bank & Thrift, A	28.80%
9.	Fidelity Select Brokerage	28.34%
10.	Fidelity Select Regional Bank	27.74%

Source: Lipper Analytical Services

TOP 10 GROWTH MUTUAL FUNDS WITH HIGHEST 5-YEAR ANNUALIZED RETURNS

1.	Franklin California Growth	25.99%
2.	Legg Mason Value	25.74%
3.	FPA Capital	24.62%
4.	Vanguard PRIMECAP	24.32%
5.	Torray Fund	24.11%
6.	Merrill Growth Fund, A	23.94%
7.	Mairs & Power Growth	23.70%
8.	Oakmark Fund	23.53%
9.	SAFECO Growth	23.52%
10.	Stand Ayer Wood: Equity	23.45%

Source: Lipper Analytical Services

TOP 10 SMALL CAP MUTUAL FUNDS WITH HIGHEST 5-YEAR ANNUALIZED RETURNS

1.	Barr Rosen: Small Cap	24.1%
2.	Baron Asset Fund	24%
3.	Franklin Small Cap Growth Adv	22.8%
4.	Lord Abbett Developing Growth A	22.8%
5.	Franklin Small Cap Growth I	22.7%
6.	Enterprise Small Co. Growth Y	22.2%
7.	Govett Smaller Companies A	21.9%
8.	Berger Small Cap Value Inst.	21.9%
9.	Berger Small Cap Value Ret.	21.8%
10.	MAS Small Cap Inst.	21.5%

Source: CDA/Wiesenberger

TOP 10 FOREIGN FUNDS BASED ON HIGHEST 5-YEAR ANNUALIZED RETURNS

1.	GAM International Fund, A	22.79%
2.	Dean Witter European Growth	22.16%
3.	Putnam Europe Growth, A	20.66%
4.	Morgan Stanley Inst. Intl. Equity, A	20.34%
5.	Merrill Lynch Eurofund, A	20.24%
6.	Pioneer Europe Fund, A	19.98%
7.	Harbor Fund International	19.77%
8.	Fidelity Europe	19.58%
9.	Wright EquiFund-Netherlands	19.39%
10.	Vanguard Intl. Equity Index Europe	19.11%

Source: Lipper Analytical Services

TOP 10 BOND FUNDS BASED ON 5-YEAR ANNUALIZED RETURNS

1.	GT Global High Income, A	17.99%
2.	GT Global High Income, B	17.22%
3.	American Century Benham Target 2020	16.72%
4.	Northeast Investors Trust	15.21%
5.	American Century Benham Target 2015	14.93%
6.	Fidelity Spartan High Income	14.60%
7.	Loomis Sayles Bond	14.26%
8.	Morgan Stanley High Yield, A	14.24%
9.	MAS Fund High Yield	14.14%
10.	Mainstay High Yield Corp., B	13.98%

Source: Lipper Analytical Services

Selecting a solid fund with below-average fees is extremely important and can make a big difference in your returns over the long run.

AVERAGE TOTAL EXPENSE RATIOS FOR DIFFERENT MUTUAL FUND CATEGORIES

1. Growth funds	1.52%
2. International funds	1.66%
3. Small cap funds	1.49%
4. Sector funds	1.64%
5. Taxable bond funds	.97%
6. Tax-free bond funds	.95%
7. Index funds	.51%

Source: Lipper Analytical Services

THE 30 COMPANIES IN THE DOW JONES INDUSTRIAL AVERAGE

AT&T

Allied Signal

Alcoa

American Express

Boeing

Caterpillar

Chevron

Coca-Cola

Disney

DuPont

Eastman Kodak

Exxon

General Electric

General Motors

Goodyear

Hewlett-Packard

IBM

International Paper

Johnson & Johnson

McDonald's

Merck

Minnesota Mining & Manufacturing (3M)

J.P. Morgan

Philip Morris

Procter & Gamble

Sears

Travelers Group

Union Carbide

United Technologies

WAL-MART

BEST OVERALL CREDIT CARDS WITH INTRODUCTORY RATE

Card Issuer Introductory rate Introductory period

Card Issuer	Introductory rate	Introductory period
AT&T Universal	(800) 66-APPLY	7.9% 12 months
Wachovia Bank	(800) 842-3262	8.5% 12 months
Long Island Savings	(800) 635-0581	8.9% 12 months
AmTrust Bank	(888) 268-7878	6.9% 6 months
Ohio Savings Bank	(800) 987-6446	6.9% 6 months
Travelers Bank & Trust	(800) 772-7775	6.9% 6 months
Citizens Bank	(800) 438-9222	5.9% 6 months

Source: Bank Rate Monitor

The *Unofficial Guide*™ Reader Questionnaire

If you would like to express your opinion about investing or this guide, please complete this questionnaire and mail it to:

The *Unofficial Guide*™ Reader Questionnaire
Macmillan Lifestyle Group
1633 Broadway, floor 7
New York, NY 10019-6785

Gender: ___ M   ___ F

Age: ___ Under 30   ___ 31–40   ___ 41–50
___ Over 50

Education: ___ High school   ___ College
___ Graduate/Professional

What is your occupation?
_____

How did you hear about this guide?
___ Friend or relative
___ Newspaper, magazine, or Internet
___ Radio or TV
___ Recommended at bookstore
___ Recommended by librarian
___ Picked it up on my own
___ Familiar with the *Unofficial Guide*™ travel series

Did you go to the bookstore specifically for a book on investing?   Yes ___   No ___

Have you used any other *Unofficial Guides*™?
Yes ___   No ___

If Yes, which ones?
_____
_____
_____

pension plan = asst mut

What other book(s) on investing have you purchased?

_____
_____
_____

Was this book:
___ more helpful than other(s)
___ less helpful than other(s)

Do you think this book was worth its price?
Yes ___   No ___

Did this book cover all topics related to investing adequately?   Yes ___   No ___

Please explain your answer:

_____
_____
_____

Were there any specific sections in this book that were of particular help to you?   Yes ___   No ___

Please explain your answer:

_____
_____
_____

On a scale of 1 to 10, with 10 being the best rating, how would you rate this guide? ___

What other titles would you like to see published in the _Unofficial Guide_™ series?

_____
_____

Are _Unofficial Guides_™ readily available in your area?   Yes ___   No ___

Other comments:

_____
_____
_____
_____

About The Author

Lynn O'Shaughnessy can tell you everything you need to know about investing. Lynn is a former *Los Angeles Times* reporter and president of an investment club that has beaten the Standard & Poor's 500 Index for the past four years. As a personal finance writer, her articles have appeared in *Mutual Funds* magazine, *Bloomberg Personal, Individual Investor,* and many more.